# The
# EARLY CHILDHOOD
# Curriculum
## A REVIEW OF CURRENT RESEARCH

## Second Edition

*Edited by*
## Carol Seefeldt

## Teachers College, Columbia University
## New York and London

Published by Teachers College Press, 1234 Amsterdam Avenue
New York, NY 10027

*Library of Congress Cataloging-in-Publication Data*

The Early childhood curriculum : a review of current research / edited
    by Carol Seefeldt.—2nd ed.
        p.      cm.—(Early childhood education series)
        Includes bibliographical references and index.
        ISBN 0-8077-3196-X
        1. Early childhood education—United States—Curricula.    2. Early
    childhood education—United States—Curricula—Research.
    I. Seefeldt, Carol.    II. Series.
    LB1139.4.E17    1992
    372.19—dc20                                                                    92-18816


    ISBN 0-8077-3196-X

    Printed on acid-free paper
    Manufactured in the United States of America
    99  98  97  96  95  94  93  92        8  7  6  5  4  3  2  1

# Contents

# Preface

"What are you teaching children, and what are they learning?" Historically, early childhood educators, embracing nativists' theories of learning, have maintained that they teach children, not content. Today, however, this response seems not only naive, but irresponsible.

As calls for sweeping curriculum reforms become common, the pressure to answer the question of what curriculum content is appropriate for young children increases. The prevalence in all areas of curriculum on drill and practice of isolated academic skills may be attributed to the inability of early childhood educators to specify what content is appropriate for young children. If early childhood educators remain unable to specify what their curriculum content is, then others will do so for them.

The second edition of this text, *The Early Childhood Curriculum: A Review of Current Research*, has been designed as a resource for early childhood educators to answer the questions of what it is they teach and what children learn in an early childhood program. The text offers graduate students and decision makers in early childhood education an overview of the various theories, research bases, and practices in curriculum content areas in early childhood education.

In Chapter 1, "Determining the Curriculum," Leslie R. Williams describes how society's attitudes and views of the nature of children have always influenced the curriculum. The social forces that led to varying views of children, and thus curricula, are described. The idea of the curriculum being inseparable from the whole child provides the basis for this chapter.

Teachers' interactions with children—what teachers actually do, how they reach decisions about appropriate educational experiences, and the strategies they use as they interact with children—are potent directors of the curriculum. Margaret Lay-Dopyera and John E. Dopyera present the history, theory, and practice of teaching strategies in Chapter 2, "Strategies for Teaching."

"But all they do is play!" Uninformed of the power of play as an educational tool, many view play as a waste of time. Early childhood educators, however, think of play as the major vehicle for learning. In Chapter 3, "A

Review of Research on Play," Doris Pronin Fromberg describes the distinctive dynamics of early play, script theory, and the relation of play to cognitive and affective development, thereby presenting a convincing rationale for play as the early childhood curriculum.

Celia Genishi, in Chapter 4, "Developing the Foundation: Oral Language and Communicative Competence," describes the research and theory on issues in language learning and curriculum. She discusses the role of the adult in encouraging children's talk and language interactions and reviews the issues in the field revolving around these interactions. The chapter covers how teachers enable children to develop communicative competence in the classroom, as well as the research on their choices and on curriculum that builds on children's oral communicative abilities.

Nita H. Barbour presents an overview of the theory, research, and practice of how children learn to read and how teachers facilitate their moving into the reading process. The questions of when children should learn to read, and by what methods, are described in Chapter 5, "Reading."

Chapter 6, "New Directions for the Early Childhood Mathematics Curriculum," by Patricia F. Campbell and Deborah A. Carey examines recent research that can inform curriculum development in mathematics. The authors present research on creating problem-solving environments, the role of the teacher, and the clustering of mathematics instruction around themes as opposed to isolated topics.

George E. Forman and Christopher Landry, in Chapter 7, "Research on Early Science Education," aim to help educators determine useful procedures to facilitate scientific thinking in young children. As a context for this educational research, they also present the cognitive development research that has established the goals for much of early science education.

In no other area of the curriculum is there as much confusion about what content to teach young children as in the social studies. The breadth and multidisciplinary nature of social studies, and of early childhood education, have led to lack of clarity of goals and objectives in both fields. The current thinking and research on what social studies content is and children's understanding of this content are discussed by Carol Seefeldt in Chapter 8, "The Social Studies in Early Childhood Education."

Bill Stinson presents recent developments in physical education in Chapter 9, "Early Childhood Trends in Movement Development." He charts the last two decades of research in early childhood motor development and movement experiences. Summarizing the research on children's individual development and movement potential, and the tasks to be performed, this chapter clarifies a child-centered approach by citing the necessity of a "working knowledge" of motor development to intelligently teach motor skills to children.

Clifford D. Alper discusses the crucial implications of current theories in music education for young children in Chapter 10, "Early Childhood Music Education." He reviews the Orff, Kodaly, and Dalcroze methods of teaching music and evaluates critically the contemporary problems in the music education research.

In Chapter 11, "Art in Early Childhood Education" by Harold J. Mc Whinnie, research in art education is reviewed with a focus on the issues of art for children between the ages of 4 and 7. Art education is conceptualized within a framework of development, cognitive theory, and new directions within recent art education theory and practice. A special focus is on Howard Gardner's theory of multiple intelligences.

The concluding chapter, "The Integrated Early Childhood Curriculum: New Interpretations Based on Research and Practice," by Rebecca S. New, presents a picture of an integrated curriculum in a cross-cultural context. Describing the curriculum of the child-care centers in the city of Reggio Emilia, Italy, New demonstrates how knowledge of separate subject-matter disciplines can be used to create a whole curriculum for whole children.

With knowledge of current research and theory in each of the curriculum content areas described in *The Early Childhood Curriculum: A Review of Current Research,* teachers will have a foundation on which to design an organized framework of content young children can and should learn, and on how they can help children achieve this learning. Then the field of early childhood education will be able to answer the difficult question of "what do you actually teach young children?"

# Acknowledgments

The significant contribution this book makes to early childhood education is the result of the expertise, energies, and time of many. First, the contributions of the authors of the individual chapters must be recognized. Each an expert in a specific area of curriculum content, the authors gave freely of their time and knowledge to write a chapter specifically for this work.

The editors at Teachers College Press—including Myra Cleary, Carol Collins, and Cynthia Fairbanks—must also be recognized. The memory of Ron Galbraith, who originally acquired this text and offered his support, encouragement, and knowledge to the design of this book, is treasured. The outstanding dedication, expertise, careful thought, and understanding of Susan Liddicoat, who gave many hours to the editing of this book, is recognized. Her conceptual and precise editing is highly valued.

Finally, the ideation and conceptual insights of Eugene Seefeldt are acknowledged. Without his thoughtful insights this book would not have been written.

# CHAPTER 1

# Determining the Curriculum

LESLIE R. WILLIAMS

"Curriculum" is a word that evokes many images in the minds of teachers, administrators, and parents. For most early educators, though, "curriculum" has a single powerful association—the image of "the whole child." Consideration of what that phrase means to those who work with young children (children from birth to age 8) and how it came to have so particular a connotation reveals some of the distinctive characteristics of early education and explains what for other educators may be considered the idiosyncratic nature of the field's curriculum literature. In early childhood education, the curriculum and the whole child tend to be seen as inseparable.

Most early educators understand "the whole child" to mean the child's complete integration of intellectual (cognitive), emotional, social, and physical capabilities. Learning in any one of these domains must necessarily involve all the others. Effective teaching, as a consequence, must draw upon those inner connections, with recognition of the distinctive ways in which young children take in and utilize knowledge of the world around them.

The task of determining the early childhood curriculum, therefore, hinges to a certain extent on discovering the nature of children. *What* young children learn is at least partially dependent upon *how* they learn. As this concept has evolved, how children learn has also increasingly come to be seen in relation to a *context*, a broad social and cultural base for children's emerging knowledge, skills, feelings, and attitudes. Experience has taught early educators that young children thrive on acknowledgment and use of their unique capacities for learning and that they show themselves to be capable of strong performance in all areas of accomplishment when taught as unitary, integrated beings.

## EARLY BEGINNINGS

The idea of educating the whole child reflects a rich tradition of comprehensiveness that has characterized early education from its beginnings.

This tradition arose as a response both to social conditions adversely affecting the lives of young children and to the moral, spiritual, pragmatic, and eventually scientific streams flowing through Western society over the past 200 years.

Historian Philippe Aries (1962) suggests that before the Romantic period, children by the age of 5 or 6 were viewed as miniature adults and were expected to learn in the same entirely language-based mode used in adult education. The one classical distinction that was made by both Plato (427–347 B.C.) and Aristotle (384–322 B.C.) was that children required strict training of character as a proper foundation for learning. In a similar vein, preparation of young scholars in medieval Europe was expected to be grounded in spiritual disciplines, so that the training of the mind would reflect the order of the Creation or divine intent. While these provisos implied the integration of the faculties of human learning, translating that assumption into curricula was not seen except in sporadic instances—for example, in the seventeenth century, Luther's incorporation of vocational instruction into courses of study; and Comenius's use of pictures as concrete referents to vocabulary studied (Braun & Edwards, 1972; Comenius, 1896/1910; Weber, 1984).

## Rousseau and the Natural Child

A clear demarcation in the image of the child came with the popularization of the work of Jean-Jacques Rousseau (1712–1788). In his educational treatise *Emile* (1762/1969), Rousseau departed from the view of children as being like adults and presented them as moving through a succession of stages, each of which had its own internal order and coherence (Gutek, 1972). Equally important was Rousseau's insistence that children learned not through the abstractions of the written word, but through direct interaction with the environment. He took the extreme position that only the natural world provided guidance in this interactive process and that society corrupted children, tarnishing their innate nobility of spirit. He recommended that children be raised in situations where contact with nature could be frequent and prolonged, where children could play without social restraint until reaching the age of reason (approximately puberty). At that time formal studies could commence without danger of distortion of the true nature of the child (Rousseau, 1762/1969).

While Rousseau's main interest was in reforming society's total conception of education and did not focus specifically on young children, his work is important to understanding the inner structures of early childhood curricula because he anticipated several of the themes that characterize work in the field to this day. His awareness of the emergence of developmental stages and stage-related learning has already been mentioned. In addition, his presentation of learning as an interactive, sensorially based process, and his recognition of play as a medium for learning, were powerful intimations of the directions to be taken in the future.

Like all issues of import in education, however, conceptions of play and processes in learning, and their relationship to the idea of teaching the whole child, have evolved over time. Ensuing changes have been responsive to broad social patterns, needs, and priorities. In every era, new program designs and curricular formulations have revealed both unique and cumulative perceptions of the role of each of these in suiting instruction to the distinctive characteristics of young children. Tracing the path of that evolution can contribute to our understanding of the fundamental questions behind curriculum research in early childhood education today.

Returning, therefore, to the predecessors of modern practice, we see that from the mid-eighteenth century onward, there was a clear line of development in the image of the whole child. Emphases on interactive processes and play became more and more apparent in the fabric of early childhood education, as each innovator passed insights to a new generation of persons serving, nurturing, and educating the young child.

## Pestalozzi and the Observant Child

Rousseau's work deeply influenced the thinking of Johann Pestalozzi (1746–1827), an Italian-Swiss schoolteacher who founded one of the first European schools to acknowledge children's developmental characteristics. Pestalozzi was convinced of the profound effect of social environment on children. When his novel *How Gertrude Teaches Her Children* (1801/1915) was first published in 1801, he was promulgating the then revolutionary notion of an intimate teaching connection between parents and their children. He assumed that children were the pliant recipients of parental instruction and were in danger of corruption by society if that teaching was not of the highest moral character.

The curriculum "Papa" Pestalozzi designed for his children equated parental guidance and strong morality with the work ethic. The result was a high-intensity work training program that prepared children to face a rapidly changing economy. Manual dexterity was stressed as a survival skill in the newly emerging industrial revolution (Gutek, 1968).

The structure behind Pestalozzi's program was even more unconventional for its day than was its outward form. Pestalozzi saw the purpose of his work as the development of children's moral, physical, and intellectual powers. While the first two were fostered through the approach described above, intellectual growth was stimulated through *Anschauung*, a perceptual-ideational process through which concepts or clear ideas were formed. *Anschauung* involved three levels of operation. Most immediately, it represented the reception in the mind of direct sensory impressions from interaction with the external environment. One step removed from that was the formation of ideas by combining sense impressions with attention, or mental concentration, and arriving at concepts by association. At the third level of operation, mental ideas would appear without a concrete referent. *Anschauung* was developed in children through guided observation and representation of the natural world. Practice in recording the numbers and forms inherent in objects and the language associated with them led to refinement of mental capacity and its application in the physical and moral realms. Thus, the whole person was educated and became a competent and coping human being (Gutek, 1968).

## Froebel and the Child as Divine Reflection

Friedrich Froebel (1782–1852) studied with Pestalozzi; but he, designing a curriculum in 1837, 50 years after Pestalozzi's first work, found his teacher's vision of the child inadequate to capture the spirit of the new age. He molded and changed that vision to encompass "self-actualization" as a legitimate goal of early childhood education. Young children, said Froebel, arrive on this earth with an impressive repertoire of inborn knowledge and skills. The role of the teacher was to bring these capabilities to fruition by making children consciously aware of and able to use all that they know.

Froebel created a curriculum that was fascinating both in its complexity and in its inherent appeal to the children of his day. It consisted of a carefully sequenced set of manipulative materials known as the *Gifts*, complemented by an equally carefully sequenced set of handwork projects which he called the *Occupations*. The Gifts and Occupations together were designed to illustrate fundamental mathematical principles that Froebel believed were part of the creative human spirit and that echoed essential workings of the cosmos, or the mind of God (Froebel, 1826/1887).

Froebel is generally considered the founder of early childhood education not only because he was the first to design a curriculum specifically for young children (Pestalozzi's work encompassed the range from early childhood through adolescence), but because he introduced play as a major medium for instruction. For the first time, children "played" in school, that is, used manipulatives specially designed to teach concepts and skills. Formal games, music, art, and outdoor activities (such as gardening and care of pets) were integrated into the daily program to supplement the use of the Gifts and the Occupations.

Froebel's notion of "play" was substantially different from modern conceptions. He saw play as a teacher-directed process, largely imitative in nature and revolving around predetermined content. But he also understood play to be a form of "creative self-activity," expressing children's emerging capabilities and reflecting their particular way of learning (Froebel, 1826/1887).

## FIRST HALF OF THE TWENTIETH CENTURY

Froebel's mystical formulation dominated curriculum design in early childhood education for 50 years. In the 1890s, however, a new generation of persons concerned with the well-being of young children and their families began to challenge the view of the child contained in the Froebelian kindergarten curriculum.

### Dewey and Progressive Education

While not rejecting the picture of children as innately creative beings, the progressive followers of John Dewey reached backward in time to reclaim some of Pestalozzi's understanding of learning through direct experience with the natural world, and forward into the new century to envision children as builders of a new social order—a democratic society. Progressive educators found the highly defined and teacher-directed Froebelian curriculum to be too removed from the challenges and problems of daily living. Instead, they suggested, a curriculum for young children should be designed to meet the circumstances children faced as members of a group living in a modern world (Dewey, 1966).

Children were thus seen as social beings, and the curriculum became a flexible grouping of activities to promote social problem-solving processes. Examples of such activities were joint efforts in the preparation of food for lunch, or small group work on representation in the classroom of a familiar institution such as the local grocery store. Through such activities, children were expected to develop a sense of mutual responsibility and an understanding of at least some of the workings of the society in which they lived (Dewey, 1902).

New conceptions of play and the use of process in teaching and learning were emerging. The nature of children as learners was being seen in relation to experience (Dewey, 1938/1963). This meant connection with real-life activities that tended to integrate subject areas and require coordination of socioemotional, psychomotor, and cognitive responses from children. Such responses frequently took the form of sociodramatic play, in which the children reenacted what they had observed or directly experienced, often adding new dimensions to the scene in ways that revealed the processes behind their growing understanding.

## Montessori and Education for Social Competence

As the Progressive Movement was gathering momentum in the United States, Maria Montessori in Italy was transforming her observations of the nature of the whole child into another process-oriented curriculum. Like Dewey, Montessori was keenly aware of societal demands on children. Instead of looking at the functioning of children in groups, however, she focused on the promotion of social competence in individuals. She saw children as very sensitive to sensorial stimulation, "capable of sustaining mental concentration when genuinely interested in their work," loving cleanliness and order, "preferring work to play and didactic materials to toys, and having a deep sense of personal dignity" (Standing, 1962, pp. 40–43). Consequently, she designed her curriculum to foster independence in self-care and individual responsibility for one's own learning. Children worked individually or with self-chosen companions, practicing skills on specially made, self-corrective manipulative materials that provided immediate feedback on children's accomplishment.

Montessori had a deep understanding of learning as process. Her curriculum was organized around several "periods" in the child's development, each of which had its particular requirements for interaction with the environment. Assuming a continuum between refinement of the senses and broader intellectual functioning, she devised procedures and didactic materials that were responsive to children's evolving learning characteristics. During the period of the "absorbent mind" (birth to age 6), and most especially in the substage of greatest sensitivity and receptivity (3 to 6 years), she engaged the children in exercises of "practical life" and sense training. Practical life work emphasized cleanliness, self-care, and care and maintenance of the learning environment. Work in sense training promoted fine powers of sensory discrimination and developed readiness for the writing, reading, and other academic learnings that followed in the primary grades (Montessori, 1912/1964).

All of the exercises were process-oriented. While the didactic materials were designed to achieve specific outcomes (such as the ability to order cylinders from largest to smallest in height), they were also made to encourage the repetition of tasks, which in Montessori's view typically precedes and follows mastery in young children. Thus, while specific accomplishment was important, how children achieved mastery and continuing opportunity to demonstrate mastery were seen to be even more significant to their emerging competence.

## The Child Development Perspective

Simultaneously with Dewey's and Montessori's separate efforts, the American Child Study Movement, under the leadership of G. Stanley Hall (1844–1924), was starting to influence early childhood practice. Observations of children's behavior in a variety of contexts began yielding powerful data that, in turn, were causing curriculum makers to rethink what were appropriate learning experiences for young children (Kessen, 1965; Weber, 1984). The complexity of "the whole child" was beginning to reveal itself and to require increasingly sensitive applications of integrated approaches to teaching and learning.

As the century advanced, the conception of the child as a social being was expanding to include an accounting of the individual child's physical and psychological growth patterns. From the 1920s through the 1950s, the attention of early educators focused successively on children's social functioning, physical development and maturational milestones, emotional health, and finally underlying cognitive skills that signaled stage-appropriate mental functioning. Drawing on the work of Gesell and Ilg, Erikson, and Piaget, among others, early childhood educators in the late 1950s generally espoused what came to be known as the "child development" point of view (Braun & Edwards, 1972; Weber, 1984).

Notable during this 30-year period was the work of such finely tuned educators as Susan Isaacs in Britain and Harriet Johnson, Caroline Pratt, and Lucy Sprague Mitchell in the United States. By mid-century, the names of Lawrence Frank, Daniel Prescott, Arthur Jersild, and James L. Hymes had been added to the list (Weber, 1984). While these early childhood advocates each had a distinct point of view, they all emphasized the centrality of process, and play as an expression of process, in the growth, development, and education of young children.

## THIRTY YEARS OF GROWTH: 1950–1980

As understanding of the processes of children's learning became more refined through extended child observation, curriculum content was increasingly linked with the everyday occurrences of children's lives. This was so partly because of the continuing influence of Dewey's thinking on classroom practice, and partly because there was new theoretical support for the power of such content from two giants in the field of child development, Erik Erikson (born 1902) and Jean Piaget (1896–1980). Mentioned above in the context of changing emphases in early childhood education, the work of these two researchers requires particular attention because of the depth and breadth of their influence on curriculum design to the present day.

## Erikson and Development Through Conflict Resolution

As a young teacher raised in Europe, Erik Erikson came under the tutelage of Anna Freud. Prepared by her for work in child therapy, he soon became intrigued by the interactions he discerned between the course of psychosexual development in young children as described in classic psychodynamic literature and the sociocultural milieu in which children were being raised.

Erikson accepted the point of departure of psychodynamic thought, that the essential nature of human beings is instinctual and manifests itself in the realm of feeling and emotion. Cognition arises from unfulfilled desire, as a secondary characteristic of human nature. He understood socioemotional development as proceeding through the resolution of a series of conflicts, each of which addresses a fundamental issue of the human psyche. Proceeding from trust versus mistrust to autonomy versus shame, to initiative versus guilt and beyond through all eight distinctive "ages of man," children (and adults) strive to achieve integration and maintain balance in the context of the particular demands their society places upon them (Erikson, 1950/1963).

Young children, said Erikson, most commonly work through their current conflicts by reconstructing them in symbolic play. For curriculum developers influenced by Erikson's formulation, play centering on day-to-day events and familiar objects became a critical element in early childhood programs. It provided an arena for children's coming to terms with their existential dilemmas and encouraged cognition through channeling of childhood fantasy.

## Piaget and the Child's Construction of Knowledge

Piaget's theory of intellectual development gave a different but equally potent justification for including play in the early childhood curriculum. Piaget concluded that the essential nature of human beings was their power to construct knowledge through adaptation to the environment. From birth, children engage in the reciprocal acts of "assimilation" and "accommodation" in order to form, extend, and expand the structures of their minds. In assimilation, children match information, concepts, and skills arising from interaction with the environment, with previously formed mental structures. Accommodation, on the other hand, requires that the structures be modified in order to make sense of the new information or concepts, or to represent new skills (Piaget & Inhelder, 1969).

These complementary processes are fueled by children's direct activity, said Piaget. Play especially exercises the assimilation process, using action and frequently language as proving grounds for newly acquired ideas. As children proceed through the four periods of intellectual development (sensorimotor, preoperational, concrete operational, and formal operational) described by Piaget, play assumes a variety of forms; and within any one period, it can have multiple functions. Sensorimotor play, for example, generally revolves around practicing physical skills acquired through use of the five senses. However, it can also be used as a medium for establishing social relationships. During the preoperational period, play might be used symbolically or constructively to solidify physical knowledge of one's surroundings, to practice solving problems in the adult world, or to create a microsociety in which to try out new capabilities or to refine social interactions (Piaget, 1962).

## Implications for Curriculum

Early childhood program designers who accepted Piaget's descriptions of child development found that they could interpret his work according to their own instructional leanings. Piaget himself did not transform his theory into specifications for classroom practice. Curriculum makers, therefore, were free to draw implications leading to a variety of approaches to addressing the cognitive characteristics of young children. The one common feature of these approaches was that abundant manipulable materials and ample time for the children to interact directly with them were seen as vital spurs to the children's continued cognitive development.

By the early 1960s, therefore, the concept of teaching the whole child through a process orientation and incorporating play experiences into the curriculum was well established. Many "child development" programs reflected a psychodynamic (Freudian, Eriksonian) or, less frequently, a Piagetian point of view that stressed the interconnection of experiences and the role of emotion, cognition, and maturation in the promotion of learning. Other programs remained more closely aligned to the earlier Deweyan point of view or to the "readiness" rationale stemming from child study. In spite of the variety of theoretical underpinnings, however, classroom practice tended to have common characteristics.

Typically, early childhood classrooms were arranged into "interest centers" such as the block corner, library, art area, family or sociodramatic play corner, and sand/water areas. Daily schedules incorporated both child-initiated and teacher-directed work periods. The areas of the room were stocked with a range of manipulable materials used, according to the orientation of the program, to promote social interaction, skill/concept development, or a combination of the two. The curriculum was derived through teachers' observations of the children's interests and developmental needs, through the possibilities presented by the learning materials themselves, and through awareness of the school content that would follow in the first grade.

## Head Start

At this time (approximately 1959–1963) the federal government intervened in early childhood education in ways that altered the course of curriculum development for the next 15 years. Distressed by descriptions of the depressed physical and intellectual condition of the nation's growing number of poor children, the United States Office of Child Development (now the Administration for Children, Youth and Families) initiated a new federally funded early childhood program—Project Head Start.

Head Start originally espoused the child development tradition in its early learning centers. The educational program was designed around a flexible schedule of child-initiated play and group-learning experiences, which were generally aimed at connecting the three domains of learning. The purpose of the program was to enable each child to develop as fully as possible all facets of his or her "being," while being prepared for the social, emotional, cognitive, linguistic, and physical demands of the first grade.

The public school expected that children would come to the first grade with a firm command of not only social behavior that would enable them to work effectively in a classroom, but also premath, prereading, and other "readiness" skills. The very name Head Start implied such a preparation. The public school's conception of curriculum at that time was, generally speaking, not developmental in nature. It was focused instead on the acquisition of specific content (the facts or substance of math, science, language, literature, and so forth). If children came to the first grade for some reason not ready to assimilate that content, they were considered to be "disadvantaged."

Head Start's mission was to ensure that children would not fail. Consequently, there were new initiatives among Head Start curriculum makers. Strongly influenced by learning theorists and analysts of school content, some of the curriculum developers in experimental projects turned away from the child development approach to direct instruction in a variety of readiness skills and a high proportion of teacher direction in each day's work.

In some of the innovative curriculum models, the interest centers charac-
terizing the early childhood classroom disappeared. They were replaced by
high-intensity, small group interactions, by practice with workbook exercises, or by other forms of focus on behavioral sequences geared to the acquisition of skills and attitudes related to upcoming school experiences
(Evans, 1975).

In other new curriculum models that made up Head Start's "Planned
Variations," the familiar interest centers remained in the classroom, but
were used in new ways to promote school-related skills and attitudes. Whatever the case, children who entered the programs were observed or assessed to see what their needs were—that is, where they were lacking
skills—and learning experiences were designed to develop those skills.
While there were some notable exceptions in program design, many of the
recommended learning activities encouraged use of materials commonly
found in public school kindergartens and first grades, such as felt circles,
squares, and triangles to teach shapes, and monthly calendars to teach passage of time.

## Curriculum Research

Between 1967 and 1973, curriculum research in early childhood education also began to take a particular turn. Instead of focusing so heavily on
the nature of the child as a learner, psychologists and early childhood educators began to explore which program designs would yield the greatest
gains in the children's performance on standardized I.Q. and readiness tests.
Some studies indicated that children did equally well in demonstration or
experimental programs that were radically different from one another (Weikart, 1969). Other studies indicated that academically based programs that
made strong use of direct instruction did result in higher scores on standardized tests (Miller & Dyer, 1975), but that these scores were not generally maintained beyond third grade without follow-up intervention in the
public school (Gray, Ramsey, & Klaus, 1982; Miller & Dyer, 1975).

The results of that wave of research raised a number of interesting
questions. What were the factors that accounted for some measure of success with some children but not with others in the same classroom? Which
programs would be best for children with particular sets of characteristics?
(Smith & Bissell, 1970). What were the contextual variables (such as focus
on the children's direct experiences and incorporation of culturally derived
content into the curriculum) that might account for heightened performance
in given situations? (Juárez & Associates, 1982). These and other concerns

surfaced through the 1970s, refocusing attention on the complexity of the whole child and the many dimensions involved in teaching young children.

## DEBATE AT THE END OF THE CENTURY

With the beginning of the 1980s a new curriculum development movement appeared. This initiative arose in response to a growing nationwide interest in providing all-day kindergartens in public schools. Unlike the Head Start program, full-day kindergartens would address the needs of all children attending public school, regardless of socioeconomic status. While promotion of a longer kindergarten day has been fueled by a variety of political, social, economic, and educational rationales, the net result has been a reassessment of the needs and responses of 5-year-olds in such extended programs.

Particularly prominent in this movement has been renewed interest in the use of traditional school subject areas in kindergarten programs. This interest has in fact sparked lively debate between those who feel that formal, academic skills such as reading and computation should be taught in kindergarten, and those who feel that acquisition of academic skills is not a developmentally appropriate goal for kindergartners.

The former group believes that school subjects should be presented as soon as possible to young children so that academic achievement can be accelerated. This point of view assumes that young children learn in fundamentally the same ways that older children do and that the key to their eventual proficiency in the use of basic skills is "time on task."

The latter group, on the other hand, argues that more important than promoting facility with use of symbols is developing young children's underlying thinking processes—the foundations for problem solving that can be applied later to traditional academic learning. The advocates for providing "the foundations" point out that the elements of all the subject areas can be integrated into learning activities designed to both respond to and promote young children's direct engagement with the world around them. Because of children's developmental characteristics, they can best grasp such content when it is highlighted in common events of interest and when the material is presented in ways that draw upon children's social, emotional, and psychomotor as well as cognitive responses. Incorporation of play into early childhood programs, the developmentalists maintain, should not be abandoned in favor of increased direct instruction, because play serves the function of relating subject matter or content to the children's particular ways of knowing.

The debate between the two opposing camps became so pronounced by the mid-1980s that the National Association for the Education of Young Children (NAEYC, the largest professional association of early childhood educators in the United States) decided it should produce a policy paper defining its position on the issue. The recently expanded statement of NAEYC (Bredekamp, 1987) has subsequently become a major rallying point for the developmentalists.

At the same time, the statement has also inspired renewed interest in a reconceptualization of the early childhood curriculum toward stronger recognition of value systems as legitimate sources of curriculum for young children (Kessler, 1990). A related curricular movement has manifested itself as part of the broader national interest in multicultural and inclusive approaches to teaching young children (Ramsey, Vold, & Williams, 1989). Both of these curricular developments retain a strong child-centered orientation, while suggesting that children's knowledge is not only individually but socially constructed (Kessler, 1990; Williams, 1991). For that reason, culture and belief systems also play a role in what and how children learn and must further expand the notion of the whole child. Knowledge in these areas is acquired largely through the children's observation of their society and playful imitation of the expectations and ways of life that they see around them.

Thus, the image of the whole child, and arguments for the roles of process and play in promoting development and learning, remain vital to the present day; and the themes that have characterized early childhood program formulations continue to reveal themselves in curriculum research. Opposing ideas introduced in some periods of innovation and exploration have served to sharpen the distinctive viewpoint—that the young child should be approached as an integrated being—permeating the field. The chapters that follow explore that viewpoint both within subject areas and across the themes traced in our brief history. The fundamental curriculum questions and the approaches to their possible resolution provided by each author suggest directions for future early childhood curriculum development.

## REFERENCES

Aries, P. (1962). *Centuries of childhood* (R. Balkick, Trans.). New York: Knopf.

Braun, S., & Edwards, E. (1972). *History and theory of early childhood education*. Worthington, OH: Charles A. Jones.

Bredekamp, S. (Ed.). (1987). *Developmentally appropriate practice in early childhood programs serving children from birth through age 8* (rev. ed.). Washington, DC: National Association for the Education of Young Children.

Comenius, J. A. (1910). *The great didactic* (M. W. Keating, Trans.). New York: Russell & Russell. (Original translation 1896)

Dewey, J. (1902). *The child and the curriculum.* Chicago: University of Chicago Press.

Dewey, J. (1963). *Experience and education.* New York: Macmillan. (Original work published 1938)

Dewey, J. (1966). *Democracy and education.* New York: Free Press.

Erikson, E. (1963). *Childhood and society.* New York: W. W. Norton. (Original work published 1950)

Evans, E. (1975). *Contemporary influences in early childhood education* (2nd ed.). New York: Holt, Rinehart & Winston.

Froebel, F. (1887). *The education of man* (W. Hailman, Trans.). New York: E. Appleton. (Original work published 1826)

Gray, S. W., Ramsey, B. K., & Klaus, R. A. (1982). *From 3 to 20: The early training project.* Baltimore: University Park Press.

Gutek, G. L. (1968). *Pestalozzi and education.* New York: Random House.

Gutek, G. L. (1972). *A history of the western educational experience.* New York: Random House.

Juárez & Associates. (1982). *An evaluation of the Head Start bilingual bicultural curriculum development project* (Contract No. HEW 105-77-1048). Washington, DC: Head Start Bureau, Administration for Children, Youth and Families, Department of Health and Human Services.

Kessen, W. (1965). *The child.* New York: John Wiley.

Kessler, S. (1990, April). *Early childhood education as caring.* Paper presented at the Annual Meeting of the American Educational Research Association, Boston.

Miller, L., & Dyer, J. L. (1975). Four preschool programs: Their dimensions and effects. *Monographs of the Society for Research in Child Development, 40*(5–6, Serial No. 162). Chicago: University of Chicago Press.

Montessori, M. (1964). *The Montessori method.* New York: Schocken Books. (Original work published 1912)

Pestalozzi, J. H. (1915). *How Gertrude teaches her children* (L. E. Holland & F. C. Turner, Trans.). Syracuse, NY: C. W. Bardeen. (Original work published 1801)

Piaget, J. (1962). *Play, dreams and imitation in childhood* (H. Weaver, Trans.). New York: W. W. Norton.

Piaget, J., & Inhelder, B. (1969). *The psychology of the child* (C. Gatlegno & F. M. Hodgson, Trans.). New York: Basic Books.

Ramsey, P. G., Vold, E. B., & Williams, L. R. (1989). *Multicultural education: A source book.* New York: Teachers College Press.

Rousseau, J.-J. (1969). *Emile or on education* (A. Bloom, Trans.). New York: Basic Books. (Original work published 1762)

Smith, M. S., & Bissell, J. S. (1970). Report analysis: The impact of Headstart. *Harvard Educational Review, 40* (1), 51–104.

Standing, E. M. (1962). *Maria Montessori: Her life and work.* New York: Mentor Omega Books.

Weber, E. (1984). *Ideas influencing early childhood education: A theoretical analysis.* New York: Teachers College Press.

Weikart, D. (1969). *A comparative study of three preschool curricula.* Presented at the biennial meeting of the Society for Research in Child Development, Santa Monica, CA.

Williams, L. R. (1991). Curriculum making in two voices: Dilemmas of inclusion in early childhood education. *Early Childhood Research Quarterly, 6* (3), 303–311.

# Chapter 2

# Strategies for Teaching

Margaret Lay-Dopyera
John E. Dopyera

This chapter focuses on the strategies early childhood educators select and use as they go about their teaching tasks. The term *strategy* as we are employing it refers to the various approaches teachers use to accomplish their objectives. There are not, to our knowledge, other existing reviews of research on teaching strategies that are appropriate for early childhood education. The compilations of Joyce, Showers, and Weil (1991) and Weil and Joyce (1978a, 1978b, 1978c), which they refer to as "teaching models," are very valuable but have limited application for teachers of young children. What is reported and discussed in this chapter has been gleaned from diverse sources but does not claim full comprehensiveness. We have not, for example, attempted to review research on alternative strategies for the arrangement of the environment or the provision of equipment and materials. There are other omissions as well. This issue will be discussed in more detail at the end of the chapter. The chapter is organized in three sections—theoretical bases, research bases, and summary and implications.

## THEORETICAL BASES

Early childhood educators, like professionals in many fields, have had little success in articulating what it is that they really do. A case is sometimes made that it must always be thus, since each teacher and each teaching situation is different. Some insist that teaching is an art and therefore cannot be successfully analyzed. The teacher as artist is assumed to create teaching strategies in response to each new situation. Perhaps such a view would be more acceptable if there were enough such artists to competently staff our programs, if there were consensus within the profession as to what excellent teaching is, and if the general public had greater respect for the professional educators. This is not the case. We have very discordant images of teaching even within the education profession. Also, low status and poor salaries suggest that teachers of the young are not perceived as respected professionals. This state of affairs might be remedied were teachers to become more reflective about what they do, so that they could better clarify for themselves, and communicate more effectively to others, what works, how it works, and with which children.

Donald Schön's books entitled *The Reflective Practitioner: How Professionals Think in Action* (1983) and *Educating the Reflective Practitioner* (1987) provide useful insights for examining the development of professional expertise. In his terms, in teaching as well as in many other occupations, we lack the ability to make sense of what makes practitioners who are artfully competent different from those who are ineffective. He contrasts a professional's "knowing-in-action" expertise with "reflecting-in-action" expertise. Educators, in general, and perhaps early educators in particular, seem to rely on "knowing-in-action." In this mode we use actions that are carried out almost automatically and that we do not think much about before or during their performance. We may be unaware that we ever learned these things. They seem to us to be natural and spontaneous responses to a given set of circumstances. We may once have had an understanding of why a particular action is appropriate in a given set of circumstances, but have long since ceased to think about it. Perhaps we learned through seeing others act in the same ways and never did really come to understand the rationale. In either case, we are unable to effectively describe what it is that we do. Nor can we adequately explain why we do it.

The development of self-confidence and earning respect from others for professional expertise, according to Schön, is more likely to be related to a "reflecting-in-action" mode. This means one notices what one is doing while doing it, thinks about how it is working, and perhaps changes the way things are being done to determine what these changes bring about. Reflecting-in-action often involves practical theorizing and experimentation—some in advance of action but much of it on the spot. Sometimes a different way of seeing the situation emerges, which then suggests a different action. Through these processes, Schön proposes, legitimate professionalism can be developed.

The consideration of research findings on teaching strategies, some of which may run counter to expectations, may be useful in leading toward a reflective stance; in addition, the conscious development of a repertoire of teaching strategies is an essential step toward reflecting-in-action. By *repertoire*, we refer to the array of alternative actions of which an individual is capable. The systematically planned expansion of repertoire requires a shift away from an assumption of a "best" way and to a gradual adoption of additional strategies. Without a repertoire of alternative strategies for potential teaching situations, the practitioner has little decision-making flexibility.

In early childhood education, practitioners' teaching strategies are sometimes so closely tied to the preferred orientation toward child development (DeVries & Kohlberg, 1987; Kohlberg, 1968; Langer, 1969; Lay-Dopyera & Dopyera, 1990) that practitioners may not scrutinize their methods. If the orientation is constructivist (interactional, cognitive-developmental), certain strategies are accepted without question; if the orientation is behaviorist (environmentalist, cultural transmission), another set of strategies are assumed and seldom questioned. The maturationist (romantic) holds to yet another set. Too often, in our opinion, these beliefs become a rigid ideology, seldom questioned and ineffectively articulated. We concur with Schön that the advancement of the profession and the enhancement of the education and development of young children would be furthered by a more active and reflective stance.

Schön also discusses the relationship between research and practice and the need for a partnership between researchers and reflective practitioners. The agenda, he says, will be generated out of dialogue between these groups and from their joint efforts. Much of the research reviewed in this chapter was initiated by researchers on the issues in which they were interested. This may have little relationship to the teaching tasks as these are viewed by practitioners. Were practitioners to adopt a stance in dialogue with researchers, a different and more extensive set of research findings would be found in such a chapter as this. The following body of research, as viewed from this perspective, must be seen as partial and suggestive.

## RESEARCH BASES

The research will be considered under the following subtopics: teacher–child relationships; classroom management strategies; teacher–child dialogue strategies; and strategies for group lessons.

### Teacher–Child Relationships

Early childhood texts and other professional literature often assert that teachers' relationships with children have a critical influence on children's development and learning. Within this concept, which is often based on something rather close to the Freudian notion of identification, it is said that the ideal relationships are those in which teachers convey warmth, acceptance, and nurturance. Agreement is not universal, however. According to the Montessori tradition, the ideal teacher is friendly but somewhat detached. Montessori children are expected to be motivated by the tasks in which they are involved, not by their relationship with the teacher. Clearly, teachers have alternative possibilities to consider as they decide how they will relate to the children in their classrooms.

And what does the research say about this issue? An early exploration of the benefits of a nurturing supportive relationship with teachers was reported by Thompson (1944), who established and studied two different nursery school curricula for matched groups of children. In one curriculum, the teacher had minimum contact with the children, permitting them to work independently throughout the program day and giving them assistance only when requested. In the other curriculum, the teacher attempted to become a warm friend who actively guided and participated in the children's play experiences in helpful and interested ways. At the end of an 8-month experimental period, the children who experienced the friendly, helpful teacher were found to be more constructive and more ascendant, showed more participation and leadership, and showed less destructive behavior than those in the other group.

A number of similar studies across the decades have used a variety of dependent measures. Comparable findings come from a more recent study. In two day care programs housed within the same university, Tzelepis, Giblin, and Agronow (1983) compared one program, with an abundance of adult-initiated contacts of a positive (less restrictive) nature, with another program in which there was much less interaction. Observations of children's behavior were made during the first and fourth weeks. Where there were fewer adult-initiated contacts, children's interactions with each other and with activities were dramatically less than in the other group. Differences were also noted in peer affiliation. In the program in which adults initiated more friendly, supportive actions, peer interaction was more complex.

Teacher attention and warmth, the above studies suggest, seem to benefit children, at least in the short term. There may be longer-term consequences as well. Shipman (1976), in a longitudinal study of economically disadvantaged children from preschool age through third grade, compared children doing better than expected and those performing more poorly than expected. Those children who did better than expected had teachers during prekindergarten and primary years who were at least moderately warm, enthusiastic, and well prepared. While only suggestive and partial, since other factors may have been as influential, this evidence does support the idea that teacher–child relationships are very important to social and emotional development and that teacher warmth may be critical to those relationships.

Montessori programs, which, as previously mentioned, place less emphasis on teacher–child relationships, were compared by Chattin-McNichols (1981) with non-Montessori programs.

> The Montessori program performs equal to or better than other programs in certain areas such as divergent production and school readiness, and is inferior in some respects to specially designed programs, for example, in comparison to Piaget-oriented programs in producing Piagetian conceptual development. Vocabulary recognition, and ratings of verbal-social participation are other areas in which programs other than Montessori produce higher gains. In the development of attentional strategies, general intelligence, achievement in academic areas, . . . the Montessori method performs as well as any other program. (p. 65)

It should be pointed out that there are many additional differences between Montessori and non-Montessori programs, besides teacher–child relationships, which may account for the cited findings.

There are other ways of describing teacher–child relationships, of course. Within a behaviorist tradition, the ideal teacher–child relationship is often characterized in terms of interchange, such as reinforcements from the teacher, particularly the extent to which those reinforcements relate directly to the appropriateness of children's behavior. Attention, appropriately directed, has been repeatedly found to be effective in changing preschool children's behavior. Warmth, in these situations, may be experienced by children but only when their behavior is in line with the teacher's expectations.

On the other hand, interesting contrasting evidence suggests that adult attention may, in some instances, prevent children from fully exercising their own resources. Garvey (1977) noted that as young as age 3, children surrounded by adults seemed to use more restricted language, in contrast to the extensive conversations the same children held by themselves in a playroom. These findings bring to mind earlier evidence (Siegel & Kohn, 1959) that dyads become more aggressive when a friendly interested adult—who does not interfere with their aggressive actions—is present, than when there is no adult present. Pellegrini (1984) similarly has found that when children play in the presence of adults they tend to engage in less mature forms of play than when they play alone. It appears that an adult who is passively present, even though friendly in orientation, does not motivate children to rely on their own resources. To build children's repertoire for independent action, however, the active involvement of a warm, friendly, attentive adult may be very important.

It is clear that teachers can bring about diverse effects by the attention strategies they choose. Although the teacher's child development orientation might be expected to accurately predict teacher–child relationships, research suggests that the patterns may not be as clear-cut as one might expect. For example, Miller and Dyer (1975) learned as they compared the program processes and effects of contrasting program models, that the program that most emphasizes teacher–child relationships—the "traditional" nursery school model—had the highest ratio of negative-to-positive feedback to children. Soar and Soar (1972) also point out the high rate of negative feedback given to children in the more "open" Follow Through classrooms in which they observed. Fagot (1973) found a similar result in a preschool study.

Rather than identifying themselves as warm, accepting teachers and simply assuming that this is the case, reflective teachers might do well to observe themselves in action to determine when and under what conditions they are warm and supportive and when they become harsh and rejecting. And reflective teachers, whether behaviorist or otherwise, might also observe how children's behavior and learning are influenced by their own warmth and attention, contingently or noncontingently given.

## Strategies for Classroom Management

Classroom management may be described as teacher behavior aimed at keeping children engaged appropriately and reducing the likelihood of behavior that requires the teacher to give children negative feedback. Much of the research on classroom management has been conducted in elementary schools rather than early childhood settings. It seems likely, however, that there are some important commonalities. On the other hand, it should be noted that in the elementary school studies, effectiveness is equated with pupils' achievement gains. The relevance of these findings for early education and for nonacademic goals has not been determined.

In a number of studies, effective teachers have been found to be those who plan ahead and who develop in advance clear notions of acceptable student behavior. Anderson, Evertson, and Emmer (1979) report that less effective teachers often appear to be unclear in their own thinking about how they want children to behave and they wait until problems develop before talking with the children about what they expect. In the third-grade classrooms in which observations were done over the course of a year, the teachers who emerged as more effective could be identified by their pattern of behavior during the first 3 weeks of school. These teachers were actively involved in communicating with their pupils about behavioral expectations and classroom procedures. Effective teachers began the year by attending to details such as arranging space for personal possessions and routines for toileting, eating, drinking, and so forth. Emmer, Evertson, and Anderson (1979) also point out that effective teachers plan ahead for various possibilities such as the need to rearrange space for special events and for the accommodation of classroom visitors.

Similar findings are reported for prekindergarten programs. Tzelepis, Giblin, and Agronow (1983) found the early weeks of a day care program to be critical. They proposed that since the initial orientation of children entering a new program is toward adults, at this stage adults can take advantage of this opportunity to informally teach children skills necessary to interact with peers, to express wants, to understand possessions and how to share, to verbalize pleasure and anger, and to begin to resolve conflict. Additionally, adults can redirect children's attention to available materials and activities. Then as children engage in parallel play, adults can encourage constructive peer interaction.

Effective teachers have also been reported by Emmer, Evertson, and Anderson (1979) to engage in the following behavior. They use a variety of means of teaching procedures: modeling, rehearsal, and incentives. And they continue to work on necessary procedures until children master them. They give very specific feedback, both positive and negative, about children's performance rather than general praise. For example, instead of saying, "You've been very good at lunch today," they would give more precise praise, such as "I notice that you remembered what to do with your cup, plate, and napkin when you finished eating." Good and Grouws (1975) studied third- and fourth-grade teachers and found that effective teachers spend less time on transitions. They also wait until all are quiet to give verbal instructions.

One's position in the classroom is important for effective management. Brophy and Evertson (1976) found that effective teachers move around the classroom more often and, when stationary, regularly scan the entire classroom. By knowing what is going on, the teacher is often able to redirect children's behavior in a constructive way or foresee the need for materials or guidance.

Anderson, Evertson, and Emmer (1979) report that effective teachers can predict what children are likely to pay attention to, or to be confused or distracted by. They use variations in voice modulation, pacing, and movement to attract and hold attention. They prevent confusion by carefully pacing directions so that they are not presenting similar activities at the same time. They require the active attention of every group member when important information is to be given. However, it may also be effective to limit the amount of information presented to young children in groups. Stallings (1975) found that when teachers give instructions to first-grade children on a one-to-one basis, the children are more persistent with tasks than when instructions are presented to a group. The younger the child, the less likely that information presented in a group setting will be efficiently received.

The great advantage in systematic structuring for effective classroom management may be reduced stress for the adult. If adult stress is avoided, children benefit, since the psychological state of the teacher is often communicated nonverbally to children, even though verbal expression is suppressed (Yinger, 1975). By building a repertoire for classroom management, teachers can reflect in action about other aspects of their teaching responsibilities.

## Teacher–Child Dialogue Strategies

Dialogue is essential in teaching young children, for a number of reasons. First, as noted above, children prior to age 6 or 7 are believed to take in information more accurately when that information is directed to them as individuals. Perhaps this is a function of teacher position or eye contact in the one-to-one encounter. Or perhaps the teacher talks to the child so as to match the child's ability to understand. Or perhaps it is the self-enhancement that comes from receiving personal attention. Whatever the reason, dialogue does seem to be essential (see Stallings, 1975).

Second, in early childhood programs as well as at home, much of the children's time is spent in play activities. Many early educators consider play to be the most effective medium for children's learning. Play often involves pretend activities in which children assume roles or manipulate toys to create imaginary scenes. It may also involve the use of manipulative materials such as sand, blocks, clay, and so forth, for purposes determined by the children without teacher direction. Other aspects of play may involve games such as "tag" or "button, button," which children invent or learn from peers or from their parents or teachers. Kamii and DeVries (1980) offer examples and guidelines for the use of group games in early education and amply illustrate the benefits of fostering these involvements. While children are playing, teachers have the opportunity to engage individuals and small groups in dialogue. Through such interchanges, children can be helped to pursue their own goals, and adults have optimal opportunity for informal teaching. As Almy, Monighan, Scales, and Van Hoorn (1984) point out in the following excerpt, it is not sufficient for teachers to merely set the stage and let children play:

> Teachers who . . . justify an important place for play in the early childhood curriculum will not lose sight of their responsibilities as instructors. They will take account of the allure of play but will also recognize children's needs to acquire information and skills in a variety of ways. Bearing in mind Piaget's view of play as assimilation, they will not neglect the accommodative aspect of learning. Preschool children, at their own level, need

to encounter the physical and the social worlds in ways that help them to clarify and understand. Teachers have responsibility in these areas as well as providing the play opportunities in which children can consolidate and make personally meaningful the experiences they have had. (p. 22)

Dialogue between teachers and children that contributes to children's learning occurs not only during free play periods, but also during many informal group activities during the program day. As Katz and Chard (1989) have recently reminded us, children learn best when engaged in meaningful work. The quality and diversity of classroom talk are believed to be enhanced when children are pleasurably absorbed in exciting investigations or in creating products related to a topic that is engaging. The schools at Reggio Emilia, Italy (see Chapter 12, this volume; New, 1990; Katz, 1990) provide a model of the type of setting that fosters dialogue. At Reggio Emilia, children's inquiry into topics such as shadows, colors, and space travel is strongly supported and ambitiously pursued. According to New (1990), one of the functions teachers at Reggio Emilia fulfill is to serve as the "memory" of the group. The development of projects and explorations is well documented through photographs and transcribed tape recordings of the children's activities and discussions. These records, created by teachers, provide the stimulus for children's reflection and further experimentation. The effects of a teacher's active tracking of children's experiences, for purposes not only of informing themselves and other adults of progress, but of providing children with their own history, have not been sufficiently investigated. We would hypothesize, however, that teacher–child dialogue is enhanced by the presence of these kinds of records.

Within rich, well-organized, or unhurried classroom settings, teachers constructively enter into dialogue with individual children or with small groups through the following types of strategies: providing descriptive feedback; reinforcing; coaching, prompting, and giving suggestions; asking questions; and modeling. Each of these will be described in turn.

*Giving descriptive feedback.*    There have been many useful guides for teachers about how to teach informally through talking with children. Memorable examples are "How to Talk with a Scribbler" (Sparling & Sparling, 1973) and "Teaching Children as They Play" (Anker, Foster, McLane, Sokel, & Weissbourd, 1974). In giving descriptive feedback, teachers observe the child's activity or attention focus and talk to him or her about it. The landmark study of Hess and Shipman (1965) reported that the degree to which mothers used elaborate language and drew children's attention was related to children's success in learning tasks. Since then, many other studies have pursued the same and related issues with similar results. Carew (1980), in a longitudinal observational study of home-reared and day care children in their second and third years, found that in day care, as in the home, children's I.Q. at age 3 was predicted by the amount of language-focused activity provided earlier by adults. According to Carew and many other researchers (e.g., Blank, 1973; Blank & Solomon, 1968, 1969), appropriate language-focused adult–child interchange appears to be required to build intelligent behavior.

*Reinforcing.* As indicated in the above section on teacher–child relationships, most early educators recognize the influence of teacher behavior on children's behavior, learning, and development. The most systematic and comprehensive presentation of research on how reinforcement works comes, of course, from the late B. F. Skinner and his associates (e.g., Skinner, 1974; Bijou & Baer, 1978). Teachers in classrooms reinforce or fail to reinforce children by the distribution of their attention to approval. They also distribute "turns," grant permissions, and regulate the use of resources. Principles derived from the research of behaviorists on the management of reinforcers (positive and negative) versus ignoring and punishment are useful for teachers to understand, regardless of their own child development orientation. Conversely, teachers are well advised to consider how they themselves are being influenced by the reinforcement of children's behavior toward them as well as the other way around. Whether viewed in behaviorist terms or otherwise, it is obvious that in teacher–child relationships influences go in both directions. Many of the hassles between teachers and children may, however, be more easily understood as reciprocal when viewed according to reinforcement principles. For example, Wittmer (1985b) found teachers of toddlers observed in Title XX Day Care seemingly to be influenced by children's behavior. When children's behavior was positive, teachers behaved toward them in a positive fashion. However, when children's behavior was negative it was predominantly followed by negative teacher behavior. Observers in schools often see this pattern and wonder why it appears to be so persistent. As Wittmer (1985a) comments, "If teachers responded to a higher proportion of child positive behaviors and used more positive techniques in response to child negative behaviors, the outcome could be more emotionally nurturant, intellectually stimulating experiences" (p. 3).

When this situation is examined in practical terms, we note that adults who react to children's negative behavior by scolding, for example, are immediately reinforced by the cessation, however temporary, of the child's misbehavior. This reinforcement leads the teacher to increased use of scolding. And since the scolding is only mildly aversive, it is not an effective punishment. In fact, the teacher's attention may be reinforcing. More negative actions are the result. Children's negative behavior followed by the teacher's negative behavior becomes cyclical in far too many school settings. As Peters, Neisworth, and Yawkey (1985) point out: "Teachers of young children have hundreds of opportunities daily to reinforce developmentally appropriate behavior; the devilish other side of the coin is that there are also hundreds of opportunities accidentally to reinforce inappropriate and developmentally destructive behavior" (p. 105).

*Coaching, prompting, and giving suggestions.* While children are engaged in pretending and other active classroom pursuits, teachers can, through judicious observation and interjection, add to children's understanding and extend children's repertoires for subsequent similar situations. The goal of intervening in children's dramatic play is to develop their abilities to engage in social interactions more adequately and to pretend, both of which are related not only to success in play but also to learning and thinking skills.

Much of the research has focused on the consequences of training "disadvantaged" children how to play. Smilansky (1968), Feitelson and Ross (1973), Rosen (1974), and Rubin, Maioni, and Hornung (1976) have all reported less frequent involvement and less complex sociodramatic play in children from low socioeconomic backgrounds. Smilansky (1968) reported that training significantly improved the quality of Israeli children's play. A number of other studies of what is sometimes called "play-training" have reported positive effects on verbal I.Q. (Saltz, Dixon, & Johnson, 1977), creative thinking (Feitelson & Ross, 1973), social-role conservation (Fink, 1974), and conservation of quantity (Golomb & Cornelius, 1977).

Two types of intervention, inside and outside, as suggested by Smilansky (1968), were emphasized by Christie (1982). In outside intervention, the teacher does not take a role in the play episode but comments to a child about specific play behaviors that might be used. Comments may take the form of questions: "What are you going to cook for dinner?"; suggestions: "You might cook spaghetti for dinner"; directions: "Put some water in the pan and then put it on the stove"; coaching: "Tell the doctor what is wrong with the baby." In inside intervention, the teacher takes a role and actually joins in the children's play and shows the children how to play roles, to use one object to represent another, to pretend particular actions, and to communicate about particular actions and roles to others involved in playing.

Rosen's (1974) study demonstrated that when teachers become actively involved with individual children during free play in modeling role playing, in asking leading questions and offering suggestions, and in greater role playing, the results are gains in group productivity and problem solving. In the Rosen intervention, teachers often directed their attention within the group to those weakest in skills. To the group they introduced new problems, ideas, themes, or incidents. For example, in house play they interjected the illness of a family member; in a mountain-climbing episode, they suggested that a member of the group had fallen over a ledge, leaving the rest of the group to consider how to help.

Coaching, prompting, and giving suggestions are viable teaching strategies in many other situations as well. The teacher's ability to enter skillfully into children's involvement with materials such as puzzles, table toys, paints, and so forth, is also significant. Interrupting a child's activity for dialogue is worthwhile if teachers can use their comments and children's responses as a basis for mutual learning. The teacher can learn about how children are thinking, and children can be helped to extend their concepts and language. Guidelines provided by Marian Blank (1973; Blank & Solomon, 1969) are particularly useful in building these skills.

*Asking questions.*     Questions were used extensively by Piaget and were considered by him to "constitute the fundamental factor in cognitive development" (1977, p. 17). Questions, within the comprehension realm of the child, that create discrepancies, pose contradictions, and require a shifting of perspective would be expected to have maximal impact on children's thinking and learning. Kamii and DeVries (1978) suggest four types of questions that encourage children to think about relationships between objects and events.

1. Making predictions: What do you think will happen if you _____?
2. Creating specific effects: Can you do _____?
3. Connecting actions with events: How did you do _____?
4. Determining causes: Why does _____ happen?

Questions that focus children's attention on transformations are also recommended by Forman and Kuschner (1977). They further propose emphasis on questions that encourage the child to think about the opposite of what he or she is talking about. The child says, "I want to play with the ball outside." The teacher might say in response, "Does that mean that you don't want to play with the ball inside?" Perhaps such teacher intervention, when used judiciously, challenges the child toward greater metalinguistic and conceptual awareness.

Siegel and Saunders (1979), in a comprehensive summary of questioning as an informal instructional model, point out that asking questions directly confronts the child's current point of view, thus leading the child to restructure his or her thoughts. They further point out the importance of waiting long enough between question and answer, accepting answers without posing alternatives, and showing approval of thoughtful answers even though they may be wrong. They advise pursuing the thinking behind incorrect answers, since both the teacher and child benefit. The teacher learns more about the child's view, and the child examines his or her own beliefs more fully. Responses to questions a child asks can also be important if the teacher takes advantage of the opportunity to get the child to consider past experiences, find appropriate information, or figure out answers independently. Children's questions can lead to genuine dialogue. Siegel and Saunders (1979) note the positive results of programs that emphasize question-asking.

*Modeling.*    Modeling, as used in this context, refers to adults' conscious enactment, for children's observation, of desirable behavior. If the person doing the modeling is admired, and/or if rewards are observed to follow the behavior, imitation of the modeled behavior can be anticipated. The efficacy of modeling has been fully documented by Bandura and Walters (1963; see also Bandura, 1969, 1973). Teachers are potent influences for children, often without realizing it. The extent to which nonrelevant as well as relevant behavior is noted and faithfully imitated is testimony to the efficacy of modeling. The teacher who sniffs and rubs her eyes because of allergy problems while showing children how to do something sometimes finds sniffing and eye rubbing incorporated by the children as part of what they have learned. The teacher's behavior and especially the behavior of admired peers or older children are potent influences for good or for ill. Teachers will generally benefit from greater awareness of how to use modeling. For example, according to Zimmerman and Rosenthal (1974), simple modeling, involving only observations of a model, as contrasted with guided practice, is more effective for helping young children learn new procedures. Zimmerman and Rosenthal (1974) also report that 4-year-olds, unlike 7-year-olds, are helped in learning from a model by being led to verbalize what is being demonstrated. Much has been written (e.g., Ross, 1981) about the effects of models, the characteristics of a good model, and ways to facilitate modeling effects that teachers may find useful.

### Strategies for Group Lessons

When, for one reason or another, it is desirable to have a group of children together in an activity that a teacher intends to actively lead, various strategies may be used. These include direct instruction, deductive lessons with advance organizers, inductive lessons for concept attainment, cooperative learning, modeling lessons, problem discussion lessons, "wonderful idea" lessons, and "play-debrief-play" lessons. Each of these will be discussed below.

*Direct instruction.*    Direct instruction undoubtedly has many varia-tions but has been characterized generically by Jacobs and Welch (1983) as using attention signals, instances and noninstances, response signals, feed-back, reinforcers, pacing, pauses, rhythm, response rates, volume, body language, enthusiasm, stimulus change, surprises, intentional mistakes, and mastery. The efficacy of direct instruction with low socioeconomic students for accomplishing specific academic and other similar highly focused objec-tives has been well documented (Becker & Gersten, 1982; Bereiter & En-gelmann, 1966; Rosenshine, 1978).

In the direct instruction approach, initially proposed by Bereiter and Engelmann (1966) and commercially packaged under the DISTAR label, the teacher's behavior is predetermined via a prepared script provided with the teaching materials. Very specific steps leading to final objectives are speci-fied. The basic techniques, however, may also be employed by teachers for lessons they design with very specific objectives. The direct instruction les-son starts off with contrasts—children are verbally presented with discrim-inations or labels along with examples of where these may be applied. The representations begin with extreme contrasts and go toward finer and finer gradations. For example, children may be asked initially to discriminate be-tween ice-cream cones and the letter *m*, but eventually, between the letters *m* and *n*. The students' role is to learn the right response, and the teacher's role is to tell the pupils whether they are right or wrong and to carefully arrange the presentation so that they will be right most of the time. Lively, rhythmic interchanges and enthusiastic reinforcement are essential to the success of the strategy.

*Deductive lessons with advance organizers.*    For Ausubel (1963, 1968), the most efficient approach to instruction is to begin a lesson with general ideas under which more differentiated ideas can be developed. Children are first given a comprehensive general presentation before seeing how exem-plars fit into an overall scheme. This is said to be particularly important for young children since they tend to jump quickly to erroneous conclusions, to generalize from limited experience, and to consider only one aspect of a problem or a situation at a time. In this approach children's discovery of knowledge is deemphasized and the meaningful presentation by the teacher of external subject matter is considered essential if misconceptions are to be avoided.

A series of studies conducted by Lawton and associates of the Wisconsin Research and Development Center for Cognitive Learning support this approach to the teaching of logical operations and social studies concepts (Lawton, 1977), hierarchical classification (Schwadener & Lawton, 1978), and concepts of conservation as identified by Piaget (Lawton & Reddy, 1983). Advance organizer lessons have also been applied to instruction in music, math, science, language, prereading, and social problem solving (Schwadener & Lawton, 1978).

In an advance organizer lesson on classification described by Schwadener and Lawton (1978), the teacher pointed out objects in the room and identified them as to their various properties: differing heights, weights, colors, and so forth. Children were then given objects to examine, manipulate, and classify according to similar properties. Throughout there were attempts to relate new concepts or examples to the more general concepts that the children gave evidence of understanding.

The preplanning of this approach appears to be most concerned with hierarchical sequencing of presentation. Once the format from general to specific is set, the teacher looks for appealing materials, concrete props, and a variety of related materials. While teaching, the teacher must be very alert to the children's existing understandings so that these may be used as a basis for new learning.

*Inductive lessons for concept attainment.*    As in the concept attainment tasks used by Bruner, Goodnow, and Austin (1956) to study children's thinking strategies, the concept attainment lesson begins with an assortment of exemplars or nonexemplars. The term *exemplar* refers to particular actions, situations, objects, or pictures selected to represent a given concept. *Nonexemplars* refer to actions, situations, objects, or pictures selected because they do *not* represent the concept. There are two approaches. In the first, the concepts to be "discovered" are predetermined by the teacher. Exemplars representing contrasts either are already grouped and displayed at the point of initial presentation or are presented one at a time and gradually sorted by the teacher according to some preset criterion, for example, zoo animals versus farm animals, or circles versus squares. The criterion for inclusion or exclusion in a particular group of objects is not told to the children. They try to figure out the underlying concept that makes one item identified as A and the next as not A.

In this type of concept attainment lesson, the teacher uses familiar materials, identifies both examples and nonexamples of the target concepts, gives students many examples, provides materials for children to test out their own ideas, and encourages children to discuss each other's ideas. The advantage of the concept attainment lesson is believed to be the development of thinking skills. The mental processes used in this lesson are seen as comparable to those used to discover or invent concepts in everyday learning.

In the second approach, the children are shown a mixed array of pictures or objects selected to represent several possible conceptual dimensions (for example, clothing that might be classified according to gender, season, or appropriateness for indoor or outdoor wear). Students sort according to a category they invent and explain their classification rationale to other children in the group. There are, in this approach, no "right" ways to categorize.

*Cooperative learning.*    Although cooperative learning, as described and promoted by Johnson & Johnson (1990), Slavin (1987, 1991), and Guskey (1990), is typically employed with older children, the basic strategy may be relevant for consideration for early childhood teaching as well. Miller (1989), for example, cites evidence for the use of cooperative learning strategies in enhancing the social integration of mainstreamed young children. In cooperative learning, small groups work together to accomplish learning tasks and are expected to assist each other in the process. Each student is responsible not only for his or her own learning but for the learning of others in the group as well. To receive the recognition or reward established for successful completion of the task, all members must reach the set goal. For accomplishment of their tasks, students must work together in face-to-face interaction and communicate effectively with each other, resolving conflicts within the group. The tasks for young children might be such things as learning to tie shoes or name primary colors.

The limitations of these procedures, as viewed by many early childhood educators, are the adult imposition of tasks and the use of external rewards for completion. Cooperative learning strategies are often paired with mastery and behaviorist approaches, with highly specified criteria for students' efforts and evidence of completion. Constructivists, however, also value cooperative learning although, for them, the specification of tasks and their completion are part of the decision making done by the group rather than fully specified by the teacher. Kohlberg and Lickona (1987), for example, describe as cooperative learning activities making group terrariums, making group murals, cooperative block building, cooperative puzzles, and so forth. In these activities the comparisons children make of their own ideas with the ideas of others lessen egocentrism and lead them to "realize the necessity of logical argument and empirical verification" (p. 179).

*Modeling lessons.*    There are situations in which a teacher may want to teach a particular skill or procedure to a group of children quite systematically. The modeling procedure cited by Charles (1981, p. 156) provides a pragmatic approach for classroom use. The following steps are recommended:

1. Choose a good model (a person who incorporates traits seen as desirable by the children, such as a popular peer leader, a somewhat older child, a favorite adult).
2. Train the model in precise behavior to be enacted and have the model demonstrate the "target" behavior to the group.
3. Call for verbal group enactment in unison of what was modeled. Ask leading questions regarding critical points, having the model reenact as necessary. Repeat verbal group enactment two or three times, making sure all participate.
4. Ask for volunteers (two) to reenact the event individually.
5. Draft two nonvolunteers.
6. Have learners immediately apply the skill or behavior to a meaningful situation.

*Problem discussion lessons.*    In a problem discussion lesson, a social problem is typically used as a focus, although other kinds of problems may be addressed. The problem may be a simulated one requiring description and/or role playing, or it may be an actual problem of concern to the group members. The goal is not to teach the "right" or "best" answer but to develop children's awareness of the need for solutions and to develop a repertoire of viable possibilities in problem situations.

Problem discussion lessons are part of the training provided by the Spivack and Shure interpersonal Problem-Solving Curriculum for 4-year-olds and 5-year-olds (Shure, 1980; Spivack, Platt, & Shure, 1976; Spivack & Shure, 1974). The curriculum is effective for increasing children's awareness of alternatives and consequences. Children become more adept at generating various strategies that have potential for solving interpersonal problems. They also learn to evaluate various alternatives in terms of their prospective consequences. Teachers' ratings indicate that after the training, children's social competence increases.

The Spivack and Shure lesson scripts include the initial development of essential vocabulary and concepts for considering and discussing alternatives. Once this has been done, the teacher poses a problem for consideration. One lesson, for example, begins by establishing that it is fair for children who have been playing with toys to put them away. The children are then told about a situation in which one of two children will not help in putting the toys away. The question that is posed is, "What can _____ do so _____ will help him put the toys away?" Responses are acknowledged and listed on a chalkboard. After each answer, the teacher repeats it and all previous suggestions and asks, "Who's got a different idea?" (Spivack & Shure, 1974, p. 176). Although the Spivack and Shure materials consist of a set of detailed scripts, the lesson strategies can be adapted for use for any problem-focused group discussion.

*"Wonderful idea" lessons.*     Eleanor Duckworth, the author of "The Having of Wonderful Ideas" (1972; as reported by Meek, 1991), describes her approach for working with groups as introducing a stimulus that is complex enough to provide something intriguing to think about. She then simply asks her students what they notice about the phenomenon. Although she has her own ideas of what may be noticed, she has no preconceived answers. The smallest comment is valued, and students learn from each other's answers and are stimulated by others' ideas to refocus and to look (or listen or feel) more closely with growing awareness and differentiation. Depending on the stimulus, children's comments often include dynamic processes they observe as well as physical characteristics. Whether the stimuli are floating objects or mirrors, there are myriad possibilities for learning as children (or adults) experiment and share their "wonderful ideas."

*Play-debrief-replay lessons.*     Selma Wasserman in her book *Serious Players in the Primary Classroom* (1990) proposes a lesson format designed to amplify the learning potential in play experiences by following a "play" period with a "debrief" period in which the children are encouraged to reflect on what they have done and observed. The teacher's questions about the play involvement increase children's understanding and alert them to new possibilities for experimentation and observation. Opportunities for "replay" follow debriefing and may occur over the next several days. In replay experiences, the same play opportunities may be available or new materials may be added.

In using the "play-debrief-replay" lesson strategy, teachers create play centers to support the development of major concepts of the curriculum—science, social studies mathematics, language arts, and creative arts. For each play center, stimulating materials are collected together that develop selected concepts, promote learning goals, and engage children in a variety of thinking operations. "Activity cards" are created for each play center, which are either read by the children or read to the children. The card describes the general purpose of the materials in the center and poses leading questions. Children typically choose between various play opportunities but are accountable for responding thoughtfully to the questions the teacher will pose during debriefing. The play is often carried out in cooperative learning groups, although this is not necessarily the case. During the play the teacher observes, rather than participating or directing the children's activities. As Wasserman points out, the "play-debrief-replay" lesson strategy is rooted in the principles of John Dewey and is frequently observed in classrooms. Formalizing the three steps, a la Wasserman, however, provides the structure for curriculum implementation using children's play as a focus.

It may be accurately noted that the last three strategies for group lessons (problem discussions, "wonderful idea" lessons, and "play-debrief-replay" lessons) might not appropriately be called lessons at all if one adheres to the narrow conception of lessons as described by Tyler (1949) or Hunter (1982). We believe that it is useful for early childhood educators to recognize the distinction between *planning for lessons with preset objectives* and *planning for activities with many alternative learning possibilities*. Both formats are valuable, but the two function differently (Lay-Dopyera & Dopyera, 1990). The presentation of activities such as soap bubbles or soup making to small intact groups, without preset objectives to be achieved, is described as follows:

> Each activity . . . provides for children with a range of abilities and has sufficient complexity to permit numerous ways for children to become involved. Various types of learning are expected from each activity. Teacher planning focuses on finding ways to stimulate and encourage children to connect new with previous experiences, to experiment, to categorize, to theorize, and to draw inferences. Each activity and set of materials is analyzed in considerable detail by the teacher as part of the planning process. With various possibilities in mind, the teacher is more alert and flexible concerning ways in which the children . . . become involved. (Lay-Dopyera & Dopyera, 1990, p. 229)

The resurgent enthusiasm for project learning or themes, as promoted by Goetz (1985), Jacobs and Borland (1986), Levin (1986), Katz and Chard (1989), Krogh (1990), and Nunnally (1990), and the growing involvement of teachers with whole language approaches (Goodman, 1986; Newman, 1985) require teacher skill in using open-ended teaching strategies for group work along with the more traditional lesson approaches.

## SUMMARY AND IMPLICATIONS

Howsan, Corrigan, Denemark, and Nash (1976) characterize teaching as a semiprofession. They point out that teaching, in contrast to occupations that can be considered true professions, is held in low esteem and has a low occupational status, a shorter training period, a less specialized and less highly developed body of knowledge and skills, and less emphasis on theoretical and conceptual bases of practice. As Spodek and Saracho (1982) point out, teachers of early childhood education enjoy even less esteem than those at other levels. In the introductory section of this chapter, we cited Schön's perspective that greater articulation and examination of work processes are necessary to develop professional expertise. The romantic view of teacher as artist is inadequate either to foster individual professional growth or to enhance teaching as a profession.

As a remedy to this situation, we urge teachers to consciously develop a repertoire for various teaching situations and to undertake reflecting-in-action. It also seems important that professional groups help to articulate what these alternatives might be, developing vocabulary and concepts to match what has remained a largely intuitive set of practices. From such a thrust we predict benefits for individual teachers, the teaching profession, and children enrolled in early childhood education programs.

The strategies discussed in this chapter should help individual teachers in assessing repertoire areas in need of development. They may also indicate the need for better articulation of what it is we really do in teaching young children. In this chapter we have considered teaching alternatives under strategies for teacher–child relationships, teacher–child dialogue, and group lessons. Teachers may choose whether to establish warm, supportive relationships with children or remain more distant, hoping not to interfere with children's autonomy and integrity; whether to provide attention freely or contingently; and what degree of structuring to provide. The classroom management section delineated areas in which teachers' choices and actions may be critical to children's involvement and learning. For example, how may the first days and weeks of school be used to orient children to procedures and expectations? What advance anticipation and preparation are helpful for effective management? Possible alternatives for teacher–child dialogue were proposed: giving descriptive feedback; reinforcing; coaching, prompting, and giving suggestions; asking questions; modeling. For group lessons we discussed strategies of direct instruction, deductive lessons with advance organizers, inductive lessons for concept attainment, cooperative learning, modeling lessons, problem discussions, "wonderful idea" lessons and "play-debrief-replay" lessons. Of course, this represents a very meager set of strategies; others are referred to in textbooks and articles but have not yet been researched. There are also, we expect, strategies used by highly competent teachers that are not well recognized, and hence little, if anything, has been written about them.

Despite its meager nature, we expect that this collection of teaching strategies may go well beyond the alternatives now available to many individual early childhood education teachers. It is fascinating to consider what else there is. We wish to challenge ourselves and our fellow professionals to engage more often in reflecting-in-action so that we may, as a profession, act more intelligently and develop a body of knowledge that helps us become adequate to our tasks of guiding the learning and development of young children.

## REFERENCES

Almy, M., Monighan, P., Scales, B., & Van Hoorn, J. (1984). Recent research on play: The teacher's perspective. In L. G. Katz (Ed.), *Current topics in early childhood education* (Vol. 5, pp. 1–25). Norwood, NJ: Ablex.

Anderson, L., Evertson, C., & Emmer, E. (1979). *Dimensions in classroom management derived from recent research.* Austin: Texas University Research and Development Center for Teacher Education. (ERIC Document Reproduction Service No. ED 175 860)

Anker, D., Foster, J., McLane, J., Sokel, J., & Weissbourd, B. (1974). Teaching children as they play. *Young Children, 29,* 203–213.

Ausubel, D. P. (1963). *The psychology of meaningful verbal learning.* New York: Grune & Stratton.

Ausubel, D. P. (1968). *Educational psychology: A cognitive view.* New York: Holt, Rinehart and Winston.

Bandura, A. (1969). Social learning theory of identification processes. In D. A. Goslin (Ed.), *Handbook of socialization theory and research* (pp. 213–262). Chicago: Rand McNally.

Bandura, A. (1973). *Aggression: A social learning analysis.* Englewood Cliffs, NJ: Prentice-Hall.

Bandura, A., & Walters, R. H. (1963). *Social learning and personality development.* New York: Holt, Rinehart and Winston.

Becker, W. C., & Gersten, R. (1982). A follow-up of Follow Through: The later effects of the Direct Instruction Model on children in fifth and sixth grades. *American Educational Research Journal, 19,* 75–92.

Bereiter, C., & Engelmann, S. (1966). *Teaching disadvantaged children in the preschool.* Englewood Cliffs, NJ: Prentice-Hall.

Bijou, S. W., & Baer, D. M. (1978). *Behavior analysis of child development.* Englewood Cliffs, NJ: Prentice-Hall.

Blank, M. (1973). *Teaching learning in the preschool: A dialogue approach.* Columbus, OH: Charles E. Merrill.

Blank, M., & Solomon, F. (1968). A tutorial program to develop abstract thinking in socially disadvantaged preschool children. *Child Development, 39* (1), 379–390.

Blank, M., & Solomon, F. (1969). How shall the disadvantaged child be taught? *Child Development, 40,* 47–61.

Brophy, J. E., & Evertson, C. M. (1976). *Learning from teaching: A developmental perspective.* Boston: Allyn & Bacon.

Bruner, J. S., Goodnow, J. J., & Austin, G. A. (1956). *A study in thinking.* New York: John Wiley.

Carew, J. V. (1980). Experience and the development of intelligence in young children at home and in day care. *Monographs of the Society for Research in Child Development, 45* (Serial No. 186).

Charles, C. M. (1981). *Building classroom discipline: From model to practice.* New York: Longman.

Chattin-McNichols, J. P. (1981). The effects of Montessori school experience. *Young Children, 36*, 49–66.

Christie, J. F. (1982). Sociodramatic play training. *Young Children, 37*, 25–32.

DeVries, R., & Kohlberg, L. (1987). *Constructivist early education: Overview and comparison with other programs.* Washington, DC: National Association for the Education of Young Children.

Duckworth, E. (1972). The having of wonderful ideas. *Harvard Educational Review, 42*, 217–231.

Emmer, E., Evertson, C., & Anderson, L. (1979). *The first weeks of class . . . and the rest of the year.* Austin: Texas University Research and Development Center for Teacher Education. (ERIC Document Reproduction Service No. ED 175 861)

Fagot, B. I. (1973). Influence of teacher behavior in the preschool. *Developmental Psychology, 9*, 198–206.

Feitelson, D., & Ross, G. S. (1973). The neglected factor—play. *Human Development, 16*, 202–223.

Fink, R. S. (1974). *The role of imaginative play in cognitive development: An experimental study.* Buffalo: State University of New York at Buffalo.

Forman, G. E., & Kuschner, D. S. (1977). *The child's construction of knowledge: Piaget for teaching children.* Monterey, CA: Brooks/Cole.

Garvey, C. (1977). *Play.* Cambridge, MA: Harvard University Press.

Goetz, E. (1985). In defense of curriculum themes. *Day Care and Early Education, 13* (1), 12–13.

Golomb, C., & Cornelius, C. B. (1977). Symbolic play and its cognitive significance. *Developmental Psychology, 13*, 246–252.

Good, T. L., & Grouws, D. A. (1975). *Process-product relationships in fourth grade mathematics classrooms.* Columbia: University of Missouri. (ERIC Document Reproduction Service No. ED 125 907)

Goodman, K. (1986). *What's whole in whole language?* Portsmouth, NH: Heinemann.

Guskey, T. R. (1990). Cooperative mastery learning strategies. *The Elementary School Journal, 9* (1), 33–42.

Hess, R. O., & Shipman, V. C. (1965). Earl experience and the socialization of cognitive modes in children. *Child Development, 36*, 869–886.

Howsan, R. B., Corrigan, D. C., Denemark, G. W., & Nash, R. J. (1976). *Educating a profession.* Washington, DC: American Association of Colleges for Teacher Education.

Hunter, M. (1982). *Mastery teaching.* El Segundo, CA: TIP Publications.

Jacobs, H., & Borland, J. (1986). The interdisciplinary concept model: Theory and practice. *Gifted Child Quarterly, 30* (4), 159–163.

Jacobs, J. A., & Welch, K. V. (1983). A generic approach to direct instruction. (ERIC Document Reproduction Service No. ED 242 177)

Johnson, D. W., & Johnson, R. T. (1990). *Cooperation and competition: Theory and research.* Edina, MN: Interaction Book Co.

Joyce, B., Showers, B., & Weil, M. (1991). *Models of teaching* (4th ed.). Englewood Cliffs, NJ: Prentice-Hall.

Kamii, C., & DeVries, R. (1978). *Physical knowledge in preschool education: Implications of Piaget's theory.* Englewood Cliffs, NJ: Prentice-Hall.

Kamii, C., & DeVries, R. (1980). *Group games in early education: Implications of Piaget's theory.* Washington, DC: National Association for the Education of Young Children.

Katz, L. (1990). Impression of Reggio Emilia preschools. *Young Children, 45* (6), 11–12.

Katz, L., & Chard, S. (1989). *Engaging children's minds: The project approach.* Norwood, NJ: Ablex.

Kohlberg, L. (1968). Early education: A cognitive-developmental view. *Child Development, 39,* 1013–1062.

Kohlberg, L., & Lickona, T. (1987). Moral discussion and the class meeting. In R. DeVries with L. Kohlberg (Eds.), *Constructivist early education: Overview and comparison with other programs* (pp. 143–181). Washington, DC: National Association for the Education of Young Children.

Krogh, S. (1990). *The integrated early childhood curriculum.* New York: McGraw-Hill.

Langer, J. (1969). *Theories of development.* New York: Holt, Rinehart and Winston.

Lawton, J. T. (1977). The use of advance organizers in the learning and retention of logical operations and social studies concepts. *American Education Research Journal, 14,* 25–43.

Lawton, J. T., & Reddy, P. (1983). *Effects of advance organizer and guided self-discovery instruction on preschool children's understanding of conservation.* Presented at the annual meeting of the American Education Research Association, Montreal. (ERIC Document Reproduction Service No. ED 230 279)

Lay-Dopyera, M., & Dopyera, J. E. (1990). *Becoming a teacher of young children* (4th ed.). New York: McGraw-Hill.

Levin, D. E. (1986). Weaving curriculum webs: Planning, guiding, and recording curriculum activities in the day care classroom. *Day Care and Early Education, 13* (4), 16–19.

Meek, A. (1991). On thinking about teaching: A conversation with Eleanor Duckworth. *Educational Leadership, 48* (6), 30–34.

Miller, K. A. (1989). Enhancing early childhood mainstreaming through cooperative learning: A brief literature review. *Child Study Journal, 19,* 285–294.

Miller, L., & Dyer, J. L. (1975). Four preschool programs: Their dimensions and effects. *Monographs of the Society for Research in Child Development, 40* (5–6, Serial No. 162).

New, R. (1990). Excellent early education: A city in Italy has it. *Young Children, 45* (6), 4–10.

Newman, J. (Ed.). (1985). *Whole language theory in use.* Portsmouth, NH: Heinemann.

Nunnally, J. C. (1990). Beyond turkeys, santas, snowmen, and hearts: How to plan innovative curriculum themes. *Young Children, 46* (1), 24–29.

Pellegrini, A. D. (1984). The social cognitive ecology of preschool classrooms: Contextual relations revisited. *International Journal of Behavioral Development, 7,* 321–332.

Peters, D. L., Neisworth, J. T., & Yawkey, T. D. (1985). *Early childhood education: From theory to practice.* Monterey, CA: Brooks/Cole.

Piaget, J. (1977). *The development of thought: Equilibration of cognitive structures.* New York: Viking.

Rosen, C. (1974). The effects of sociodramatic play on problem-solving behavior among culturally disadvantaged preschool children. *Child Development, 45,* 920–927.

Rosenshine, B. V. (1978). Academic engaged time, content covered, and direct instruction. *Journal of Education, 160,* 38–66.

Ross, A. O. (1981). *Child behavior therapy: Principles, procedures, and empirical basis.* New York: John Wiley.

Rubin, K. H., Maioni, T. L., & Hornung, M. (1976). Free play behavior in middle- and lower-class preschoolers: Parten and Piaget revisited. *Child Development, 47,* 414–419.

Saltz, E., Dixon, D., & Johnson, J. (1977). Training disadvantaged preschoolers on various fantasy activities: Effects on cognitive functioning and impulse control. *Child Development, 48,* 367–380.

Schön, D. A. (1983). *The reflective practitioner: How professionals think in action.* New York: Basic Books.

Schön, D. A. (1987). *Educating the reflective practitioner.* San Francisco: Jossey-Bass.

Schwadener, E., & Lawton, J. T. (1978). *The effects of two types of advance organizer presentations on preschool children's classifications, relations, and transfer task performance.* Madison: University of Wisconsin Center on Cognitive Learning. (ERIC Document Reproduction Service No. ED 152 413)

Shipman, V. (1976). *Notable early characteristics of high and low achieving black low-SES children* (Progress Report 76–21). Princeton, NJ: Educational Testing Service.

Shure, M. B. (1980). Real-life problem-solving for parents and children: An approach to social competence. In D. P. Rathjen & J. P. Foreyt (Eds.), *Social competence* (pp. 54–68). Elmsford, NY: Pergamon Press.

Siegel, I. E., & Kohn, L. G. (1959). Permissiveness, permission, and aggression: The effect of adult presence or absence on aggression in children's play. *Child Development, 30,* 131–142.

Siegel, I. E., & Saunders, R. (1979). An inquiry into inquiry: Question asking as an instructional model. In L. G. Katz (Ed.), *Current topics in early childhood education* (Vol. 2., pp. 169–193). Norwood, NJ: Ablex.

Skinner, B. F. (1974). *About behaviorism.* New York: Knopf.

Slavin, R. E. (1987). Cooperative learning: Where behavioral and humanistic approaches to classroom motivation meet. *The Elementary School Journal, 88* (1), 29–37.

Slavin, R. E. (1991). Synthesis of research on cooperative learning. *Educational Leadership, 48* (5), 71–82.

Smilansky, S. (1968). *The effects of sociodramatic play on disadvantaged preschool children.* New York: John Wiley.

Soar, R. S., & Soar, R. U. (1972). An empirical analysis of selected Follow Through programs: An example of a process approach to evaluation in early childhood education. In I. Gordon (Ed.), *71st Yearbook of the National Society for the Study of Education* (Part II, pp. 229–259). Chicago: University of Chicago Press.

Sparling, J. J., & Sparling, M. C. (1973). How to talk to a scribbler. *Young Children, 28,* 333–341.

Spivack, G., Platt, J. J., & Shure, M. B. (1976). *The problem-solving approach to adjustment: A guide to research and intervention.* San Francisco: Jossey-Bass.

Spivack, G., & Shure, M. B. (1974). *Social adjustment of young children's cognitive approach to solving real life problems.* San Francisco: Jossey-Bass.

Spodek, B., & Saracho, O. N. (1982). The preparation and certification of early childhood personnel. In B. Spodek (Ed.), *Handbook of research in early childhood education.* New York: Free Press.

Stallings, J. (1975). Implementation and child effects of teaching practices in Follow Through classrooms. *Monographs of the Society for Research in Child Development, 40* (Serial No. 163).

Thompson, G. G. (1944). The social and emotional development of preschool children under two types of educational programs. *Psychological Monographs, 56* (5, Whole No. 258).

Tyler, R. W. (1949). *Basic principles of curriculum and instruction.* Chicago: University of Chicago Press.

Tzelepis, A., Giblin, P. T., & Agronow, S. J. (1983). Effects of adult caregivers' behaviors on the activities, social interactions, and investments of nascent preschool day-care groups. *Journal of Applied Developmental Psychology, 4,* 201–216.

Wasserman, S. (1990). *Serious players in the primary classroom.* New York: Teachers College Press.

Weil, M., & Joyce, B. (1978a). *Information processing models of teaching: Expanding your teaching repertoire.* Englewood Cliffs, NJ: Prentice-Hall.

Weil, M., & Joyce, B. (1978b). *Personal models of teaching: Expanding your teaching repertoire.* Englewood Cliffs, NJ: Prentice-Hall.

Weil, M., & Joyce, B. (1978c). *Social models of teaching: Expanding your teaching repertoire.* Englewood Cliffs, NJ: Prentice-Hall.

Wittmer, D. S. (1985a). *Looking in the window: An analysis of caregiver interactions with twos and threes in Title XX day care.* Doctoral dissertation, Syracuse University, Syracuse, NY.

Wittmer, D. S. (1985b). *Summary of findings of "Looking in the window: An analysis of caregiver interactions with twos and threes in Title XX day care."* Unpublished manuscript.

Yinger, J. (1975). *Problem-solving with children.* San Francisco: Far West Laboratory for Educational Research and Development.

Zimmerman, B. J., & Rosenthal, T. C. (1974). Observational learning of rule-governing behavior by children. *Psychological Bulletin, 81,* 29–42.

# CHAPTER 3

# A Review of Research on Play

DORIS PRONIN FROMBERG

Why would we want children to play in early childhood classes? How would we provide worthwhile conditions? In exploring ways to answer these questions, this chapter builds upon various reviews of research about the play of young children. Of particular note are reviews that are in their various ways intensive, distinctive, and worthwhile (Almy, Monighan, Scales, & Van Hoorn, 1984; Bergen, 1988; Christie & Johnsen, 1983; Fein & Rivkin, 1986; Pellegrini, 1985; Rubin, Fein, & Vanderberg, 1983; Schwartzman, 1978; Singer, 1973; Wortham, 1985).

The purpose of the synthesis of research in this chapter is to suggest what research and practice might contribute to transforming education. The format includes a definition of play, some theories that contribute to contemporary views, and a look at the varied research that these theories generate. These materials suggest implications for teaching practice.

## DEFINING PLAY

*Play* functions as both a verb and a noun. Rather than a category, property, or stage of behavior, play is a *relative* activity. The shifting functions in different settings may contribute to many researchers' problems in defining play.

Perhaps because play is relative behavior, scholars have studied it from the differing perspectives of historians (Huizinga), philosophers (Ellul, Dewey, Langer), linguists (Cazden, Chukovsky, Kirschenblatt-Gimblett, Weir), anthropologists (Aldis, Bateson, Blurton Jones, Schwartzman, Sutton-Smith, Smith), and psychologists (Almy, Monighan-Nourot, Scales, & Van Hoorn; Bretherton; Bruner, Jolly, & Sylva; Fein; Freud; Lieberman; Peller; Piaget; Pulaski; Singer; Vygotsky; Werner), to list only some. From these varied perspectives, scholars and researchers have considered the child as solitary, playing with objects or imagination; as well as a social player with one or more peers, children of varied ages, parent figures, and other

adults. They have considered the immediate contexts in which play occurs, the content, the interaction of context and content, and the cultural
environment. They have considered the player's experience as "optimal"
(Csikszentmihalyi, 1988) when the player "is unaware of time passing," with
play being "satisfying and focused enough in the present to transcend the
moment" (Fromberg, 1990, p. 224). They have differentiated play from exploration. They have divided social play into structured games-with-rules
and sports, as contrasted with the more evolving forms of sociodramatic play.
This chapter concentrates on representational and interactive play.

As we watch children play, it seems a matter of common sense to ask
what it is that they are doing. Yet there is a tendency for adults to confuse
what children are doing with how significant play may be for other purposes
than the child's immediate purpose of pretense. Indeed, when researchers
come to look at play, they have a way of seeing play from the unique theoretical perspectives of their own specialties and values. Within this limited
space, the focus will be on those theories that are more current than mainly
historical, except where contrast may serve to highlight an issue.

First, I propose a definition of play that might suffice as a foil to parry
with the various theoretical perspectives. Then those perspectives can ri-
poste. Young children's play is:

*Symbolic,* in that it represents reality with an "as if" or "what if" atti-
tude
*Meaningful,* in that it connects or relates experiences
*Active,* in that children are doing things
*Pleasurable,* even when children are engaged seriously in activity
*Voluntary* and *intrinsically motivated,* whether the motives are curios-
ity, mastery, affiliation, or others
*Rule-governed,* whether implicitly or explicitly expressed
*Episodic,* characterized by emerging and shifting goals that children
develop spontaneously

The content of play is influenced by children's experiences and also by
the context in which they find themselves. Context may include the physical
environment, time, other children or adults, and cultural sanctions and expectations. Since context helps to define play, various theorists tend to see
the functions of play somewhat differently.

## THEORIZING ABOUT PLAY

Two broad theoretical perspectives on play are discussed below—the
more or less psychological and the more or less cultural. These theoretical
positions emphasize different ways of looking at the same activity.

## The Psychological Perspective

Jean Piaget, a psychologist who also employed the perspectives of an epistemologist and biologist, offers a powerful definition of play that evolved from the stage-based structure of his cognitive theory of child development. He sees children taking an active role in forming their play symbols. Building on the object play of solitary children, he proposes that play can be "pure assimilation," but that it is the "ratio," the "relationship," or "predominance," of assimilation over accommodation that defines an activity as play (1962, pp. 90, 103, 164, 150). In emphasizing assimilation, he sees play as a state of imbalance. Using similar terms, Dewey (1933) suggests that play gives "prominence" or places "emphasis" on activity, "without much reference to its outcomes" (p. 285). However, he cautions that when there is no outcome play can "degenerate into fooling, and work into drudgery. . . . To be playful and serious at the same time is possible, and it defines the ideal mental condition" (p. 286). His work suggests the following continuum: fooling—play—work—drudgery. For example, work or drudgery may come to feel like play in certain circumstances.

*Present-time behavior with a past- or future-orientation.*    For Piaget (1962), play can "distort" reality to fit the child's current level of understanding (pp. 104, 164). However, other psychologists (Vygotsky; Bruner, Jolly, & Sylva) and anthropologists (Schwartzman, Sutton-Smith) speak of Piaget's description of play as assimilation that "distorts" reality, as if the word "distorts" had a negative connotation. Schwartzman (1978) prefers the term *allusion*, suggesting that play is a defining context "which produces a text characterized by allusion (not distortion or illusion), [and] transformation (not preservation)" (p. 330), an orientation toward the future.

By "distorting" reality, Piaget (1962) suggests that children's play focuses on past experiences "to transform reality and to deform and subordinate reality to the desires of the self" (1966, pp. 111–112). In contrast, Vygotsky (1978) suggests that children at play act "against immediate impulse" by subordinating themselves to rules. There is a paradox in Vygotsky's dialectic between pleasure in being "emancipated from situational constraints" while acting spontaneously, and subordinating oneself to the rules of play as the "path to maximal pleasure in play" (p. 99). In this way, children at play exercise their greatest self-control and behave "in advance of development" (p. 129). Vygotsky contends that "play creates a zone of proximal development" (p. 102) that is a context for instruction that is oriented toward the future development of children.

If a major benefit of play for Vygotsky is the creation of an advancement of development, the major benefit of play for others is its creative, "combinatorial" (Bruner, Jolly, & Sylva, 1976, p. 153; Sutton-Smith, 1979, p. 315), and "generative" aspect (Bruner & Sherwood, 1976, p. 277). For Piaget, it would be the ongoing consolidation by children of their experiences, a process that leads toward construction of internal representations of the world. Piaget posits play as a transition between egocentric thought and the development of reciprocity. Vygotsky (1976) sees play as a bridge ("pivot") that joins objects and actions with their representation in thought. Until children can separate the thought from the object or action, they must have something to act as a "pivot" in the form of a meaningful substitute, for example, "a stick denoting a horse" (p. 546).

*Making connections and substitutions.* It is interesting to consider how the process of making connections and substitutions occurs. Piaget (1962, 1976) suggests the elegant dynamic of "cognitive conflict" similar to the concept of "cognitive dissonance" (Festinger, 1957). There is an element of novelty or surprise caused by the discrepancy between the partial resemblance and the partial difference, which stimulates fresh perceptions. The contrast and movement between familiar and strange stimulate perception. Cognitive conflict in this sense, and cognitive dissonance in the sense of the discrepancy between what one expects and what one finds, represents one of the powerful conditions for learning that is available for teachers.

*Wish fulfillment and mastery.* Investigators have agreed that children use play to represent wish fulfillment (Erikson; Freud; Peller; Piaget; Sutton-Smith & Kelly-Byrne; Vygotsky). Vygotsky's (1976) view suggests that play reflects "generalized affects" rather than "isolated wishes" and that the "union of affect and perception" is characteristic of early childhood (pp. 540, 545). They also concur that play helps children to feel in control and to experience a sense of mastery. Thus, children come to understand the limits of their own power to control the environment (Corsaro, 1986, 1988, 1990). "Seeing the consequences of one's actions in a game develops the sense of predictable and controllable environment" (Coleman, 1976, p. 462). Other commentators see play as a way in which children attempt to cope with their environment and as a "temporary refuge" (Eisen, 1988, p. 107), as well as a way to learn to "reconcile" themselves to varied levels of success and influence (Opie & Opie, 1976, p. 396). Children also control the intensity of play activity, as in "play fighting" (Aldis, 1975, p. 180). These views parallel the idea that children have a need to feel competent and capable of influencing their world (White, 1959).

*Intrinsic motivation.* Psychologists also see play as intrinsically motivated (Moore & Anderson, 1968). Whatever the motives at the outset, it is useful to refer to Allport's (1958) construct of "functional autonomy" in which he noted that activity, perhaps begun with a distant goal in mind, may become intrinsically satisfying in itself without reference to the less playful goal. In this way, work or drudgery may come to feel playful. By way of contrast, consider that a less playful goal may become "workful" or exploratory. Still another way to define play is to contrast it with exploration.

*Distinguishing between exploration and play.*    Hutt (1976) captures an essential orientation when she states, "In play the emphasis changes from the question of 'what does this object do?' (which is exploration) to 'what can I do with this object?' (which is play) (p. 211). She bases her ideas on "arousal" theory, associated with Berlyne's (1960) work, which proposes that when humans face high arousal or uncertainty, they attempt to reduce it by exploratory behavior that provides information. Play for her "only occurs in a known environment" (Hutt, 1976, p. 211).

Wohlwill (1984) concurs, contending that nursery school children's exploratory behavior precedes play, which occurs when arousal stimulation is more moderate. He cites Gibson's (1979) work on "affordance-directed activity," which suggests that manipulative exploration at the physical, rather than at the cognitive or imaginal level, may be transitional between exploration and play in its transformational possibilities. While Collard (1979) agrees with these views, she adds, "The infant learns the perceptual properties of objects primarily through exploration and the action or function properties of objects primarily through play" (p. 52).

*Assessing play.*    Situational context makes a difference in children's play competence (Corrigan, 1987; Ellis, 1984; Lee, 1989). Familiar and private settings appear to facilitate more creative and competent play (Dansky, 1985; Fein, 1987; Kelly-Byrne, 1989; Olszewski, 1987). In a "strange situation, the range and diversity of play became considerably restricted and the tempo was reduced. Nothing happened to the structural variables" (Fein, 1985, p. 26). Having studied play's physical manifestations in heart rate and biorhythms, one investigator observed that children deemed hyperactive in a traditional classroom were indistinguishable in play (Ellis, 1979). In a similar vein, observers found children to be more aggressive in school and school playground settings than "in the street or in the wild places" (Opie & Opie, 1976, p. 399).

These findings suggest that we might expect children to behave in *relation* to contexts and constraints. This implies that relative rather than absolute accomplishments need documentation. Some researchers, for example, suggest that social activity provides more complexity than objects (Ellis, 1979; Ellis & Scholtz, 1978) and that language use is more complex with peers than with teachers (Hutt, 1976). The finding of another study that younger children's language was more advanced with their older siblings than with peers (Zukow, 1989) tends to support the position that it is relevant to define the child's competence as it relates to a particular context.

## The Cultural Perspective

The preceding positions have emphasized a psychological perspective, although there have been contrasts with more sociocultural or anthropological views. Now, play will be discussed from a cultural viewpoint, emphasizing the contextual and *relative* aspects of play. Some investigators have contended that what may be play in one time and place may be ritual or religious, frivolous, or technical behavior elsewhere (Csikszentmihayli, 1976; Kirschenblatt-Gimblett, 1979; Lancy, 1984; Scales, Almy, Nicolopoulou, & Ervin-Tripp, 1991). The cultural context also determines who may, or is likely to, engage in various kinds of play (Geertz, 1976; Morgan, 1982; Whiting & Edwards, 1988).

*Play as a categorization frame.* Some commentators identify the concept of a play frame, background, or context. Our culture teaches us what to expect and how to categorize reality and pretense play (Bateson, 1971, 1972, 1976, 1979). In this way, play is progress in the "evolution of communication" and "metacommunication" (1976, pp. 121, 125). Bateson suggests that children demonstrate by their behavior that they can categorize play and not-play as they enter into and step outside the framework of play situations.

Studies of North African immigrant families in Israel found that parents taught their preschool children to categorize objects, kinship structures, and myths in unique ways (Janiv, 1976) that appeared to influence their play (Smilansky, 1968). In a longitudinal study in the United States, Heath (1983) found that North Carolina urban middle class black and white children arrived at school with similar backgrounds, whereas the play and language use of rural working class black and white children differed from one another and from the middle class children. The rural black children brought to school strengths such as creative narratives, rich metaphors, humor, and fluid alternative uses of time and space. Teachers typically did not appreciate these strengths until the intermediate grades, by which time many children had become alienated and discouraged. The rural working class white children tended to receive approval at home for single "correct" behaviors and the use of playthings in a single correct way. This limited approach served them in the school's primary grades but did not serve them as they encountered the need to make connections in the intermediate grades.

Understanding children's category systems and the emphases of their early play experiences suggests the need to appreciate, rather than rank-order, differences. The metacommunication that takes place in social play makes it possible for children to pretend together as they accept or reject each other's play premises, plans, and suggestions. This metacommunication is not the same as metacognition, Piaget's (1976) notion of mature self-awareness. In contrast to Piaget's (1962) position that play as "pure assimilation" reflects development, there is conjecture that young children also acquire knowledge and develop cognitively as they engage in social play (Bretherton, 1985).

Still another way to consider the fruitful notion of metacommunication in play is to consider that symbolic representation takes place every time children play with objects as "pivots" that bridge the gap between real and make-believe, or when they collaborate with others to "map" a play territory together. The verbal rituals of play that help to categorize oneself and others in the play frame make it possible to transform relationships within the system (Garvey, 1979).

*Play as leading development.*    In this respect, play seems to lead development (Leslie, 1987; Nelson et al., 1986; Reiber & Carton, 1987). This is evident when the surface structures of children's play reveal their deeper propositional structures (Garvey, 1979). Some researchers would concur, finding that 2-year-olds appeared to understand, cooperate in, and contribute to joint pretend play earlier, and to engage in play with longer themes, when at home with older siblings (Dunn & Dale, 1984). It would make sense for those who subscribe to these views to pursue a line of research that studies the relationship of play and language, cognitive functioning, imagination, and social competence in varied settings. A review of such research follows the next section, which discusses theory and research about the dynamics and development of play.

## PLAY DYNAMICS AND DEVELOPMENT

Looking at play with a psychological as well as a cultural emphasis reveals that the child integrates the shared symbols of social players with the personal, representational aspects of play, while interacting within situational and cultural contexts.

### Transformational Dynamics

The representational nature of social play also has been considered in the "script model" that several investigators have studied (Auwarter, 1986;

Bretherton, 1984; Eiser, 1989; Forbes & Yablick, 1984; Garvey & Kramer, 1989; Kreye, 1984; Mandler, 1983; Nelson et al., 1986; Roskos, 1990; Schank & Abelson, 1977). Script theory takes the position that children develop sociodramatic play content out of the event knowledge that they acquire in daily life within their distinct cultural contexts. Event knowledge might include such routines as food acquisition, preparation, and consumption; relations between adults and children in varied culturally defined situations; and experiences and responsibilities for participating in family or community events.

Young children amass experiences that they then play out together within a combined process of shared predictability and collaborative novelty in a temporal sequence and within particular, culturally defined spaces. A temporal sequence might include events surrounding attendance at a health clinic or food-gathering event. Spaces might be playing "farming" alongside a field in which mothers engage in farming (Whiting et al., 1988) or making faces behind the teacher's back in a classroom (Corsaro, 1990).

Children enter the play frame and interact together with some shared event schemata and some evolving scenes that emerge as they negotiate, collaborate, and coordinate their activities within their script sequence. Such play scripts serve as evidence of the recursive relation between the shared cultural understandings of young children and their capacity to interactively plan, share, enact, elaborate, and further develop thematic content.

Script theory investigators propose that, as figurative frameworks, event schemata provide sequential "links between elements of scripts . . . in contrast to the links between members of . . . classification hierarchies that are based on similarity" (Bretherton, 1984, p. 272; Bretherton, 1989). Other investigators observed that a story narrative "grammar" and parallel problem-solving capacity undergirded children's pretend play (Eckler & Weininger, 1989).

In a way, script theory posits a kind of syntactic structure and context for sociodramatic play. Scripts contain a finite set of *figurative* structures that can generate an infinite set of combinations, a kind of grammar for play. While children understand the signals of play such as voice change, posture, gestures, or facial expression, they seem to follow certain organizational rules that are more or less complex. Their play explicitly represents their implicit understanding of the "script."

Among the interpretations of script theory, there are references to "cognitive templates" (Whyte & Owens, 1989), "affective representational templates" (Fein, 1985, p. 26; 1987), "cognitive seeds" (Lucariello & Rifkin, 1986, p. 203), and manipulable "mental models" (Leslie, 1987; Perner, 1988, 1991). Among interpreters, there is caution that script theory would be too convergent, since children's emotional preoccupations are fluid and relative to particular contexts (Fein, 1985). However, it is not at all clear that the "figurative" structures of script theory and the opportunities for divergent experiences in play need to be mutually exclusive.

The isomorphic nature of script theory is worth studying because it has an intriguing potential for leading in divergent directions. *Isomorphic structures* have been postulated in a number of fields concerned with exploring transformational knowledge. Dream symbols in psychology (Jung, 1968/1970), autotelic folk models in game theory (Moore & Anderson, 1968), mythic themes in anthropology (Levi-Strauss, 1949/1969a, 1964/1969b), recursive loops in interdisciplinary theory (Hofstadter, 1980), perceptual models in communications theory (McLuhan, 1963) and curriculum theory (Fromberg, 1977, 1982, 1987), generative structures in linguistics (Chomsky, 1972), and DNA in genetics research (Pfeiffer, 1962) indicate the diverse directions in which such issues have traveled.

Several other positions point to the isomorphic character of play. Seeing play as an opportunity to practice subroutines of behavior, Bruner and Sherwood (1984) talk about the "syntax" of the game, "patterned variation within a constraining rule set [that] seems crucial to the mastery of competence and generativeness (p. 283). Koestler (1967) talks about thinking as consisting of "rules . . . capable of varied flexible strategies (p. 182). Sutton-Smith (1971) assumes that play precedes game elements by a progression of "ludic infrastructures" (p. 299).

Even Piaget (1962) posits that intuitive sensorimotor schemas that are related to individual objects evolve into "infralogical or spatio-temporal operations [that] relate not the objects . . . but elements of those objects" (p. 271). However, a gestalt psychologist (Levine, 1984) takes issue with what she perceives to be Piaget's too practical cognition, proposing that the logic of play is the logic of metaphor that proceeds by the juxtaposition and connection of sometimes disparate phenomena through their isomorphic relationships. A similar criticism is that Piaget subordinates imagination to reason (Gilmore, 1971).

*Affective considerations.*    Schwartzman (1978), an anthropologist, has entitled an entire book about play *Transformations*, denoting and documenting the generative character of play. She also highlights the affective element in play, as children learn about "authority," "control," "manipulation," and "dominance" (1979, p. 252). She would support the notion that the psychological and social aspects of play change in relation to communication content (text) that occurs in the play context.

From another vantage point, Fein (1985) attributes an affective relativity to play. Further, she sees "pretense as an orientation in which the immediate environment is deliberately treated in a divergent manner" (p. 21).

Lieberman (1977) proposes that there is a quality of "playfulness" that contributes to divergent thinking. Csikszentmihayli (1979) touches on the idea of playfulness when he talks about a "state of flow" in play. He focuses on the experiential state of the person who is playing and who has achieved "a subjectively perceived balance" between "challenge and skill," spontaneity and control (p. 261). This state-of-flow experience may be compared with Dewey's (1934) views on art as a dialectic between "spontaneity and order" that is common to play and aesthetic experience. However, he notes that art "as esthetic experience . . . involves a definite reconstruction of objective materials" (p. 279). Huizinga (1955) also speaks of play as creating order and having an "aesthetic factor" (p. 10). Eisner (1990) points to the shared representational power and significance of art and play. These views would point to the study of play as related to associative fluency and creativity.

The dynamics of play theory include processes that are predominantly a blend of *cognition* and *affect,* such as cognitive dissonance, cognitive conflict; challenge; and pivotal and transformational, including isomorphic, models. Other play processes that are predominantly *social* involve metacommunication, collaborative rule-building, and scripts that connect neatly with isomorphic models of the play process. Thus, the isomorphic imagery shared within the social/cultural context becomes part of the child's individual/personal perspective. Additional attention to these dynamics follows.

*More on metacommunication and context.*    Piaget et al. (1965) make the point that when children build rules together as they play, they become more independent and increase their ability to see points of view other than their own, the process of *decentering* from oneself and one's immediate environment. We might see the ongoing social feedback in sociodramatic play as a kind of coaching system that helps children build their social and cognitive skills. For example, a study of the natural play of preschoolers found that they ask for feedback from one another by various conventional statements that they add to their play-related comments (Chafel, 1984). Statements such as "OK?" "See?" "Right?" and "Don't we?" seek confirmation, information, compliance, argument, and attention. As they play, they are able to move outside the play frame for brief negotiations about how to keep the play going and then maintain pretense during the play.

Giffin (1984) found that children agreed to rules that helped them sustain their transformation of reality "with the least possible acknowledgment of the playframe" (p. 88) because they prefer to act "rather than organize if at all possible" (p. 93). She proposes three "rules" by which children act: an "implicit pretend"; a "strict adherence," whereby play transformations are consistent with the script; and "incorporation," when others adapt to the recommended transformations of reality (pp. 89–91).

Nelson and Seidman (1984) confirm Giffin's work. For them, "the shared script . . . contributes a background context within which roles are defined, props are specified, and a sequence of actions is understood" (p. 50). In varied play contexts, they found dyads of nursery school children engaged in scripted play. Among the older children, they found play events with a greater number of more expansive and extended scripts. Other support exists for developmental trends (Goncu & Kessel, 1988).

As a contrast to studies of children who know each other, Forys and McCune-Nicolich (1984) found "that pretending facilitated the social interaction of unfamiliar young peers" (pp. 174–175), although one dyad in their small sample engaged in mainly nonverbal negotiation. Thus, these metacommunicative processes lead to varied outcomes among young 3-year-olds.

*More on cognitive dissonance, cognitive conflict.*    Children at play are continually perceiving and using *contrasts,* an essential condition of learning. The negotiations of social play in particular appear to involve an oscillation process between what you expect in somebody else's behavior and what you find. This oscillation stimulates the decentration that characterizes development in cognition, socialization, and play.

For Freud (1916/1960), "A joke is judgment which produces a comic contrast," (p. 10) and play "is the first stage of jokes" (p. 128). McGhee (1984) proposes that humor is an intellectual subset of play. Freud (1925/1958) also sees contrasts in the child's clear distinction between play and reality. Were a child (or an adult) not able to contrast play and reality, he or she might be daydreaming. It may, indeed, be that the underlying motives of play and intellectual challenge share common aspects of contrasts and cognitive dissonance. Clearly, individual readiness to perceive contrasts and experience cognitive dissonance varies.

### Individual Differences

The study of individual differences provides another contribution to understanding the dynamics of play. Using naturalistic observations in a longitudinal study, Shotwell, Wolf, and Gardner (1979) and Gardner (1982) have distinguished between the styles of "patterners" and "dramatists" in playing with symbols. Patterners appear to be intrigued by the world of objects. Dramatists prefer the world of people. These researchers suggest that each style appears to be a valid route toward general symbolic competence. They attribute the roots of these unique styles to underlying "mental structures" (Shotwell, Wolf, & Gardner, 1979, p. 130) and personality. These styles appear to parallel Adler's (1923) introvert–extrovert categories.

J. L. Singer (1973) reports findings concerning a related difference— individuals who display a profile of high or low fantasy in their play. Others support his findings (Connolly & Doyle, 1984; Freyberg, 1973; Moran, Sawyers, Fu, & Milgram, 1984; Pulaski, 1973) and in addition find that kindergarten children come to school with varied ability to show initiative in using equipment imaginatively (Feitelson & Ross, 1973). J. L. Singer and D. Singer (1979) found that high-imagination children report greater contact with parents who model or provide specific opportunities for fantasy play. High-imagination children manifest a capacity to wait quietly for a longer period of time, reporting fantasy play as they do so. They also scored higher in imaginative storytelling, made more analogic kinds of statements, and were more persevering than low-fantasy children.

Fein (1985) identified and studied "master players," defined as children who engage in extended social pretend play, according to their teachers and trained observers. She identified components of play that are characterized by fluidity, flexibility, risk-taking, and affective relationships.

## The Sequence of Development

Investigators have found that children between 14 and 38 months begin with solitary pretend play and match their behavior to others in social play before they are able to coordinate social pretend play in complementary ways (Howes, Unger, & Seidner, 1989). They wonder if toddlers who are familiar with one another engage in "ritualized interactions" that might function as "scripts" (p. 83). This is consistent with the view that children engage in pretend play at about 18 months of age, by representing a model of reality with an as-if model, a phase that precedes coordinated social pretend play in the third year (Perner, 1991).

Other researchers also have reported a progression in children's play from solitary and beginning joint play (2-year-olds), more relatedness and talk (2½-year-olds), and then reciprocal role playing (3-year-olds) (Miller & Garvey, 1984). Decontextual and fictional variation in pretend play appears in another study to be a function of socioeconomic community and day care center (Nevius, 1989).

Language development appears to parallel and have a recursive relationship with decontextualized play and social cognition within these studies (Shore, 1990). The contextual significance of scaffolding in this process appears in a longitudinal study that followed 28 toddlers at 16, 20, 24, 28, and 32 months, and found that nonverbal imitation occurred at 20 months with an adult and 2 months later with a peer; verbal directives at 28 months with an adult and 2 months later with a peer (Eckerman & Didow, 1989). When older children interacted with toddlers (Howes & Farver, 1987), and older children interacted with their younger siblings, young children's play and language were more advanced than with peers, regardless of socioeconomic or national background (Zukow, 1989). On the other hand, another study found that language use is more complex with peers than with teachers (Hutt, 1976).

Although the sequence present in various developmental studies follows the pattern suggested by Parten (1971), it is possible that more sophisticated thinking may require solitary play. For example, there is a consensus among researchers that although children become increasingly competent and complex in their sociodramatic play through 5 years of age, such play declines among 6-year-olds, perhaps because of schooling and the internalization of imagination (Cole & LaVoie, 1985; Voss, 1987). Between 5 and 7 years of age, the nature of children's concern appears to shift from actions within the pretense to purposes of the actions (Forbes & Yablick, 1984). The following sections deal with findings concerning children's interactions with objects and then with others.

*Interactions with objects.*    Children who use objects and toys alone and with others engage in a similar sequence of strategies. Fein (1975, 1985) studied children between 22 and 30 months of age and found that it was more difficult for the younger children to pretend substitutions with less prototypical objects or with more than one symbolic transformation. The play of older children was more diverse and complex. Fein (1985) concluded that transformations "designate the process whereby characteristics of the immediate environment become subordinated to what is essentially a mentally initiated activity" (p. 295). Confirming Fein's (1975) findings, others (Copple, Cocking, & Matthews, 1984) agreed, and observed a developmental progression of object choices of almost-4- to 5-year-olds, as follows: "functional assimilation" followed by "literal representation," and then "symbolic representation" (p. 120). Others concur, noting that a double substitution would depress pretend play more than a single substitution (Bretherton, O'Connell, Shore, & Bates, 1984). However, they suggest that there is probably an upper limit to the effectiveness of modeling, implying that it varies in different contexts.

Observing nine middle class children between 1 and 7 years of age longitudinally at home (Wolf, Rygh, & Altshuler, 1984), other researchers noted that children began to talk to and treat toys differently than persons at around 18 months. Children's symbolic capacities become explicit through language, gesture, and their expression in play. The investigators identified a first phase, between 1 and 5 years of age, when children begin to implicitly understand that they are "independent agents" as others are (p. 205). A second phase involves recognizing that "beyond performing actions, human actors also undergo internal experiences" (p. 205). These researchers found gender differences. Boys tended to use a third-person stance and emphasized object use. Girls tended to speak through a character and emphasized internal experience. While they used their social understanding differently, by 3 years of age all were able to describe their characters as agents and experiencers.

Another study found that unstructured toys elicited more pretend play, and 2½- to 5-year-old boys played with them longer, only when they were presented before structured toys (McGhee, Etheridge, & Berg, 1984). The experimenters suggested that children may be more receptive to less realistic, unstructured toys if they have begun with symbolic rather than realistic objects. They wondered if a longitudinal study might reveal a longer attention span with unstructured toys after children had had enough time with the structured toys for the novelty to pass.

Children in other studies who used low-specificity toys engaged in more interactive play and maintained a shared social script more continuously than children who used high-specificity props (McLoyd, 1983; Wanska, Pohlman, & Bedrosian, 1989). Another investigator varied play training to improve story recall among preschool children (Mann, 1984). After hearing a story, children rehearsed it using both realistic and unrealistic props. The experimenter, while finding a significant correlation between recall (a problem-solving task that required divergent thinking) and realistic props, inferred that when subjects used unrealistic props, they relied on their "imaging capacities to a greater extent" (p. 373). This study reports no pilot testing or second observer to strengthen the reliability of observations. Whether the sequence of exposure to realistic toys was a significant study variable is a question that begs for longitudinal research.

*Interactions with others.*   If they might meet, in dialogue, the more psychological or more sociocultural investigators cited above might all agree that there is a significant interaction between the child's developmental capacity and the play context. Garvey (1979) made a related observation after studying 40 dyads of 3-year-olds and 48 children between almost 3 and 5½ years of age in a laboratory setting. She found that the younger children's interactive speech showed a more complex, advanced propositional structure than might be apparent from the surface elements of play. She used the term "scaffolding" (p. 114) to denote the switches that children make between acting within and directing the play frame. These findings suggest that metacommunication in the play context advances development.

Pellegrini (1984c) reports similar findings in a study of 10 three-year-olds and 10 four-year-olds from middle class homes. He found that children in art, blocks, and housekeeping activities engaged in more mature social cognitive play when there were other children than when there was an adult present. He suggests that the presence of other children provided more opportunity for cognitive conflicts.

At the same time, others have found otherwise, that is, that an adult presence—with toddlers from varied backgrounds (Eckerman & Didow, 1989) and preschoolers from low income families—stimulated more complex play and language (Miller & Garvey, 1984; Smilansky, 1968; Sylva, 1984). Pellegrini (1984c) wondered whether his middle class children were less likely than the low income population to express disagreement with an adult.

These studies have focused mainly on what development transpires when children play with objects and with others, and its relation to their social competence. Depending on one's theoretical position, one sees play as extending cognitive, linguistic, and social learning, or as reinforcing what children already have learned. Children extend their imagination and improve associative fluency, or lack the capacity for imagining what is not or has not been present. If one holds that intervention in play can improve children's learning and imagination, then one would create a different environment for children than if one disagreed.

Researchers also have wondered whether play, or "improved" play, could change the course of development. Therefore, they have pursued bodies of study that attempt to find out if modeling, or otherwise stimulating children to be more playful, could influence social competence, creativity, cognitive development, and language development. The section that follows discusses these attempts.

## THE RELATIONSHIP OF PLAY AND DEVELOPMENT

The relative nature of play and development, both culturally and individually, seems to be established. Therefore, as we look at the sequence of play development, it makes sense to expect trends with variations rather than fixed results.

### Social Development

In general, social and moral development take place as young children interact with others. The social negotiations of pretend play are a particularly potent and influential realm of experience. After studying the symbolic play of toddlers, one team of researchers concluded that play can be enhanced or depressed by contextual variation (Bretherton, O'Connell, Shore, & Bates, 1984). They contended that it is more important "to discover the range of a child's ability under different contextual conditions than to attempt to establish whether he or she has the ability in an absolute sense" (p. 294). Using a laboratory setting as well as home visits, this team found that when adults modeled play behavior, the complexity of children's use of toys was enhanced at three levels of reference: (1) "self-reference," where children pretend to feed themselves; (2) "other-reference," where children pretend that the doll is a real baby; and (3) other "agent–patient," where children pretend to play both roles of a play interaction with two dolls or animal figures. The more advanced language of children at 28 months than at 20 months enhanced the reciprocal relations play between the two toys. However, these young children did not prefer a less realistic substitute prop, and some of the more sophisticated players protested its presence. The researchers did not discuss whether individual children started out more or less object-dependent or whether the object substitution was a result of adult intervention.

Another investigator concluded that social pretend play of children between 20 and 31 months, after modeling, both reflects and contributes to decentration (Fenson, 1984). Using the modeling levels of other-reference and other agent–patient, he proposed that children progress in turn through the processes of decentering, decontextualization, and integration (Fenson, 1984, 1985). Development, from this perspective, proceeds from a focus on the self toward active other-directed acts. The indicators of decontextualization are symbolic transformation, substitutions, and inventive acts, as children become less dependent on prototypical representation. An increasing ability to combine individual action sequences into multischeme combinations characterizes integration. There was no gender effect on language but there was an increasing predominance of speech in children's pretend play with age. However, he found more integrative play among girls.

Other studies support the notion that toddlers played for a longer time and with greater complexity when their parents played with them, modeled play behaviors, and verbally appreciated children's play (Denham, Renwick, & Holt, 1991; Slade, 1987a; Stevenson, Leavitt, Thompson, & Roach, 1988). Children adjusted the content and reduced the complexity of their play with children of different ages and younger siblings (Brownell, 1990; Slade, 1987a; Whiting et al., 1988). More secure children also spent more time in pretend play, which might reflect and contribute to their autonomy as organizers and planners (Slade, 1987b). A related finding is that children who received more child-care changes, often associated with more stressed families, manifested less competent play (Howes & Stewart, 1987). More competent and more cooperative, less argumentative players were the object of peer acceptance (Ladd, Price, & Hart, 1988; Rubin, 1985) and positive teacher assessment of sociability and school adjustment (Ladd & Price, 1987). Researchers with parallel findings state that "social behavior was more mature [and reciprocal] in pretend play than in nonpretend activities" (Connolly, Doyle, & Reznick, 1988, pp. 311–312), although not necessarily more flexible. Pellegrini (1988) found that more cooperative players experience social acceptance, perhaps as a result of their capacity to flexibly solve social problems through such means as rough-and-tumble play, rather than aggression. Whether players' perceived cooperation reflects their capacity to be more or less flexible and/or compliant is an issue for future study.

## Imagination

There is controversy surrounding the body of research that deals with the influence of play on children's creativity. Feitelson and Ross (1973) hypothesize that thematic play influences children's creativity and that it does not develop automatically but through modeling. They reason that children's creativity could be increased if they were taught to play thematically. They found more combinatorial play on post-tests after kindergarten children received tutoring and encouragement in the use of combinatorial play and unstructured props.

While they pretested children for their predispositions to imaginative play, Pellegrini (1984a) did not. However, he intervened by asking kindergarten children divergent questions in order to facilitate associative fluency and found that questions stimulating "descriptive exploration and difference exploration" were "both effective facilitators of associative fluency" (p. 249). When he used the same procedures on a transfer task, these results were confirmed, along with the observation that using both kinds of questions together was more successful than either strategy alone. The sequence of questions used was first descriptive; next, similar; and then different. It may be that the powerful process of learning through contrasts was a contributing variable.

In another intervention study, the researcher trained 80 low income 5-year-olds in groups of four to play more imaginatively, using unstructured materials around four themes (Freyberg, 1973). She found improvements in verbal communication, sentence length and complexity, sensitivity to others, spontaneity, creative use of play material, inventiveness and originality, labeling, attention span, and positive affect. She suggests that "engaging in activities that in themselves involve more organization and longer and more complex schemata would be facilitating to cognitive development" (p. 133).

Other researchers found that nursery school children who played with unstructured materials produced significantly more nonstandard responses in an alternative-uses test than children in the control group or those who were asked to imitate tasks (Dansky & Silverman, 1976). Dansky (1986) concluded that "the amount of make-believe displayed during the 10 minutes just prior to testing was directly correlated with the number of unusual uses given . . . [and that] . . . make-believe enhanced fluency irrespective of the particular form it took" (p. 73). He attributes the level of associative fluency to individual differences among children and situational variables. A related study found that those who had engaged in divergent play before testing scored higher on fluency and originality measures (Pepler & Ross, 1982). Divergent players seemed to be more willing to try alternatives, when compared with children who had played with convergent materials that suggested a narrower range of options or had observed play with either type of materials. Convergent materials seemed to constrain the activities of the children. The researchers cautioned that the effects were short-term and that longitudinal study is needed to confirm these findings.

Lieberman (1977) reported that 92 upper middle class kindergarten children who were assessed to be more playful did better on divergent tasks. She defined playfulness "as physical, social, and cognitive spontaneity, manifest joy, and a sense of humor" (p. 23). Hutt and Bhavnani (1976) report similar findings after studying nursery school children and reexamining 48 of them when they were between 7 and 10 years of age.

Pulaski (1973), using procedures similar to those of Singer, above, found that unstructured toys stimulated a greater variety of play themes than more realistic toys. However, 36 high-fantasy middle class kindergarten through second-grade children in a laboratory setting included more imaginary details in their stories, which were better organized. In comparison with low-fantasy children, they also were able to integrate more than one category of a toy and to become more deeply absorbed in their play, while accepting interruption and change more easily.

Observations of young children in their natural group settings suggested that pairs of children were most effective in stimulating each other's imagination and that groups of three or more did better than a child alone (Bruner, 1980, 1986). Thus, within the limitations and questions raised, these studies support the paradigm that children who are stimulated to play more imaginatively show improved ability to make new connections.

Simon and Smith (1985a, 1985b, 1985c) and Smith and Whitney (1987) challenge the validity of research methods used in the body of associative fluency and play research, questioning the presence of subconscious experimenter bias as well as whether play had occurred. Using blind procedures as a precaution against experimenter testing effects, they did not confirm the body of findings that correlate play and associative fluency.

Their work has extended an ongoing dialogue within this paradigm (see also Dansky, 1985). Others who attempted to control against experimenter bias and retested children 3 years later found that children's play was related to associative fluency mainly for boys, but not girls (Clark, Griffing, & Johnson, 1989). They suggest that boys may have "a divergent cognitive style" (p. 87). The volleying of related studies is likely to continue.

### Cognitive Development

*Contextual Factors.*    Smilansky's position, like others' (Corsaro, 1990; Feitelson & Ross, 1973; Ogbu, 1988; Rogoff, 1990; Scales, Almy, Nicolopoulou, & Ervin-Tripp, 1991) leans toward the notion that the contents of sociodramatic play and cognitive development depend on cultural and contextual factors. Thus, different environmental experiences, and historical and cultural expectations, affect children's perceptions, practices, preferences, and achievements in distinct ways.

With her particular cognitive goals in view, Smilansky (1968) suggests that young children need adult intervention in their play. She observes that less advanced sociodramatic play covaries with academic failure and a disadvantaged background (in relation to her educational setting). When teachers intervened to stimulate the sociodramatic play of disadvantaged preschool children in their classrooms, they found that children became more flexible planners, used language more elaborately and expansively, sustained play for longer periods, and improved their use of pretense. Teachers attempted to vary the intervention on the basis of the different skills with which individual children came to school. Smilansky worked through the teachers of 420 preschool and kindergarten children who "taught" sociodramatic play over 67 hours during 9 weeks. She attributes the startling results over this brief period to the children's readiness for learning these skills. Freyberg (1973) agrees with these conclusions.

Contrary findings are reported by Eifermann (1971). She used the observations of 150 observers of 14,000 elementary school children in informal, unstructured play settings at school and in their neighborhoods. Eifermann found that a similar population of 6- to 8-year-olds in her sample displayed more, not less, social symbolic play than the other children. Eifermann proposes that low income children may develop symbolic play at a later age.

Levenstein (1976, 1985), however, hypothesizes that play skills need to be taught and that mothers of children from low income families could learn to assist their toddlers in improving play skills. She takes the position that children's play is related to problem solving, academic skills, classroom attitudes, and I.Q. Studying 54 children between 20- and 43 months of age from low income families, Levenstein developed a training program shared with 33 mothers and their children at home. Toy demonstrators taught the mothers verbal stimulation techniques and various ways to use materials. The demonstrators visited each home regularly, modeled the use of materials, and left the toys and books. Levenstein found significant increases in the children's I.Q., which are replicated in four studies.

Schwartzman (1984) cautions us to be careful about labeling children as "nonimaginative, noncreative, nonconceptual" (p. 58). Differences to her are not necessarily deficient but merely stylistic. However, Schwartzman (1985) agrees with other researchers that play tutoring is useful in some contexts as long as participants maintain spontaneity and playfulness.

A play intervention study with 12 middle class 3- to 5-year-olds found that intensive dramatic play, including individual, dyadic, and triadic play, for each child resulted in a significant improvement in the number of cognitive constructs elicited from the experimental group on a sorting task (Ghiaci & Richardson, 1980). These findings were sustained in another posttest one month later. Similar findings in a related series of studies found that children were able to provide theoretical justifications for situations after play, suggesting that the task setting influenced their capacity to deal with problem content (Dias & Harris, 1988).

Sylva, Bruner, and Genova (1976) studied problem solving with 180 three- to five-year-olds. Treatments involved free play with materials, observing an adult, or no treatment. They found that the children who had prior free-play experience with the materials solved the problem as well as those who had been shown the principle by an adult. While both groups used an orderly approach, there were more all-or-nothing strategists among children in the observation group and more systematic progressions from simple to increasingly complex steps among children in the free-play group. They concluded that "the effect of prior play seems to be not only in combinatorial practice, but also in shifting emphasis in a task from ends to means, from product to process" (p. 256).

Believing that opportunities to play could influence development, Golomb (1979) and Golomb, Gowing, and Friedman (1982) created a strategy to stimulate the conservation of quantity among young children who were pretested and post-tested in a clinical Piagetian manner. (Conserving quantity refers to children's learning that a quantity remains the same even though its appearance may change, for example, when a liquid is poured from a tall, thin container into a short, wide container.) Experimenters provided an intervention procedure with nonconserving children—75 three- to five-year-olds and 47 four- to five-and-a-half-year-olds. Their use of pretense play with individual children led them to conclude that it facilitated the acquisition of conservation of quantity. They suggested that their subjects used intuitive and unreflective reversibility, which they propose is a spontaneous precursor to genuine reversibility of operational thought.

A related study that touches on 26 three-year-olds' early moral development within the family included story stems (problem narratives) with doll play and props in both laboratory and home settings (Buchsbaum & Emde, 1990). They found the children, at younger ages than Piagetian researchers might predict, capable of offering coherent and "alternative prosocial choices in a moral dilemma . . . when the task is altered so as to be accessible to younger children both in terms of its affective significance and the mode of required response" (p. 150). They relate their research to script theory as a representational form that derives its content and power from contextual factors.

*Gender.* There is a confluence of findings that girls and boys receive attention for different types of behaviors from their parents (Caldera, Huston, & O'Brien, 1989; Roggman & Peery, 1989), especially fathers (Bradley & Gobbart, 1989), and from their teachers (Fagot, 1988; Golomb, Gowing, & Friedman, 1982; Serbin, 1978). Adults give girls more physical proximity, comments, and questions, while boys receive more corrections and less proximity. In general, boys receive attention for assertive, contrary behavior and respond best to child-initiated pretense play, whereas girls tend to follow the teacher and adult-initiated pretense.

In one preschool, the researcher observed that teachers appeared to reinforce proximity-seeking in girls, but that 10 minutes after the teacher placed herself in the block corner, usually populated by boys, girls as well as boys played (Serbin, 1978). This study also found that "just the presence of a peer, especially an opposite sex peer, is likely to make a child conform to sex-role stereotypes" (p. 90). It is interesting to observe, therefore, that when there is a sufficient quantity of blocks, there are no gender differences in their use (Rogers, 1985). Access to the traditionally male domain of blocks, in which young children can develop their visual-spatial skills, is related significantly to mathematical learning (Maccoby & Jacklin, 1974). Teacher awareness of gender patterns in choices of play centers and themes is important for educational equity, therefore, in light of these findings as well as a study, in a middle class laboratory school, that found older preschoolers choosing same-sex children for play (Urberg & Kaplan, 1989). There was more intense interactive play in smaller groups of homogeneous age. Other research indicates that, while there were no differences in the frequency of imaginative play, the play content of 24 middle class boys and girls differed by the time they entered preschool (Greif, 1976). The 4½-year-old children in this study demonstrated stereotyped role play. Male roles had more status and girls were willing to play them, while boys were less willing to play female roles.

Another researcher (Black, 1989) found that girls engaged in longer episodes of shared pretense, suggesting (following Gilligan, 1982) that girls might value the interaction while boys' goals were to gain "acceptance of their own suggestions" (p. 390). Finding that gender preferences for toys were apparent at 13 months of age, Duveen and Lloyd (1990) noted that at 4 years of age, boys (but not girls) used toys to mark gender differences, perhaps as a way of asserting superiority. In a related finding, others found that boys initiated more play topics to which more girls responded and that girls engaged in "more sophisticated, constructive play [when playing with blocks] with boys" (Pellegrini & Perlmutter, 1989, p. 295).

Other investigators have found that, with the exception of boys from separated/divorced families (Kier & Fouts, 1989), boys tend to engage in more active play, rough-and-tumble play, games-with-rules, and games involving spatial relations (Blurton Jones, 1976; Henniger, 1985; Humphreys & Smith, 1984; Paley, 1984; Parker, 1984; Pellegrini, 1987). Within rough-and-tumble play, the children may perceive themselves to be collaborative rather than confrontational, regardless of adult conclusions. Boys' play is dramatically different from the predominantly housekeeping play of girls, even when thematic content varies (Dodge & Frost, 1986). The section that follows discusses how such thematic play may influence language development as well as how investigators provide intervention.

## Language Development

Cazden (1971) reports observations of children's language during play in a classroom housekeeping corner. While the quantity of language was plentiful, the syntax and language content were repetitious rather than elaborative and expansive. Other researchers have found that children use more varied and extensive language when teachers provide materials for varied themes (Dodge & Frost, 1986; Levy, Schaefer, & Phelps, 1986).

There is a recently growing, distinctive body of applied research concerning classroom provision of alternative sociodramatic play themes (e.g., bank, office, post office, restaurant, veterinary office, hospital, pet shop) that include literacy materials as play props, and their influence on children's increased use of literacy skills (Christie, 1991; Morrow, 1990; Neuman & Roskos, 1991; Schrader, 1989, 1990; Vukelich, 1991). These studies document a powerfully recursive relationship between play and literacy development within the classroom context of thematic learning centers. In effect, the play provides a collaborative medium in which children may practice literacy skills, mutually develop scripts based on event knowledge, provide mutual scaffolding, and further expand and extend literacy use. Studies tend to support the notion that play as the locus of children's power can prevail when the teacher intervenes to model and extend rather than direct.

Another line of research considers the parallel development of structural correspondence between early vocal articulations and gestures, early language and symbolic play, and combinatorial language and combinatorial play (McCune-Nicolich, 1981). This study of parallel development predicts that the onset of decentered play and differentiated language use would occur about the same time. In a study of 18 young children, two-thirds of the population confirmed this hypothesis (McCune, 1985).

In addition to looking at how language and play coincide developmentally, there has been discussion about the significance of children's play with language itself. Researchers have suggested that children enjoy playing with language because it makes them feel in control (Cazden, 1976; Chukovsky, 1963; Freud, 1928/1959, 1916/1960; Garvey, 1977; Kirschenblatt-Gimblett, 1979; Weir, 1976). They have observed such play as sounds or words repeated for their own sake as well as in riddles, jokes, and metaphors. Thus, just as pretend play may suggest "the hallmark of an emerging artistic and literary ability" (Bretherton, 1988, p. 211), playing with language may have poetic as well as metalinguistic functions.

Compared with adults, children may treat language with more awareness in play and less awareness in ordinary communications (Cazden, 1976). While there are individual differences in metalinguistic awareness, Cazden (1976) proposes a sequence of awareness beginning with words, then syllables, followed by sounds and then rules dealing with structure.

*Story recall.*    There also are intervention studies concerning how play influences the recall of stories. They found that children's story comprehension improved after training in thematic fantasy play. In one study, role playing, rather than adult-led discussion, appeared to facilitate the ability to retell stories by stimulating the verbal skills that children needed for recall (Pellegrini & Galda, 1982). The investigators imply that the metacommunication children used in order to maintain the play frame made it possible for the children to move between their own role and their peers' role interpretations.

Another study concurs with these findings and stresses the importance of giving children repeated opportunities to play out stories in small groups (Williamson & Silvern, 1984). Additional studies found that children up to 80 months of age as well as less able primary age children were most able to benefit from such intervention (Williamson & Silvern, 1991).

Peer-directed play as well as adult-directed play facilitates story recall (Pellegrini, 1984b), but the most effective play training with 92 low income children appears to include a combination of fantasy, verbalization, and conflict (Pellegrini, 1985). Adding that children show fuller story recall when they engage in imaginative play actions themselves, rather than through puppets, a related study with 60 middle class 5-year-olds supports this finding (Marbach & Yawkey, 1980). Children's shared negotiations in play also appear to support Vygotsky's notion of play as leading development, when researchers conclude that the "representational nature of symbolic play necessitated their [children's] use of metalanguage" (Galda, Pellegrini, & Cox, 1989, p. 303).

Throughout the studies that consider the relation of young children's play and their language development, there flows a strong current that carries the message: Social pretend play involves the development of scripts that evolve collaboratively. The negotiation processes provide a scaffolding similar to that of an editor and author. These images suggest that young children's increasing oral language skills are the foundations upon which they build their skills as writers, learning about how to communicate with an audience and what voices to use.

## IMPLICATIONS FOR FUTURE RESEARCH

### Avoiding Limitations of Past Research

*Size of samples.*   With few exceptions, most experimental studies of play have involved small samples. When one considers that 80 subjects may have been involved in three or four treatments, findings shrink to the 20 subjects who confirmed the investigator's hypothesis. The trend toward ethnographic research focused on young children's play, however, can lead to an expanded, significant body of case material.

*Context.*   Increasing numbers of studies are taking place in classroom settings. If a significant purpose of research is to understand development and practice in order to improve the conditions of children's and teachers' interactions with one another, then the need for additional study and insights into ongoing group settings would follow.

Inasmuch as most of the studies in the literature have been carried out in laboratory settings for brief periods of time, we need to consider, for young children in particular, how a familiar adult presence would make a difference in performance. Some studies have attempted to acclimate children through preliminary efforts that involved parents and familiarization with researchers. We need ways to understand what happens to children in alternative contexts over longer periods. There have been increasing calls for observations of children in a variety of their natural habitats (Blurton Jones, 1976; Eifermann, 1976; Schwartzman, 1984, 1985; Singer, 1973; Smith & Simon, 1984). For investigators, this may mean catching things when they happen rather than trying to induce them to occur in ways that fit into a busy adult's schedule. In naturalistic observations, researchers may focus on a particular sort of behavior as it appears. However, they can understand it more fully because of its context in terms of time, sequence of activity, relationships of protagonists, and how typical it is for the population.

Many of the studies of solitary players may need to be replicated in the context of peer interaction. Inasmuch as play is a relative activity, it would make sense to account for the human as well as the physical context in which studies occur.

## Collaborative Research

Using a collaborative, naturalistic approach, researchers increasingly reassess and reformulate the role of early childhood teachers as coresearchers working with college teachers. To have the most relevant impact on curriculum, researchers plan collaboratively with teachers to develop those questions that need answering in order to improve the conditions of children and teachers in school. Teachers, with some job redefinition, are in an exceptional position to collaborate in the collection of data. It would be illuminating if such observation could take place simultaneously with an outside observer, and if children's impressions also were studied.

Participation in study design, implementation, and intervention is another role for teachers. Smilansky (1968) reports that teachers played a significant role in her study, albeit after initial resistance to trying things with their school children that they had done comfortably with their own offspring at home.

Significant teacher involvement in intervention studies may encourage the administrators of such studies to undertake a longer-term commitment to longitudinal research and to timely post-tests and pretests in order to find out the extent to which the intervention was stable over time or transferred to other tasks. Moreover, such participation will make it possible to study many more than the comparatively small numbers of children who have been studied until now.

Another form of collaborative research is the development of a systematic body of case studies. Focusing on issues of shared concern, a network of data collectors might study particular cases and amass their findings (see Munro, 1991).

## Studying Play Content and Context

*Functional study.*   We would do well to extend studies to consider the diversity of play forms as well as to distinguish between transformations based on the surface elements of behaviors and the functional relations be-

tween them. In particular, there is room for studying the intersections between script theory and other isomorphic imagery as children use play as
part of the construction of their cognitive and social paradigms.

*Integrative study.*    Another way to look at research is to look at play as
an integrative experience. Studies have tended to look at either the affective, cognitive, social, linguistic, or other specific aspect of play. We need to
plan studies that investigate the interaction, within varied contexts, of affect,
cognition, and play; and of social, linguistic, and cognitive development, and
play. An integrative approach can better provide a body of evidence to support a balanced curriculum that refers to real rather than dissected human
beings.

McCune-Nicolich and Fenson (1984) suggest studying the developmental trends that occur in individual children over time from several perspectives—decentration, decontextualization, and integration. It is worthwhile
to investigate the interrelation of trends, the relative sequence of their appearance, and their relation to other areas, such as language in particular
contexts.

The contextual studies concerned with metacommunication and script
models begin to deal with more interactive elements than the solitary study
of children in laboratory settings. However, as this body of literature
evolves, it would be useful to explore alternative intervention treatments in
classrooms. In addition to extending such bodies of study as the inclusion of
literacy materials in thematic sociodramatic play centers (Christie, 1991),
research in the following directions, to name just a few, can help inform
better curriculum decisions: the level of prop structures, the identification
of concrete activities that generate cognitive conflict during different developmental phases, the identification of isomorphic patterns underlying children's natural play, and the identification of individual children's variations.

Singer (1973) reminds us that "our conventional methods are biased
towards particular aptitudes that are symbolic and concrete" (p. 201). It is
also likely that we need to extend the literature on the relationship of play,
associative fluency, and the young child's artistic and poetic development.
Implications for curriculum are discussed below within the context and limitations of existing research, theoretical formulations, and my own bias.

## IMPLICATIONS FOR CURRICULUM DEVELOPMENT

### Teacher Attitude

The research on play indicates that it is an important part of the lives
of young children. Play has lymphatic, in the sense of pervasive and inter-

connected, implications for their education. While the research on play has not dealt directly with the impact of teacher attitudes toward play, Torrance (1962) reports that teachers perceive creative children as more of a problem than garden-variety achievers. We expect that the spontaneous nature of play will be a burden to teachers with this attitude. More teachers need to be joyful and playful as they work with young children, ready to accept the unexpected connection or alternative with good humor and patience.

## Teacher Provisions

*Modeling.* Teachers need to model play behavior that stimulates development through challenge. This would mean attracting children to play by providing a variety of options with which they can feel comfortable and in which they perceive a chance for success. The best options are those that children can actively structure and for which there may be more than only one possible outcome. Rather than try to motivate children by gimmicks, teachers should let the materials and activities entice the children to be intrinsically motivated.

Part of the teacher's task is to vary the level of structure for different children in order to facilitate varied enactments and symbolic progress. Thus, the teacher would help children extend rather than merely replay and repeat experiences (Tizard, 1977).

Inasmuch as children come to school with different experiences, providing materials and opportunities will yield different outcomes. It makes sense to observe how children categorize and play out their experiences. Therefore, teachers actively bring children into play activities in varied ways, sometimes by taking roles, creating contrasts, or entering a play frame with an extendable model or suggestion.

*Questioning.* Modeling also takes place when a teacher asks questions that suggest a variety of possible responses. Such questions and situations that suggest more than one way to proceed are likely to encourage an openness to various problem solutions. If there is only one material or method, children receive the message that independent thinking is unwelcome. An array of possibilities, however, might encourage play.

*Planning.* Children need enough time to play out their themes. Paley (1984) found that some of her kindergarten children needed unusual amounts of time to engage in sociodramatic play before they could focus on artwork at a table. There is evidence that 30 minutes provides a minimum amount of time within which young children might develop a sociodramatic play theme (Christie, Johnsen, & Peckover, 1988). Beyond minimal time, there is need for one or more long blocks of time during the school day. Thematic learning centers with 6- to 8-week shifts in content focus are important provisions for children's play throughout the primary grades as well as in kindergartens and nursery schools.

Other children need some time to be alone in the unique fantasy world we create in classrooms. Therefore, teachers organize space for privacy as well as participation with others. Gardner (1982) describes one child who engaged in pretend play throughout his drawing and another child who created dramatic action with words and gestures after a minimal drawing. Thus, while their teacher provided the materials and the opportunity, the children were able to create their own structures and pace.

Children need the time and opportunity to explore new materials and situations as well as to play. In order to strike a balance, teachers need to infuse novelty, variety, and fresh challenges as required by the varied backgrounds of the children. When teachers effectively pace the *contrasts* between the strange and the familiar, children are able to perceive a new figure when it is contrasted clearly against a known background. To the extent that children construct their learning in self-directed ways, they acquire increasingly realistic expectations about the future and a sense of confidence and control.

In these ways, teachers create classroom cultures that define and tolerate different levels and types of play. When teachers find children making opportunities to play at unplanned times or in unexpected places, it is likely that the children need more time to play or that immediate expectations are daunting. When effective teachers involve children in games, they focus in a comfortable way on the game-playing process rather than on only the outcome.

*Playing with language.*    In addition to questions, modeling, materials, time, and space, teachers can encourage children to play with words through legitimizing peer interaction and providing child-controlled literacy materials. Certainly, poets and linguists would recommend encouraging and appreciating the nondiscursive uses of language by children.

Teachers can improve story comprehension with small groups by playfully questioning and asking children to predict what might happen in stories, telling the stories, and then having the children play roles. Practice improves this process: A teacher who plays a bigger early role as an exemplar can later reduce her or his participation. Paley (1984) reports harnessing rough-and-tumble and superhero play with which she felt uncomfortable by asking children to "save" their ideas for use in a collaborative language-experience setting.

## Planning for Cooperative Play

Interage play as well as peer play helps children to learn as they see attainable models. In a sense, playmates are natural examples of new figures highlighted against familiar backgrounds. Therefore, teachers try to help children who tend to be isolates to move into parallel and then collaborative play with other children. For isolates as well as others, playing with children of different ages may assist the development of more complex and extended play forms. Interage play traditionally has been more common around the world than our relatively recent practice of grouping children according to the calendar (Schwartzman, 1985; Whiting et al., 1988; Zukow, 1989).

Group playing with ideas (brainstorming) may aid the creative process (Lieberman, 1977). Certainly, social play situations provide opportunities for the development of decentration and reciprocal relations through cognitive conflicts. In addition, as teachers plan sociodramatic play areas that involve varied, imaginative settings in addition to only housekeeping, there are opportunities for children's language and social competence to develop. Teachers who try, by being present and supportive, to make girls as well as boys feel welcome in the block corner provide equitable access to visual-spatial learnings.

## Providing Worthwhile Experiences

This is a time when extreme views are pressing on early childhood education. There is a push in one direction toward limiting the function of public schools to the three R's and stating facts, crisply advanced. There is advocacy from the opposite direction for a folklorist tradition in early childhood education, vaguely propounded.

We need a more valid basis for developing curriculum than decision making that is based solely on what children can learn, or what certain factions want them to learn, or what tradition has dictated. We need to consider what is worthwhile learning. This is the deeper moral issue that can guide us to ethical decisions.

There is abundant evidence, accruing at meteoric rates, indicating the power of play as a developmental lymphatic system. In the course of early childhood development, play almost seems to be a cauldron in which, at different times and in different contexts, various proportions of cultural, social, cognitive, linguistic, creative, aesthetic, and emotional ingredients blend.

We might playfully entertain the notion that play serves to merge the hypothetical functions of the right and left hemispheres of the brain. In this way, normal children manage to maintain a balance in their experience as human beings. The implications of current interest in imagery and metacognition can be considered as part of the concern for children to have "thinking skills."

Imagery processes interacting with metacognitive processes serve problem solving. *Imagery* is the creative aspect of experience and the capacity of human beings to make connections. For young children, it is an early form of symbolic representation in such activities as sociodramatic play and personal analogy. There has been conjecture that the right hemisphere of the brain, dealing with metaphoric and aesthetic ways of knowing the world, can be developed and strengthened by experiences that are rich in imagery. *Metacognition* is the development of self-awareness about one's own thinking. It takes place in a gradual process as we have experiences, get feedback from our environments, and experience cognitive dissonance. Although children attain this capacity around the ages of 11 and 12 years, development is continuous beforehand (Piaget, 1976). Perner (1991) suggests that, in early childhood, multiple mental models serve as part of the development toward metarepresentation that becomes manifest in children's pretend play. There has been conjecture that improved metacognition can strengthen and develop the functions of the brain's left hemisphere, dealing with logical ways of knowing the world. Working jointly, the processes of imagery and metacognition function in the service of problem solving.

To attempt to "teach" young children these integrative skills separate from direct, concrete experiences is akin to trying to learn to ride a bicycle with a stationary exercycle. To use workbooks for these functions that develop naturally with healthy play is to be irrelevant if not downright abusive.

For young children, play is a way to strengthen worthwhile, meaningful learning and cooperation with others rather than merely acquiring facts alone. Play may well be the ultimate relativist integrator of development. As a moral issue, the role of play as part of early education touches on many dimensions of development and can affect the sheer joy of living fully. The transformational potential of play in itself is a potent lever for making new connections in a rapidly changing world.

Thus, teachers of young children have an ethical responsibility to create situations that can help to improve the conditions of learning and life in schools. We need to intervene in indirect and playful ways to the extent of our own potential capacities for professionalism and playfulness.

## REFERENCES

Adler, A. (1923). *The practice and theory of individual psychology.* London: Routledge & Kegan Paul.

Aldis, D. (1975). *Play fighting.* New York: Academic Press.

Allport, G. W. (1958). The functional autonomy of motives. In C. L. Stacey & M. F. DeMartino (Eds.), *Understanding human motives* (pp. 68–81). Cleveland: Howard Allen.

Almy, M., Monighan, P., Scales, B., & Van Hoorn, J. (1984). Recent research on play: The teacher's perspective. In L. G. Katz (Ed.), *Current topics in early childhood education* (Vol. 5, pp. 1–25). Norwood, NJ: Ablex.

Auwarter, M. (1986). Development of communicative skills: The construction of fictional reality in children's play. In J. Cook-Gumperz, W. A. Corsaro, & J. Streeck (Eds.), *Children's worlds and children's language* (pp. 205–230). New York: Mouton de Gruyter.

Bateson, G. (1971). The message "this is play." In R. E. Herron & B. Sutton-Smith (Eds.), *Child's play* (pp. 261–266). New York: John Wiley.

Bateson, G. (1972). *Steps to an ecology of mind.* New York: Ballantine.

Bateson, G. (1976). A theory of play and fantasy. In J. S. Bruner, A. Jolly, & K. Sylva (Eds.), *Play—its role in development and evolution* (pp. 119–129). New York: Basic Books.

Bateson, G. (1979). *Mind and nature.* New York: E. P. Dutton.

Bergen, D. (Ed.) (1988). *Play: A medium for learning and development.* Portsmouth, NH: Heinemann.

Berlyne, D. E. (1960). *Conflict, arousal and curiosity.* New York: McGraw-Hill.

Black, B. (1989). Interactive pretense: Social and symbolic skills in preschool play groups. *Merrill-Palmer Quarterly, 35* (4), 379–397.

Blurton Jones, N. (1976). Rough-and-tumble play among nursery school children. In J. S. Bruner, A. Jolly, & K. Sylva (Eds.), *Play—its role in development and evolution* (pp. 352–362). New York: Basic Books.

Bradley, B. S., & Gobbart, S. K. (1989). Determinants of gender-typed play in toddlers. *Journal of Genetic Psychology, 150* (4), 453–455.

Bretherton, I. (Ed.). (1984). *Symbolic play: The development of social understanding.* New York: Academic Press.

Bretherton, I. (1985). Pretense: Practicing and playing with social understanding. In C. C. Brown & A. W. Gottfried (Eds.), *Play interactions* (pp. 69–79). Skillman, NJ: Johnson & Johnson.

Bretherton, I. (1988). Reality and fantasy in make-believe play. In D. Bergen (Ed.), *Play: A medium for learning and development* (pp. 209–211). Portsmouth, NH: Heinemann.

Bretherton, I. (1989). Pretense: The forms and function of make-believe play. *Developmental Review, 9* (4), 383–401.

Bretherton, I., O'Connell, B., Shore, C., & Bates, E. (1984). The effect of contextual variation on symbolic play development from 20 to 28 months. In I. Bretherton (Ed.), *Symbolic play: The development of social understanding* (pp. 271–298). New York: Academic Press.

Brownell, C. A. (1990). Peer social skills in toddlers: Competencies and constraints illustrated by same-age and mixed-age interaction. *Child Development, 61,* 838–848.

Bruner, J. S. (1980). *Under five in Britain.* Ypsilanti, MI: High/Scope.

Bruner, J. S. (1986). Play, thought and language. *Prospects, 16,* 77–83.

Bruner, J. S., Jolly, A., & Sylva, K. (Eds.). (1976). *Play—its role in development and evolution.* New York: Basic Books.

Bruner, J. S., & Sherwood, V. (1976). Peekaboo and the learning of rule structures. In Bruner, J. S., Jolly, A., & Sylva, K. (Eds.), *Play—its role in development and evolution* (pp. 276–285). New York: Basic Books.

Buchsbaum, H. K., & Emde, R. N. (1990). Play narratives in 36-month-old children. *The Psychoanalytic Study of the Child, 45,* 129–155.

Caldera, Y. M., Huston, A. C., & O'Brien, M. (1989). Social interactions and play patterns of parents and toddlers with feminine, masculine, and neutral toys. *Child Development, 60,* 70–76.

Cazden, C. (1971). Language programs for young children: Notes from England and Wales. In C. S. Lavatelli (Eds.), *Language training in early childhood education* (pp. 119–153). Urbana, IL: Educational Resources and Information Center.

Cazden, C. B. (1976). Play with language and meta-linguistic awareness: One dimension of language experience. In J. S. Bruner, A. Jolly, & K. Sylva (Eds.), *Play—its role in development and evolution* (pp. 603–608). New York: Basic Books.

Chafel, J. A. (1984). "Call the police, okay?" Social comparison by young children during play in preschool. *Early Child Development and Care, 14,* 201–216.

Chomsky, N. (1972). *Language and mind* (enl. ed). New York: Harcourt Brace Jovanovich.

Christie, J. F. (Ed.). (1991). *Play and early literacy development.* Albany: State University of New York Press.

Christie, J. F., & Johnsen, E. P. (1983). The role of play in social-intellectual development. *Review of Educational Research, 53,* 93–115.

Christie, J. F., Johnsen, E. P., & Peckover, R. B. (1988). The effects of play period duration on children's play patterns. *Journal of Research in Childhood Education, 3* (2), 123–131.

Chukovsky, K. (1963). *From two to five* (M. Morton, Trans. & Ed.). Berkeley: University of California Press.

Clark, P. M., Griffing, P. S., & Johnson, L. G. (1989). Symbolic play and ideational fluency as aspects of the evolving divergent cognitive style in young children. *Early Child Development and Care, 51,* 77–88.

Cole, D., & LaVoie, J. C. (1985). Fantasy play and related cognitive development in 2- to 6-year-olds. *Developmental Psychology, 21* (2), 233–240.

Coleman, J. S. (1976). Learning through games. In J. S. Bruner, A. Jolly, & K. Sylva (Eds.), *Play—its role in development and evolution* (pp. 460–463). New York: Basic Books.

Collard, R. R. (1979). Exploration and play. In B. Sutton-Smith (Ed.), *Play and learning* (pp. 45–68). New York: Gardner.

Connolly, J. A., & Doyle, A. (1984). Relation of social fantasy play to social competence in preschoolers. *Developmental Psychology, 20,* 797–806.

Connolly, J. A., Doyle, A. B., & Reznick, E. (1988). Social pretend play and social interaction in preschoolers. *Journal of Applied Developmental Psychology, 9*, 301–313.

Copple, C. C., Cocking, R. R., & Matthews, W. S. (1984). Objects, symbols, and substitutions: The nature of the cognitive activity during symbolic play. In T. D. Yawkey & A. D. Pellegrini (Eds.), *Child's play: Developmental and applied* (pp. 105–123). Hillsdale, NJ: Lawrence Erlbaum.

Corrigan, R. (1987). A developmental sequence of actor-object pretend play in young children. *Merrill-Palmer Quarterly, 33*, 87–106.

Corsaro, W. A. (1986). Routines in peer culture. In J. Cook-Gumperz, W. A. Corsaro, & J. Streeck (Eds.), *Children's worlds and children's language* (pp. 231–251). New York: Mouton de Gruyter.

Corsaro, W. A. (1988). Routines in the peer culture of American and Italian nursery school children. *Sociology of Education, 61*, 1–14.

Corsaro, W. A. (1990). The underlife of the nursery school: Young children's social representations of adult rules. In G. Duveen & B. Lloyd (Eds.), *Social representations and the development of knowledge* (pp. 11–26). New York: Cambridge University Press.

Csikszentmihalyi, M. (1976). The Americanization of rock-climbing. In J. S. Bruner, A. Jolly, & K. Sylva (Eds.), *Play—its role in development and evolution* (pp. 484–488). New York: Basic Books.

Csikszentmihalyi, M. (1979). The concept of flow. In B. Sutton-Smith (Ed.), *Play and learning* (pp. 257–274). New York: Gardner.

Csikszentmihalyi, M. (1988). Introduction; The flow of experience and its significance for human psychology; The future of flow. In M. Csikszentmihalyi & I. S. Csikszentmihalyi (Eds.), *Optimal experience: Psychological studies in flow consciousness* (pp. 3–14; 15–35; 364–383). New York: Cambridge University Press.

Dansky, J. L. (1985). Questioning "A Paradigm Questioned": A commentary on Simon and Smith. *Merrill-Palmer Quarterly, 31*, 279–284.

Dansky, J. L. (1986). Play and creativity in young children. In K. Blanchard, W. W. Anderson, G. E. Chick, & E. P. Johnsen (Eds.), *The many faces of play* (pp. 69–79). Champaign, IL: Human Kinetics.

Dansky, J. L., & Silverman, I. W. (1976). Effects of play on associative fluency in pre-school children. In J. S. Bruner, A. Jolly, & K. Sylva (Eds.), *Play—its role in development and evolution* (pp. 650–654). New York: Basic Books.

Denham, S. A., Renwick, S. M., & Holt, R. W. (1991). Working and playing together: Prediction of preschool social-emotional competence from mother–child interaction. *Child Development, 62*, 242–249.

Dewey, J. (1933). *How we think*. Boston: Heath.

Dewey, J. (1934). *Art as experience*. New York: Capricorn.

Dias, M. G., & Harris, P. L. (1988). The effect of make-believe play on deductive reasoning. *British Journal of Developmental Psychology, 6*, 207–221.

Dodge, M. K., & Frost, J. L. (1986). Children's dramatic play: Influence of thematic and nonthematic settings. *Childhood Education, 62*, 166–170.

Dunn, J., & Dale, N. (1984). I a daddy: 2-year-olds' collaboration in joint pretend with sibling and with mother. In I. Bretherton (Ed.), *Symbolic play: The development of social understanding* (pp. 131–157). New York: Academic Press.

Duveen, G., & Lloyd, B. (1990). A semiotic analysis of the development of social representations of gender. In G. Duveen & B. Lloyd (Eds.), *Social representations and the development of knowledge* (pp. 27–46). New York: Cambridge University Press.

Eckerman, C. P., & Didow, S. M. (1989). *Developmental Psychology, 25* (5), 794–804.

Eckler, J. A., & Weininger, O. (1989). Structural parallels between pretend play and narratives. *Developmental Psychology, 25* (5), 736–743.

Eifermann, R. K. (1971). Social play in childhood. In R. E. Herron & B. Sutton-Smith (Eds.), *Child's Play* (pp. 270–297). New York: Wiley.

Eifermann, R. K. (1976). It's child's play. In J. S. Bruner, A. Jolly, & K. Sylva (Eds.), *Play—its role in development and evolution* (pp. 442–455). New York: Basic Books.

Eisen, G. (1988). *Children and play in the Holocaust: Games among the shadows.* Amherst: University of Massachusetts Press.

Eiser, C. (1989). Let's play doctors and nurses: A script analysis of children's play. *Early Child Development and Care, 49,* 17–23.

Eisner, E. W. (1990). The role of art and play in children's cognitive development. In E. Klugman & S. Smilansky (Eds.), *Children's play and learning: Perspectives and policy implications* (pp. 43–56). New York: Teachers College Press.

Ellis, M. J. (1979). The complexity of objects and peers. In B. Sutton-Smith (Ed.), *Play and learning* (pp. 157–174). New York: Gardner.

Ellis, M. J. (1984). Play, novelty, and stimulus seeking. In T. D. Yawkey & A. D. Pellegrini (Eds.), *Child's play: Developmental and applied* (pp. 203–218). Hillsdale, NJ: Lawrence Erlbaum.

Ellis, M. J., & Scholtz, G. J. L. (1978). *Activity and play of children.* Englewood Cliffs, NJ: Prentice-Hall.

Ellul, J. (1965). *The technological society* (J. Wilkinson, Trans.). New York: Knopf.

Erikson, E. H. (1976). Play and actuality. In J. S. Bruner, A. Jolly, & K. Sylva (Eds.), *Play—its role in development and evolution* (pp. 688–703). New York: Basic Books.

Fagot, B. I. (1988). Toddlers' play and sex stereotyping. In D. Bergen (Ed.), *Play: A medium for learning and development* (pp. 133–135). Portsmouth, NH: Heinemann.

Fein, G. G. (1975). A transformational analysis of pretending. *Developmental Psychology, 11,* 291–296.

Fein, G. G. (1985). The affective psychology of play. In C. C. Brown & A. W. Gottfried (Eds.), *Play interactions* (pp. 19–28). Skillman, NJ: Johnson & Johnson.

Fein, G. G. (1987). Pretend play: Creativity and consciousness. In D. Gorlitz & J. F. Wohlwill (Eds.), *Curiosity, imagination, and play* (pp. 281–304). Hillsdale, NJ: Lawrence Erlbaum.

Fein, G. G., & Rivkin, M. (Eds.). (1986). *The young child at play.* Washington, DC: National Association for the Education of Young Children.

Feitelson, D., & Ross, G. S. (1973). The neglected factor—play. *Human Development, 16*, 202–223.

Fenson, L. (1984). Developmental trends for action and speech in pretend play. In I. Bretherton (Ed.), *Symbolic play: The development of social understanding* (pp. 249–270). New York: Academic Press.

Fenson, L. (1985). The developmental progression of exploration and play. In C. C. Brown & A. W. Gottfried (Eds.), *Play interactions* (pp. 31–36). Skillman, NJ: Johnson & Johnson.

Festinger, L. (1957). *Cognitive dissonance.* New York: Harper.

Forbes, D., & Yablick, G. (1984). The organization of dramatic content in children's fantasy play. In F. Kessel & A. Goncu (Eds.), *Analyzing children's play dialogues* (pp. 23–36). San Francisco: Jossey-Bass.

Forys, S. K., & McCune-Nicolich, L. (1984). Shared pretend: Sociodramatic play at 3 years of age. In I. Bretherton (Ed.), *Symbolic play: The development of social understanding* (pp. 159–191). New York: Academic Press.

Freud, S. (1958). The relation of the poet to daydreaming (I. F. Grant Duff, Trans.). *On creativity and the unconscious.* New York: Harper & Row. (Original work published 1925)

Freud, S. (1959). *Beyond the pleasure principle* (J. Strachey, Trans.). New York: Bantam. (Original work published 1928)

Freud, S. (1960). *Jokes and their relation to the unconscious* (J. Strachey, Trans.). New York: W. W. Norton. (Original work published 1916)

Freyberg, J. T. (1973). Increasing the imaginative play of urban disadvantaged children through systematic training. In J. L. Singer (Ed.), *The child's world of make-believe: Experimental studies of imaginative play* (pp. 129–154). New York: Academic Press.

Fromberg, D. P. (1977). *Early childhood education: A perceptual models curriculum.* New York: John Wiley.

Fromberg, D. P. (1982). Transformational knowledge: Perceptual models as a cooperative content base for the early education of children. In S. Hill & B. J. Barnes (Eds.), *Young children and their families* (pp. 191–206). Lexington, MA: Lexington Books.

Fromberg, D. P. (1987). *The full-day kindergarten.* New York: Teachers College Press.

Fromberg, D. P. (1990). Play issues in early childhood education. In C. Seefeldt (Ed.), *Continuing issues in early childhood education* (pp. 223–243). Columbus, OH: Charles E. Merrill.

Galda, L., Pellegrini, A. D., & Cox, S. (1989). The short-term, longitudinal study of preschoolers' emergent literacy. *Research in the Teaching of English, 23* (3), 292–309.

Gardner, H. (1982). *Art, mind, and brain: A cognitive approach to creativity.* New York: Basic Books.

Garvey, C. (1977). Play and learning. In B. Tizard & D. Harvey (Eds.), *The biology of play* (pp. 74–99). Philadelphia: Lippincott.

Garvey, C. (1979). Communicational controls in social play. In B. Sutton-Smith (Ed.), *Play and learning* (pp. 109–125). New York: Gardner.

Garvey, C., & Kramer, T. L. (1989). The language of social pretend play. *Developmental Review 9* (4), 364–382.

Geertz, C. (1976). Deep play: A description of the Balinese cockfight. In J. S. Bruner, A. Jolly, & K. Sylva (Eds.), *Play—its role in development and evolution* (pp. 656–674). New York: Basic Books.

Ghiaci, G., & Richardson, J. T. E. (1980). The effects of dramatic play upon cognitive structure and development. *Journal of Genetic Psychology, 136*, 77–83.

Gibson, J. J. (1979). *The ecological approach to visual perception.* Boston: Houghton Mifflin.

Giffin, H. (1984). The coordination of meaning in the creation of a shared make-believe reality. In I. Bretherton (Ed.), *Symbolic play: The development of social understanding* (pp. 73–100). New York: Academic Press.

Gilligan, C. (1982). *In a different voice: Psychological theory and women's development.* Cambridge, MA: Harvard University Press.

Gilmore, J. B. (1971). Play: A special behavior. In R. E. Herron & B. Sutton-Smith (Eds.), *Child's play* (pp. 311–319). New York: John Wiley.

Golomb, C. (1979). Pretense play: A cognitive perspective. In N. R. Smith & M. B. Franklin (Eds.), *Symbolic functioning in childhood* (pp. 101–116). Hillsdale, NJ: Lawrence Erlbaum.

Golomb, C., Gowing, E. D. G., & Friedman, L. (1982). Play and cognition: Studies of pretense play and conservation of quantity. *Journal of Experimental Child Psychology, 33*, 257–279.

Goncu, A., & Kessel, F. (1988). Preschoolers' collaborative construction in planning and maintaining imaginative play. *International Journal of Behavioral Development, 11* (3), 327–344.

Greif, E. B. (1976). Sex role playing in pre-school children. In J. S. Bruner, A. Jolly, & K. Sylva (Eds.), *Play—its role in development and evolution* (pp. 385–391). New York: Basic Books.

Heath, S. B. (1983). *Ways with words: Language, life, and work in communities and classrooms.* New York: Cambridge University Press.

Henniger, M. L. (1985). Preschool children's play behaviors in an indoor and outdoor environment. In J. L. Frost & S. Sunderlin (Eds.), *When children play.* Wheaton, MD: Association for Childhood Education International.

Hofstadter, D. (1980). *Godel, Escher, Bach: An eternal golden braid.* New York: Vintage.

Howes, C., & Farver, J. (1987). Social pretend play in 2-year-olds: Effects of age of partner. *Early Childhood Research Quarterly, 2* (4), 305–314.

Howes, C., & Stewart, P. (1987). Child's play with adults, toys, and peers: An examination of family and child-care influences. *Developmental Psychology, 23* (3), 423–430.

Howes, C., Unger, O., & Seidner, L. B. (1989). Social pretend play in toddlers: Parallels with social play and with solitary pretend. *Child Development, 60* (1), 77–84.

Huizinga, J. (1955). *Homo ludens: A study of the play elements of culture.* Boston: Beacon.

Humphreys, A. P., & Smith, P. K. (1984). Rough-and-tumble in preschool and playground. In P. K. Smith (Ed.), *Play in animals and humans* (pp. 241–266). New York: Basil Blackwell.

Hutt, C. (1976). Exploration and play in children. In J. S. Bruner, A. Jolly, & K. Sylva (Eds.), *Play—its role in development and evolution* (pp. 202–215). New York: Basic Books.

Hutt, C., & Bhavnani, T. (1976). Predictions from play. In J. S. Bruner, A. Jolly, & K. Sylva (Eds.), *Play—its role in development and evolution* (pp. 216–219). New York: Basic Books.

Janiv, N. N. (1976). *Kedmah.* Presented at the Bicentennial Conference on Early Childhood Education, Coral Gables, FL.

Jung, C. G. (1970). *Analytical psychology.* New York: Vintage. (Original work published 1968)

Kelly-Byrne, D. (1989). *A child's play life: An ethnographic study.* New York: Teachers College Press.

Kier, C. A., & Fouts, G. T. (1989). Sibling play in divorced and married-parent families. *Journal of Reproductive and Infant Psychology, 7,* 139–146.

Kirschenblatt-Gimblett, B. (1979). Speech play and verbal art. In B. Sutton-Smith (Ed.), *Play and learning* (pp. 219–238). New York: Gardner.

Koestler, A. (1976). *The ghost in the machine.* New York: Macmillan.

Kreye, M. (1984). Conceptual organization in the play of preschool children: Effects of meaning, context, and mother–child interaction. In I. Bretherton (Ed.), *Symbolic play: The development of social understanding* (pp. 299–336). New York: Academic Press.

Ladd, G. W., & Price, J. M. (1987). Predicting children's social and school adjustment following the transition from preschool to kindergarten. *Child Development, 58,* 1168–1189.

Ladd, G. W., Price, J. M., & Hart, C. H. (1988). Predicting preschoolers' peer status from their playground behaviors. *Child Development, 59,* 986–992.

Lancy, D. F. (1984). Play in anthropological perspective. In P. K. Smith (Ed.), *Play in animals and humans* (pp. 292–303). New York: Basil Blackwell.

Langer, S. (1948). *Philosophy in a new key.* New York: Mentor. (Original work published 1942)

Lee, P. C. (1989). Is the young child egocentric or sociocentric? *Teachers College Record, 90* (3), 375–391.

Leslie, A. J. (1987). Pretense and representation: The origins of "theory of mind." *Psychological Review, 94* (4), 412–426.

Levenstein, P. (1976). Cognitive development through verbalized play: The mother–child home programme. In J. S. Bruner, A. Jolly, & K. Sylva (Eds.), *Play—its role in development and evolution* (pp. 286–297). New York: Basic Books.

Levenstein, P. (1985). Mothers' interactive play behavior in play sessions and children's educational achievements. In C. C. Brown & A. W. Gottfried (Eds.), *Play interactions* (pp. 160–167). Skillman, NJ: Johnson & Johnson.

Levine, S. (1984). A critique of the Piagetian presuppositions of the role of play in human development and a suggested alternative: Metaphoric logic which organizes the play experiences is the foundation for rational creativity. *Journal of Creative Behavior, 18,* 90–107.

Levi-Strauss, C. (1969a). *The elementary structures of kinship* (J. H. Bell, Trans.). Boston: Beacon. (Original work published 1949)

Levi-Strauss, C. (1969b). *The raw and the cooked* (J. Weightman & D. Weightman, Trans.). New York: Harper Torchbooks. (Original work published 1964)

Levy, A. K., Schaefer, L., & Phelps, P. C. (1986). Increased preschool effectiveness: Enhancing the language abilities of 3- and 4-year-old children through planned sociodramatic play. *Early Childhood Research Quarterly, 1,* 133–140.

Lieberman, J. N. (1977). *Playfulness: Its relationships to imagination and creativity.* New York: Academic Press.

Lucariello, J., & Rifkin, A. (1986). Event representation as the basis for categorical knowledge. In K. Nelson et al., *Event knowledge: Structure and function in development* (pp. 189–203). Hillsdale, NJ: Lawrence Erlbaum.

Maccoby, E. E., & Jacklin, C. T. (1974). *The psychology of sex differences.* Stanford, CA: Stanford University Press.

Mandler, J. M. (1983). Representation. In P. H. Mussen (Ed.), *Handbook of child psychology* (Vol. 3, pp. 420–494). New York: John Wiley.

Mann, B. L. (1984). Effects of realistic and unrealistic props on symbolic play. In T. D. Yawkey & A. D. Pellegrini (Eds.), *Child's play: Developmental and applied* (pp. 359–376). Hillsdale, NJ: Lawrence Erlbaum.

Marbach, E. S., & Yawkey, T. D. (1980). The effect of imaginative play actions on language development in five-year-old children. *Psychology in the Schools, 17,* 257–263.

McCune, L. (1985). Play-language relationships and symbolic development. In C. C. Brown & A. W. Gottfried (Eds.), *Play interactions* (pp. 38–45). Skillman, NJ: Johnson & Johnson.

McCune-Nicolich, L. (1981). Toward symbolic functioning: Structure of early pretend games and potential parallels with language. *Child Development, 52,* 785–797.

McCune-Nicolich, L., & Fenson, L. (1984). Methodological issues in studying early pretend play. In P. K. Smith (Ed.), *Play in animals and humans* (pp. 81–104). New York: Basil Blackwell.

McGhee, P. E. (1984). Play, incongruity, and humor. In T. D. Yawkey & A. D. Pellegrini (Eds.), *Child's play: Developmental and applied* (pp. 219–236). Hillsdale, NJ: Lawrence Erlbaum.

McGhee, P. E., Etheridge, L., & Berg, N. A. (1984). Effect of level of toy structure on preschool children's pretend play. *Journal of Catholic Education, 144,* 209–217.

McLoyd, V. C. (1983). The effects of the structure of play objects on the pretend play of low-income preschool children. *Child Development, 54,* 626–635.

McLuhan, M. (1963). We need a new picture of knowledge. In A. Frazier (Ed.), *New insights and the curriculum* (pp. 57–70). Washington, DC: Association for Supervision and Curriculum Development.

Miller, P., & Garvey, C. (1984). Mother–baby role play: Its origins in social support. In I. Bretherton (Ed.), *Symbolic play: The development of social understanding* (pp. 101–131). New York: Academic Press.

Moore, O. K., & Anderson, A. R. (1968). The responsive environments project. In R. D. Hess & R. M. Bear (Eds.), *Early education* (pp. 171–189). Chicago: Aldine.

Moran, J. D., III, Sawyers, J. K., Fu, V. R., & Milgram, R. M. (1984). Predicting imaginative play in preschool children. *Gifted Child Quarterly, 28,* 92–94.

Morgan, R. (1982). *The anatomy of freedom: Physics and global politics.* Garden City, NY: Anchor.

Morrow, L. M. (1990). Preparing the classroom environment to promote literacy during play. *Early Childhood Research Quarterly, 5* (4), 537–554.

Munro, J. (1991). Case study development. *Journal of Early Childhood Teacher Education, 12* (1), 14.

Nelson, K., & Seidman, S. (1984). Playing with scripts. In I. Bretherton (Ed.), *Symbolic play: The development of social understanding* (pp. 45–71). New York: Academic Press.

Nelson, K., et al. (1986). *Event knowledge: Structure and function in development.* Hillsdale, NJ: Lawrence Erlbaum.

Neuman, S. B., & Roskos, K. (1991). The influence of literacy-enriched play centers on preschoolers' conceptions of the functions of print. In J. F. Christie (Ed.), *Play and early literacy development* (pp. 167–187). Albany: State University of New York Press.

Nevius, J. (1989). Relations between young Mexican American children and play paradigms. *Journal of Genetic Psychology, 150* (4), 45–71.

Ogbu, J. U. (1988). Culture, development, and education. In A. D. Pellegrini (Ed.), *Psychological bases for early education* (pp. 245–273). New York: John Wiley.

Olszewski, P. (1987). Individual differences in preschool children's production of verbal fantasy play. *Merrill-Palmer Quarterly, 33* (1), 69–86.

Opie, I., & Opie, P. (1976). Street games: Counting-out and chasing. In J. S. Bruner, A. Jolly, & K. Sylva (Eds.), *Play—its role in development and evolution* (pp. 394–412). New York: Basic Books.

Paley, V. G. (1984). *Boys and girls: Superheroes in the doll corner.* Chicago: University of Chicago Press.

Parker, S. T. (1984). Playing for keeps: An evolutionary perspective on human games. In P. K. Smith (Ed.), *Play in animals and humans* (pp. 271–293). New York: Basil Blackwell.

Parten, M. (1971). Social play among preschool children. In R. E. Herron & B. Sutton-Smith (Eds.), *Child's play* (pp. 83–95). New York: John Wiley.

Pellegrini, A. D. (1984a). The effects of exploration and play in young children's associative fluency: A review and extension of training studies. In T. D. Yawkey & A. D. Pellegrini (Eds.), *Child's play: Developmental and applied* (pp. 237–253). Hillsdale, NJ: Lawrence Erlbaum.

Pellegrini, A. D. (1984b). Identifying causal elements in the thematic-fantasy play paradigm. *American Educational Research Journal, 21*, 691–701.

Pellegrini, A. D. (1984c). The social cognitive ecology of preschool classrooms: Contextual relations revisited. *International Journal of Behavioral Development, 7*, 321–332.

Pellegrini, A. D. (1985). The relations between symbolic play and literate behavior: A review and critique of the empirical literature. *Review of Educational Research, 55*, 107–121.

Pellegrini, A. D. (1987). Rough-and-tumble play: Developmental and educational significance. *Educational Psychologist, 22*, 23–43.

Pellegrini, A. D. (1988). Elementary-school children's rough-and-tumble play and social competence. *Developmental Psychology, 24* (6), 802–806.

Pellegrini, A. D., & Galda, L. (1982). The effects of thematic-fantasy play training on the development of children's story comprehension. *American Educational Research Journal, 19*, 443–452.

Pellegrini, A. D., & Perlmutter, J. C. (1989). Classroom contextual effects on children's play. *Developmental Psychology, 25* (2), 289–296.

Pepler, D. J., & Ross, H. S. (1982). The effects of play on convergent and divergent problem-solving. *Child Development, 52*, 1202–1210.

Perner, J. (1988). Developing semantics for theories of mind: From propositional attitudes to mental representation. In J. S. Astington & O. Harris (Eds.), *Developmental theories of mind* (pp. 141–172). New York: Cambridge University Press.

Perner, J. (1991). *Understanding and the representational mind.* Cambridge, MA: MIT Press.

Pfeiffer, J. (1962). *The thinking machine.* Philadelphia: Lippincott.

Piaget, J. (1962). *Play, dreams, and imitation in childhood* (C. Gattegno & M. F. Hodgson, Trans.). New York: W. W. Norton.

Piaget, J. (1966). Response to Brian Sutton-Smith. *Psychological Review, 73*, 111–112.

Piaget, J. (1976). *The grasp of consciousness.* Cambridge, MA: Harvard University Press.

Piaget, J., et al. (1965). *The moral judgment of the child* (M. Gabain, Trans.). New York: Free Press.

Pulaski, M. A. (1973). Toys and imaginative play. In J. L. Singer (Ed.), *The child's world of make-believe: Experimental studies of imaginative play* (pp. 73–103). New York: Academic Press.

Reiber, R. W., & Carton, A. S. (Eds.) (1987). *The collected works of L. S. Vygotsky: Vol. 1. Problems of general psychology* (Minick, N., Trans.). New York: Plenum.

Rogers, D. L. (1985). Relationships between block play and the social development of children. *Early Child Development and Care, 20*, 245–261.

Roggman, L. A., & Peery, J. C. (1989). Parent–infant social play in brief encounters: Early gender differences. *Child Study Journal, 19* (1), 65–79.

Rogoff, B. (1990). *Apprenticeship in thinking: Cognitive development in social context.* New York: Oxford University Press.

Roskos, K. (1990). A taxonomic view of pretend play activity among 4- and 5-year-old children. *Early Childhood Research Quarterly, 5* (4), 495–512.

Rubin, K. H. (1985). Play, peer interaction, and social development. In C. C. Brown & A. W. Gottfried (Eds.), *Play interactions* (pp. 88–96). Skillman, NJ: Johnson & Johnson.

Rubin, K. H., Fein, G. G., & Vanderberg, B. (1983). Play. In P. H. Mussen & E. Hetherington (Eds.), *Handbook of child psychology* (Vol. 4, pp. 693–774). New York: John Wiley.

Scales, B., Almy, M., Nicolopoulou, A., & Ervin-Tripp, S. (Eds.). (1991). *Play and the social context of development.* New York: Teachers College Press.

Schank, R., & Abelson, R. (1977). *Scripts, plans, goals and understanding: An inquiry into human knowledge.* Hillsdale, NJ: Lawrence Erlbaum.

Schrader, C. T. (1989). Written language use within the context of young children's symbolic play. *Early Childhood Research Quarterly, 4* (2), 225–244.

Schrader, C. T. (1990). Symbolic play as a curricular tool for early literacy development. *Early Childhood Research Quarterly, 5* (1), 79–103.

Schwartzman, H. B. (1978). *Transformations: The anthropology of children's play.* New York: Plenum.

Schwartzman, H. B. (1979). The sociocultural context of play. In B. Sutton-Smith (Ed.), *Play and learning* (pp. 239–255). New York: Gardner.

Schwartzman, H. B. (1984). Imaginative play: Deficit or difference? In T. D. Yawkey & A. D. Pellegrini (Eds.), *Child's play: Developmental and applied* (pp. 49–62). Hillsdale, NJ: Lawrence Erlbaum.

Schwartzman, H. B. (1985). Child-structured play: A cross-cultural perspective. In C. C. Brown & A. W. Gottfried (Eds.), *Play interactions* (pp. 11–19). Skillman, NJ: Johnson & Johnson.

Serbin, L. A. (1978). Teachers, peers, and play preferences: An environmental approach to sex typing in the preschool. In B. Sprung (Ed.), *Perspectives on nonsexist early childhood education* (pp. 79–93). New York: Teachers College Press.

Shore, C. (1990). Combinatorial play, conceptual development, and early multiword speech. *Developmental Psychology, 22* (2), 184–190.

Shotwell, J. M., Wolf, D., & Gardner, H. (1979). Exploring symbolization: Styles of achievement. In B. Sutton-Smith (Ed.), *Play and learning* (pp. 127–156). New York: Gardner.

Simon, T., & Smith, P. K. (1985a). A role for play in children's problem-solving: Time to think again. In J. L. Frost & S. Sunderlin (Eds.), *When children play: Proceedings of the International Conference on Play and Play Environments* (pp. 55–59). Wheaton, MD: Association for Childhood Education International.

Simon, T., & Smith, P. K. (1985b). Play and problem solving: A paradigm questioned. *Merrill-Palmer Quarterly, 31* (3), 265–277.

Simon, T., & Smith, P. K. (1985c). Problems with a play paradigm: A reply to Dansky. *Merrill-Palmer Quarterly, 32* (2), 205–209.

Singer, J. L. (Ed.). (1973). *The child's world of make-believe: Experimental studies of imaginative play.* New York: Academic Press.

Singer, J. L., & Singer, D. (1979). The values of imagination. In B. Sutton-Smith (Ed.), *Play and learning* (pp. 195–218). New York: Gardner.

Slade, A. (1987a). A longitudinal study of maternal involvement and symbolic play during the toddler period. *Child Development, 58,* 367–375.

Slade, A. (1987b). Quality of attachment and early symbolic play. *Developmental Psychology, 23* (1), 78–85.

Smilansky, S. (1968). *The effects of sociodramatic play on disadvantaged preschool children.* New York: John Wiley.

Smith, P. K., & Simon, T. (1984). Object play, problem-solving and creativity in children. In P. K. Smith (Ed.), *Play in animals and humans* (pp. 199–216). New York: Basil Blackwell.

Smith, P. K., & Whitney, S. (1987). Play and associative fluency: Experimenter effects may be responsible for previous positive findings. *Developmental Psychology, 23* (1), 49–53.

Stevenson, J. B., Leavitt, L. A., Thompson, R. H., & Roach, M. A. (1988). A social relations model analysis of parent and child play. *Developmental Psychology, 24* (1), 101–108.

Sutton-Smith, B. A syntax for play and games. In R. E. Herron & B. Sutton-Smith (Eds.), *Child's Play* (pp. 298–307). New York: Wiley.

Sutton-Smith, B. (Ed.). (1979). *Play and learning.* New York: Gardner.

Sutton-Smith, B., & Kelly-Byrne, D. (1984). The phenomenon of bipolarity in play theories. In T. D. Yawkey & A. D. Pellegrini (Eds.), *Child's play: Developmental and applied* (pp. 29–47). Hillsdale, NJ: Lawrence Erlbaum.

Sylva, K. (1984). A hard-nosed look at the fruits of play. *Early Child Development and Care, 15,* 171–184.

Sylva, K., Bruner, J. S., & Genova, P. (1976). The role of play in the problem-solving of children 3–5 years old. In J. S. Bruner, A. Jolly, & K. Sylva (Eds.), *Play—its role in development and evolution* (pp. 244–257). New York: Basic Books.

Tizard, B. (1977). Play: The child's way of learning. In B. Tizard & D. Harvey (Eds.), *The biology of play* (pp. 199–208). Philadelphia: Lippincott.

Torrance, E. P. (1962). *Guiding creative talent.* Englewood Cliffs, NJ: Prentice-Hall.

Urberg, K. A., & Kaplan, M. G. (1989). An observational study of race-, age-, and sex-heterogeneous interaction in preschoolers. *Journal of Applied Developmental Psychology, 10* (3), 299–311.

Voss, H-G. (1987). An empirical study of exploration-play sequences in early childhood. In D. Gorlitz & J. F. Wohlwill (Eds.), *Curiosity, imagination, and play* (pp. 152–179). Hillsdale, NJ: Lawrence Erlbaum.

Vukelich, C. (1991). Materials and modeling: Promoting literacy during play. In J. F. Christie (Ed.), *Play and early literacy development* (pp. 215–231). Albany: State University of New York Press.

Vygotsky, L. S. (1976). Play and its role in the mental development of the child. In J. S. Bruner, A. Jolly, & K. Sylva (Eds.), *Play—its role in development and evolution* (pp. 537–554). New York: Basic Books.

Vygotsky, L. S. (1978). *Mind in society: The development of higher psychological processes* (M. Cole, V. John-Steiner, S. Scribner, & E. Souberman (Eds.). Cambridge, MA: Harvard University Press.

Wanska, S. K., Pohlman, J. C., & Bedrosian, J. L. (1989). Topic maintenance in preschoolers' conversation in three play situations. *Early Childhood Research Quarterly, 4* (3), 393–402.

Weir, R. (1976). Playing with language. In J. S. Bruner, A. Jolly, & K. Sylva (Eds.), *Play—its role in development and evolution* (pp. 609–618). New York: Basic Books.

Werner, H. (1948). *Comparative psychology of mental development* (rev. ed.). New York: International Universities Press.

White, R. W. (1959). Motivation reconsidered: The concept of competence. *Psychological Review, 65,* 297–333.

Whiting, B. B., & Edwards, C. P. (1988). *Children of different worlds: The formation of social behavior.* Cambridge, MA: Harvard University Press.

Whyte, J., & Owens, A. (1989). Language and symbolic play: Some findings from a study of autistic children. *Irish Journal of Psychology, 10* (2), 317–332.

Williamson, P. A., & Silvern, S. B. (1984). Creative dramatic play and language comprehension. In T. D. Yawkey & A. D. Pellegrini (Eds.), *Child's play: Developmental and applied* (pp. 347–358). Hillsdale, NJ: Lawrence Erlbaum.

Williamson, P. A., & Silvern, S. B. (1991). Thematic-fantasy play and story comprehension. In J. F. Christie (Ed.), *Play and early literacy development* (pp. 69–90). Albany: State University of New York Press.

Wohlwill, J. F. (1984). Relationships between exploration and play. In T. D. Yawkey & A. D. Pellegrini (Eds.), *Child's play: Developmental and applied* (pp. 143–170). Hillsdale, NJ: Lawrence Erlbaum.

Wolf, D. H., Rygh, J., & Altshuler, J. (1984). Agency and experience: Actions and states in play narratives. In I. Bretherton (Ed.), *Symbolic play: The development of social understanding* (pp. 195–217). New York: Academic Press.

Wortham, S. C. (1985). A history of outdoor play 1900–1985: Theories of play and play environments. In J. L. Frost & S. Sunderlin (Eds.), *When children play: Proceedings of the International Conference on Play and Play Environments* (pp. 3–7). Wheaton, MD: Association for Childhood Education International.

Zukow, P. G. (1989). Siblings as effective socializing agents: Evidence from central Mexico. In P. G. Zukow (Ed.), *Sibling interaction across cultures: Theoretical and methodological issues* (pp. 79–105). New York: Springer-Verlag.

# CHAPTER 4

# Developing the Foundation: Oral Language and Communicative Competence

CELIA GENISHI

From their earliest days, children are participants in the world around them. Oral language, the focus of this chapter, offers them access to a number of communities within that world. In the classroom community, young children might sound like these kindergartners sitting at the art table.

KEVIN: I'm not a boy. I'm a bully.
DAWNN: I'm not a girl. I'm a girly.                    (Wang, 1989, p. 5)

Or they may sound like Alma, who is retelling with puppets the story of *Caps for Sale* (Slobodkina, 1968) to an adult. Quite sophisticated, she uses English to narrate the story and Spanish to give "stage directions."

He was going and going. And then, he sit down. And then the . . . *a ver, se va a sentar, agárralas, a ver, agárralas, se va a sentar.* [let's see, he's going to sit down, pick them up, let's see, pick them up, he's going to sit down.] And slowly . . . *ahora, es tí, ése se va a sentar,* [now, it's you, that one is going to sit down.]                    (Seawell, 1985, p. 124)

Alma, Dawnn, and Kevin show that they know about the ways words, sentences, and ideas are constructed through language. And they demonstrate what they know about the world. Like an increasing number of young children, Alma is aware that there are languages other than the one she uses at home. She is a member of a Spanish-speaking community at the same time that she is entering the English-speaking world and the community of the literate, in which stories are told and retold in speech and print. Kevin and Dawnn know how to contrast negative and affirmative statements and how to play with them. In their gender-related joking, they seem to know that "changing" into a bully or girly is just for fun.

How did Alma, Dawnn, and Kevin become the speakers and learners that they are? Should adults expect all children to use language as these three have? How large a role has the adult played to encourage talk and interaction? What issues in the field of early childhood education are reflected in these interactions and influence the kind of curriculum children will experience? The content of this chapter addresses these questions by focusing on the following topics related to the processes of language acquisition: the historical context of language in early childhood education; the nature of language and its acquisition; developing communicative competence in the classroom: issues and choices; and curricula that build on children's oral communicative abilities.

## THE HISTORICAL CONTEXT

In the last 25 years, language has become a special issue in early childhood education in the United States. The social programs and movements of the 1960s and 1970s, including Head Start and the women's movement, affected public expectations for preschool and primary education. People looked to compensatory programs like Head Start as forces for social and economic reform. A variety of social groups, including ethnic minorities, participated in changing the structure and look of early education, especially at the preschool level. Parents became an integral part of administrative groups for Head Start and sometimes for day care centers and schools.

Because the dialect or language of minority group children is often different from that of middle class children, traditional views of language in schools have been challenged since the 1960s. Twenty or more years ago most people assumed that there was only one kind of English with which teachers needed to be concerned: standard (newscasters' or textbook) English. When educators or researchers wrote about varieties or different dialects of English, they often wrote about them as if dialects were inappropriate and incorrect. For example, in a report of pioneering research about the language of elementary school children, Loban (1963) stated in his summary of findings: "For Negro subjects with southern background, using appropriately the verb *to be* proves to be 12 times as troublesome as for northern Caucasian or Negro subjects" (p. 85).

Later, in the 1960s and 1970s, linguists like Labov (1970) demonstrated that speakers of nonstandard dialects of English, including what many call black English, use forms of the verb *to be* in ways that are consistently different from standard English forms. These different uses are not "troublesome" within the black English-speaking community. For instance, using any form of *to be* as in, "Richard be sick," suggests that Richard's condition is habitual. In contrast, "Richard sick" conveys the message that his sickness is temporary; Richard probably is not a sickly person.

By 1985 a number of books had been written about black English (Brooks, 1985; Burling, 1973; Dillard, 1972; Labov, 1972; Piestrup, 1973). Many authors emphasized the fact that *everyone* uses a dialect and that the term *dialect* is neutral, not negative. Educators' understanding of variation in language grew, so that they no longer assumed that standard English was the only acceptable dialect for classroom settings. When the federal Bilingual Education Act of 1968 marked the recognition that a growing number of U.S. students spoke a language other than English, the horizons of language education expanded even further. Broadened views of language led educators to reconsider their goals for young children's learning at the same time that parents and practitioners called for "culturally relevant" education. Taking into account the culture and previous experiences of children led to the creation of some innovative programs and curricula. These included the frequent use of languages other than English, for example, the Rough Rock Navajo and the Tucson (Spanish) Language Experience models (John & Horner, 1971), or the incorporation of black English features into materials for the teaching of reading (Simpkins, Simpkins, & Holt, 1977).

By the 1980s, policy makers and the public wondered about the effectiveness of compensatory programs, even though some studies (for example, Schweinhart & Weikart, 1980) showed the long-term benefits of Head Start. As a group, minority children still achieve less well in school than majority or mainstream children. Educators and researchers continue to ask why this happens. They study children's home and school environments as they try to discover what kinds of experiences and curricula might improve learning and teaching for all groups. So in recent decades the educator's domain of concern has extended beyond the classroom to the home.

In the 1990s language is still a primary issue in the field. Since 1987 there has been much discussion of the need for "developmentally appropriate" practices (Bredekamp, 1987) and for curricula that are responsive to the diversity of young children and their families (see Chapter 1, this volume). How aspects of language learning fit within appropriate ways of educating children is a subject of debate, revolving around topics such as "dialect differences," "multiculturalism," and "developmentally appropriate" curriculum. Each topic reflects persistent concerns of educators and parents, and each will be discussed below in the section "Developing Communicative Competence in the Classroom: Issues and Choices."

In linguistics and language acquisition, researchers have expanded their areas of study in tandem with educators. Linguists now focus on functions of language across different situations, along with rules related to its forms. Researchers discuss the growth of communication, not just language, and the boundary between spoken and written uses of language is blurred. Further, the processes of acquisition that they study are those of working class and minority, not just middle class, children. The findings of researchers whose work is most pertinent to early childhood language education are discussed in the next section.

## LANGUAGE AND THE PROCESSES OF ACQUISITION

We take for granted our ability to make language do what we need it to do. In or out of the classroom, language gives our thoughts substance. As we talk to ourselves, language helps us to remember, plan, understand what happens to us, and formulate ideas. Language is part of the individual's uniquely human ways of knowing, feeling, and being. As we use language with others, it shapes our identities and social lives. The way our own language sounds to listeners leads them to make judgments about where we are from, what our occupation is, how friendly or clever we are.

We easily see what language does, and we can see this without having to describe what it is. Understanding what language is, how it is structured, how it works, is the task of linguists who describe language in terms of components. These are summarized below to show just how impressive—for adult and child—the feat of learning a language is.

Each language component is made up of parts and the rules that enable speakers to combine those parts. *Phonology* refers to the sounds of a language. English speakers easily produce the sounds of English, and without knowing the word *ruddle* they will know that it sounds like a possible English word whereas *fwoodr* does not. English speakers also know the *morphology* of their language, or the rules for how morphemes are combined to form words. (Words like *happy, look*, or *jump* or parts of words like *-ing* or *un-* are morphemes.) Speakers know, then, that the addition of *-ing* to a certain kind of word means an action is ongoing, as in *looking* or *jumping*. They know that *un-* preceding a word changes its meaning in a specific way, as in *unhappy*. Linguists who see the morpheme as the main unit of meaning in a language refer to morphology as the core of the semantic or meaning-related component.

The way we combine morphemes in an utterance or sentence is known as *syntax*. We know that in this sentence, "Carla is jumping," the morphemes are arranged in a way that makes sense to English speakers. We say *Carla* before *is* and *is* before *jumping*. We would not ordinarily say "Jumping is Carla" or "Carla jumping is," although we could say "Is Carla jumping?" and change the meaning of the sentence. We are no longer telling; we are asking. Linguists would describe the change from a declarative ("Carla is jumping") to a question ("Is Carla jumping?") in terms of the syntactic rules the speaker knows about forming questions. One of these rules for question formation has to do with saying *is* before *Carla*.

Finally, *pragmatics* relates not to combining morphemes within sentences, but combining sentences with other sentences. Here linguists are concerned with rules for carrying on conversations, for using language in human interaction. Because rules of usage are different for different groups (for example, Minnesotans may find appropriate something that Texans think is offensive), pragmatic rules are slippery. They include rules about what kind of answer may follow a question in order to be judged polite or appropriate in a particular situation. For example, saying a simple, "Yes," after someone asks, "Do you know how to get to 14th Street?" is not appropriate, whereas following the "Yes" with directions to 14th Street is.

In summary, we know a great many rules, rules for combining sounds into morphemes, morphemes into words, words into sentences, sentences into conversations. The wonder is that no one explicitly teaches us these rules. Yet like kindergartners Kevin, Dawnn, and Alma, we apply them without being aware of them. We know them in a subconscious way, and that knowledge—sometimes called *linguistic competence*—enables us to use language as we need to.

Most people easily go through life without defining the components of language or reflecting on the marvels of the human mind that enable people to learn and use language. They have no need to study it or understand how an individual learns it. Why should early childhood educators understand what language is and how it comes to be? One reason is that language acquisition is a major part of human development. In fact, when it comes to oral language, children have experienced a rich and spontaneous "curriculum" since birth. Understanding what they know and how they come to know it can aid the teacher in planning activities and teaching strategies that build on children's ways of leaning. Another reason to know about this aspect of development is that language is at the center of school learning. Almost every area of the curriculum entails language in the teaching/learning process. Third, increasing numbers of children enter early childhood settings with a language other than English. Knowing that children acquire a first language so well at an early age helps teachers see that children are healthy learners, regardless of what language they use. How do children come to know the language they bring with them to the classroom?

## Learning Language Through Interaction

The process of learning language is enormously complicated. Thus theories that explain how children acquire it cannot be simple. For example, according to a strict *innatist* theory, a person's genes are the sole source of language and communicative development; a child born with no physical handicaps should learn language. Unfortunately, researchers know that this is not the case. A child whose physical needs are met but who lacks any opportunity for social interaction does not become a language user (Curtiss, 1977). At the other extreme, a strict *behaviorist* theory grounds communicative development only in the environment—what is outside the learner. From this point of view, children learn what they hear around them through imitation, repetition, and reinforcement. Children do imitate what they hear, and they learn the language of those around them; but they also say things they have never heard before, such as "goed" or "footses" or "Why you putted it there?" They use these forms even when no one reinforces or encourages them to do so. These forms—what adults would call mistakes—suggest that a full explanation of how children acquire language must include children's ability to think and formulate rules for themselves.

Current theories about language acquisition are neither strictly innatist or behaviorist. Most child language specialists believe that acquiring language depends on interaction between nature and nurture, between genes and the environment. Human beings are biologically prepared to use language in ways that no other organism is. What is with a person at birth, however, must be cultivated by an environment consisting of other people, objects, and actions, the essentials of interaction and bases of development. The theoretical approach of many researchers of children's communication is, therefore, termed *interactionist* and *constructivist* (Piaget & Inhelder, 1969; Vygotsky, 1978). The process of acquisition is based on the interaction of inborn abilities to formulate rules, act physically upon the environment, and seek social interaction. The child constructs, through her or his own activity and thinking in varied social situations, knowledge about how language works.

### Early Language or Early Communication?

In the 1960s and early 1970s, child language researchers focused on the development of *language*, primarily the syntactic rules of child speakers. What word did they say first? How did children combine their first two words? Were the combinations similar to adult forms? By the mid-1970s researchers had taken a step back, toward infancy, to investigate the foundations of language. Researchers broadened their focus to study the growth of *communicative competence*, a person's ability to speak and act appropriately in different social situations. This competence depends on many kinds of knowledge: knowledge of linguistic rules (the speaker's linguistic competence), as well as of social rules for appropriate verbal and nonverbal behavior. Young children are in the process of learning these complicated rules for communicating, which develop in a broad range of contexts.

To see how children become communicators, some researchers studied early "conversations" like this one.

INFANT: Baba daba.
MOTHER: Where was it? It was far away, wasn't it? It wasn't right around here? Noooo.
[Infant babbles]
MOTHER: It wasn't right around here, was it? No.
[Infant babbles]
MOTHER: Yes, you were ridin' an old horsie. Ridin' an old horsie. You saw cows. Did you see co-o-ows? Cows go mooo. Cows go mooo.

This child's construction of communication is at first embedded in one-sided conversations between mother and son. With a babbling sound, cry, or vigorous movement of the arms and legs, infants let others know that they have messages to send. To document the ways in which communication develops, Stern (1977) watched mothers and children, between birth and age 6 months, "dance" with each other. From the first weeks of life, each partner accommodated the other; the child's smile was followed by the mother's smile, for example. These early behaviors are elementary, but researchers believe they underlie more complex interaction in the future.

During and after the first 6 months of life, infants communicate in nonverbal ways, and they also vocalize—or coo and babble—using sounds that will eventually be combined into adultlike words. Some time after the first birthday, most children begin to verbalize. They use words like *juice, car,* or *up* to refer to their concrete world. As they become competent communicators, the dance between care givers and themselves continues as each child expands his or her role in interaction to coordinate words with previously learned nonverbal behaviors and actions.

Nelson (1973) studied early words by documenting the first 50 words of 18 one- to two-year-olds. She found that most of these words were nouns like *sock, key,* and *shoe,* which named things that were common in the child's environment, movable, and handled by the children themselves. These objects were the basis for children's actions; first words were grounded in sensory and physical activity. More recently Nelson (1985, 1986) has investigated early words as part of a broader process of children's conceptual development. She sees as critical the ordinary and repeated experiences of infants' lives. What the child comes to know and remember is an *event* or whole episode of an activity like feeding or bathing. Over time this event is mentally represented and broken down or analyzed into component parts. These are eventually labeled, but only after many occurrences of the event. Thus, the child's actions, experience, and cognitive abilities to represent, remember, and analyze all contribute to the making of a young language user.

Although Nelson, whose ideas are compatible with Piagetian theory, provides insights into how children learn words as a by-product of sensory and physical experiences, other researchers (Barrett, 1982; Clark, 1983) propose alternatives to Nelson's approach. According to these researchers, children may first name common objects in their environment, but to acquire the full meaning of a word, they may need to go through a subconscious analysis of its features. They note features that are functional (how is a shoe used?) and perceptual (what is its shape, size, texture, and so on?). At first, children may only refer to their shoes as shoes; then they may focus on noticeable features, for example, the shoes' shape. For a short while they may call both shoes and house slippers "shoes," but over time they are finally able to identify the features that set shoes apart from boots and slippers. At this point, children have acquired the bundle of features and concepts that define the word. Along the way, young children, intent on communicating about what is new to them, make the most of what they already know to make sense of experience (Wong Fillmore, 1976).

Beyond the stage of using one word at a time, children continue to expand their vocabularies with an impressive effortlessness and speed. Miller and Gildea (1987) point out that the average number of words learned in a day as children acquire their first language is about 10, a number that suggests a large number of "events" and experiences from which to draw new concepts and words. (See Genishi, 1988b, for further discussion of word learning.) In addition, researchers have found that varied experiences are critical not just at the early childhood level. Snow, Barnes, Chandler, Goodman, and Hemphill (1991) indicate that second through sixth graders who make progress in literacy learning in the classroom had teachers who stressed vocabulary learning *in context*, that is, in all content areas. They used diverse materials, such as maps, trade books, comic books, and encyclopedias, and experience-broadening activities such as field trips. Thus, the need for experience as a source of verbal knowledge extends beyond the early childhood years.

## Combining Words: The Development of Syntax

Linguists and psychologists interested in child language in the 1960s focused not on the acquisition of words but on rules of syntax, which guide the ways we combine words to form grammatical utterances. Pioneers in this search included Brown and his collaborators (Brown, Cazden, & Bellugi, 1969; Miller & Ervin, 1964). These and other psycholinguists recorded and studied thousands of utterances to discover the rules children subconsciously use to combine their first words in conversations. An example is this conversation between Karen, 19 months old, and her father, who is watching television and attending to his daughter and an adult visitor.

> KAREN: Mommy tape. Mommy tape. Mommy tape. Mommy tape. Mommy tape.
> FATHER: Invisible mending tape. ("translating" for other adult)
> ADULT: Oh!
> FATHER: You can have *this* much (shows with his thumb and index finger how long the piece can be).
> KAREN: Daddy knee (pointing toward his face).
>
> (Genishi & Dyson, 1984, p. 46)

The rules underlying Karen's two-word utterances are part of her early grammar; over a period of years she will construct a number of grammars, not just one. By using a simple rule for combining a noun with another noun ("Mommy tape"), Karen has managed to start a conversation about tape. She refers to the mending tape as her mother's; later she cryptically calls Daddy's face his "knee," perhaps making a joke. In another conversation, she may apply a rule to combine noun and verb, as in "Daddy sleep." In a few weeks or months she might say "Mommy's tape" and "Daddy's knee," and eventually she might add *-ed* to all verbs to form a past tense, as in *walked, goed,* or *hided,* probably even to verbs that have irregular past forms (*went, hid*). These constructions are especially informative when they occur consistently, since they reveal what the child's own rules are. Well before kindergarten age, then, children's speech reflects their knowledge of basic syntactic rules.

In addition to noting spontaneous child utterances like "two feets," "Bubba eating," or "Gram goed," researchers tested children's rules experimentally. Berko (1958) created an ingenious test for tapping children's knowledge of specific rules for combining morphemes, or parts of words, to form other words. Berko used nonsense words, such as *wug, gling,* and *spow,* to see whether children aged 4 to 7 years could look at a picture related to the word and then form an appropriate new word. A child might respond that a picture of more than one *wug* (drawn like a cartoon animal) was a picture of *wugs.* Or the experimenter might show a picture of a man doing something he called *spowing* to see if the child could say that the man *spowed* yesterday. Berko concluded that children who were able to produce such forms as plural, progressive, and past with nonsense words also knew rules for producing these forms with ordinary English words. Along with their spontaneous "mistakes" (*goed, hided*) in conversation, children's responses on the Berko test prove that children learn language by means other than strict imitation of adult forms. Instead they subconsciously construct and apply the rules of their developing grammars.

Researchers in the 1970s shifted their focus from syntax to meaning, or semantics. Their question became: What do children's early word combinations mean? One syntactic structure could have more than one meaning; for example, "Mommy juice" could mean, "Mommy's juice," or "Mommy, give me juice," and so on. Brown believed a satisfactory explanation of possible meanings was based on a "rich interpretation." According to this view, young speakers are able to convey a variety of basic meanings and relationships (Brown, 1973). "Mommy juice" might express the relationship technically called possession or agent (the "doer") + object (what "receives" the action). At other times children use language to convey the meaning of nomination (naming things, as in "this doggie") or of nonexistence (remarking on the disappearance of a person or object, as in "allgone car"). Those meanings will continue to be the foundation of what speakers say well beyond the time when two-word utterances are heard. The utterances and rules underlying them eventually become much more elaborate, but behind the technical terms describing any utterance, Brown believed there was always an active, thinking, meaning-seeking, and meaning-creating child.

### Later Syntactic and Semantic Development

Most research on language acquisition has focused on children under 5 years old, and most recently on children under 2 years of age. Still there is much "complexification" that develops after the early stages. Somewhere between 2 and 4, for example, children not only use multiword utterances but also begin to use complex sentences that include more than one idea or proposition. Instead of saying two separate simple sentences, "I like the game. The game is at my friend's house," the child can say, "I like the game, and it's at my friend's house," or—using more advanced rules for combining ideas in a single sentence—"I like the game that's at my friend's house." "I'm going to the store. Then, "Lee Marie comes over," might later be stated, "I'm going to the store before Lee Marie comes over." To accomplish these combinations, children master certain rules of syntax that enable them to eliminate some words, add others, and change the word order if necessary. By learning a few rules about incorporating one sentence or idea within another, children can eventually produce countless numbers and varieties of sentences that they could not before.

Children also learn rules for forming other types of sentences. When they can consistently say, "Does Dan have the book?" instead of, "Dan has the book?" they speak as if they know a basic rule for forming questions. That is, they must use a form of *do* and invert the order of subject and verb

("Does Dan have . . ." instead of "Dan have . . ."). Another form children master is the negative sentence. A 6-year-old's utterance, "I don't want to sleep any more," shows mastery of adult rules for negative sentence formation, whereas her earlier, "I not sleep," does not. Researchers have come to realize that such rules develop over a period of years. In the case of special structures, requiring the use of *ask* and *tell*, for instance, children may not master adult constructions until age 9 or 10 (Chomsky, 1969). In experimental settings, children under 9 years old may confuse the meanings of *ask* and *tell*, so that they interpret, "Ask Joan what her address is," the same way as, "Tell Joan what her address is." Part of the dialogue between experimenter and child might sound like this.

ADULT: Ask Joan what her address is.
CHILD: (said to Joan) 4 Maple Street.
ADULT: Now tell Joan what her address is.
CHILD: (also said to Joan) 4 Maple Street.

The child here responds to *ask* as if it means the same as *tell*. Classroom teachers have observed similar confusions, especially when they require children to ask questions. Children often tell an answer instead. The problem seems to be that the child does not fully understand the meanings of *ask* or *question* in a testlike situation.

Differences in word meaning that seem obvious to adults may be unclear to children, for throughout middle childhood they continue to work out semantic as well as syntactic puzzles. Semantic development in the school years occurs gradually and, like the acquisition of first word meanings, is bound up with experience and the development of concepts. Children learn new vocabulary though instruction and through unplanned exposure in conversation, which for some centers around books. Few child language researchers have studied semantic refinements learned by school-aged children, largely because the focus in the elementary years shifts from talk to words in print. (For example, on reading and children's developing vocabulary knowledge, see Mason, Herman, & Au, 1991.) With respect to spoken language, Asch and Nerlove (1960) provided an interesting study of "double function" words, such as *bright, sweet,* and *cold.* By interviewing children between 3 and 12 years old, they found that the youngest subjects could talk about the physical definition of such words but not the psychological one. Objects could be bright or sweet, but people could not. Almost all 12-year-olds, though, understood both meanings. If the definitions of these dual function words develop over a period of years, full understandings of subtler distinctions must also take time. A first grader, for example, might understand that *skinny* and *thin* are similar in meaning, but for a period of time may not understand what makes a skinny person different from a thin one; similarly, an adolescent or adult may only gradually learn, without instruction, the nuanced distinction between *strong* and *powerful* or *fashionable* and *trendy*.

Whether we consider syntactic or semantic development, researchers tell us that no development takes place unless children are actively and thoughtfully engaged with the world around them. We have so far focused on the language that is acquired, with little regard for the characteristics of the world outside the child. The next topic is the social context surrounding the child: the activities and human interactions that support the development of language and communication.

## Contexts for the Development of Communicative Competence

We know that all physically normal children learn to communicate in a first language. We know too that children learning the same language differ in the rate at which they learn language but follow the same general sequence as they learn linguistic forms. A particular 2-year-old may be able to say more than a 3-year-old neighbor, but in the course of development, both will utter one word before two, and simple sentences before complex sentences. What in the child's environment is absolutely necessary for this leaning to take place? Researchers are far from knowing the answer. This section presents examples of interaction in different contexts to illustrate the range of situations that successfully support communicative development.

> ADULT: Bo-o-at. Puppy dog. What's a dog say, Robert? What's a dog say, huh?
> CHILD: [Babbles]
> ADULT: Hey, Chrissy, what's a dog say? What's a dog say? Arf, arf, arf!
> CHILD: [Screams happily]
> ADULT: No-o-se. No-o-se. Where's Chrissy nose? Um hmmmm. Bird. Bird. Can you flap your wings like a bird? Like this. That's what birds do. They fly. They go wheee!
> CHILD: [Noises]
> ADULT: The birds. Whatcha got, Brian? Watcha got? Uh boo!
>
> (Genishi & Dyson, 1984, p. 65)

This conversation was overheard in the infant room of a day care center, where the care giver shared a picture book with three children. Her talk had many of the characteristics, which adults may find cute or silly, of "baby talk," or adult-talk-to-children (ATC). Researchers have been interested in this way of adjusting one's speech for young children, because they suspect that it provides a simplified model for child language learners (Schachter & Strage, 1982). Some of the features of ATC are

1. Short utterances
2. Lots of repetition
3. Vowel lengthening (as in no-o-se)
4. Exaggerated intonation (extreme ups and downs)
5. Lots of questions

Much of the research that describes ATC has been done with middle class standard English-speaking mothers and children. And many middle class families, whatever their ethnicity, engage in conversations similar to the one above. One of its features is that the adult often asks questions to which she already knows the answer. After the child responds, nonverbally or verbally, the adult encouragingly asks another question. Researchers have called this and other gamelike exchanges a *routine* (Snow, Dubber, & De Blauw, 1982) or *format* (Bruner, 1983) and have found that in some homes the routine changes over time. When the adult and child first establish the routine, the adult is the initiator. In a few weeks or months, adult and child may switch roles, so that the child may initiate and ask, "What's this? What's that?" When the routine is book reading, the child may eventually memorize part of the text and take the adult's place as "reader," well before he or she is a conventional reader.

Routines are to many middle class adults a staple of adult–child interaction both at home and in school. Heath (1983b) has pointed out that not every child has engaged in this kind of talk and that adults who are not middle class may judge this talk to be pointless. A grandmother in a working class black community had this to say about her grandson Teegie's learning and talking: "He gotta learn to know 'bout dis world, can't nobody tell 'im. . . . Gotta watch hisself by watchin' other folks. Ain't no use me tellin' im: Learn dis, learn dat. What's dis? What's dat?" (Heath, 1983b, p. 84). Teegie's grandmother captures the child-rearing values and life circumstances of her own community when she emphasizes Teegie's ability to figure things out on his own, to "know 'bout dis world." As she implies, children in other communities may hear frequent lesson-like routines in which adults often ask, "What's this? What's that?"

Researchers who have studied other cultural groups have observed other ways of interacting, which do not rely on features of ATC. In the Piedmont Carolinas of the United States, Health (1983b) recorded this exchange in a black American mill town she calls Trackton. Lem, 18 months old, sits on the porch, playing with a toy truck while his mother and her neighbor talk about Miss Lula's visit to the doctor.

LILLIE MAE: Miz Lula done went to de doctor.

MATTIE: Her leg botherin' her?

LEM: Went to (rolling his truck and banging it against the board that separates the two halves of the porch) de doctor, doc leg, Miz Lu Lu Lu, rah, rah, rah.

LILLIE MAE: I reckon so, she was complainin' yesterday 'bout her feet so swelled she couldn't get no shoes on.          (Heath, 1983b, p. 92)

Here Lem, Lillie Mae, and Mattie are engaged in a very different kind of conversation from the one involving Robert, Chrissy, and Brian at the day care center. Heath observed that children between 12 and 24 months of age are often not central to conversations between adults. Lem seems to pay careful attention to and pick up bits of the adults' talk so that he can play contentedly with them on his own. According to Heath, he is in a stage of conversational development called "repetition with variation"; he repeats some things that he hears and then varies them. This follows a period of time when children simply repeat part of what they hear and precedes the stage called "participation" when adults attend to a child's comments or questions, especially when they change the topic of a conversation.

In contrast with middle class interactions in which adults assume that even infants are automatically part of a conversation, these working class examples illustrate a different view of the child's role in conversation. In Lem's community adults like Lillie Mae and Mattie are just as caring as middle class care givers; their apparent lack of attention to what Lem says is not evidence of disinterest in his development. Instead it reflects their knowledge and belief that the young child initially is not a conversationalist, but *becomes* a full participant in conversation over time. Adults in Trackton also use syntactic features of black English that are not found in middle class speakers' English. Thus Lem naturally uses black English features as well.

The communicative ways of working class white families also vary from a middle class "standard," as Heath (1983b) and Miller (1982) in South Baltimore, and Tizard and Hughes (1984) in the United Kingdom, have vividly documented. And in more geographically distant Papua, New Guinea, Schieffelin (1979) found that adults do *not* use "baby talk" features in their speech and believe that any parent should be discouraged from using them so that their children can lean language normally. Thus, different communities have their own beliefs about language socialization processes: how adults should talk to children and how children learn to talk. As Heath (1983b) puts it, they all have their own "ways with words." No one "way" is superior to another, and families everywhere raise children who learn the complex social and linguistic rules of their community.

To summarize briefly the major points of this section:

1. Language is an enormously complex system through which people construct and convey meaning. Its main components are *semantics* (the system of meanings), *phonology* (the sound system), *syntax* (the rules for combining morphemes in sentences), and *pragmatics* (the rules underlying conversations).
2. Imitation is not the key to acquiring language. The active, thinking, meaning-seeking, and meaning-constructing child in interaction with people and things gradually figures out for herself or himself the intricacies of language and communication.
3. All normal children develop communicative competence within their own communities. Different communities' ways of talking and communicating may vary widely, and researchers are just beginning to study these ways in communities that are not middle class. Thus, we cannot make judgments about what social contexts are "better" than others or what specific features in the contexts are essential for children's communicative development to occur.

## DEVELOPING COMMUNICATIVE COMPETENCE IN THE CLASSROOM: ISSUES AND CHOICES

Everyone agrees that it is crucial to respect the out-of-school social contexts in which children learned their families' ways of communicating, but not everyone agrees on how to act on that respect. How educators value a child's dialect or language and how they teach about language in early childhood settings depend largely on each educator's values and personal understandings of a curriculum that is responsive to a wide range of children. Embedded in the construction of such a curriculum are some overlapping topics, including *multiculturalism, dialect differences,* and *developmentally appropriate practice.* These topics may become controversial issues primarily when children in the same setting have diverse social and linguistic backgrounds or when the backgrounds and therefore the language and culture of children differ from the teacher's or school's. In this section issues most closely related to language education are considered as a prelude to a look at examples of classroom practices.

### Multiculturalism and Language Choice

Questions have been raised about *whose* culture, language, or dialect should dominate in both classrooms and other institutions. Some answers to the questions are presented here in the context of a broad vision of multicultural education, whose advocates work toward "awareness of, respect for, and enjoyment of the diversity of our society and world" (Ramsey, Vold, & Williams, 1989, p. ix). In this view multicultural education is not restricted to minority group children and aims toward equity for all members of society (see also Derman-Sparks & the ABC Task Force, 1989). This definition provides no facile prescriptions for educators who wish to bring multiculturalism to life in the classroom, but it does provide space for *choices* that educators can make, for example, regarding dialect or language use.

*Dialects and "success" in school.*    Research consistently shows that children who are academically successful in school, especially in language arts and reading, come from homes where the ways of interacting are similar to those of the school; or they come from homes in which parents or adults share the school's values and goals (Durkin, 1966, 1982; Heath, 1983b; Wells, 1986). Put another way, children whose out-of-school experiences have *not* provided them with a "hidden curriculum"—including the school's ways with words—may have difficulty with academic tasks.

What should schools do to make the "hidden curriculum" visible to all children? In terms of language, many would say that one of the school's obligations is to "teach" children the forms and content of "school talk," or standard English. Unfortunately, no one has demonstrated that a second dialect can be taught, at least in direct, lesson-like ways. Few studies look carefully at changes in dialect use in individual speakers over time, and long-term evaluations of instructional methods are also lacking (but see Stockman, 1984, for a study of acquisition of black English). Past attempts to teach standard English forms in highly structured ways have not succeeded, whereas teachers' acceptance and encouragement of children's own language forms have led to greater learning (Cullinan, Jaggar, & Strickland, 1974; Piestrup, 1973; Rentel & Kennedy, 1972).

Current attempts to emphasize the use of standard English throughout a curriculum developed for African-American preschoolers show mixed results (Hale-Benson, 1990). In this program, adults model the use of standard English and correct in nonpunitive ways children's use of nonstandard forms. However, standardized measures used for evaluation, such as the McCarthy Scales of Children's Abilities and the Metropolitan Reading Readiness Test, do not show clear benefits. For a variety of possible reasons, including some participating teachers' lack of experience, Hale-Benson reports that children in the program did not do significantly better than a control group.

*Different languages and the match between home and school.*
Teachers in early childhood settings and statisticians both note that the number of children in the United States speaking languages other than English

at home is increasing significantly. It has been predicted that by the year
2000, there will be 7.7 million children from non-English language backgrounds from birth through age 14 in the United States. This is an increase
of about 37% since 1976 (Oxford-Carpenter et al., 1984). The number of
non-English-speaking children is highest in urban areas. For example, in
New York City at least 10% of all children enrolled from kindergarten to
grade 12 are termed "limited English proficient." Of this group, 69% are
Spanish speakers (New York City Board of Education, 1988–89).

Questions about appropriate programs for these children are complex
and, as with dialect issues, revolve around choices that are not only linguistic, but also social and political (Escobedo, in preparation). With respect to
young children's second-language learning, researchers agree on two points:
(1) learning two or more languages in early childhood is in itself not harmful
or "confusing" and in fact may be beneficial to cognitive development (Hakuta & Diaz, 1984); and (2) learning a second language, like learning the first,
occurs over a period of time, sometimes years (Cummins, 1979; Wong Fillmore, 1991). A third point is more controversial. Based on a limited number
of studies, researchers support the maintenance of the home language while
learners develop a second language. That is, they say *adding* a second language to a simultaneously growing foundation in the first language strength-
ens learning in general (Cummins, 1979). Thus a transitional program that
employs children's home language for only a short period of time, for example, a year, may be ineffective for most second-language learners.

Regarding choices among curricula, parents and teachers vary. Some
would like the home language maintained in school as a way of supporting
the children's culture, so that Spanish-speaking children would use Spanish
for part of the day at school. But often parents are more concerned with
their children's learning English than maintaining their home language
(Wong Fillmore, 1991). In many parts of the United States, alternatives to
exclusively English-speaking classrooms are lacking. Particularly at the
prekindergarten level, there are few programs and curricula that are widely
available and even fewer that have been both explicitly described and carefully evaluated (for detailed descriptions and evaluations, see DeGaetano,
1990; Chesterfield & Chavez, 1982; and citations in Soto, 1991). The current
consensus regarding appropriate curricula, even with older learners, is that
explicit teaching about the *forms* of English is not useful; being able to *use*
English, as well as hear it in comprehensible ways, is critical (Krashen &
Terrell, 1983).

In keeping with this emphasis on language use, classroom teachers
Fournier, Lansdowne, Pastenes, and Steen and teacher educator Hudelson
(in press) describe a second-grade, Spanish–English bilingual classroom that
emphasizes the use of both languages in every part of the curriculum. They

do not claim that this classroom is typical of other bilingual classrooms, but they present their own rationale for a language-rich, "whole language," teacher-evaluated program. Too, they present enough detail to aid others in developing their own curricula for children of diverse backgrounds, not just bilinguals.

### What Is Multiculturally and Developmentally Appropriate?

For purposes of this chapter, a program that is both multicultural and developmentally appropriate *takes into account the nature of each learner.* In this kind of program, teachers are trusted to know their children as individuals with particular social, cultural, and linguistic histories, in order to base the curriculum on that personal knowledge, combined with knowledge of human development and early childhood curricula. The way that teachers plan for children is not determined by scores on a "readiness test," and the activities in their curricula are not dictated by a publisher or textbook. Published materials may play a role, but teachers' judgments, guided by children's responses and actions, are primary. This broad, child-oriented notion of developmental appropriateness has been a familiar one to early childhood teachers for many years. Descriptions and elaborations of appropriate curricula within today's context are becoming available (this volume is an example; see also Bredekamp, 1987; Harris, 1991; Katz & Chard, 1989; Raines & Canady, 1990).

At the same time, educators legitimately ask whether there can be a *single* developmentally appropriate approach that meets all children's needs. For example, speaking from an African-American perspective, Delpit (1988) presents an eloquent argument in favor of carefully considering approaches that narrow rather than broaden children's options. For example, according to some definitions, programs that are referred to as "child-centered," "whole language," or "process-oriented" include little direct teaching of skills (including letter–sound correspondences) to children. Yet, direct teaching is what many African-American parents expect and want. From Delpit's point of view, waiting for children who lack such skills to "discover" them on their own is a failure to teach. Other educators make similar points (Schickedanz, 1989) and conclude that most children need a combination of approaches that include teaching specific information and skills, along with time for the holistic activities that lead to discovery and understanding. Using a musical analogy, Delpit (1988) highlights the need for teachers to combine approaches and "to coach those [student] voices to produce notes that will be heard clearly in the larger society" (p. 296). Access to the larger society—to its social and economic opportunities—is what virtually every family wants for its children. The characteristics of class-rooms that may enhance this access are considered next.

## LANGUAGE IN THE CLASSROOM

Language in the classroom takes many forms. In some classrooms it's inaudible as children sit quietly filling in worksheets, which contain little written language. In others it's both audible and visible as children interact through talk and print as if they are participating in a language "bath" (Lind-fors, 1987). Still other settings are audibly distinctive as children and some-times teachers use languages other than English. And a single classroom or setting can vary in the course of a day: It can incorporate talk-filled times and periods of silence, as well as episodes like this one in a second-grade classroom.

> TEACHER: OK, boys and girls, do any of these words rhyme? See if you can find a word that rhymes with another word. Kevin, can you find two words that rhyme?
> KEVIN: *Meat* and *seat.*
> TEACHER: Good, *meat* and *seat.* Right. See how these words look a lot alike? What's different about these words, Kevin?
> KEVIN: The first letter.
> TEACHER: Just the beginning letter. Do you know two of them that rhyme, Shanda?
> SHANDA: *Seal* and *deal.*
> TEACHER: Good, any others?
> RANDY: *Seal* and *real.*

The skills and phonics focus of this lesson contrasts with a conversation about the tooth fairy that kindergartners had with their teacher Ms. Coffee. They later link the discussion to a recent unit on money.

> SARAH: They're smiling about my loose tooth. You'd better stop smiling about my loose tooth.
> MS. COFFEE: They're probably thinking about all of the money you're going to get when you get it from the tooth fairy. Does the tooth fairy come to your house?
> CHILDREN: Yeah.
> MS. COFFEE: How much money do you usually get, or have you ever lost a tooth?
> SARAH: (Her answer must be negative.)
> MS. COFFEE: Then you don't know how much money you get, do you?

SARAH: I know, but one time I had money, um, when I had my wart fell off . . . when I gave them the wart, and then they had to take the wart away, and then they gave me some money.
(Archer, Coffee, & Genishi, 1985, p. 272)

Within the context of previously presented concerns, these two examples may both be called "developmentally appropriate," depending on children's abilities and interests and the nature of other classroom activities. The *balance* that teachers achieve between more and less skills-oriented activities seems to determine how appropriate a program is. This section contains descriptions of classroom research and practice that work toward combining children's needs for specific information and spontaneous expression, toward expanding their communicative competence, and toward being both multicultural and developmentally appropriate.

## The Importance of Story

The use of story, whether told orally, written down, or created through the dramatic play of children, is essential to the communication of human experience. It is also an important link among members of the same family, across families, across communities and different cultures, and across oral and written modes of language. The current popularity of literature-based and whole language programs has enhanced the role of story from early childhood through the elementary grades (Dyson & Genishi, in press; Galda & Cullinan, 1991).

*Stories and cultural variation.*     Educators tend to assume that children who have had stories told or read to them are likely to join the world of the literate with ease since stories told should be bridges to stories read. Recent research, however, shows this is not always the case. Cazden (1988) gives a striking demonstration of how, like a parent's ways of interacting with children, the sound of a story can vary with the teller. Many adults naturally and subconsciously make judgments about stories that don't sound like the pretend-worlds or favorite stories they know. Cazden (1988) collected such judgments, based on 12 (5 black and 7 white) graduate students' responses to the following contribution to sharing time:

AT GRANDMOTHER'S
On George Washington's birthday I'm goin' ice my grandmother
we never haven't seen her since a long time
and and she lives right near us
and she's and she's gonna
I'm gonna spend the night over her house

and every weekend she comes to take me
like on Saturdays and Sundays away from home
and I spend the night over her house
and one day I spoiled her dinner
and we were having we were
she paid ten dollars
and I got eggs and stuff
and I didn't even eat anything.
                    (pp. 17–18)

The students' responses to first grader Leona's story varied; white raters judged it negatively, saying it was "a terrible story" and that the child would have problems with school work. In contrast, the black respondents viewed it positively; they said it was easy to understand and full of detail and interest. In fact, three of the black raters thought it was the best of the five stories they'd heard. Such divergent responses show that stories, like other ways of communicating, embody the social and linguistic styles and values of particular cultures. Thus, stories are similar to other culturally derived genres and dialects: There is nothing inherently "better" about one style of storytelling over another, just as there is nothing inherently better about one dialect over another (on stories of personal experience from minority perspectives, see Miller, Potts, & Fung, 1989). Unlike Leona's story, the stories in most children's books and textbooks reflect a single style—often structured around one topic or event and with a clear beginning, middle, and end. These conventional stories can be appreciated along with other, less school-like styles, and through exposure and interaction can be learned in the classroom (Heath, 1983a).

*Story as drama: Playing roles.* "In play a child behaves beyond his average age, above his daily behavior; in play it is as though he were a head taller than himself" (Vygotsky, 1978, p. 102). Child-watchers know that when children engage in pretend or dramatic play, they take on characteristics of people who behave and speak differently from themselves. Children can display sophisticated powers to observe and mimic as they imitate their parents, doctors, or speakers of other languages.

MARI: *Hablamos en inglés. Hablamos en inglés.* [Let's speak in English. Let's speak in English.]
DIANA: (A little later) I'm gonna call you—I'm gonna friends is you— (talking to toy telephone).
ADELITA: I'm friends.
DIANA: I already told you. I'm gonna call you at H.E.B. [a supermarket]. One, two, eight, nine (dialing the toy telephone).

ADELITA: I'm gonna sit me down, OK?

DIANA: OK. Don't cry. You promise to me.

DIANA: (Later to Adelita) Ouch, ouch, ouch, ouch. Ouch. *Dije que te salieras, Adelita. ¿Sabes qué quiere decir "ouch"? Que te salgas.* [Ouch. I told you to get out, Adelita. Do you know what *ouch* means? To get out.]                                              (Genishi & Dyson, 1984, p. 122)

In this exchange, Spanish speaker Mari prompts the others to speak English, though she herself speaks none. Her classmates at a Head Start center in Texas follow her cue and stretch their language so that part of their play becomes a short practice session in English, which is becoming their second language. This was one of the few examples of English that the author heard in a 2-month period. It shows Diana's and Adelita's English to be elementary but understandable—despite Diana's unique translation of "ouch." Like children learning a first language, the two girls construct in their second language their own understandings of its many rules. Errors are naturally a part of this constructive and interactive process.

Children can also enact familiar stories when adults set up book corners and let children take charge of the activity. Mexican-American kindergartners Erica and Oscar, not yet conventional readers, use puppets to act out the tale of the three little pigs.

ERICA: The Three Little Pigs. The mother said, "Bye, my little pigs got to go." The first little pig met a little man with a bundle of straw. "Please, please leave me have those straw. I can build a house."

OSCAR: *Se lo comió.* [He ate him.]

ERICA: "And I'll huff and huff, and I'll blow your house in. . . ." "Little pig, little pig, let me in." "Not by the hair of my chinny, chinny, chin." "Then I'll puff—" (Erica carries on with the story, as Oscar reminds her twice)

OSCAR: *Se lo comio-o-o-ó! Erica, Erica, se lo comió. El, el marranito.* [He ate him. Erica, Erica, he ate him. The, the little pig.] (By now Oscar is exasperated with Erica for not noticing the picture that he pointed out, showing the pig's fate.)

(Adapted from Seawell, 1985, pp. 84–85)

Spanish speaker Oscar understands what is happening in this English story, as he and Erica, an English learner, maintain a bilingual dialogue.

The dramatic play setting, enjoyable and usually free from adult intervention, truly encourages talk that is "a head taller" than the ordinary. It can also push children to take others' points of view, as they create scripts for their characters (Nelson & Gruendel, 1979). Representing through play talk the way others think or present themselves can enrich children linguistically and cognitively, whether they are bilingual or monolingual (Nourot & Van Hoorn, 1991). Thus, opportunities for dramatic play, so often limited to preschools and kindergartens, would also benefit children in the primary grades, as the next example demonstrates.

Ms. Raney, a second-grade teacher, has her children act out different roles as they read the play *The Bremen Town Musicians* together.

> DOG: Good morning.
> DONKEY: Good morning. Where is your—where's your Mastah?
> DOG: I'm running away from her.
> DONKEY: That's funnah. I'm runnin' away from mine. For many years it's been nothing but work, work, work. Now that I'm old and tired, he wants to get rid of me. . . . Where are you going?
> (Genishi & Dyson, 1984, p. 201)

To teach children about their own language, Ms. Raney audiotapes her children in different speaking situations, so that they can hear themselves sound casual in some and more formal in others—as Ms. Raney says, more "how they talk on TV." Alex, as the donkey, talks in TV talk, though at another time he described a picture in this way: "Dat cah right dere goin' to hit da cub [curb]'n dat cah right dere goin' ta hit da ho'se'n dat cah right dere goin' to hit da do-ug [dog]" (Genishi & Dyson, 1984, p. 201). When playing the donkey, Alex uses some features of the sound system of standard English, pronouncing crisply and carefully (*going*, instead of *goin'*), whereas in the second example, he uses many features of his own community's dialect, black English. Ms. Raney has her children both dramatize plays in standard English and speak in their own dialect in less formal situations. Without the use of repetitious language drills, she acts upon a belief that children should grow in their communicative competence, by adding standard English to their repertoires while they develop as speakers, writers, and readers.

*Learning through story: How is it assessed?*    Just as no one has proven that drill-like teaching of standard English or a second language is effective over time, no one has proven that language-based activities like dramatic play, often a feature of whole language programs, contribute in measurable ways to school learning. In fact, the task of assessing such activities and programs is as much a challenge as the task of describing developmentally appropriate curricula. (See Schickedanz, 1990, and Stahl & Miller, 1989, for a discussion of assessment issues related to whole language.) Standardized assessment measures, such as general intelligence tests or readiness instruments, are widely available; but these show only what children do at a point in time in a testing situation. They are inappropriate for depicting what children can do on an ongoing basis and they seldom help the teacher assess informally in a way that helps her or him refine the curriculum for individual children.

There is now strong interest in developing *alternative* or *authentic* forms of assessment that link appropriate curriculum with child-oriented assessment (Genishi, in press; National Association for the Education of Young Children & National Association of Early Childhood Specialists in State Departments of Education, 1991). These alternatives often rely on ways of assessing that early childhood teachers have always used, such as careful observation and anecdotal records. They can also be procedures or checklists that focus on a particular aspect of development or learning, for example, children's progress in language and literacy learning (Centre for Primary Language Education, 1988; Chittenden & Courtney, 1989; Genishi & Dyson, 1984; Goodman, Goodman, & Hood, 1989). The audiotape recorder can be a valuable aid in this kind of assessment. Further, teachers tell their own stories of assessment by presenting detailed portraits of what children say and do in play and other settings (Genishi, in press; Paley, 1981, 1986a, 1986b, 1990).

Researchers also provide a demonstration of assessment that goes beyond standardized measures as they ask how the use of stories and trade books affects both curriculum and assessment. Morrow and Weinstein (1986), for example, evaluated children's use of library centers in the classroom and found that children with access to literature did just as well on standardized tests as those using traditional textbooks. In addition, the children who read literature *enjoyed* reading and read more books during free-choice time. Enjoyment is something that standardized tests do not measure but seems an important dimension in learning that is truly appropriate.

Relying on careful observation over time, Dyson (1989, 1992) captures both intellectual struggle and enjoyment as she documents children's ways of becoming literate. First grader Jake, one of the children Dyson observed for 2 years in an urban magnet school, is faced with a problem of choice. His teacher, Margaret, has become concerned that Jake's favorite journal topic of bubble-cars has put Jake into a creative rut. Jake explains:

> JAKE: It's [writing] not as easy as you really think it is nowadays, 'cause you see, now I can't be writing about my bubble-car all the time.
> MANUEL: Why?
> JAKE: 'Cause Margaret says so.
> MANUEL: She doesn't want any bubble-car stories?
> JAKE: Yeah.
> JESS: She hates 'em.

JAKE: No, she doesn't. She's getting tired of 'em. That's all. That's why
they're not as easy as they used to be.                (Dyson, 1989, p. 158)

Through talk, Jake soon finds a new topic, his friend, Manuel. His new story
will be called "Me and Manuel," something that he will enjoy and that may
encourage new forms of writing. Although this is a bit of "data" from a long-
term study, it is also a way of assessing Jake's learning—his thinking made
visible through talking and writing with friends.

The many facets of story, then, provide showcases for children's abilities
in language at the same time that they present teachers with opportunities
for intervention. The intervention may be direct when a first grader
struggles with the spelling of a word that she wants to "get right," or it may
be more subtle as when Margaret urged Jake to shift journal topics. Teachers
themselves can assess such specific aspects of language use and more general qualities like fluency in oral storytelling, complexity of speech, extent
of bilingualism, or imaginativeness in dramatic play by careful watching and
listening. These aspects of *oral* language are not often measured by standardized tests but are important to teachers who aim to extend children's
communicative competence.

## Talking Across the Curriculum

Much of what is accessible to young children is embedded in the talk
of stories, although areas like social studies, art, science, and math also offer
opportunities for talk about shared experiences. A child's drawing easily
leads to a discussion of its content or a conversation about the child's name,
which she or he has written or asked the teacher to write. In an earlier
example from Ms. Coffee's kindergarten, children and teacher made a connection between the tooth fairy and their social studies unit on money, a
topic that clearly overlaps with math. Science, too, when taught with children's ways of learning in mind, is another area of learning that is enhanced
through talk.

Chittenden (1990) reports on a collaboration among 22 kindergarten
and primary-grade teachers and himself, which capitalized on discussion as
a way of teaching about science and assessing children's learning. The focus
on discussion was an "attempt to capture a dimension of classroom life that
ordinarily remains undocumented—namely, children's talk" (Chittenden,
1990, p. 241). Through talk the curriculum was extended, negotiated
through questioning and debating such issues as whether one could feel the
earth move as it rotated. During a unit on earth/sun/moon, children said
things like the following:

My sister said that the planet takes a bite out of the moon.
You know what? My cousin thinks there's no such thing as a planet up in
    the sky.
I know [earth is round] because I have an earth in my house. It has yellow
    and green.
The earth is a circle. I looked in a book.
I saw stars on the ceiling in the museum.
                    (Chittenden, 1990, p. 237)

The topic of discussion was sources of information about the earth, sun, and
moon. Children most often cited as authorities books and other children,
such as cousins and friends. Although this study centered on science, the
use of ongoing discussions easily extends across the curriculum. Again, an
audiotape recorder can be invaluable for preserving children's thinking,
building upon it, and assessing it.

Almost every activity presents an opportunity for talk when teachers
allow it to. The computer, the object of scrutiny and controversy in some
early childhood programs, is a machine that could be socially isolating and
impersonal. But like many other things, it can also prompt talk. In the following example, first graders are using a computer program to create designs on their screens:

FLORA: Help him. He doesn't know how to do it.
MARGARET: (to Juan) Want me to help you?
JUAN: Yeah.
MARGARET: OK. First, press that one down (demonstrates). (Juan
    presses the key while Margaret presses another.) There.
JUAN: I can do it.
MARGARET: OK, and you keep pushing that one (goes back to her own
    computer, but quickly checks Juan's again). Now you need to make
    your plus (a cross-like shape), so you go up here and you do that,
    and go here, like that (she touches the screen as she traces a cross).
    If you need help, just ask me, OK?

Computer activity among first graders and younger children can be talk-
generating and cooperative (Genishi, 1988a; Genishi, McCollum, & Strand,
1985). The easily viewed computer screen can lead to children's learning
from and helping each other.


## CONCLUSIONS

Everything in this chapter acts in praise of children's enormous accomplishments as communicators at home and in school. Returning to the ques-

tions about Alma's, Dawnn's, and Kevin's talk at the beginning of the chapter, we now know that like all children, the three have become speakers and learners through a complex process over time. With the human gift for learning language and in interaction with people and objects, they have figured out huge numbers of rules, related to the phonology, syntax, semantics, and pragmatics of their own dialect. As active, thinking children, they have been at the core of the learning process.

We know too that Dawnn's and Kevin's playful talk demonstrates tiny bits of their linguistic and communicative competence and that their ways of communicating in standard English are not the ways of every child. Alma's English is budding as she becomes bilingual, perhaps with greater ease than other children from her community. Further, other children may or may not be as captivated by drama and story as she is. If every child's communicative development could be viewed like a kaleidoscope that is constantly moving, individual teachers would see only a few of the intricate patters that make up the whole of children's communicative histories.

The classroom or center is only one setting in which that history evolves. So much more of it has been embedded in children's own communities where the events and conversations of everyday life have a seamless look and feel. For some children, the seamlessness of the years outside of school ends abruptly when they enter a setting where adults talk and behave differently from their parents or friends. Unless there are opportunities to learn "school talk," in partnership with supportive others, a center or school may become an uncomfortable and difficult place for the child.

Teachers ease the transition to school when, in all areas of the curriculum,

1. They nurture talk between adults and children and between children that serves a variety of purposes or functions—to inform, tell stories, pretend, have fun, discuss, plan, and so on.
2. They provide for and engage the children in activities that are the focus of talk, since talk flows when people have something to talk about or tell each other.
3. Conversations are comfortable for both child and teacher—talk is fluent because the communicators are absorbed in getting their messages across, and their conversations are meaning-oriented, not form-oriented.

Though the language forms—and sometimes the language—that a child uses may not always match the teacher's, the communicative purposes of the two can match. In developmentally appropriate settings, educators choose collaboratively with parents the range of purposes to be included, depending on their values and views of language and learning.

The teacher plays a critical role in deciding whether oral language is inaudible or provides a "language bath" for children throughout the day. Before children read and write with ease, talk is the adult's versatile and ready tool for finding out what children know, what their individual social histories are, which adult meanings elude them, and how they view their experiences. In the processes of teaching and learning, teachers provide engaging and varied activities as they nourish talk and thus make visible some of the children's thinking. Thus teachers draw on their own knowledge of development and language as they try to see what children see, with the goal of helping them experience and know more.

## REFERENCES

Archer, C., Coffee, M., & Genishi, C. (1985). Research currents: Responding to children. *Language Arts, 62,* 270–276.

Asch, S. E., & Nerlove, H. (1960). The development of double function terms in children: An exploratory investigation. In B. Kaplan & S. Wapner (Eds.), *Perspectives in psychological theory: Essays in honor of Heinz Werner* (pp. 47–60). New York: International Universities Press.

Barrett, M. D. (1982). Distinguishing between prototypes: The early acquisition of the meaning of object names. In S. Kuczaj II (Ed.), *Language development: Vol. 1. Syntax and semantics* (pp. 313–334). Hillside, NJ: Lawrence Erlbaum.

Berko, J. (1958). The child's learning of English morphology. *Word, 14,* 150–177.

Bredekamp, S. (Ed.). (1987). *Developmentally appropriate practice in early childhood programs serving children from birth through age 8* (rev. ed.). Washington, DC: National Association for the Education of Young Children.

Brooks, C. K. (Ed.). (1985). *Tapping potential: English and language arts for the black learner.* Urbana, IL: National Council of Teachers of English.

Brown, R. (1973). *A first language: The early stages.* Cambridge, MA: Harvard University Press.

Bruner, J. S. (1983). *Child's talk.* New York: W. W. Norton.

Burling, R. (1973). *English in black and white.* New York: Holt, Rinehart and Winston.

Cazden, C. B. (1988). *Classroom discourse: The language of teaching and learning.* Portsmouth, NH: Heinemann.

Centre for Primary Language Education. (1988). *Primary language record: A handbook for teachers.* Portsmouth, NH: Heinemann.

Chesterfield, R., & Chávez, R. (1982). *An evaluation of the Head Start bilingual bicultural curriculum development project* (Final Report Contract No. HEW 105–77–1048). Los Angeles: Juárez & Associates.

Chittenden, E. (1990). Young children's discussions of science topics. In G. Hein (Ed.), *The assessment of hands-on elementary science programs.* Monograph of the North Dakota Study Group on Evaluation. Grand Forks, ND: University of North Dakota Press.

Chittenden, E., & Courtney, R. (1989). Assessment of young children's reading: Documentation as an alternative to testing. In D. S. Strickland & L. M. Morrow (Eds.), *Emerging literacy: Young children learn to read and write* (pp. 107–120). Newark, DE: International Reading Association.

Chomsky, C. (1969). *The acquisition of syntax in children from 5–10*. Cambridge, MA: MIT Press.

Clark, E. V. (1983). Meanings and concepts. In P. H. Mussen (Ed.), *Handbook of child psychology* (4th ed., Vol. 3, pp. 787–840). New York: John Wiley.

Cullinan, B. E., Jaggar, A. M., & Strickland, D. (1974). Language expansion for black children in the primary grades: A research report. *Young Children, 29* (1), 98–112.

Cummins, J. (1979). Linguistic interdependence and the educational development of bilingual children. *Review of Educational Research, 49,* 222–251.

Curtiss, S. (1977). *Genie: A psycholinguistic study of a modern-day "Wild-Child."* New York: Academic Press.

DeGaetano, Y. (1990). *A cross cultural approach to teaching: A case study.* Unpublished doctoral dissertation, Teachers College, Columbia University, New York.

Delpit, L. D. (1988). The silenced dialogue: Power and pedagogy in educating other people's children. *Harvard Educational Review, 58* (3), 280–298.

Derman-Sparks, L. & the ABC Task Force. (1989). *Anti-bias curriculum: Tools for empowering young children.* Washington, DC: National Association for the Education of Young Children.

Dillard, J. L. (1972). *Black English: Its history and usage.* New York: Vintage.

Durkin, D. (1966). *Children who read early: Two longitudinal studies.* New York: Teachers College Press.

Dyson, A. Haas. (1989). *Multiple worlds of child writers: Friends learning to write.* New York: Teachers College Press.

Dyson, A. Haas. (1992). The case of the singing scientist: A performance perspective on the "stages" of school literacy. *Written Communication, 9,* 3–47.

Dyson, A. Haas, & Genishi, C. (in press). Visions of children as language users: Research on language and language education in early childhood. In B. Spodek (Ed.), *Handbook of research on young children.* New York: Macmillan.

Escobedo, T. H. (in preparation). Curriculum issues in early education for culturally and linguistically diverse populations. In E. E. Garcia (Ed.), *The Mexican-American child.*

Fournier, J., Lansdowne, B., Pastenes, Z., Steen, P., & Hudelson, S. (in press). Learning with, about, and from children: Life in a bilingual classroom. In C. Genishi (Ed.), *Ways of assessing children and curriculum: Stories of early childhood practice.* New York: Teachers College Press.

Galda, L., & Cullinan, B. (1991). Literature for literacy: What research says about the benefits of using trade books in the classroom. In J. Jensen, J. Flood, D. Lapp, & J. R. Squire (Eds.), *Handbook of research on teaching the English language arts* (pp. 397–403). Sponsored by the National Council of Teachers of English and the International Reading Association. New York: Macmillan.

Genishi, C. (1988a). Kindergartners and computers: A case study of six children. *Elementary School Journal, 89,* 185–202.

Genishi, C. (1988b). Research in review: Children's language: Learning words from experience. *Young Children, 44* (1), 16–23.

Genishi, C. (Ed.). (in press). *Ways of assessing children and curriculum: Stories of early childhood practice.* New York: Teachers College Press.

Genishi, C., & Dyson, A. Haas (1984). *Language assessment in the early years.* Norwood, NJ: Ablex.

Genishi, C., McCollum, P., & Strand, E. (1985). Research currents: The interactional richness of children's computer use. *Language Arts, 62,* 526–532.

Goodman, K. S., Goodman, Y. M., & Hood, W. J. (Eds.). (1989). *The whole language evaluation book.* Portsmouth, NH: Heinemann.

Hakuta, K., & Diaz, R. (1984). The relationship between bilingualism and cognitive ability: A critical discussion and some new longitudinal data. In K. E. Nelson (Ed.), *Children's language* (Vol. 5, pp. 319–344). Hillsdale, NJ: Lawrence Erlbaum.

Hale-Benson, J. (1990). Visions of children: African-American early childhood education program. *Early Childhood Research Quarterly, 5,* 199–213.

Harris, V. J. (1991). Research in review: Multicultural curriculum: African American children's literature. *Young Children, 46,* (2), 37–44.

Heath, S. B. (1983a). Research currents: A lot of talk about nothing. *Language Arts, 60,* 999–1007.

Heath, S. B. (1983b). *Ways with words: language, life, and work in communities and classrooms.* New York: Cambridge University Press.

John, V., & Horner, V. (1971). *Early childhood bilingual education.* New York: Modern Language Association.

Katz, L. G., & Chard, S. C. (1989). *Engaging children's minds: The project approach.* Norwood, NJ: Ablex.

Krashen, S., & Terrell, T. (1983). *The natural approach: Language acquisition in the classroom.* Hayward, CA: Alemany Press.

Labov, W. (1970). The logic of nonstandard English. In F. Williams (Ed.), *Language and poverty* (pp. 153–189). Chicago: Markham.

Labov, W. (1972). *Language in the inner city: Studies in the black English vernacular.* Philadelphia: University of Pennsylvania.

Lindfors, J. W. (1987). *Children's language and learning* (rev. ed.). Englewood Cliffs, NJ: Prentice-Hall.

Loban, W. D. (1963). *The language of elementary school children.* Urbana, IL: National Council of Teachers of English.

Mason, J. M., Herman, P. A., & Au, K. H. (1991). Reading: Children's developing knowledge of words. In J. Flood, J. M. Jensen, D. Lapp, & J. R. Squire (Eds.), *Handbook of research on teaching the English language arts* (pp. 721–731). New York: Macmillan.

Miller, G. A., & Gildea, P. M. (1987, September). How children learn words. *Scientific American,* pp. 94–99.

Miller, P. (1982). *Amy, Wendy, and Beth.* Austin: University of Texas Press.

Miller, P., Potts, R., & Fung, H. (1989). Minority perspectives on narrative development. Paper presented at the annual meeting of the American Educational Research Association, San Francisco.

Miller, W., & Ervin, S. M. (1964). The development of grammar in child language. In U. Bellugi & R. Brown (Eds.), The acquisition of language. *Monographs of the Society for Research in Child Development, 29*, 9–34 (1, Serial No. 92).

Morrow, L. M., & Weinstein, C. S. (1986). Encouraging voluntary reading: The impact of a literature program on children's use of library centers. *Reading Research Quarterly, 21*, 330–346.

National Association for the Education of Young Children & National Association of Early Childhood Specialists in State Departments of Education. (1991). Guidelines for appropriate curriculum content and assessment in programs serving children ages 3 through 8. *Young Children, 46* (3), 21–38.

Nelson, K. (1973). Structure and strategy in learning to talk. *Monographs of the Society for Research in Child Development, 38* (1–2, Serial No. 149).

Nelson, K. (1985). *Making sense: The acquisitions of shared meaning.* New York: Academic Press.

Nelson, K. (Ed.). (1986). *Event knowledge: Structure and function in development.* New York: Academic Press.

Nelson, K., & Gruendel, J. M. (1979). At morning it's lunchtime: A scriptal view of children's dialogues. *Discourse Processes, 2*, 73–94.

New York City Board of Education. (1988–89). *Answers to frequently asked questions about limited English proficient students and bilingual/ESL programs.* New York: Board of Education, Division of Multilingual and Multicultural Education.

Nourot, P. M., & Van Hoorn, J. (1991). Research in review: Symbolic play in preschool and primary settings. *Young Children, 46* (6), 40–50.

Oxford-Carpenter, R., Pol, L., Lopez, D., Stupp, P., Gendell, M., & Peng, S. (1984). *Demographic projections of non-English-language background and limited-English-proficient persons in the United States to the year 2000 by state, age, and language group.* Rosslyn, VA: InterAmerica Research Associates.

Paley, V. (1981). *Wally's stories.* Cambridge, MA: Harvard University Press.

Paley, V. (1986a). *Mollie is three: Growing up in school.* Chicago: University of Chicago Press.

Paley, V. G. (1986b). On listening to what the children say. *Harvard Educational Review, 56*, 122–130.

Paley, V. G. (1990). *The boy who would be a helicopter: The uses of storytelling in the classroom.* Cambridge, MA: Harvard University Press.

Piaget, J., & Inhelder, B. (1969). *The psychology of the child* (C. Gattegno & F. M. Hodgson, Trans.). New York: Basic Books.

Piestrup, A. (1973). *Black dialect interference and accommodation of reading instruction in first grade.* Berkeley: University of California, Language-Behavior Research Laboratory.

Raines, S., & Canady, R. (1990). *The whole language kindergarten*. New York: Teachers College Press.

Ramsey, P. G., Vold, E. B., & Williams, L. R. (Eds.). (1989). *Multicultural education: A source book*. New York: Garland.

Rentel, V., & Kennedy, J. (1972). Effects of pattern drill on the phonology, syntax, and reading achievement of rural Appalachian children. *American Educational Research Journal, 9*, 87–100.

Schachter, F. F., & Strage, A. A. (1982). Adult's talk and children's language development. In S. G. Moore & C. R. Cooper (Eds.), *The young child: Review of research* (Vol. 3, pp. 79–96). Washington, DC: National Association for the Education of Young Children.

Schickedanz, J. A. (1989). The place of specific skills in preschool and kindergarten. In D. S. Strickland & L. M. Morrow (Eds.), *Emerging literacy: Young children learn to read and write* (pp. 96–106). Newark, DE: International Reading Association.

Schickedanz, J. A. (1990). The jury is still out on the effects of whole language and language experience approaches for beginning reading: A critique of Stahl and Miller's study. *Review of Educational Research, 60*, 127–131.

Schieffelin, B. B. (1979). Getting it together: An ethnographic approach to the study of the development of communicative competence. In E. Ochs & B. B. Schieffelin (Eds.), *Developmental pragmatics* (pp. 73–108). New York: Academic Press.

Schweinhart, L. J., & Weikart, D. P. (1980). Young children grow up: Effects of the Perry Preschool Program on youths through age 15. *Monographs of the High Scope Educational Research Foundation* (7). Ypsilanti, MI: High Scope.

Seawell, R. P. M. (1985). *A micro-ethnographic study of a Spanish/English bilingual kindergarten in which literature and puppet play were used as a method of enhancing language growth*. Unpublished doctoral dissertation, University of Texas, Austin.

Simpkins, G., Simpkins, C., & Holt, G. (1977). *Bridge: A cross-culture reading program*. Boston: Houghton Mifflin.

Slobodkina, E. (1968). *Caps for sale*. New York: Harper & Row.

Snow, C. E., Barnes, W. S., Chandler, J., Goodman, I. F., & Hemphill, L. (1991). *Unfulfilled expectations: Home and school influences on literacy*. Cambridge, MA: Harvard University Press.

Snow, C. E., Dubber, C., & De Blauw, A. (1982). Routines in mother–child interaction. In L. Feagans & D. C. Farran (Eds.), *The language of children reared in poverty: Implications for evaluation and intervention* (pp. 53–72). New York: Academic Press.

Soto, L. D. (1991). Research in review: Understanding bilingual/bicultural young children. *Young Children, 46* (2), 30–36.

Stahl, S. A., & Miller, P. D. (1989). Whole language and language experience approaches for beginning reading: A quantitative research synthesis. *Review of Educational Research, 59* (1), 87–116.

Stern, D. (1977). *The first relationship: Infant and mother.* Cambridge, MA: Harvard University Press.

Stockman, I. (1984). *A developmental study of Black English* (Phase 1, Final Report). (ERIC Document Reproduction Service No. ED 245 555.)

Tizard, B., & Hughes, M. (1984). *Young children leaning.* Cambridge, MA: Harvard University Press.

Vygotsky, L. S. (1978). *Mind in society: The development of higher psychological processes* (M. Cole, V. John-Steiner, S. Scribner, & E. Souberman, Eds.). Cambridge, MA: Harvard University Press.

Wang, M-H. (1989). *Playful language.* Unpublished term paper, Ohio State University, Columbus.

Wells, G. (1986). *The meaning makers: Children learning language and using language to learn.* Portsmouth, NH: Heinemann.

Wong Fillmore, L. (1976). *The second time around: Cognitive and social strategies in second language acquisition*, Parts 1 & 2. Unpublished doctoral dissertation, Stanford University, Stanford, CA.

Wong Fillmore, L. (1991). Language and cultural issues in early education. In S. L. Kagan (Ed.), *The care and education of America's young children: Obstacles and opportunities: Part I. The 90th Yearbook of the National Society for the Study of Education* (pp. 30–49). Chicago: National Society for the Study of Education.

*Acknowledgment.*    I'm grateful to Sal Vascellaro, a doctoral student in early childhood education at Teachers College, Columbia University, for suggestions for revision and clarification of the first (1987) version of this chapter.

# CHAPTER 5

# Reading

NITA H. BARBOUR

Researchers and reading specialists have for much of the twentieth century attempted to determine the best method of teaching reading to young children. Generally discussions and investigations centered around whether children should receive phonics instruction before undertaking the reading process or, before beginning formal reading instruction, should develop a repertoire of sight words with the expectation that they would figure out the relationship of letters to sounds. Jeanne Chall (1967), in *Learning to Read: The Great Debate*, attempted to end the controversy as she analyzed the results of comparative studies conducted between 1912 and 1965. She concluded that the phonics method had an edge over the whole word approach for reading achievement, but the evidence was not overwhelming.

At intervals since then, large research projects have been undertaken with the hope of providing better solutions for reading instruction in America's schools. Though results have been enlightening, solutions were not necessarily applicable to constantly changing societal patterns that affect children's learning. The "great debate" continued in the late 1980s (Carbo, 1988; Chall, 1989), and the focus of the argument, in spite of years of emphasis on phonics teaching in public schools, was still on the efficacy of different models—teaching phonics versus teaching for meaning. Moreover, the models research overlooks the literacy skills development that enables children to become effective and efficient readers in their later years. Both Turner (1989) and Taylor (1989) suggest that these "debates" present a reductionist's perspective of research and ignore the work that has been done over the last 20 years by educational psychologists, linguists, sociologists, and anthropologists, as well as teachers doing action research in the classroom. Taylor (1989) points out that these later investigators emphasize a new direction that research must take; that is, literacy must be understood from the perspective of the child as he or she begins the reading and writing process. Some researchers and theorists are now suggesting that the role of the teacher and of the contexts in which literacy is taught and learned is more important than a particular method (Hiebert, 1991; Smith, 1988). Goodman (1984) argues that former research has been multidisciplinary rather than interdisciplinary and suggests that an interdisciplinary approach to reading must be pursued in order to address better the problems of literacy in schools.

The central questions of when children should begin reading instruction, what form this instruction should take, and what factors contribute to or deter literacy development continue to be examined. Political, social, and economic forces put pressures on schools to provide instruction that produces a highly literate society. Reports in the 1980s summarized the research, and in the 1985 Commission on Reading report (Anderson, Hiebert, Scott & Wilkinson, 1985) recommendations for different aspects of teaching reading were made as a result of this research. However, this report did not stop the debate regarding the teaching of reading.

Marilyn Jager Adams in conjunction with the Center for the Study of Reading began a study of beginning reading programs and the quality of phonics instruction. Her book, *Beginning to Read: Thinking and Learning about Print* (1990), has been both praised and criticized by reading theorists and reading specialists (Adams et al., 1991). Adams argues that her massive analysis of the reading research supports the notion that in order to learn to read children must understand the alphabetic principle, but that learning this principle is not done in an hierarchical fashion, nor is it the only part of the reading process. She notes that as children learn to read text, teachers need to recognize that children have two sources upon which reading skills will be built—the text is one source, but children's prior knowledge is another. She also indicates that "teaching of phonemic awareness, letter and word recognition must be developed in authentic reading and writing situations where children have opportunities to reflect on the forms, functions and meanings of text" (Adams, 1990, p. 422).

Researchers and theorists are calling for an end to the arguments about methods and paradigms regarding reading, and instead are pleading for the need for an emphasis on ways to develop literacy so that all children can learn to read (Adams et al., 1991; Hiebert, 1991; Stanovich, 1990).

Observational and ethnographic studies in the past recommended classroom climates conducive to reading achievement. From this continued research and new studies, classroom teachers can discover modes of interactions that have been found to facilitate growth in reading. Certainly, teachers who make constructive use of research area able to interpret individual children's literacy development and understand how specific types of environments and techniques facilitate that development.

The purpose of this chapter is to present a general overview of the research in reading. It is impossible, however, to do a complete review, as reading is one of the most highly researched areas in education. This chapter is limited to examples of (1) various views of reading, (2) research on factors that influence literacy development, and (3) research on strategies that enhance children's reading and writing development. As teachers reflect on these three areas, they may be able to redefine their own thinking and then reconstruct or find support for the practices they use in their classrooms.

## DEFINITIONS OF READING

Reading is defined in different ways; however, nearly all definitions have the common elements of print, language, and comprehension. Authorities also view reading as an activity that involves a combination of certain motor, perceptual, and linguistic functions. Heller (1991) indicates that the differing definitions of reading depend on the view one takes of three essential elements—skills, products, and processes. Thus reading may be defined in three different ways as "complex unitary skills made up of numerous sub-skills acquired through instruction, . . . the products of skills acquisition, with comprehension being the visible, quantifiable, measurable aspect, . . . or processes an individual undertakes to construct meaning from print or to construct meaning using print respectively" (p. 3).

Finn (1990) categorizes definitions of reading into three broad categories, each category having a basis in learning theory: empiricist, rationalist, and interactivist. Empiricists reflect behaviorist models of reading. Their focus is on the skills approach emphasizing the relationship of print to language as the important focus in reading. They view the beginning reader as progressing from learning the various parts of words to understanding the whole passage, maintaining that reading is first translating graphic symbols into the corresponding speech sounds. The empiricists believe that only after this latter task has been accomplished can the learner attach meaning to the symbols (Bateman, 1983). These theorists have been strong advocates of the phonics emphasis in teaching beginning reading, and in the current literature are often described as advocating a "bottom-up" approach to reading.

The rationalists focus on the relationship between language and meaning. They see the reader as interpreting and building meaning in context before analyzing the subparts of the graphic form. Smith (1988) takes issue with the behaviorist view—asserting that it is a mechanistic view of reading that requires a decoding of the print, which puts "the reader under the control of the text" (p. 2). For him reading is a rational and purposeful task. "Reading is seen as a creative and constructive activity having four distinctive and fundamental characteristics—it is purposeful, selective, anticipa-tory, and based on comprehension, all matters where the reader must clearly exercise control" (pp. 3–4). Readers have a purpose as they seek information and select and test hypotheses in order to answer questions regarding the text. Readers anticipate what the text will mean because of prior experiences, knowledge, and feelings. They understand the text be-cause they modify their expectations to meet the specifications of the writer. The rationalists advocate the "meaning" or holistic approach to beginning reading, and in the present literature on reading are often described as ad-vocating a "top-down" approach.

Interactivists, or constructivists, have a balanced perspective, main-taining that reading is a transactional process (Goodman, 1984; Rosenblatt, 1989). In this new paradigm advocates believe that a reader must simulta-neously extract information about print as well as make hypotheses regard-ing the meaning of the text. Information from both sources interacts until finally the meaning of the text is clear (Rumelhart, 1977). Reading involves the context of the print, as well as what the reader brings to the reading act. "Every reading act is an event, a transaction involving a particular reader and a particular configuration of marks on a page, and occurring at a partic-ular time in a particular context. Meaning does not reside ready-made in the text or in the reader; it happens during the transaction between reader and text" (Rosenblatt, 1989, p. 157).

In the past decade constructivists have been examining the manner in which children come to literacy. As this interest in literacy events pro-gresses, the definition of reading for meaning becomes linked with writing, so that reading and writing become viewed as interactive processes. As a child becomes involved with the process of reading, attempts at writing are viewed as underlying skills of reading. Drawing and language use around these events (Dyson, 1990) become important elements in the development of reading skills, so that reading is seen as an integrative language arts pro-cess.

Whichever of the three viewpoints is followed, it is clear that reading is a complex process. It is not a simple linear pursuit proceeding from one subskill to the next until the act of reading is accomplished. It is the accu-mulation of a wide range of skills that requires practice if children are to become active readers who seek information and enjoyment from the printed page. As Marie Clay (1991) so vividly points out, the viewpoint one takes can affect children's growth in reading, either enriching or hindering their progress. For example, a teacher's rigid adherence to a particular view-point may mean that some children will have difficulty learning to read in that classroom. What is more important is for teachers to understand the differing perspectives and be able to deal with the different ways that children have of becoming literate. Only then will there be schools to accommodate the individual literacy requirements of all children.

## FACTORS THAT INFLUENCE LITERACY DEVELOPMENT

Most educators and theorists would agree with Clay. In order to determine some of the specific factors related to literacy development, researchers have examined the relationships between reading achievement and age, intelligence, gender, visual skills, auditory skills, letter knowledge, word consciousness, metalinguistic ability, or environmental factors. Though establishing a strong correlational link between any of these factors and reading achievement does not mean these factors are prerequisites for reading, research findings help teachers identify which children may need assistance either before specific formal instruction begins or as reading instruction is taking place.

### Age

Chronological age seems to have little relationship to when a child is capable of learning to read. Coltheart (1979) reports that the age at which children are formally taught to read varies from country to country: for example, it is five years in Israel, Great Britain, and Hong Kong; six in France, the United States, and Japan; and seven in Denmark, Sweden, and Ecuador. If there were an optimal age, then the programs in some of these countries would be more successful with beginning readers; no such evidence exists.

In the United States, instruction has tended to begin by age 6, because events in the 1930s (for example, major reading studies, the developmental theorists' influence, and the testing movement) led people to believe that a mental age of 6.5 was necessary for reasonable growth in reading. The Morphett and Washburne, and Dolch and Bloomster studies greatly influenced the notion that there was a mental age that children should reach before reading instruction started. After finding that children with mental ages of 6.5 made better reading progress than did those with less maturity, Morphett and Washburne (1931/1983) concluded that if reading instruction were postponed until children reached 6.5 years, this would reduce their chances of failure. Dolch and Bloomster (1937) found a high correlation between phonic ability and mental age, and concluded that a child could not be expected to use phonics much before the age of 7.

Gates (1937) examined different methods of teaching reading and found that if teachers recognized individual differences and adjusted to them, low achievers could successfully learn to read. He concluded that whether the child could learn to read at a particular time depended more on the type of instruction than on a particular mental age. In spite of this contrast between the Gates study and other studies, the concept of a specific mental age for readiness gained much more prominence in this country than did the concept of adjusting instruction to the child's need.

In the 1960s there were challenges to the notion that reading instruction should not commence until a child had reached the mental age of 6.5. Research on the early reader was one such challenge.

Dolores Durkin carried out three longitudinal studies of early readers. In two of these studies Durkin (1966, 1974–75) identified children who could already read without having had any formal instruction. These children were followed through sixth grade to determine if they maintained their advantage as proficient readers. These early readers did indeed maintain their higher reading scores throughout their 6 years in elementary school.

Studies have been designed to determine if teaching reading to younger children is appropriate. Results tend to be mixed. In her third study Durkin (1977) found that though children taught to read before entering first grade scored higher on reading tests during grades 1 and 2, by the end of third and fourth grades the two groups did not score significantly differently. McKee, Brezeniski, and Harrison (1966) reported that children taught to read in kindergarten maintained their advantage only if their first-grade instruction was similar to their kindergarten instruction. Sutton (1969) reported a study that had young children learn to read by providing a rich reading environment rather than specific instruction. Sutton found those children who did learn to read continued to show more progress through third grade than did their classmates who started to read in first grade.

The research on early readers has led to an examination of children's literacy experiences before entering school. These studies have led to a recognition of children's developmental progression toward literacy. Children exposed to stories, an environment rich in print, and opportunities to draw and write develop responses to literature and to writing in a progressively more sophisticated way. Thus, these researchers suggest that there is no point in time when children are "ready to read," but they are constantly in the process of developing literacy skills or *emerging* toward literacy (Hiebert, 1988; Teale & Sulzby, 1986).

## Intelligence

Intelligence is another factor to be considered. On the average, early readers have higher intelligence scores than their peers. However, Heilman, Blair, and Rupley (1986) found in a review of several studies that high I.Q. is not a prerequisite for early reading. Cassidy and Vukelich (1980) noted that there were as many nonreaders among their sampling of gifted children as there were readers. High intelligence seems to help, but it is neither a prerequisite nor a guarantee that very young children will profit from beginning reading instruction (Durkin, 1977; Sampson & Briggs, 1981; Torrey, 1979).

### Gender

Gender differences in reading achievement tend to be explained by cultural expectations. Girls in the early years of reading instruction tend to achieve higher scores than boys (Gates, 1961; Johnson, 1973–74). One hypothesis offered is that in American culture reading is a sedentary activity and girls are socialized to be more passive than boys. Thus, girls are rewarded for quiet reading behavior. A second theory is that reading materials are more interesting for girls. Finally, the major role models that children have for reading are their female kindergarten and primary school teachers. There is no clear evidence from the research, however, that boys should begin reading instruction any later than girls (Dwyer, 1973).

Kincade and Kleine (1990) suggest that there may be some gender differences in children's recall ability due to instructional factors. In their study of children's recall ability of text under two different conditions, cued recall and free recall, boys did significantly better under the cued conditions and girls did better under free recall. The researchers suggest that boys may need more structure than girls—a situation that may be accommodated as teachers become more adept at adjusting instruction to a child's literacy development.

### Visual Skills

Vision plays an important role in learning to read, but it is difficult to discern to what extent vision is related to reading failures. One important visual factor is visual discrimination. Since it is believed to be related to reading achievement, there are many prereading activities in schools designed to improve visual discrimination. Children perform many activities requiring them to note likenesses and differences in objects and pictures, and to relate much of this to size, color, and shape.

Children who are weak in the ability to see likenesses and differences in shapes, patterns, and forms have difficulty in recognizing words and letters (Spache, 1976). Spache argues that there is a developmental pattern of visual discrimination, that is, children progress from discrimination of three-dimensional materials, to two-dimensional materials, and finally to reproducing and matching two-dimensional forms.

Other researchers attempted to determine if perceptual training could enhance a child's readiness for reading. Barrett (1965) concluded that discrimination of letters and words was a better predictor of reading than discrimination of shapes and forms. A 1978 research review by Weaver and Shonkoff concluded that perceptual training to help children "discriminate, recognize and produce letters of the alphabet" (p. 40) was more helpful than perceptual training to help children discriminate geometric shapes and pictures. In her research in Auckland, New Zealand, Clay (1991) found that children's letter identification scores after a year of schooling showed a higher correlation with reading progress than with any other variable. Children's ability to scan the letters of a word and their manner of categorizing, labeling, and distinguishing them from other letters is important learning and separates children who make rapid progress in reading from those who make slower progress.

Children may need some experience in discriminating similarities and differences in shapes and patterns. However, it appears that these experiences will not necessarily enhance children's readiness for reading. Children need direct experience with discrimination of letters and words as a part of their reading instruction if they are to learn to read.

## Auditory Skills

Auditory skills, like visual skills, encompass a number of component parts: auditory acuity, discrimination, blending, comprehension, and memory. Children who have difficulties in one or more of these areas may have some difficulties in learning to read. Research has attempted to determine if auditory discrimination or the ability to hear likenesses and differences between the smallest unit of sound (phonemes) is a predictor of reading achievement.

Smith (1988) notes that children do not need skill in auditory perception in order to read. There may be, however, some types of reading instruction that might require the child to have certain auditory skills in order to achieve. The relationship between auditory discrimination—or ability to segment the phonemes into component parts—and reading ability has been studied by Bond and Dykstra (1967) and Fox and Routh (1976). They found positive correlations between ability to discriminate phonemes and readiness to read. Paradis and Peterson (1975) and Rozin, Bressman, and Taft (1974) noted that children from lower income backgrounds and inner-city children had greater difficulty in discriminating between sounds.

Though there is correlational evidence of the relationship between distinguishing sounds and reading, there is no clear indication that a cause-and-effect relationship exists. Phonemic analysis may be greatly improved as one learns to read. Goldstein (1976) determined that phonemic analysis was both a predictor and a consequence. Children who were sensitive to the differences in sounds were able to read with greater ease, but learning to read also helped improve the ability to discriminate sounds for all the children in the study.

From several reviews of this topic (Adams, 1990; Ball & Blachman, 1991; Ehri, 1979; Lyon, 1977), one can conclude that auditory discrimination or phonemic awareness skills are necessary for reading, and learning to read is important for developing phonemic awareness. However, developing these skills in nonreaders will not ensure that they will learn to read. In the studies there were good readers who had poor auditory skills and poor readers who were able to discriminate sounds adequately (Lyon, 1977).

## Letter Knowledge

Knowledge of letters has been viewed as an important factor in beginning reading, and some studies have indicated that letter naming and letter recognition are the best predictors of reading success, especially in the primary grades (Barrett, 1965; Muehl & DiNello, 1976). Studies indicate that early readers have a knowledge of letter names (Bissex, 1980; Torrey, 1979).

Although there is evidence that letter knowledge is an important factor in reading, teaching of letter names to children does not necessarily result in their successfully learning to read (Muehl & Kremenack, 1966; Speer & Lamb, 1976). Some theorists suggest that letter knowledge is a result of a child's interest in books and his or her intrinsic language competence (Gibson & Levin, 1975).

Most children are surrounded by a great deal of print in their environment, but there is disagreement among authorities as to whether children learn to abstract the necessary graphic clues for reading from this environment in the same natural way that they learn oral language, or whether children need such prerequisite skills as letter recognition or phoneme segmentation before they can read the print.

Goodman and Goodman (1979) and Harste, Woodward, and Burke (1984) maintain that children learn to read in the preschool years as they begin to identify symbols from their environment. For example, they can read things such as the labels on food packages, the Gulf or Exxon signs on gas stations, or the McDonald's sign on the fast-food restaurant. At first children recognize these signs because of the context in which they are found. Gradually, after many experiences, the print itself becomes familiar and the words can be recognized when seen in a new context, and finally individual letters can be segmented out and recognized.

In a critique of the letter-name knowledge research, Ehri (1983) points out that in the last 10 years research on letter-name knowledge has focused on the child's developing awareness of the letter-sound mapping system. English orthography is alphabetic and the sounds of many letters closely resemble the letter names. That children demonstrate this awareness is clear from the research relating to children's early writings (Chomsky, 1977; Harste, Woodward, & Burke, 1984; Paul, 1976). Children who are encouraged to write and to use their spelling will use the letter names they hear in the words in their writings. Thus they might write "PPL" for *people*, or "KOT" for *coat*, or "DRD" for *dirty*. Paul (1976) has even suggested that there is a progression in this skill. That is, children seem to note first the initial consonant or long vowel (letter-name) sounds, progress to identifying letters for the final phoneme or syllable, and then finally begin to separate out and identify short vowel sounds as separate letters. Thus a child might progress in recognizing and writing the letters in the word *come* by first writing "K" (a letter to represent the initial sound of the word). Then he or she would begin to recognize initial and final letters, writing "DM" for *dumb* or "KT" for *coat*. Finally the child would indicate an awareness of the separation of letters sounds within a word by writing "KUM" (*come*), or "DUM" (*dumb*), or "BITN" (*biting*). It would be only after much experience with the word that the child would finally write the correct orthography of most commonly used words. At that stage the child would have learned the word and would no longer be writing the word as letter and sound segments. The "invented spelling" seems to be a means for mapping the letter-sound system rather than a means for identifying words.

The question as to whether children need to know the letter name in order to read or whether they can figure out the process by lots of experience with the print environment is not totally clear. Masonheimer, Drum, and Ehri (1984) found that children could be classified into two groups depending on mastery of the alphabet: (1) contextual-dependent children, who had not mastered the alphabet and were unable to read words in isolation, and (2) contextual-independent children, who had mastered the alphabet and were able to read words in isolation. It seems that children need to know letter names in order to be able to read words out of context. Nevertheless, it is still not clear whether direct teaching of the letter names helps children move from contextual dependence to contextual independence, or whether children figure out the letter names because of interest and curiosity.

The research does suggest that teachers should provide a classroom environment where letter name and recognition are a part of the program and where children have an opportunity to ask questions and receive answers regarding the letters they see in books or printed on various signs and charts in the classroom. Alphabet songs and games also provide the opportunity for children to acquire letter knowledge. Mastering knowledge of the alphabet does not, however, guarantee reading success. Learning letters should be a part of the total reading process, not just a prerequisite to reading instruction.

## Word Knowledge

Children entering school have wide variations in their vocabulary development, and certainly language facility plays an important role in later reading success. The extent of a child's vocabulary has been a predictor of future reading success (Artley, 1948; Robinson, 1963). Children who did well earlier on different vocabulary tasks had higher scores later in reading achievement.

Meaningful words are easier to learn to read. Thus, the words selected for sight recognition may affect children's reading achievement. De Hirsch, Jansky, and Langford (1966), Biemiller (1977–78), and Lesgold and Resnick (1982) found a high correlation between first-grade reading achievement and children's ability to recognize words they had been taught that had special meaning for them, such as their name, important dates, or words like *monster* or *candy.*

While vocabulary is important for a child's reading achievement, it is not clear that attempting to teach children an extensive sight vocabulary improves their reading ability. Jackson and Biemiller (1985) compared the time it took precocious readers and average readers to read letters in isolation, words in isolation, and connected text. They concluded rapid word identification facilitated rapid reading and comprehension of text, but was not a prerequisite for it.

Extensive studies are being conducted on word consciousness and how that relates to reading. Many children, when they enter school, are not aware of the subunits of language, that is, that sentences can be divided into words and words into letters and sounds. In addition, children also may have difficulty in interpreting the terminology used for teaching reading, such as letter, word, sound, beginning, and ending.

Ehri (1979) examined the relationship between word consciousness and ability to read. From several correlational studies, she found that beginning readers did much better on word analysis tasks than did nonreaders. She suggests that there is perhaps an interactive process taking place where learning to read helps the child to understand the function of words better and thus to adjust to print. At the same time, the child's knowledge and understanding of the spoken word help with reading the printed language.

## Metalinguistic Ability

The relationship between the child's metalinguistic ability—being able to separate language from its meaning and to analyze and reflect upon the form of language—and reading achievement has been explored (Flavell, 1976). For example, a child would know not only that *man* is someone like Daddy or Uncle Joe, but also that it is a word and can be separated into both letter and sound parts (*m-a-n*). Further, he or she would know strategies for segmenting the word. The ability to develop these strategies for this segmentation requires the child to decenter, and recognize that things (ideas, objects) can have more than one characteristic. *Man* can have a "meaning quality," but *man* can also have "linguistic qualities," such as sounds and letters that are arranged in a certain order and that relate to one another (Templeton, 1980). It is important in learning to read that the beginner realize that words can be broken down into sound segments.

Clay (1991) suggests that children not only discover sounds of single letters but very early will learn to focus on units of letters that always appear together and are always pronounced the same way. The larger the unit and the more units that the child discovers and uses in both reading and writing experiences, the more efficient a reader he or she becomes. In the early stages of learning to read, these remembered clusters may serve as a key to recall the word the next time it is viewed in print or when it is needed for writing. For example, a child may recognize, store in memory the letters and sounds of *jl*, and then be able to recognize the word *jail* the next time he or she sees it in print (Ehri, 1989).

Researchers describe different levels of children's phonemic awareness as they experience writing and reading. Ehri (1989) has identified four stages of development.

1. *Precommunicative*—producing scribbles or strings of letters to represent ideas.
2. *Semiphonetic*—knowing names and sounds of some letters and beginning to use them to represent words.
3. *Phonetic*—believing that the sound they hear must be represented by a different letter.
4. *Morphemic*—using the conventional spelling of the word and learning spelling patterns across words.

Ryan, McNamara, and Kenney (1977), Ehri (1979), and Allan (1982) examined the relationship between children's awareness of lexical tasks and their reading achievement. Ryan, McNamara, and Kenney (1977) tested differences between better and poorer readers in awareness of sounds as words and as nonwords. Ehri (1979) examined the word consciousness of beginning readers compared with that of prereaders. Though there were some differences, both research studies found high correlations between children's lexical awareness and reading achievement. There seems to be some evidence that children who have not achieved lexical awareness are less able readers.

Metalinguistic knowledge, as it relates to the discourse level of a whole passage, has also been examined to determine how the discourse affects children's reading comprehension ability. The processes involved in story comprehension and different story grammars—how stories are constructed—have been examined by Applebee (1978) and Stein and Glenn (1982). A common grammar or story format, for example, is a story set in a time and place (which may be indefinite) in which characters are introduced so that a problem is set up, the hero or heroine departs to solve the problem, and through a series of events the problem is resolved. The hero or heroine returns, often wiser for the experience. Children appear to remember better stories that conform to the typical story formats.

In an extensive study of reading as a complex system of skills, Forrest-Pressley and Waller (1984) found that performance on reading skills and on the ability to verbalize or strategize increased with grade and reading ability. The ability to use the skills tended to be a better predictor of reading ability than did the ability to verbalize about language (a metalinguistic function). High performance without high verbalization, and vice versa, was rarely found. The study did not shed light on whether it is productive to instruct students in metacognitive skills with the intent of improving reading ability. However, since the verbalization measures did help to explain the students' level of reading, the researchers concluded, "The implication of this observation put simply is that teachers, perhaps, should talk to students about how and what they know and why they do things the way they do" (p. 123).

## Environmental Factors

The effects of home environment on children's reading achievement have been studied by several researchers. When early researchers examined the relationship between socioeconomic status and reading achievement, high correlations were found (Chomsky, 1972; Justman, 1965). Later research studies, however, have examined other factors in home and school, in addition to socioeconomic status, that could account for differences.

Walberg and Tsai (1985) examined 9-year-olds in an attempt to determine some of the factors that affect reading. Socioeconomic status and ethnicity were not highly correlated to reading achievement, but stimulus materials for reading in the home were. Walker and Kuerbitz (1979) noted that children who had been read to at home achieved higher reading scores at the end of first grade than did their counterparts.

Thus, it has been concluded that socioeconomic background may have some influence, but it is only a minor factor. It is the family background that plays the important role in terms of reading (Teale, 1986; Torrey, 1979; Wigfield & Asher, 1984). These studies confirm conclusions from Durkin's (1966) study of early readers. Children with higher reading achievement and early readers come from homes where parents engage in a wide range of literary events such as reading a great deal themselves, reading a great deal to their children, and providing a rich print environment. Other important factors are availability of writing materials, encouragement to write, responsive parents or siblings when children ask for help in spelling, and educational TV programs that focus on reading. In all the studies, there are strong suggestions that the initiative for reading activities comes from the children. They want to be read to and often ask for the same book over and over. They request the information they need in performing both reading and writing tasks. These experiences provide children with an awareness of print.

Studies on such literacy events occurring in homes of different socioeconomic status indicate that there are vast differences in the amounts of literacy events and that children from homes with fewer of these events tend to do more poorly in school (Feitelson & Goldstein, 1986; Heath, 1983; Teale, 1986). From some of these studies and from her experiences with her own child, Adams (1990) calculated that her child had between 1,000 and 1,700 hours of storybook reading alone and countless other hours of interactions about print. Conversely, some children in the studies had as little as 25 hours of storybook reading and perhaps 200 hours of interactions regarding print. Such differing environmental effects will require different approaches and responses to children's early attempts at acquiring reading skills.

In summary, the research supports the idea that reading is an accumulation of many skills, that these skills are acquired in an interactive way, and that each child's process of learning and experiential background are unique. There are few specific prerequisites for learning to read and no precise time when reading instruction should begin, since reading is an ongoing emerging process involving awareness of print and functions of text. The process begins at home as parents respond to the child's interest in books and print, progresses during the school years as teachers facilitate comprehension and interest through helping the child to perfect the subskills of reading, and continues into adulthood as one practices and refines the ability to acquire information and to receive enjoyment from various types of text.


## METHODS AND STRATEGIES FOR TEACHING READING

### Methods Research

Much of the early methods research compared an "innovative" approach (either meaning or phonics) with the current or traditional approach (either meaning or phonics) used in a particular community. The results of these studies suggested that the "innovative" approach produced greater achievement than did the traditional approach (Pflaum, Walberg, Kargianes, & Racher, 1980). Because of ambiguity, Hawthorne effects, and inconclusive results of such studies, three major research studies were conducted in the 1960s and 1970s to further assess the best method. In the 1980s whole language approaches and research, based on Marie Clay's work in New Zealand, were undertaken (Harste, 1985; Reutzel & Cooter, 1990; Ribowsky, 1985).

Chall's (1967) research, as mentioned earlier, examined the efficacy of two differing approaches, the meaning approach versus the phonics approach. The U.S. Office of Education attempted broader-based research in the Cooperative Reading Research Project, which examined five different approaches (Bond & Dykstra, 1967). The 20 Follow Through Projects of the 1970s examined children's progress when they were taught using a particular model from preschool through third grade (Stebbins, St. Pierre, Proper, Anderson, & Cerva, 1977). Stahl and Miller (1989) reviewed studies that compared whole language approaches with basal reading approaches. Adams (1990) in her extensive review of research includes examinations of differing approaches to reading.

Though conclusions from these studies are challenged and debated (Adams et al., 1991; Carbo, 1988; Edelsky, 1990; Schickedanz, 1990), the vast amount of research on what method is best does not indicate that a single method or model is superior in developing general reading skills. The fact that, in all the methods research studies, there were wide variations among students who were taught by the same approach indicates that many other factors affect reading outcomes. Such results have led reading specialists to recommend that multifaceted or eclectic approaches be adopted for classroom practice (Durkin, 1989; May, 1990), so that the unique development of each child can be accommodated, and that debates about and em-

phasis on methods research be suspended in favor of observational research
in order to determine how different children learn to read.

## Observational Research

A great deal of research has been undertaken to examine the teacher
and classroom variables that affect children's progress in reading and writing. Cochran-Smith and Lytle (1990) point out that most of the research falls
into two categories, which they classify as process-product research and
qualitative or interpretative research. The process-product research tends
to correlate teacher behaviors with student achievement. The qualitative/
interpretative research examines differences in children because of home,
school, and community differences, as well as children's levels of understanding as they progress in literacy.

*Process-product research.* Observational studies of the process-
product variety have identified about 350 different variables that affect classroom learning (Dunkin & Biddle, 1974). The variables pertain to such elements as teacher–pupil interaction during instruction, teachers' solutions to
problems that arise in the classroom, amount and type of content covered,
student's success rate, and general classroom climate (Barr, 1984; Rosenshine & Stevens, 1984). Various other components in addition to classroom
environment can affect reading outcome. Samuels (1981) has summarized
these as the human element (teachers, aides, parents, librarians, administrators), materials (textbooks, audiovisual materials, teacher-constructed
materials), and procedures (curriculum and evaluation mandates, schedules
and routines, school district organization and size). Hiebert (1991) emphasizes the importance of practitioners understanding the complexity of creating classroom environments that support literacy. For example, whole
group instruction might be an effective strategy for a specific skill and for a
particular age group, and not for other skills or a different age group of
students. As studies reveal the variables that affect learning to read, practitioners need guidance in implementing programs that encompass a multi-
plicity of variables.

In the many observational studies, correlations have been noted between many of the different components and reading. Academic learning
time (ALT), or the amount of time a child is engaged in an academic task, is
one of the components that has been found consistently to correlate with
reading achievement or school learning (Fisher et al., 1978). The Beginning
Teacher Evaluation Study found that ALT (and thus achievement) increased
when the task the child was to complete was related to a very specific area
of learning and was not too difficult for the child. Monitoring of the task by

the teacher and giving appropriate feedback also affect ALT (Fisher et al., 1978). Grouping students for instruction increases ALT per student and thus reading achievement. In small groups children receive more instruction from the teacher, more praise, and more feedback. A combination of these factors is more productive for learning (Stallings & Kaskowitz, 1974). Kean, Summers, Ravietz, and Farber (1979) found that children in first through fourth grades had higher achievement if they were in classes that were taught by some combination of small group/large group instruction. These children achieved better reading scores than did their counterparts who were taught in classes where teachers conducted lessons only individually, only in small groups, or only in large groups.

Other studies examine group size and types of interaction in particular situations. For example, Morrow and Smith's (1990) study of the effects of class size on comprehension of stories during storybook readings indicated that children read to in small groups were better able to respond to comprehension questions, made more comments, and asked more questions about the stories than did children read to in either large group settings or on a one-on-one basis. Rosenshine and Stevens (1984) point out the important components of teacher–student interactions. They conclude that successful teachers give more instruction per student, more opportunity for children to practice skills, and more feedback on the correctness of these skills. They also monitor each child's behavior better and keep each child more involved in the reading task.

*Qualitative or interpretative research.*    Insights into children's literacy development because of home and school influences are provided by qualitative studies. Ethnographers have reported that children come to school with varying degrees of literacy development because of how parents or the community in which they live view and use literacy. Too often schools are geared to provide instruction based on certain expectations of literacy instead of using the strengths of different children (Heath, 1983; Teale, 1986).

This type of research has also provided insights into children's levels of understanding and using print. Case studies of single children's development in reading and writing (Baghdan, 1984; Bissex, 1980; Calkins, 1983) give insights into what children do in acquiring awareness of print and how they process this information. Studies also are suggesting there are levels of awareness that children achieve that serve as important building blocks for further learning. Snow and Ninio (1986) describe five rules that children acquire as they are read to.

1. Books are for reading, not for handling, building with, and so forth.
2. In reading a book, it is the book that controls what the reader is to think, not vice versa.

3. Pictures are intended to elicit words that signify their meaning.
4. Pictures can represent more than one object to be named, and they can represent actions and events.
5. Books represent another world that is separate from the real world but has characters and events that can be compared with real-world events.

A great deal of research has been done stressing the importance of the other language arts areas to learning to read. Jana Mason (1989) has edited a book that describes different researchers' discoveries of the reading–writing connection. Dyson (1986, 1990) examines how children's writing and drawings include more sophisticated text as they begin to see relationships between their drawings and their text and as they discuss what they are doing with their friends.

All the researchers suggest implications for the classroom teacher, but changing classrooms to implement such results is slow or nonexistent. Cochran-Smith and Lytle (1990) state that most of this research has been done by university researchers. As has been the situation for decades, teachers have been the object of the studies and yet are expected to find the research useful and to implement the findings into their classroom practice. They suggest that perhaps the questions that university researchers ask are not the ones that teachers would ask to inform and improve their own teaching practices. The importance of teachers' voices being heard to inform us of better practices is also suggested by Hiebert (1991).

## Skills/Strategies Research

No matter what method one uses or what philosophy one espouses, the main purpose of reading is comprehension. However, in order to achieve that comprehension, certain skills must be acquired. Let us consider studies suggesting strategies for developing phonics skills, sight-word identification, comprehension skills, and writing skills, which in turn enhance reading.

*Phonics.*    Beginning readers must understand and use alphabetic principles. In schools where basal reader texts are used, children learn these principles as they master rules and generalizations about phonics. The utility of phonics generalizations in basal readers has been examined by several researchers. The number of words that have certain letter combinations, and when to apply successfully the rules for those combinations, were noted. For example, Clymer (1963) found that of the 45 generalizations on words that contain certain letter combinations, only 18 worked as often as 75% of the time. He maintained that many generalizations that are taught are of limited value. However, Burmeister (1971) determined that rules that work most often were not always the most useful to teach to elementary children because they may not be reading the words to which these rules apply. She developed a list of different rules that she felt would be most useful to teach.

Since the purpose of phonics is to teach alphabetic principles, the rules that children learn should have operational use. From the principles, children should be able to identify known words rapidly and to figure out unfamiliar words. Therefore, only the most important and regular phonics rules should be taught (Anderson, Hiebert, Scott, & Wilkinson, 1985). In spite of these studies, basal readers still provide lessons for all 45 generalizations. Taylor, Frye, and Goetz (1990) in their study found that most students were able to pass phonics skills tests before these skills were introduced in the basal reading program. Instead of following the dictates of the basals in making decisions about which rules to focus on, teachers need to be aware of whether children know the principle, the utility of each rule as a help in decoding, and the likelihood of children finding examples of its application in their reading.

The synthetic approach and the analytic approach are the most common strategies for teaching phonics with the basal readers. In the synthetic approach, sounds in words are identified separately and then blended in order to form words. Children first learn a number of letter sounds from words in their speaking and listening vocabulary, then identify these sounds in isolation. The next step is to separate out the individual sounds from the known words. The final and most important step is blending the sounds together (Engelmann & Bruner, 1974).

The analytic approach to phonics instruction never uses the sound in isolation, but teaches the sound as it is heard in a series of words. For example, the letter *b* is the first sound one hears in the words *baby, boy, basket,* or *Billy.* Children are then encouraged to think of other words that they know that begin like *baby, boy,* and so forth. As they develop skill in thinking of other words, they are encouraged to identify unknown words by their similarity to known words. For example, if children know *cat* and know the sounds of other initial letters, then they should be able to figure out *mat, sat, rat* (May, 1990).

Research on phonics as to which method is best is somewhat inconclusive, though Pflaum et al. (1980), Johnson and Baumann (1984), and Williams (1985), in reviewing phonics instruction strategies, concluded that there was increasing evidence that a synthetic approach was more effective in teaching letter–sound correspondence and in helping children transfer this skill to unknown words. The most important skill for transferring phonics analysis skills to new words is the skill of blending isolated letters into recognizable words (Johnson & Baumann, 1984). Alternatively, other research has shown that the strategy of substituting letters in known words to figure out unknown words (part of the analytic strategy) is a very effective means of helping children understand how letters combine to make meaningful words (Cunningham, 1979).

Ehri (1989), from her research on teaching spelling to young children, maintains that spelling contributes to reading and reading contributes to spelling. In writing, children notice how letters and sounds are related, and this process creates an interest not only in how specific words are spelled, but in how the spelling system works in general. Reading exposes children to the correct spellings of words in which they have become interested and helps them to store these words in memory. Though spelling is important, Ehri does not suggest a specific method of teaching spelling. Goodman, Smith, Meredith, and Goodman (1987) recommend that alternative ways of helping children discover phonics rules are possible in a whole language classroom. As children write they use invented spellings and begin to formulate possible rules to remember the correct spellings. The more useful rules are the ones they will remember, as they develop proofreading techniques to improve their stories. Dictionary skills are developed in authentic ways, when children need to verify the correct spelling of words for a story. Trachtenburg (1990) suggests using children's literature in a whole-part-whole sequence to enhance phonics instruction. Students would first read and enjoy a piece of literature that contained a high utility phonic element. Next, those who needed assistance would receive instruction and then practice in using the skill. Finally, the students would apply the new skill in their reading of a different high quality literary text.

*Sight words.*   In basal reading programs, sight words are commonly taught to young children before they begin reading. The rationale for this practice is that children can begin immediately to make meaning from the printed page. Words that children already know can also serve as a starting point for phonics instruction. The research on the most effective way to teach sight words presents conflicting views.

Some advocates of teaching sight words suggest it is better to teach the word in context, using picture clues or oral or written phrases and sentences, so that as children attach meaning to the word they see its communication value and thus remember it longer. This is often viewed as helpful, especially for function words that are difficult to define in isolation (Ehri, 1978; Goodman, 1967).

Other advocates suggest children learn words best in isolation when their attention is not distracted by other stimuli but is focused on the word so that they note its distinctive features, such as configuration, length of word, and letter placement. These advocates maintain that the child's attention is attracted to the picture or other words in the sentence, when taught in context, and thus the child does not attend to the target word (Samuels, 1967; Singer, Samuels, & Spiroff, 1973–74). Rose and Furr (1984) concluded from their study that, especially for learning-disabled readers, illustrations interfered with learning isolated words.

Ceprano (1981) reports on a study comparing children's learning of words by the isolation method and the context method. She also assessed the children on the ability to recognize words in a sentence and on the ability to recognize words in isolation. She found that children taught by the isolation method did better on the isolation test, and children taught by the context method did better on the sentence test. She concluded that learning words in isolation facilitates the child's learning of graphemes and phonemes, but learning words in context facilitates the child's learning of syntax and meaning.

From an emergent literacy perspective, children learn sight words from the reading and writing experiences provided in the classroom. Shapiro and Gunderson (1988) found that children who were taught in a whole language classroom generated their own sight words. These words were more in number than found in basal reading series. High frequency words were used as often, but low frequency words appeared to be more current and relevant, since these words tended to come from class projects and children's interests. Children had little or no difficulty reading each other's writing due to the number of high frequency words used, and children's overall reading and writing appeared to be enhanced because of the wider range of low frequency words.

*Comprehension.*    Researchers examining the comprehension process indicate that it is interactive. Various types of knowledge are important to the understanding of a text. In addition to understanding the process of comprehension, teachers need to know how to teach comprehension. Durkin (1978–79), in a survey of fourth-grade classrooms, noted that teachers did much more comprehension testing than teaching. Most teachers of reading follow the Directed Reading Activity (DRA) approach suggested in the manuals (Mason & Osborne, 1982; Shannon, 1983). However, whole language advocates recommend the use of literature as the basis for teaching reading, with individualized conferences and response groups to instruct students (Goodman, Smith, Meredith, & Goodman, 1987; May, 1990; Vacca, Vacca, & Grove, 1991).

Different reading specialists suggest strategies for teaching comprehension. Three of the approaches found in the literature are the Directed Reading Activity (DRA) or the Directed Reading/Thinking Activity (DRTA) found in most basal series, the Reciprocal Questioning (ReQuest) model first developed by Manzo (1969) for remedial reading students, and Response Groups, used by those advocating a literature approach to reading (Hansen, 1987). In the DRA and DRTA model the teacher directs the children's reading by asking them literal, predicting, verifying, inferring, and critical questions about the text as the children are reading passages from the text. In the ReQuest model the teacher and students take turns asking questions about the text. The teacher carefully selects the type of questions so that predicting, inferring, and summarizing, as well as literal, questions are asked. The teacher models new types of questions to get students involved. In Response Groups children also learn to ask questions about the text, but the teaching begins in individual conferences where teachers ask authentic questions (to which they do not know the answers) of the children regarding their understanding of the text. As children develop awareness of what they are expected to understand from their reading, teachers help them to understand what knowledge they already have that helps them interpret the text.

Preparation just prior to reading is usually the first step in the different strategies for facilitating comprehension. Research suggests that an important preparatory step for increasing comprehension is providing prior knowledge or activating the child's existing knowledge. In one study, researchers (Brown, Smiley, Day, & Townsend, 1977) gave two groups of children different sets of background information about an Indian tribe they were to read about. A third group got information about Spanish people irrelevant to the story. Both groups with Indian information recalled 24% more story information than the group with Spanish information. The recall errors of the two groups with Indian information were consistent with their background information. The authors concluded that helping children gain information prior to a story facilitates understanding and recall of the story, but the information can also color the understanding of the story (Brown, Smiley, Day, & Townsend, 1977). Beck, Omanson, and McKeown (1982) had similar findings, but emphasized that information focusing on the central theme of the story was more effective than generalized information.

Prior questioning and establishing comprehension goals before reading the passage are other frequently used preparatory strategies. These questions and goals alert children to what they should be looking for in the text (Levin & Pressley, 1981). These strategies are especially beneficial if the material to be read is difficult for children to understand (Hartley & Davis, 1976).

A third preparation strategy is clarifying content through pictures that can help "set the stage" for the reading. However, these pictures must be directly related to the text or they may be a hindrance (Rice, Doan, & Brown, 1981). Arnold and Brooks (1976) determined that pictures were more helpful than statements about the reading. Pictures included in the text have also been reported as helping students recall more information about a text (Guttman, Levin, & Pressley, 1977). It seems that pictures are extremely beneficial for slow learners in assisting comprehension (Bender & Levin, 1978).

The second phase in the teaching of reading process is the reading of the text itself. There has been controversy over the form that reading should take. Often the reading is done orally by children, without any prereading, going around the group in what is known as round-robin reading. Some children reading in this fashion stumble over words, read in a jerky manner, and get frequent corrections from classmates or the teacher. Anderson, Mason, and Shirley (1984) suggest that the children who are following along are not paying attention, and thus are not engaged in learning.

During oral reading, teachers correct and evaluate children's progress. Correcting errors as children make them has been shown to deter comprehension unless the teacher is careful (Allington, 1984). Anderson et al. (1985) indicate that children show greater gains in reading when corrections are made only for those errors that distort meaning. The child is given time to make the correction, and the teacher provides clues if this is unsuccessful. Finally, it seems important to have the child reread the sentence correctly in order to ensure better comprehension.

Oral reading can enhance comprehension if children have an opportunity to read the passage silently before reading aloud. Repeated readings have proven beneficial to poor readers, who have shown marked improvement in their ability to read new selections more accurately and in their comprehension skills (Samuels, 1985). Research indicates that the amount of silent or independent reading is related to children's gain in reading (Greany, 1980; Walberg & Tsai, 1984).

Postquestioning and discussion strategies with emphasis on developing different types of reading responses to the content of the text are strategies that teachers have used to assist and/or assess children's understanding of the content of a story. School-aged children and even some preschoolers have a sense of story grammars (Applebee, 1978; Whaley, 1981). When this knowledge is activated, children are better able to understand and remember details and events from the text (Bower, Black, & Turner, 1979). These questions and discussions, of either text content or story structure, when they are directed to helping children integrate prior knowledge, have been found to improve reading achievement significantly (Beck, Omanson, & McKeown, 1982; Hansen, 1981). Morrow's (1984) research lends support for providing both types of questions, regarding content and story structure, to aid children's comprehension.

*Writing and reading connections.*   As discussed earlier, the research in emergent literacy emphasizes the interactive nature of language arts skills. As children recreate experiences, draw or scribble to express their ideas, and play with writing, they are guided into the realization that writing is communication, and that to communicate truly, certain conventions must be followed if anyone else is to read their writing (Clay, 1991; Stotsky, 1983). Researchers have found that children move through a continual development both in understanding and producing print (Chomsky, 1972; Dobson, 1989; Sulzby, 1985). However, children's writing development does not always parallel their reading development.

Dobson (1989) identified five levels of print awareness that kindergarten and first-grade children discover as they interact with books and try their skill at writing.

1. Books contain meaning, and it is through reading that meaning is discovered.
2. The written text matches the spoken text.
3. One determines that match by applying letter–sound associations.
4. Words are separate units segregated by space.
5. Morphemes have constant spellings, but there can be a new combination of these spellings for a new meaning.

She found parallels of these insights in children's attempts at writing. She also noted that children's writing revealed more and more booklike language.

Sulzby, Barnhart, and Hieshima (1989) analyzed children's writing and rereading strategies over a 2-year period. They found developmental patterns in both the reading and writing. Children's emergent skills in rereading their early writings paralleled their emergent skills in reading from their favorite storybooks. The reading and writing emergent skills did not always develop simultaneously. For example, some children continued to scribble, use drawings, or use letter strings even late in the kindergarten year, but used a more advanced literacy skill, such as tracking their scribbles and retelling the story in a consistent manner. And some children who were using invented spelling were not able to track their writing when rereading.

In whole language classrooms teachers have been using strategies that connect reading and writing (Kawakami-Arakaki, Oshiro, & Farran, 1989; Teale & Martinez, 1989). (For curriculum suggestions, see May, 1990; Heller, 1991; Vacca, Vacca, & Grove, 1991.) Levistik (1990) highlights ways that classroom teachers use literature, writing, and content relating to historical events to increase children's ability and skills in reading, writing, and concept development.

International Business Machines Corporation has developed a formal Write-to-Read program for use by kindergarten and first-grade teachers. Children use the computer to write and correct stories even as they are learning to read. The Educational Testing Service has done an extensive study of this program and found that the kindergartners had a significant advantage over the control group in reading. By first grade, both groups of children were doing equally well on standardized tests of reading, but kindergarten and first-grade children in the Write-to-Read program wrote creative stories better than children in the regular programs (Murphy & Appel, 1984). In reviewing research related to the reading–writing connection, Harp (1987) and Holbrook (1987) pointed out that as children learned to write about their reading in varying contexts and shared this writing, they showed significant gains in reading comprehension and concept development.

## SUMMARY

Reading is a complex process. While research continues to identify more and more of the elements of this process, vast amounts of research have not given definitive answers to what the best methods for teaching are, nor does the research provide evidence that leads theorists to agree on how children learn to read. Though some might continue to argue over the best time for reading instruction to begin, many adhere to the notion that literacy begins early, is a function of experience, and continues in an ongoing pattern until death. However, research does offer sound theoretical bases and suggestions, and gives directions that can be helpful to teachers.

Though research can help teachers understand children's developmental patterns in learning to read, teachers must still develop skill in observing children, using theoretical concepts as a basis to determine what each child is in fact doing as he or she acquires the skill of reading. Age, intelligence, gender, environment, visual and auditory skills, letter and word knowledge, and metalinguistic abilities are all very important considerations in the reading process. From the research on method and strategy, it appears there is no one method that is better than any other or that will work for all children. However, the extensive research on emergent literacy and the recognition of the interactive aspect of the reading and writing process provide important information for teachers. Specific methods or strategies research, as well as the accumulation of ethnographic studies and case studies, inform teachers of different approaches that can be used and of the importance of helping children use skills developed in one area of speaking, reading, and writing to enhance skills in another area. Learning how to adapt this information so that children of differing literacy experiences and development can find success in schools is a challenge for teachers, administrators, university professors, and researchers.

## REFERENCES

Adams, M. J. (1990). *Beginning to read: Thinking and learning about print.* Cambridge, MA: MIT Press.

Adams, M. J., Allington, R. L., Chaney, J. H., Goodman, Y. M., Kapinus, B. A., McGee, L. M., Richgels, D. J., Schwartz, S. J., Shannon, P., Smitten, B., & Williams, J. P. (1991). Beginning to read: A critique by literacy professionals and a response by Marilyn Jager Adams. *The Reading Teacher, 44* (6), 370–395.

Allan, K. K. (1982). The development of young children's metalinguistic understanding of the word. *Journal of Educational Research, 76,* 89–93.

Allington, R. L. (1984). Oral reading. In P. D. Pearson (Ed.), *Handbook of reading research* (pp. 829–864). New York: Longman.

Anderson, R. C., Hiebert, E. H., Scott, J. A., & Wilkinson, I. A. G. (1985). *Becoming a nation of readers: The report of the Commission on Reading.* Washington, DC: National Institute of Education.

Anderson, R. C., Mason, J., & Shirley, L. (1984). The reading group: An experimental investigation of a labyrinth. *Reading Research Quarterly, 20,* 6–38.

Applebee, A. (1978). *Child's concept of story: Ages 2–17.* Chicago: University of Chicago Press.

Arnold, D. J., & Brooks, D. H. (1976). Influence of contextual organizing material on children's listening comprehension. *Journal of Educational Psychology, 68,* 711–716.

Artley, A. S. (1948). A study of certain factors presumed to be associated with reading and speech difficulties. *Journal of Speech and Hearing Disorders, 13,* 351–360.

Baghdan, M. (1984). *Our daughter learns to read and write: A case study from birth to three.* Newark, DE: International Reading Association.

Ball, E. W., & Blachman, B. A. (1991). Does phoneme awareness training in kindergarten make a difference in early word recognition and developmental spelling? *Reading Research Quarterly, 26* (1), 49–66.

Barr, R. (1984). Beginning reading instruction: From debate to reformation. In P. D. Pearson (Ed.), *Handbook of reading research* (pp. 545–581). New York: Longman.

Barrett, T. C. (1965). The relationship between measures of prereading visual discrimination and first grade reading achievement: A review of the literature. *Reading Research Quarterly, 1,* 51–76.

Bateman, B. (1983). A commentary on Johns' critique of Gumen and Hughes' study: Measuring the effects of intensive phonics vs. gradual phonics in beginning reading. In L. M. Gentile, M. L. Kamil, & J. S. Blanchard (Eds.), *Reading research revisited* (pp. 105–113). Columbus, OH: Charles E. Merrill.

Beck, I. L., Omanson, R. C., & McKeown, M. G. (1982). An instructional redesign of reading lessons: Effects on comprehension. *Reading Research Quarterly, 17,* 462–481.

Bender, B. G., & Levin, J. R. (1978). Pictures, imagery and retarded children's prose learning. *Journal of Educational Psychology, 20,* 583–588.

Biemiller, A. J. (1977–78). Relations between oral reading rates for letters, words and simple text in the development of reading achievement. *Reading Research Quarterly, 13,* 223–253.

Bissex, G. L. (1980). *GNYS at WRK: A child learns to write and read.* Cambridge, MA: Harvard University Press.

Bond, G. L., & Dykstra, R. (1967). The cooperative research program in first grade reading instruction. *Reading Research Quarterly, 2,* 5–142.

Bower, G. H., Black, J. B., & Turner, T. J. (1979). Scripts in memory for text. *Cognitive Psychology, 11,* 177–220.

Brown, A. L., Smiley, S. S., Day, J. D., & Townsend, M. A. R. (1977). Intrusion of a thematic idea in children's comprehension and retention of stories. *Child Development, 48,* 1454–1466.

Burmeister, L. E. (1971). Content of a phonics program based on particularly useful generalizations. In N. B. Smith (Ed.), *Reading methods and teacher improvements* (pp. 27–39). Newark, DE: International Reading Association.

Calkins, L. M. (1983). *Lessons from a child.* Portsmouth, NH: Heinemann.

Carbo, M. (1988). Debunking the great phonics myth. *Phi Delta Kappan, 70* (3), 226–240.

Cassidy, J., & Vukelich, C. (1980). Do the gifted read early? *The Reading Teacher, 33,* 578–582.

Ceprano, M. A. (1981). A review of selected research on methods of teaching sight words. *The Reading Teacher, 35,* 314–322.

Chall, J. S. (1967). *Learning to read: The great debate.* New York: McGraw-Hill.

Chall, J. S. (1989). Learning to read: The great debate 20 years later—a response to "Debunking the great phonics myth." *Phi Delta Kappan, 70* (7), 521–538.

Chomsky, C. (1972). Stages in language development and reading exposure. *Harvard Educational Review, 42,* 1–33.

Chomsky, C. (1979). Approaching reading through invented spelling. In L. B. Resnick & P. A. Weaver (Eds.), *Theory and practice of early reading* (Vol. 2, pp. 43–65). Hillsdale, NJ: Lawrence Erlbaum.

Clay, M. M. (1991). *Becoming literate: The construction of inner control.* Portsmouth, NH: Heinemann.

Clymer, T. (1963). The utility of phonic generalizations in primary grades. *The Reading Teacher, 16,* 252–258.

Cochran-Smith, M., & Lytle, S. L. (1990). Research on teaching and teacher research: The issues that divide. *Educational Researchers, 19* (2), 2–11.

Coltheart, M. (1979). When can children learn to read—and when should they be taught? In G. T. Waller & G. E. MacKinnon (Eds.), *Reading research: Advances in theory and practice* (Vol. 1, pp. 1–31). New York: Academic Press.

Cunningham, P. M. (1979). A compare/contrast theory of mediated word identification. *The Reading Teacher, 32,* 774–778.

De Hirsch, K., Jansky, J. J., & Langford, W. S. (1966). *Predicting reading failure.* New York: Harper & Row.

Dobson, L. (1989). Connections in learning to write and read: A study of children's development through kindergarten and first grade. In J. Mason (Ed.), *Reading and writing connections* (pp. 83–105). Boston: Allyn & Bacon.

Dolch, E. W., & Bloomster, M. (1937). Phonic readiness. *Elementary School Journal, 38,* 201–205.

Dunkin, M. J., & Biddle, B. J. (1974). *The study of teaching.* New York: Holt, Rinehart and Winston.

Durkin, D. D. (1966). *Children who read early.* New York: Teachers College Press.

Durkin, D. D. (1974–75). A six year study of children who learned to read at the age of four. *Reading Research Quarterly, 10,* 9–61.

Durkin, D. D. (1977). Facts about pre-first grade reading. In L. O. Ollila (Ed.), *The kindergarten child and reading* (pp. 1–12). Newark, DE: International Reading Association.

Durkin, D. D. (1978–79). What classroom observation reveals about reading comprehension instruction. *Reading Research Quarterly, 14,* 481–533.

Durkin, D. D. (1989). *Teaching them to read.* Boston: Allyn & Bacon.

Dwyer, C. A. (1973). Sex differences in reading: An evaluation of current theories. *Review of Educational Research, 43,* 455–467.

Dyson, A. H. (1986). Transitions and tensions: Interrelationships between the drawing, talking, and dictating of young children. *Research in the Teaching of English, 20* (4), 379–408.

Dyson, A. H. (1990). Symbol makers, symbol weavers: How children link play, pictures, and print. *Young Children, 45* (2), 50–57.

Edelsky, C. (1990). Whose agenda is this anyway? A response to McKenna, Robinson, and Miller. *Educational Researcher, 19* (8), 7–11.

Ehri, L. C. (1978). Beginning reading from a psycholinguistic perspective: Amalgamation of word identification. In F. B. Murray (Ed.), *The recognition of words* (pp. 1–33). Newark, DE: International Reading Association.

Ehri, L. C. (1979). Linguistic insight: Threshold of reading acquisition. In T. G. Waller & G. E. MacKinnon (Eds.), *Reading research: Advances in theory and practice* (pp. 63–117). New York: Academic Press.

Ehri, L. C. (1983). Summaries and critique of five studies related to letter name knowledge and learning to read. In L. M. Gentile, M. L. Kamil, & J. S. Blanchard (Eds.), *Reading research revisited* (pp. 129–154). Columbus, OH: Charles E. Merrill.

Ehri, L. C. (1989). Movement into word reading and spelling: How spelling contributes to reading. In J. Mason (Ed.), *Reading and writing connections* (pp. 65–83). Boston: Allyn & Bacon.

Engelmann, S., & Bruner, E. C. (1974). *DISTAR reading* I: *An instructional system.* Chicago: Science Research Associates.

Feitelson, D., & Goldstein, Z. (1986). Patterns of book ownership and reading to young children in Israeli school-oriented and nonschool-oriented families. *The Reading Teacher, 39,* 924–930.

Finn, P. J. (1990). *Helping children to learn to read.* New York: Longman.

Fisher, C. W., Filby, N. N., Marliave, R., Cahen, L. S., Dishaw, M. M., Moore, J. E., & Berliner, D. C. (1978). *Beginning Teacher Evaluation Study* (Technical report, V–1). San Francisco: Far West Laboratory.

Flavell, J. (1976). Metacognitive aspects of problem solving. In L. B. Resnick (Ed.), *The nature of intelligence* (pp. 231–235). Hillsdale, NJ: Lawrence Erlbaum.

Forrest-Pressley, D. L., & Waller, T. G. (1984). *Cognition, metacognition and reading.* New York: Springer-Verlag.

Fox, R., & Routh, D. K. (1976). Phonemic analysis and synthesis as word attack skills. *Journal of Educational Psychology, 68,* 70–74.

Gates, A. I. (1937). The necessary mental age for beginning reading. *Elementary School Journal, 37,* 497–508.

Gates, A. I. (1961). Sex differences in reading ability. *Elementary School Journal, 51,* 431–434.

Gibson, E. J., & Levin, H. (1975). *The psychology of reading.* Cambridge, MA: MIT Press.

Goldstein, D. M. (1976). Cognitive linguistic functioning and learning to read in preschoolers. *Journal of Educational Psychology, 68,* 680–688.

Goodman, K. S. (1967). Reading: A psycholinguistic guessing game. *Journal of Reading Specialist, 4,* 126–135.

Goodman, K. S. (1984). Unity in reading. In A. C. Purvis & O. Niles (Eds.), *Becoming readers in a complex society* (pp. 79–115). Chicago: University of Chicago Press.

Goodman, K. S., & Goodman, Y. M. (1979). Learning to read is natural. In L. B. Resnick & P. A. Weaver (Eds.), *Theory and practice of early reading* (Vol. 1, pp. 137–155). Hillsdale, NJ: Lawrence Erlbaum.

Goodman, K. S., Smith, E. B., Meredith, R., & Goodman, Y. M. (1987). *Language and thinking in school. A whole-language curriculum.* New York: Richard C. Owen.

Greany, V. (1980). Factors related to amount and type of leisure time reading. *Reading Research Quarterly, 15,* 337–357.

Guttman, W., Levin, J. R., & Pressley, M. (1977). Pictures, partial pictures and young children's oral prose learning. *Journal of Educational Psychology, 69,* 473–480.

Hansen, J. (1981). The effects of inference training and practice on young children's reading comprehension. *Reading Research Quarterly, 16,* 391–417.

Hansen, J. (1987). *When writers read.* Portsmouth, NH: Heinemann.

Harp, B. (1987). Why are your kids writing during reading time? *The Reading Teacher, 41* (1), 88–90.

Harste, J. C. (1985). Becoming a nation of readers: Beyond risk. In J. C. Harste

(Ed.), *Toward practical theory: A state of practice assessment of reading comprehension instruction*. Bloomington: Language Education Department, Indiana University.

Harste, J. C., Woodward, V., & Burke, C. L. (1984). *Language stories and literacy lessons*. Portsmouth, NH: Heinemann.

Hartley, J., & Davis, I. K. (1976). Preinstructional strategies: The role of pretests, behavioral objectives, overviews and advance organizers. *Review of Educational Research, 46*, 239–265.

Heath, S. B. (1983). *Ways with words: Language, life, and work in communities and classrooms*. New York: Cambridge University Press.

Heilman, A. W., Blair, T. R., & Rupley, W. H. (1986). *Principles and practices of teaching reading*. Columbus, OH: Charles E. Merrill.

Heller, M. F. (1991). *Reading–writing connections: From theory to practice*. New York: Longman.

Hiebert, E. H. (1988). The role of literacy experiences in early childhood programs. *The Elementary School Journal, 89* (2), 161–171.

Hiebert, E. H. (1991). Literacy contexts and literacy processes. *Language Arts, 68*, 134–139.

Holbrook, H. T. (1987). Writing to learn in the social studies. *The Reading Teacher, 41* (2), 216–219.

Jackson, N. E., & Biemiller, A. J. (1985). Letter, word and text reading times of precocious and average readers. *Child Development, 56*, 196–206.

Johnson, D. D. (1973–74). Sex differences in reading across cultures. *Reading Research Quarterly, 9*, 67–86.

Johnson, D. D., & Baumann, J. F. (1984). Word identification. In P. D. Pearson (Ed.), *Handbook of reading research* (pp. 583–608). New York: Longman.

Justman, J. (1965). Academic aptitude and reading test scores of disadvantaged children showing varying degree of mobility. *Journal of Educational Measurement, 2*, 151–155.

Kawakami-Arakaki, A. J., Oshiro, M. E., & Farran, D. C. (1989). Research to practice: Integrating reading and writing in a kindergarten curriculum. In J. Mason (Ed.), *Reading and writing connections* (pp. 199–219). Boston: Allyn & Bacon.

Kean, M., Summers, A., Ravietz, M., & Farber, I. (1979). *What works in reading*. Philadelphia: School District of Philadelphia.

Kincade, K. M., & Kleine, P. F. (1990, April). *Children's reading task by gender interactions: Implications for research and practice*. Paper presented at the annual meeting of the American Educational Research Association, Boston.

Lesgold, A. M., & Resnick, L. B. (1982). How reading difficulties develop: Perspective from a longitudinal study. In J. P. Das, R. F. Mulcahy, & A. E. Wall (Eds.), *Theory and research in learning disabilities* (pp. 155–187). New York: Plenum.

Levin, J. R., & Pressley, M. (1981). Improving children's prose comprehension: Selected strategies that seem to succeed. In C. M. Santa & B. L. Hayes (Eds.), *Children's prose comprehension: Research and practice* (pp. 27–53). Newark, DE: International Reading Association.

Levistik, L. S. (1990). Mediating content through literary texts. *Language Arts, 67* (8), 848–852.

Lyon, R. (1977). Auditory-perceptual training: The state of the art. *Journal of Learning Disabilities, 10,* 564–572.

Manzo, A. V. (1969). The request procedure. *Journal of Reading, 11,* 123–126.

Mason, J. (Ed.). (1989). *Reading and writing connections.* Boston: Allyn & Bacon.

Mason, J., & Osborne, J. (1982). *When do children begin "reading to learn"? A survey in grades two through five.* Urbana: University of Illinois, Center for the Study of Reading.

Masonheimer, P. E., Drum, P. A., & Ehri, L. C. (1984). Does environmental print identification lead children into word reading? *Journal of Reading Behavior, 14,* 257–271.

May, F. B. (1990). *Reading as communication: An interactive approach.* Columbus, OH: Charles E. Merrill.

McKee, P., Brezeniski, J. E., & Harrison, A. L. (1966). *The effectiveness of teaching reading in kindergarten* (Cooperative Research Project No. 5-0381). Denver: Denver Public Schools and Colorado State Department of Education.

Morphett, M. V., & Washburne, C. (1983). When should children begin to read? *Elementary School Journal, 31,* 496–503. Reprinted in L. M. Gentile, M. L. Kamil, & J. S. Blanchard (Eds.), *Reading research revisited* (pp. 163–171). Columbus, OH: Charles E. Merrill. (Original work published 1931)

Morrow, L. M. (1984). Reading stories to young children: Effects of story structure and traditional questioning strategies on comprehension. *Journal of Reading Behavior, 16,* 273–288.

Morrow, L. M., & Smith, J. K. (1990). The effects of group size on interactive storybook reading. *Reading Research Quarterly, 15* (3), 213–231.

Muehl, S., & DiNello, M. C. (1976). Early first grade skills related to subsequent reading performance: A seven year follow-up. *Journal of Reading Behavior, 8,* 67–81.

Muehl, S., & Kremenak, S. (1966). Ability to match information within and between auditory and visual sense modalities and subsequent reading achievement. *Journal of Educational Psychology, 57,* 230–239.

Murphy, R. T., & Appel, L. R. (1984). *Evaluation of the writing to read instructional system, 1982–1984.* Princeton, NJ: Educational Testing Service.

Paradis, E. E., & Peterson, J. (1975). Readiness training implications from research. *The Reading Teacher, 28,* 445–448.

Paul, R. (1976). Invented spelling in kindergarten. *Young Children, 32,* 95–200.

Pflaum, S. W., Walberg, H. J., Kargianes, M. L., & Racher, S. P. (1980). Reading instruction: A quantitative method. *Educational Researcher, 9,* 12–18.

Reutzel, D. R., & Cooter, R. B. (1990). Whole language: Comparative effects on first-grade reading achievement. *Journal of Educational Research, 83* (5), 252–257.

Ribowsky, H. (1985). The effects of a code emphasis approach and a whole language approach upon emergent literacy of kindergarten children (Report No. CS–008–397). (ERIC Document Reproduction Service No. ED 269 720)

Rice, D. R., Doan, R. L., & Brown, S. J. (1981). The effects of pictures on reading comprehension, speed and interest of second grade students. *Reading Improvement, 18,* 308–312.

Robinson, H. M. (1963). Vocabulary: Speaking, listening, reading and writing. In H. A. Robinson (Ed.), *Reading and the language arts* (pp. 167–176). Chicago: University of Chicago Press.

Rose, T. L., & Furr, P. M. (1984). Negative effects of illustrations as word cues. *Journal of Learning Disabilities, 17,* 334–337.

Rosenblatt, L. M. (1989). Writing and reading: The transactional theory. In J. Mason (Ed.), *Reading and writing connections* (pp. 153–177). Boston: Allyn & Bacon.

Rosenshine, B., & Stevens, R. (1984). Classroom instruction in reading. In P. D. Pearson (Ed.), *Handbook of reading research* (pp. 745–798). New York: Longman.

Rozin, P., Bressman, B., & Taft, M. (1974). Do children understand the basic relationship between speech and writing? The mow-motorcycle text. *Journal of Reading Behavior, 6,* 327–334.

Rumelhart, D. E. (1977). Toward an interactive model of reading. In S. Dornic (Ed.), *Attention and performance* (pp. 573–607). Hillsdale, NJ: Lawrence Erlbaum.

Ryan, E. B., McNamara, S. R., & Kenney, M. (1977). Lexical awareness and reading performance among beginning readers. *Journal of Reading Behavior, 9,* 399–400.

Sampson, M. R., & Briggs, L. D. (1981). What does research say about beginning reading? *Reading Horizons, 21,* 114–118.

Samuels, S. J. (1967). Attentional process in reading: The effects of pictures on the acquisition of reading response. *Journal of Educational Psychology, 50,* 337–342.

Samuels, S. J. (1981). Characteristics of exemplary reading programs. In T. J. Guthrie (Ed.), *Comprehension and teaching: Research Reviews* (pp. 253–273). Newark, DE: International Reading Association.

Samuels, S. J. (1985). Automaticity and repeated reading. In J. Osborn, P. T. Wilson, & R. C. Anderson (Eds.), *Reading education: Foundations for a literate America* (pp. 215–230). Lexington, MA: Lexington Books.

Schickedanz, J. A. (1990). The jury is still out on the effects of whole language and language experience approaches for beginning reading: A critique of Stahl and Miller's study. *Review of Educational Research, 60* (1), 127–131.

Shannon, P. (1983). The use of commercial reading materials in American elementary schools. *Reading Research Quarterly, 19,* 68–85.

Shapiro, J., & Gunderson, L. (1988). A comparison of vocabulary generated by grade 1 students in whole language classrooms and basal reader vocabulary. *Reading Research and Instruction, 27* (2), 40–46.

Singer, H. S., Samuels, J., and Spiroff, J. (1973–74). The effects of pictures and contextual conditions on learning responses to printed words. *Reading Research Quarterly, 9,* 555–567.

Smith, F. (1988). *Understanding reading: A psycholinguistic analysis of reading and learning to read*. Hillsdale, NJ: Lawrence Erlbaum.

Snow, C. E., & Ninio, A. (1986). The contracts of literacy: What children learn from learning to read books. In W. H. Teale & E. Sulzby (Eds.), *Emergent literacy: Writing and reading* (pp. 116–139). Norwood, NJ: Ablex.

Spache, E. (1976). *Reading activities for child involvement*. Boston: Allyn & Bacon.

Speer, O. B., & Lamb, G. S. (1976). First grade reading ability and fluency in naming verbal symbols. *The Reading Teacher, 29*, 572–576.

Stahl, S. A., & Miller, P. D. (1989). Whole language and language experience approaches for beginning reading: A quantitative research synthesis. *Review of Educational Research, 59* (1), 87–116.

Stallings, J. A., & Kaskowitz, D. (1974). *Follow-through classroom observation evaluation, 1972–73*. Menlo Park, CA: Stanford Research Institute.

Stanovich, K. E. (1990). A call for an end to the paradigm wars in reading research. *Journal of Reading Behavior, 22* (3), 221–231.

Stebbins, L. B., St. Pierre, R. G., Proper, E. C., Anderson, R. B., & Cerva, T. R. (1977). *Education as experimentation: A planned variation model: Vol. IV-A. An evaluation of follow-through*. Cambridge, MA: Abt Associates.

Stein, N. L., & Glenn, C. G. (1982). Children's concept of time: Story schemata and prose processing. In W. Friedman (Ed.), *The developmental psychology of time* (pp. 255–283). New York: Academic Press.

Stotsky, S. (1983). Research on reading/writing relationships: A synthesis and suggested directions. *Language Arts, 60* (5), 627–642.

Sulzby, E. (1985). Kindergartners as writers and readers. In M. Farr (Ed.), *Advances in writing research: Vol. 1. Children's early writing development* (pp. 127–139). Norwood, NJ: Ablex.

Sulzby, E., Barnhart, J., & Hieshima, J. A. (1989). Forms of writing and rereading from writing: A preliminary report. In J. Mason (Ed.), *Reading and writing connections* (pp. 41–63). Boston: Allyn & Bacon.

Sutton, M. H. (1969). Children who learned to read in kindergarten: A longitudinal study. *The Reading Teacher, 22*, 595–602, 683.

Taylor, B. M., Frye, J. B., & Goetz, T. M. (1990). Reducing the number of reading skill activities in the elementary classroom. *Journal of Reading Behavior, 22* (2), 167–179.

Taylor, D. (1989). Toward a unified theory of literacy learning and instructional practices. *Phi Delta Kappan, 71* (3), 184–193.

Teale, W. H. (1986). Home background and young children's literacy development. In W. H. Teale & E. Sulzby (Eds.), *Emergent literacy: Writing and reading* (pp. 173–207). Norwood, NJ: Ablex.

Teale, W. H., & Martinez, M. G. (1989). Connecting writing: Fostering literacy in kindergarten children. In J. Mason (Ed.), *Reading and writing connections* (pp. 177–199). Boston: Allyn & Bacon.

Teale, W. H., & Sulzby, E. (1986). Emergent literacy as a perspective for examining how young children become writers and readers. In W. H. Teale & E. Sulzby

(Eds.), *Emergent literacy: Writing and reading* (pp. vii–xxv). Norwood, NJ: Ablex.

Templeton, S. (1980). Young children invent words: Developing concepts of "wordness." *The Reading Teacher, 33,* 454–459.

Torrey, J. W. (1979). Reading that comes naturally: The early reader. In T. G. Waller & G. E. MacKinnon, *Reading research: Advances in theory and practice* (pp. 117–145). New York: Academic Press.

Trachtenburg, P. (1990). Using children's literature to enhance phonics instruction. *The Reading Teacher, 43* (9), 648–654.

Turner, R. L. (1989). The "great" debate—can both Carbo and Chall be right? *Phi Delta Kappan, 71* (4), 276–283.

Vacca, J. L., Vacca, R. T., & Grove, M. K. (1991). *Reading and learning to read.* Boston: Little, Brown.

Walberg, H. J., & Tsai, S. (1984). Reading achievement and diminishing returns to time. *Journal of Educational Psychology, 76,* 442–451.

Walberg, H. J., & Tsai, S. (1985). Correlates of reading achievement and attitude: A national assessment study. *Journal of Educational Research, 78,* 159–167.

Walker, G. H., & Kuerbitz, I. E. (1979). Reading to preschoolers as an aid to successful beginning reading. *Reading Improvement, 16,* 149–154.

Weaver, P., & Shonkoff, F. (1978). *Research within reach: A research-guided response to concerns of reading educators.* Washington, DC: U.S. Department of Health, Education and Welfare.

Whaley, J. F. (1981). Readers' expectations for story structure. *Reading Research Quarterly, 17,* 90–114.

Wigfield, A., & Asher, S. R. (1984). Social and motivational influences on reading. In P. D. Pearson (Ed.), *Handbook of reading research* (pp. 423–452). New York: Longman.

Williams, J. P. (1985). The case for explicit decoding instruction. In J. Osborne, P. T. Wilson, & R. C. Anderson (Eds.), *Reading education: Foundations for a literate America* (pp. 205–215). Lexington, MA: Lexington Books.

# CHAPTER 6

# New Directions for the Early Childhood Mathematics Curriculum

PATRICIA F. CAMPBELL AND DEBORAH A. CAREY

Recent reports guiding curriculum reform in mathematics education suggest that learning mathematics is a problem-solving activity (e.g., Commission on Standards for School Mathematics, 1989; Commission on Teaching Standards for School Mathematics, 1991; National Research Council, 1989). These reports were informed by a substantial body of research developed over the past decade about how children learn mathematics, particularly about how children come to understand number and quantitative relations. Rather than suggesting that mathematics is a set of skills and procedures that children must acquire, mathematics is perceived of as a way of thinking about "relationships among mathematical entities and between mathematical statements and situations involving quantities, relationships, and patterns" (Resnick, 1988, p. 33). If mathematics instruction is to foster thinking, then it must shift to a focus on problem-solving tasks because problem solving is the context for developing children's mathematical thinking. Therefore, in designing an appropriate mathematics curriculum for young children, a critical factor is the creation of a problem-solving environment from which mathematical ideas can emerge.

This chapter examines recent research that may inform curriculum development in early childhood mathematics. Theoretical perspectives for defining an appropriate mathematics curriculum are considered first. Second, because knowledge about children's thinking can provide a framework for defining curriculum (Carpenter, 1988), interpretations of research on chil-

The work reported herein was supported by grants from the National Science Foundation to the first author (MDR–89554692) and to the second author (MDR–8550236). Any opinions, findings, and conclusions expressed in this publication are those of the authors, and no endorsement from the National Science Foundation should be inferred.

dren's mathematical thinking are presented. The chapter then reviews issues that must be addressed when creating problem-solving environments,
drawing from current research projects that consider teacher roles and
teacher decision making. Suggestions are also offered as to how mathematical concepts can be clustered around themes rather than dealt with as isolated topics in the primary classroom.

## THEORETICAL PERSPECTIVES ON TEACHING AND LEARNING MATHEMATICS

"In reality, no one can *teach* mathematics. Effective teachers are those
who can stimulate students to *learn* mathematics. Educational research offers compelling evidence that students learn mathematics well only when
they *construct* their own mathematical understanding" (National Research
Council, 1989, p. 58). This citation offers a perspective on mathematics
teaching and learning that mathematics education researchers began to advance in the late 1970s. In 1989, two documents were published to envision
the meaning of this perspective in mathematics classrooms and to provide
standards for revising the school mathematics curriculum toward this vision
in order to reform and revitalize mathematics instruction (Commission on
Standards for School Mathematics, 1989; National Research Council, 1989).
Judging by the consensus by which these two documents have been received by scholars, practitioners, and policy makers, it may be stated that
the mathematics education community accepts four themes regarding the
nature of mathematics and mathematical knowledge.

1. Mathematics is a growing, dynamic discipline.
2. Students actively and personally construct their mathematical
   knowledge.
3. Understanding in mathematics comes from perceiving relationships
   either between or within mathematical ideas.
4. Knowledge may be fostered through social interaction.

### Mathematics—A Dynamic Discipline

"Knowledge is not a basket of facts" (Anderson, 1984, p. 5), and mathematics is not a static network of rules that are conveyed by teachers and
absorbed by students for recall upon demand. Mathematics is the active
science of searching for order and pattern in the world around us (National
Research Council, 1989). To know and understand mathematics is to "do"
mathematics. The National Council of Teachers of Mathematics calls for a

mathematics curriculum that engages children in instructional activity that causes them to explore, examine, quantify, order, relate, invent, use, represent, verify, interpret, justify, and communicate (Commission on Standards for School Mathematics, 1989). Because mathematics revolves around the investigation of problems derived from this search for order and pattern, it continues to grow. As students solve one problem, it should give rise to further questions for investigation. Mathematics curriculum and instruction must emphasize the power and potential of mathematics, the interrelatedness of mathematical ideas, and the development of quantitative reasoning, as well as the confidence to undertake such investigation (Romberg & Tufte, 1987).

## Construction of Knowledge

This perception of mathematics and of a mathematics curriculum does not coincide with instruction wherein bits of information that compose a network of established rules and procedures are transmitted to children (via either textbooks, worksheets, or teacher demonstration). The current theoretical perspective is that students actively construct mathematical knowledge; they do not absorb mathematics, nor do they passively receive it. Its basic tenet is that understanding is constructed by actively processing and relating new information or experiences to what was already known or by connecting ideas that were previously understood but isolated from each other. Thus, learning is more than simply accumulating bits of information. Learning means new insights in the way that one thinks about something. However, these insights come from within; they are not meaningless responses in a manner previously prescribed by an authority figure (cf. Baroody, 1987). This perspective, generally termed *constructivism*, is rooted in the writings of Piaget but extended through the recent work of researchers in psychology and mathematics education (e.g., Resnick, 1983b; von Glasersfeld, 1991).

In their studies of mathematical knowledge, researchers are beginning to distinguish between conceptual knowledge and procedural knowledge. Conceptual knowledge refers to the knowledge of relationships. Mathematical concepts—that is, principles and constraints that define or characterize ideas and experiences—are relationships; yet these concepts can be related or integrated with other concepts. Children develop conceptual knowledge when they construct relationships between pieces of information. Procedural knowledge entails (1) the written symbols that are used to represent mathematical ideas, and (2) the rules and procedures that are used when solving mathematics problems. These procedures should entail strategies that foster the solution of problems while preserving or enriching the constructed meaning of mathematical concepts. Thus procedural knowledge should have a conceptual base and generally has a symbolic referent (Gelman & Greeno, 1989; Hiebert & Lefevre, 1986).

## Mathematics Instruction

This constructivist view of mathematics learning has implications for instruction. There are numerous studies in progress in primary mathematics classrooms that are investigating instruction based on a constructivist model. These studies are generally applying one of two instructional approaches, each of which relies on research-based knowledge of the development of children's learning of mathematics, but differs in what it defines to be the optimal learning environment.

One approach utilizes visible representations (manipulative materials, diagrams, and/or symbols) to characterize the desired mathematical relationship or concept in a form that is felt to be more meaningful or accessible to the child. The critical points of the instruction revolve around making connections between the varying representations (e.g., between objects and numerals) as a means of clarifying the mathematical concept (Fuson & Briars, 1990; Hiebert & Wearne, 1992; Resnick, 1983a, 1983b). The level of direction provided by the teacher regarding manipulation of the symbolic or concrete referents varies in these studies, but it is often quite directive during the initial lessons. A question raised regarding this instructional approach is what meaning is attached to these visible representations by the child (Baroody, 1989; Cobb et al., 1991). The issue is as follows: The teacher or adult readily identifies the intended mathematical structure within the referent. But is that referent meaningful to the child? Does the child interpret the same mathematical structure perceived by the adult, some variant on that structure, or no structure at all (Nesher, 1989)? Further, if a teacher directly instructs or demonstrates a procedure, either symbolically or with manipulatives, does that limit the probability that the child will reason and make sense of the activity? Might the child simply attempt to mimic the teacher's actions (Cobb, 1988)? Questions regarding children's mathematical sense making are addressed later in the chapter in terms of children's use of place-value manipulatives.

Another approach being studied also involves the use of manipulatives but limits teachers' direct instruction. This approach uses cognitive-based research as a means of identifying mathematical activities wherein children are engaged in solving problems that are challenging but conceptually attainable (Cobb, 1988). These activities may also be intended to provoke the child to relate existing understandings, to construct new knowledge, or to develop strategies or procedures. Because circumstantially based knowledge may be applied by a child when solving problems based in a context that is familiar to that child (Leinhardt, 1988), these instructional activities may evolve from experiences common and familiar to children. In this approach, the teacher does not demand a particular procedure or expect the children to use their materials in a prescribed manner. This approach is not simply discovery learning. Rather, the teacher must pose tasks that may stimulate appropriate conceptual reorganizations in his or her students. This then requires the teacher to understand the expected developmental sequence of mathematical understandings, as well as the current levels of mathematical understandings held by the children.

Researchers in mathematics education also differ regarding the use of manipulative materials within this approach. While some researchers (e.g., Cobb et al., 1991; Fennema, Carpenter, & Peterson, 1989a) utilize manipulatives, they do so after first considering the degree to which a referent might foster children's own thinking and the potential for that referent to assist the children in communicating their meaning to each other and to the teacher (Fischbein, 1987). However, Kamii (1990; Kamii & Joseph, 1988) opposes the use of manipulatives such as bundles of counting sticks, saying that young children do not abstract concepts from concrete referents nor do they internalize concepts from the external, physical environment.

## Social Interaction and the Learning of Mathematics

If mathematical knowledge is actively constructed by "doing" mathematics, then learners must be engaged in instructional activity that encourages them to investigate, represent, interpret, and relate ideas. It has been hypothesized that construction of understandings may be facilitated when students share their interpretations or conjectures, offer verification or explain their reasoning, or, if necessary, justify their perceptions (Lampert, 1990; Resnick, 1988). Cobb and his colleagues (Cobb et al., 1991) posit that classrooms that foster this type of social interaction permit the children and the teacher to "mutually construct taken-to-be-shared mathematical interpretations and understandings" (p. 6). Currently, there are a number of research studies that are investigating the teaching and learning of mathematics within classrooms that seek to employ these social settings (e.g., Lampert, 1990; Yackel, Cobb, Wood, Wheatley, & Merkel, 1990). A common characteristic of the social interaction in many of these classrooms is the sharing of approaches or strategies by the children without evaluation or judgment by the teacher. The teacher or other children may raise questions, but, in order to enhance children's trust and willingness to talk about mathematics and to support their confidence to investigate further problems, the teacher does not judge the correctness of the understandings constructed by the children.

CHILDREN'S MATHEMATICAL THINKING

## Developing Number Sense

"The major objective of elementary school mathematics should be to develop number sense" (National Research Council, 1989, p. 46). This recommendation identifies a critical distinction between traditional mathematics programs for young children and a mathematics curriculum that supports and fosters children's understanding. Although researchers in cognitive psychology and mathematics education have not clarified either a definition or a theoretical model of number sense (Greeno, 1991; Sowder & Schappelle, 1989), a consensus regarding the characteristics of number sense is emerging. The NCTM *Curriculum and Evaluation Standards* (Commission on Standards for School Mathematics, 1989) notes that children who have number sense understand the meaning of number as they are able to define many different relationships among numbers. In addition to recognizing the relative size of numbers and the effect of operating on numbers, these children define their own referents for use in measuring common objects and events. Number sense is a flexible way of thinking about numbers, and it presupposes a child's belief that mathematics should and does make sense (Carpenter, 1989; Resnick, 1989; Silver, 1989). Because it entails flexible thinking about numerical situations, it is presumed that number sense advances problem solving, supports children's construction of more enriched understandings, and perpetuates its own development.

According to a cognitivist perspective, if a child has a concept of a number, then the child has constructed a meaning for that number in terms of its relationship to other numbers. For example, five is

Two and three
One more than four
A lot less than 30
Only a little less than seven
As many fingers as are on one hand
With five more, 10 altogether

An early childhood curriculum that fosters the development of number sense permits children to understand number as more than the product of counting.

*Early constructs of quantity.*   The next section of this chapter addresses research regarding the development of meaningful counting, from rote counting to place-value numeration concepts. But first, we will consider the development of a concept of number. Through experiences in the home, young children develop primitive notions of quantity. As children begin to solve problems in their environment involving quantity, they begin to construct meaning for number (Fuson, 1989; Gelman & Meck, 1986; Saxe, Guberman, & Gearhart, 1987). Steffe and his colleagues (Cobb, 1987; Steffe, Cobb, & von Glasersfeld, 1988) have investigated the types of entities or settings for which children display increasingly sophisticated meanings for number. They note that initially children count collections of objects and learn to construct sets of a given size, but require physical objects to which they attach their numerical words. With growth, children begin to quantify not only objects but also motions that they themselves create (pointing to locations, putting up fingers). Eventually, children abstract counting. When a child abstracts counting, the child's construction of meaning for a number (e.g., "five") is independent of the presence of concrete objects or motor activity. To a child who is an abstract counter, number refers not only to any set, image, or action that contains or depicts that many items, but also to the sequence bounded by that number (e.g., "1, 2, 3, 4, 5"). Thus, abstract counters can count the act of counting. For example, in the problem, *Marissa has 7 stickers. How many more stickers does she need to have 11 stickers?* an abstract counter may respond, "8, 9, 10, 11 . . . She needs 4 more stickers."

*Part-whole constructions.*   A number may be associated with a set of objects. However, that set can also be separated into subsets, and each of those subsets also has a referent number. This critical partitioning relationship within number is generally termed part-part-whole. Resnick (1983a) noted the importance of this construction, stating:

> Probably the major conceptual achievement of the early school years is the interpretation of numbers in terms of part and whole relationships. With the application of a Part-Whole schema to quantity, it becomes possible for children to think about numbers as compositions of other numbers. This enrichment of number understanding permits forms of mathematical problem solving and interpretation that are not available to younger children. (p. 114)

With a part-whole construction, children may relate the concepts of number, addition, and subtraction (Baroody, Ginsburg, & Waxman, 1983); reach the most advanced problem-solving level for addition and subtraction problems (Riley, Greeno, & Heller, 1983); and support the conceptual adjustments involved when learning place value (Resnick, 1983a). Fischer (1990) noted that a kindergarten mathematics curriculum based on a part-part-whole approach fostered children's development of number concepts and facilitated their construction of strategies to solve addition and subtraction word problems, even though addition and subtraction applications were not taught.

## Counting and Numeration

*Early counting.*    The ability to find out *how many* is a powerful tool that children use as they begin to model and solve problems. Researchers offer differing perspectives regarding the meaning and growth of counting. Some researchers contend that children first learn a rote sequence of number words without reference to the objects being counted and then make the transition to coordinating each number word in the sequence with an object in a set to determine the cardinality of the set (Fuson, 1989). These researchers do not presume that initial "attempt[s] to carry out counting activity" (p. 398) indicate a manifestation of implicit counting principles. Others suggest that even very young children have some implicit principled understanding of counting because they respond to the presence of quantity in their environment (Gelman & Greeno, 1989; Strauss & Curtis, 1984). Despite differences in defining an initial principled knowledge of counting, it is generally accepted that explicit knowledge of counting is a prerequisite for increasing, decreasing, and comparing quantities (Greeno, Riley, & Gelman, 1984). In most instances, the ability to count rationally enables children to solve simple word problems.

Gelman and Gallistel (1978) define five principles of counting.

1. *Stable order*—Counting names are used in a stable order.
2. *One-one correspondence*—Every object is assigned one and only one unique counting name.
3. *Cardinality*—The last counting name identifies the number in the set.
4. *Order irrelevance*—Objects may be counted in any order, and a change in the order does not affect the total.
5. *Abstraction*—Any set, or collection, of objects may be counted.

Gelman and Meck (1986) posit that the first three principles represent a developmental sequence in learning how to count, although Fuson (1991) suggests the sequence in which these principles are acquired may depend on the size of the set counted. Fuson (1991) characterizes five levels of qualitative change in children's use of number words within a counting task. For example, initially children must begin their counting sequence with the words, "one, two, three,. . . ." As their understanding of number matures, they are able to begin a count with a number other than one.

*Numeration.*    Children initially use number words to represent *unitary conceptual structures*, where each number word refers to a single item in a collection of objects (Fuson, 1990). For example, a child counting a set of 26 blocks will count "1, 2, 3, . . . 24, 25, 26" and will interpret the number word "twenty-six" as referring to the total collection of 26 single objects. This interpretation of number does not reflect an understanding of our base-ten number system but does allow a child to operate with numbers larger than 10. A more sophisticated structure for multidigit numbers is constructed by children when they "disembed" groups of 10 objects from the total collection recognizing that an item may simultaneously be assigned to a group (one of 10 objects) and to the collection (one of 26 objects) (Steffe, Cobb, & von Glasersfeld, 1988). When children disembed, they have begun "to construct *multiunit conceptual structures* in which the meanings or referents of the number words are collections of entities" (Fuson, 1990, p. 273). For example, a child understands that 26 is composed of two 10s (group of 10 objects) and 6 single objects. Each single object (the remaining six) represents an additional unit to be counted, a *unit of one.* Understanding multiunit structures is the foundation for developing place-value concepts. Unless children are able to construct the multiunits, their understanding of operations on multidigit numbers is limited (Cobb & Wheatley, 1988).

The complexity of interpreting multidigit numbers is influenced by language. Recent work by Fuson (1990, 1991; Fuson & Kwon, 1991) suggests that the English system of number words does not support the conceptual components of multiunit numbers. There are irregularities in the English system that make it difficult to count and to identify the tens and ones structure in two-digit numbers. For example, as children learn the counting word sequence, there is consistency in counting *within* decades (e.g., 1, 2, 3, . . . 7, 8, 9; 21, 22, 23, . . . 27, 28, 29), but children have difficulty bridging *across* decades (e.g., 21, 22, . . . 28, 29,??). In terms of supporting conceptual structures, 26 is named "twenty-six" in the English language. The named value representation for 26 in several Asian languages (e.g., Chinese, Japanese, Korean), is "two ten six," making explicit the idea that the number is composed of two units of 10 and six units of one. In English the link between the number word for numbers between 10 and 20 and the conceptual structure of the number is even less transparent. For example, in the number word "thirteen" there is little support for children's construction of 13 as one unit of 10 and three units of one. There is much discussion about the appropriate placement of the study of numbers between 10 and 20 in the curriculum because of the inconsistencies within the number names that identify the teens (Baroody, 1990; Fuson, 1990). In a comparison of the children who spoke English or an Asian language, Fuson and Kwon (1991) reported that speakers of the Asian languages seemed to construct multiunit conceptual structures for two-digit numbers, and the English-speaking cohort constructed only unitary conceptual structures. The Asian languages, which emphasize the conceptual structure of numbers, were found to influence children's understanding of multiunits. Essentially, the string of English counting words implies a unitary meaning for numbers and does not encourage children to think of number with the more sophisticated construction of multiunits.

The transition from counting by ones to counting by tens, hundreds, and so on, is necessary in order for children to develop effective problem-solving strategies and meaning for place value. Successful manipulation of symbols within computation problems does not imply this transition. Children may compute accurately without understanding (Kamii & Joseph, 1988; Lindquist, 1989). Several tasks have been developed to assess children's understanding of number and numeration (Bednarz & Janvier, 1982; Cobb & Wheatley, 1988; Hiebert & Wearne, 1992; Ross, 1989). For example, Kamii (1985, 1989) describes a digit correspondence task where a child is shown the numeral 16 and asked to construct a set with 16 chips. Then the child is asked which part of the set is represented by each of the digits in the numeral, first focusing on the 6, then on the 1. Children who do not understand place value often correctly respond that the 6 represents six chips in the set, but they assign only one chip, rather than 10 chips, to the numeral 1, the tens digit. This response indicates that the multidigit number is perceived of as a series of concatenated single digits, and the relative position of the digits is not significant (Fuson, 1990). As a result of this assessment, Kamii (1989) posits that direct instruction with traditional addition and subtraction algorithms, where columns of numbers are treated as single units and operated on from right to left, inhibits children's understanding.

*Place-value instruction.*   Understanding how children make the transition from unitary to multiunit conceptual structures has direct implications for instruction. Fuson and Briars (1990) report a series of studies where first- and second-grade teachers used base-ten blocks (see Figure 6.1) to support children's construction of multiunit conceptual structures and an understanding of place-value concepts. This structured teaching/learning setting was characterized by the study of advanced counting strategies for adding and subtracting sums to 18, followed by work with groupings of 10. Children

**Figure 6.1    Base-ten blocks**

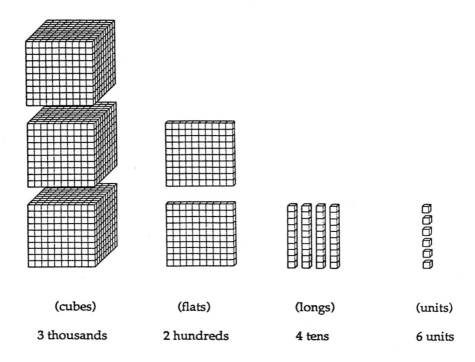

|  |  |  |  |
|---|---|---|---|
| (cubes) | (flats) | (longs) | (units) |
| 3 thousands | 2 hundreds | 4 tens | 6 units |

3,246

were then taught how to link actions on the base-ten blocks with written procedures for adding and subtracting multidigit numbers; trading ten-for-one was always ordered from right to left. The use of base-ten blocks seemed to support the construction of multiunits for second graders and above-average first graders. Average and below-average first graders maintained a unitary counting sequence, but they did not construct multiunit conceptual structures. When problem-solving instruction is carefully designed to facilitate the link between children's actions on concrete models and symbolic representations, it has been reported that children's understanding of place value increases (Hiebert & Wearne, 1992).

In general, the use of concrete models to facilitate young children's mathematical thinking has been accepted as an appropriate teaching strategy. However, the use of manipulatives, such as base-ten blocks or unifix cubes, to help children make the transition from constructing unitary to constructing multiunit conceptual structures raises two specific issues (Baroody, 1989; Kamii, 1989).

First, if manipulatives are used in instruction, there is a caution about what children are actually learning from them. Ross (1989) suggests that concrete embodiments have their limitations and may be successfully manipulated without meaning. A manipulative can be treated as a symbol system. Children may learn the rules and procedures associated with a given manipulative material without ever establishing the link between that manipulative and the concept it is to embody. For example, the relationship of ten-for-one already exists in base-ten blocks where 1 ten is a rod of 10 units and 1 hundred is a flat of 10 tens. With the blocks, children can practice trading 10 units for 1 ten, and 10 tens for 1 hundred. They can successfully group a set of 26 units and trade the grouped units for 2 tens. However, when asked to count the resulting collection of 2 tens and 6 ones, a young child who has not mentally constructed 10 as a unit will proceed to count the entire collection by ones or count the first 10 as a unit and then continue counting by ones, "10, 11, 12, 13, . . . 26." A child who has mentally constructed 10 as a unit will count, "10, 20, 21, 22, 23, 24, 25, 26." Unless young children are asked to communicate their thinking, it is not clear what they understand about a task involving concrete models or what mathematical concept they have constructed.

The second issue regarding manipulatives is the question of relevance. Kamii (1989) asserts that requiring children to physically construct sets of 10 with manipulatives is not helpful because construction of multiple groupings can only be an intellectual activity; she holds that place value cannot be perceived from concrete materials.

Young children need to engage in a variety of counting tasks where quantity is partitioned into parts and the parts are subsequently related to the whole quantity. In kindergarten and first grade, children may investigate how many ways a set of objects (e.g., 9 chips) may be separated into two or more part (e.g., three sets of 3 chips; 5 chips and 4 more chips). In first and second grade, this partitioning supports place-value construction as children understand, for example, 34 as three sets of 10 and 4 more. This flexibility with numbers is evident when a child who solves a problem such as 27 + 35 states: "20 plus 30 is 50 . . . 7 more is 57 . . . and 5 more, . . . 58, 59, 60, 61, 62." This solution strategy clearly demonstrates a mature understanding of number. The power of the part-whole construct for number is its flexibility. In a curriculum that encourages the flexible use of the part-whole construct, addition and subtraction problems are open to many solution strategies, limited only by the numerical insights of the child. For example, another child may solve this same problem by counting: "35, . . . [+10] 45, . . . [+10] 55, . . . [+7], 56, 57, 58, 59, 60, 61, 62." Both of these solution strategies are examples of informal algorithms that children construct building on their understanding of multidigit numbers and their ability to coordinate the counting of tens and ones. Informal algorithms are accessible to children who understand part-whole relationships. Researchers are currently studying the influence of children's informal solution strategies on their understanding of formal computation algorithms (Carpenter & Fennema, 1990). This work may have profound influence on the sequencing of topics in early childhood mathematics.

## Development of Problem-Solving Abilities

During the past 10 years, studies on children's thinking have yielded a well-developed body of research defining addition and subtraction word problems as well as the strategies young children use to solve those problems (Briars & Larkin, 1984; Carpenter & Moser, 1983, 1984; Carpenter, Moser, & Romberg, 1982; Riley, Greeno, & Heller, 1983). Addition and subtraction problems have been classified according to the action or relationship of the quantities in the word problem (Carpenter & Moser, 1983; Riley, Greeno, & Heller, 1983). The relative difficulty of these problems is determined by children's solution strategies.

Research indicates that prior to formal instruction children can successfully solve simple word problems by directly modeling the action in the problem with concrete objects and then counting the objects. Young children then develop more advanced strategies for solving problems, moving from modeling, to advanced counting strategies, to use of derived facts, to the recall of number facts. Even young children who generally use direct modeling to solve problems may use derived facts or recall strategies occasionally, depending on the problem type and the size of the numbers involved. For example, we can consider this problem: *Anna had some balloons. She gave 7 of them to her best friend. Now Anna has 5 balloons left. How many balloons did Anna have to start with?* Children who use a derived fact to solve this problem may recognize that $7 = 5 + 2$, therefore $5 + 5 = 10$ and $10 + 2 = 12$, the solution. Children become more flexible in their choice of solution strategy as a result of change in their conceptual knowledge (Carpenter, 1985).

Young children's successful problem-solving abilities are well documented (Carpenter & Moser, 1984; De Corte & Verschaffel, 1987; Riley & Greeno, 1988). However, children's problem-solving experiences in traditional classrooms are limited (Stigler, Fuson, Ham, & Kim, 1986). In most programs children are restricted to simple word problems where two sets are joined or some amount is removed from a set. Because these types of problems do not challenge children's thinking, particularly in terms of the solution strategies required to solve them, the current early childhood curriculum can be considered impoverished. Children should be given a variety of word problems to solve. Further, the implication of this research for curriculum development is clear: "It is not necessary to defer instruction on word problems until computational skills have been mastered" (Romberg & Carpenter, 1986, p. 855).

The decision about what problems to consider should be determined by the teacher's knowledge of the relative difficulty of the problem types and knowledge of individual children's solution strategies. The critical curriculum issue is not whether the problem can be classified as addition or subtraction. For example, we can consider the following problem: *Keisha saved 6 pennies. How many more pennies does she need to save to have 10 pennies altogether?* This type of problem has traditionally been referred to as a missing addend problem. This problem, determined by some to be too difficult for first-grade children (Kamii, 1987), can be solved by subtracting 6 from 10. This subtractive solution strategy requires an explicit understanding of the part-whole relationship. However, first-grade children are very successful at solving this problem using an appropriate additive solution strategy (e.g., 6, . . . 7, 8, 9, 10, . . . 4 pennies) (Briars & Larkin, 1984; Carpenter & Moser, 1984; De Corte & Verschaffel, 1987; Riley, Greeno, & Heller, 1983). Solving the symbolic missing addend problem, $6 + \_\_ = 10$, without the support of a problem context is a difficult task for young children. The experience of solving meaningful word problems that can be represented by a missing addend sentence should not be confused with solving symbolic computation problems with missing addends. These are two distinct tasks that require different knowledge.

Young children also can solve multiplication (grouping) and division (partitioning) word problems by direct modeling (Kouba, 1989). The development of children's solution strategies for these problems is similar to that for addition and subtraction. Direct modeling is replaced by counting strategies and eventually by derived facts and recall. Because young children do not view multiplication as commutative, modeling three sets of 5 is a different task than modeling five sets of 3. As a result of this distinction, children also perceive division problems differently. In a problem such as *Max has 12 marbles. He wants to put 4 marbles in each bag. How many bags will he need?*, children construct a set of 12 objects and then make groups of 4. When all the objects have been grouped, the number of groups is counted for the solution. In a problem such as *Max has 12 marbles and 3 bags. If he puts the same number of marbles in each bag, how many marbles are in each bag?*, children construct a set of 12 objects and then deal them out into 3 piles until all the objects are dealt. The number of objects in a pile is counted for the solution. Both solution strategies directly model the problem situation; therefore, children's actions on the objects are different for the two problems. These problems are challenging, yet they are appropriate in the early childhood curriculum because they can be modeled meaningfully by young children and they build on children's understanding of addition and subtraction.

Curriculum decisions about what types of problems to include in early childhood mathematics should be made by considering whether the problem is set in a meaningful context for children, portraying appropriate mathematical structures. Young children solve problems that go beyond simple addition and subtraction events.


## Representation

Young children understand number and can solve problems without using written symbols. Children are introduced to the use of symbols to represent mathematical concepts so they may develop meaning for written symbolic representations. The process of connecting written symbols with real-world referents, such as objects or actions on objects, develops meaning for symbols (Hiebert, 1988). The links young children establish between a symbol and its referent need to be transparent before young children are expected to manipulate symbols as abstract quantities.

Number sentences (i.e., $a + b = \_\_$, $a - b = \_\_$) are symbolic representations used by young children to directly model the action described in problems. The use of number sentences is an extension of children's problem-solving abilities, and reflects their solution strategies. As children become more flexible in their choice of solution strategy, they are able to use a variety of appropriate number sentences. We can consider the problem: *Casey had some pennies. She lost 5 of them. Now she has 7 pennies left. How many pennies did Casey have to start with?* First-grade children link the representation $\_\_ - 5 = 7$ with this problem when given a choice of several alternative number sentences (Carey, 1991). As children develop a more generalized part-whole schema, they also use $7 + 5 = \_\_$ as an appropriate representation for this problem. Adding the two parts given in the problem is an explicit representation of the part-whole relationship. This is a more sophisticated representation because it does not directly translate from the problem situation. Although children can solve problems, there are differences in the number sentences used to represent the problems.

Decisions about what representations are appropriate are determined by how young children think about a problem.

## Geometric Concepts and Spatial Sense

> Mathematics curricula at all levels must introduce more of the breadth and power of the mathematical sciences. As mathematics is more than calculation, so education in mathematics must be more than mastery of arithmetic. Geometry . . . [is] as important as numbers in achieving mathematical power. . . . To prepare students to use mathematics in the twenty-first century, today's curriculum must evoke the full spectrum of the mathematical sciences. (National Research Council, 1989, p. 43)

The traditional mathematics curriculum for young children has been dominated by the study of number and numerical relationships. A recent study noted that *less than 7%* of the pages in basal mathematics textbooks for kindergarten through fourth grade conveyed geometry (Fuys, Geddes, & Tischler, 1988). In the United States, there is no coherent, accepted geometry curriculum for children (Usiskin, 1987).

If mathematics is perceived as the search for order, pattern, and relationships to characterize ideas and experiences, then geometry and spatial sense should be central topics in a mathematics curriculum for young children. Through hands-on experiences with the geometric nature of their world, young children may construct geometric ideas. The traditional geometry curriculum for young children has emphasized vocabulary, focusing on verbal definitions and rules. Current research indicates that children in the upper primary grades generally do not use these "learned" definitions and rules when they solve problems involving geometry and space. Instead, they rely on the conceptual structures they constructed from real-life experiences, both in school and at home. This reliance on informally constructed geometric concepts as opposed to verbal definitions has been noted not only for children who have incomplete recall of definitions and rules as presented in school, but also for children who can accurately restate the verbal rules and definitions (Clements & Battista, 1989). Instruction can foster young children's geometric understandings and improve their spatial-perception abilities, but the instruction should provoke children to reflect on the manipulation of geometric structures and to construct concepts interpreting perceived relationships (Clements & Battista, 1990; Del Grande, 1987). Although research suggests a framework for developing curriculum and instruction in geometry (van Hiele, 1986), and although calls for change are clear, incorporation of geometry and spatial sense in school mathematics remains an important yet prodigious charge.

## CREATING PROBLEM-SOLVING ENVIRONMENTS

### The Role of the Teacher

The early childhood mathematics curriculum is influenced by teachers' instructional decisions. Decisions should be based on what is known about the development of children's thinking and the thinking evidenced by individual children in the classroom. Mathematics instruction facilitates a child's construction of knowledge when a teacher knows what a child understands about a concept and how that concept is developed. Teachers' knowledge of their children's problem-solving skills is related to student learning (Carpenter, Fennema, Peterson, Chiang, & Loef, 1989; Fennema, Carpenter, & Peterson, 1989b). The assessment of problem-solving skills need not be accomplished as a formal task; it can occur during instruction. When teachers observe children's approaches to problems, when they listen to children's explanations, when they challenge children to clarify their thinking, and when they evaluate the level of sophistication inherent in children's individual solutions, teachers are assessing. Assessing children's thinking is a continuing process and an important part of effective instruction. Appropriate assessment and instructional tasks can be determined as a result of teachers' questioning, listening to, and observing children. This type of ongoing instruction/assessment is a natural context for children to do and to communicate mathematics. Communication in classrooms serves two purposes: (1) it fosters children's development of patterns of verbal communication as they talk about mathematics, and (2) it allows teachers to learn about their children's thinking.

### Learning Contexts

Curriculum focusing on problem solving needs resources for realistic, engaging problems. The best resources are the experiences of the children, either planned experiences occurring within the school setting or experiences from outside the classroom that are common to all the children. The critical issue is to conceive of problems that are meaningful to *each* child and are part of *every* child's environment (Resnick, in press). For example, kindergarten or first-grade children may collect data regarding the number of doors where they live. The data collected by each child are unique, yet readily accessible. This data can then be utilized to frame problems, to stimulate graphing, and to foster both interactive and mathematical language development. These data may give rise to many questions that integrate mathematics with other curriculum areas.

## CHALLENGE FOR THE FUTURE

This is a vibrant period for mathematics education as educators from all avenues (scholars, practitioners, and policy makers) seek to reform and revitalize mathematics curriculum and instruction. The premise of this chapter is that these changes in mathematics education must begin in the early childhood years.

When mathematics is perceived as meaningful, understandable, and challenging, a child experiences the power of mathematics.

> Mathematics . . . provide[s] one of the few disciplines in which the growing student can, by exercising only the power inherent in his or her own mind, reach conclusions with full assurance. More than most other school subjects, mathematics offers special opportunities for children to learn the power of thought as distinct from the power of authority. This is a very important lesson to learn, an essential step in the emergence of independent thinking. (National Research Council, 1989, p. 4)

In this chapter we have reviewed research that may direct and guide curriculum reform to meet the challenge implied above. An early childhood mathematics "curriculum should include a broad range of content, . . . emphasize the application of mathematics, . . . be conceptually oriented, . . . actively involve children in doing mathematics, . . . [and] emphasize the development of children's mathematical thinking and reasoning abilities" (Commission on Standards for School Mathematics, 1989, pp. 18–19).

## REFERENCES

Anderson, R. C. (1984). Some reflections on the acquisition of knowledge. *Educational Researcher, 13* (9), 5–10.

Baroody, A. J. (1987). *Children's mathematical thinking: A developmental framework for preschool, primary, and special education teachers.* New York: Teachers College Press.

Baroody, A. J. (1989). Manipulatives don't come with guarantees. *Arithmetic Teacher, 37* (2), 4–5.

Baroody, A. J. (1990). How and when should place-value concepts and skills be taught? *Journal for Research in Mathematics Education, 21,* 281–286.

Baroody, A. J., Ginsburg, H. P., & Waxman, B. (1983). Children's use of mathematical structure. *Journal for Research in Mathematics Education, 14,* 156–168.

Bednarz, N., & Janvier, B. (1982). The understanding of numeration in the primary school. *Educational Studies in Mathematics, 13,* 33–37.

Briars, D. J., & Larkin, J. G. (1984). An integrated model of skills in solving elementary word problems. *Cognition and Instruction, 1,* 245–296.

Carey, D. (1991). Number sentences: Linking addition and subtraction word problems and symbols. *Journal for Research in Mathematics Education, 22*, 265–280.

Carpenter, T. P. (1985). Learning to add and subtract: An exercise in problem solving. In E. A. Silver (Ed.), *Teaching and learning mathematical problem solving: Multiple research perspectives* (pp. 17–40). Hillsdale, NJ: Lawrence Erlbaum.

Carpenter, T. P. (1988). Teaching as problem solving. In R. I. Charles & E. A. Silver (Eds.), *The teaching and assessing of mathematical problem solving* (pp. 187–202). Reston, VA: Lawrence Erlbaum/National Council of Teachers of Mathematics.

Carpenter, T. P. (1989). Number sense and other nonsense. In J. T. Sowder & B. P. Schappelle (Eds.), *Establishing foundations for research on number sense and related topics: Report of a conference* (pp. 89–91). San Diego, CA: Center for Research in Mathematics and Science Education, San Diego State University.

Carpenter, T. P., & Fennema, E. (1990). Developing understanding for multidigit operations. In K. Fuson & T. P. Carpenter (Eds.), *Learning and teaching place value and multidigit addition and subtraction* (pp. 43–48). Madison: Wisconsin Center for Education Research, University of Wisconsin–Madison.

Carpenter, T. P., Fennema, E., Peterson, P. L., Chiang, C-P., & Loef, M. (1989). Using knowledge of children's mathematics thinking in classroom teaching: An experimental study. *American Educational Research Journal, 26*, 499–531.

Carpenter, T. P., & Moser, J. M. (1983). The acquisition of addition and subtraction concepts. In R. Lesh & M. Landau (Eds.), *Acquisition of mathematics: Concepts and processes* (pp. 7–44). New York: Academic Press.

Carpenter, T. P., & Moser, J. M. (1984). The acquisition of addition and subtraction concepts in grades one through three. *Journal for Research in Mathematics Education, 15*, 179–202.

Carpenter, T. P., Moser, J. M., & Romberg, T. A. (Eds.). (1982). *Addition and subtraction: A cognitive perspective.* Hillsdale, NJ: Lawrence Erlbaum.

Clements, D. H., & Battista, M. T. (1989). Learning of geometric concepts in a Logo environment. *Journal for Research in Mathematics Education, 20*, 450–467.

Clements, D. H., & Battista, M. T. (1990). The effects of Logo on children's conceptualizations of angle and polygons. *Journal for Research in Mathematics Education, 21*, 356–371.

Cobb, P. (1987). An analysis of three models of early number development. *Journal for Research in Mathematics Education, 18*, 163–179.

Cobb, P. (1988). The tension between theories of learning and instruction in mathematics education. *Educational Psychologist, 23*, 87–103.

Cobb, P., & Wheatley, G. (1988). Children's initial understandings of ten. *Focus on Learning Problems in Mathematics, 10* (3), 1–28.

Cobb, P., Wood, T., Yackel, E., Nicholls, J., Wheatley, G., Trigatti, B., & Perlwitz, M. (1991). Assessment of a problem-centered mathematics project. *Journal for Research in Mathematics Education, 22*, 3–29.

Commission on Standards for School Mathematics. (1989). *Curriculum and evalua-*

*tion standards for school mathematics*. Reston, VA: National Council of Teachers of Mathematics.

Commission on Teaching Standards for School Mathematics. (1991). *Professional standards for teaching mathematics*. Reston, VA: National Council of Teachers of Mathematics.

De Corte, E., & Verschaffel, L. (1987). The effect of semantic structure on first graders' strategies for solving addition and subtraction word problems. *Journal for Research in Mathematics Education, 18*, 363–381.

Del Grande, J. (1987). Spatial perception and primary geometry. In M. M. Lindquist (Ed.), *Learning and teaching geometry, K–12* (pp. 126–135). Reston, VA: National Council of Teachers of Mathematics.

Fennema, E., Carpenter, T. P., & Peterson, P. L. (1989a). Learning mathematics with understanding: Cognitively guided instruction. In J. Brophy (Ed.), *Advances in research on teaching* (Vol. 1, pp. 195–219). Greenwich, CT: JAI Press.

Fennema, E., Carpenter, T. P., & Peterson, P. L. (1989b). Teachers' decision-making and cognitively guided instruction: A new paradigm for curriculum development. In N. Ellerton & M. Clements (Eds.), *School mathematics: The challenge to change* (pp. 174–187). Geelong, Victoria, Australia: Deakin University Press.

Fischbein, E. (1987). *Instruction in science and mathematics: An educational approach*. Dordrecht, Holland: D. Reidel.

Fischer, F. E. (1990). A part-part-whole curriculum for teaching number in the kindergarten. *Journal for Research in Mathematics Education, 21*, 207–215.

Fuson, K. C. (1989). *Children's counting and concepts of number*. New York: Springer-Verlag.

Fuson, K. C. (1990). Conceptual structures for multiunit numbers: Implications for learning and teaching multidigit addition, subtraction, and place value. *Cognition and Instruction, 7*, 343–403.

Fuson, K. C. (1990). Issues in place-value and multidigit addition and subtraction learning and teaching. *Journal for Research in Mathematics Education, 21*, 273–280.

Fuson, K. C. (1991). Children's early counting: Saying the number–word sequence, counting objects, and understanding cardinality. In K. Durkin & B. Shire, (Eds.), *Language in mathematical education* (pp. 27–39). Milton Keynes, England: Open University Press.

Fuson, K. C., & Briars, D. J. (1990). Using a base-ten blocks learning/teaching approach for first- and second-grade place value and multidigit addition and subtraction. *Journal for Research in Mathematics Education, 21*, 180–206.

Fuson, K. C., & Kwon, Y. (1991). Chinese-based regular and European irregular systems of number words: The disadvantages for English-speaking children. In K. Durkin & B. Shire (Eds.), *Language in mathematical education* (pp. 211–226). Milton Keynes, England: Open University Press.

Fuys, D., Geddes, D., & Tischler, R. (1988). The van Hiele model of thinking in geometry among adolescents. *Journal for Research in Mathematics Education Monograph, 3.*

Gelman, R., & Gallistel, C. R. (1978). *The child's understanding of number.* Cambridge, MA: Harvard University Press.

Gelman, R., & Greeno, J. G. (1989). On the nature of competence: Principles for understanding in a domain. In L. B. Resnick (Ed.), *Knowing, learning and instruction: Essays in honor of Robert Glaser* (pp. 125–186). Hillsdale, NJ: Lawrence Erlbaum.

Gelman, R., & Meck, E. (1986). The notion of principle: The case of counting. In J. Hiebert (Ed.), *Conceptual and procedural knowledge: The case of mathematics* (pp. 29–57). Hillsdale, NJ: Lawrence Erlbaum.

Greeno, J. G. (1991). Number sense as situated knowing in a conceptual domain. *Journal for Research in Mathematics Education, 22,* 170–218.

Greeno, J. G., Riley, M. S., & Gelman, R. (1984). Conceptual competence and children's counting. *Cognitive Psychology, 16,* 94–143.

Hiebert, J. (1988). A theory of developing competence with written mathematical symbols. *Educational Studies in Mathematics, 19,* 333–355.

Hiebert, J., & Lefevre, P. (1986). Conceptual and procedural knowledge in mathematics: An introductory analysis. In J. Hiebert (Ed.), *Conceptual and procedural knowledge: The case of mathematics* (pp. 1–27). Hillsdale, NJ: Lawrence Erlbaum.

Hiebert, J., & Wearne, D. (1992). Teaching and learning place value with understanding in first grade. *Journal for Research in Mathematics Education, 23,* 98–122.

Kamii, C. (1985). *Young children reinvent arithmetic.* New York: Teachers College Press.

Kamii, C. (1987). Children's thinking or their writing of correct answers? *Arithmetic Teacher, 35* (3), 2.

Kamii, C. (1989). *Young children continue to reinvent arithmetic–2nd grade.* New York: Teachers College Press.

Kamii, C. (1990). Constructivism and beginning arithmetic (K–2). In T. J. Cooney & C. R. Hirsch (Eds.), *Teaching and learning mathematics in the 1990s* (pp. 22–30). Reston, VA: National Council of Teachers of Mathematics.

Kamii, C., & Joseph L. (1988). Teaching place value and double-column addition. *Arithmetic Teacher, 35* (6), 48–52.

Kouba, V. (1989). Children's solution strategies for equivalent set multiplication and division word problems. *Journal for Research in Mathematics Education, 20,* 147–158.

Lampert, M. (1990). When the problem is not the question and the solution is not the answer: Mathematical knowing and teaching. *American Educational Research Journal, 27,* 29–63.

Leinhardt, G. (1988). Getting to know: Tracing students' mathematical knowledge from intuition to competence. *Educational Psychologist, 23,* 119–144.

Lindquist, M. M. (Ed.). (1989). *Results from the fourth mathematics assessment of the National Assessment of Educational Progress.* Reston, VA: National Council of Teachers of Mathematics.

National Research Council. (1989). *Everybody counts: A report to the nation on the future of mathematics education.* Washington, DC: National Academy Press.

Nesher, P. (1989). Microworlds in mathematical education: A pedagogical realism. In L. B. Resnick (Ed.), *Knowing, learning and instruction: Essays in honor of Robert Glaser* (pp. 187–215). Hillsdale, NJ: Lawrence Erlbaum.

Resnick, L. B. (1983a). A developmental theory of number understanding. In H. P. Ginsburg (Ed.), *The development of mathematical thinking* (pp. 109–151). New York: Academic Press.

Resnick, L. B. (1983b). Towards a cognitive theory of instruction. In S. G. Paris, G. M. Olson, & W. H. Stevenson (Eds.), *Learning and motivation in the class-room* (pp. 5–38). Hillsdale, NJ: Lawrence Erlbaum.

Resnick, L. B. (1988). Treating mathematics as an ill-structured discipline. In R. I. Charles & E. A. Silver (Eds.), *The teaching and assessing of mathematical problem solving* (pp. 32–60). Reston, VA: Lawrence Erlbaum/National Council of Teachers of Mathematics.

Resnick, L. B. (1989). Defining, assessing, and teaching number sense. In J. T. Sowder & B. P. Schappelle (Eds.), *Establishing foundations for research on number sense and related topics: Report of a conference* (pp. 35–39). San Diego, CA: Center for Research in Mathematics and Science Education, San Diego State University.

Resnick, L. B. (in press). Developing thinking abilities in arithmetic class. In A. Demetriou, M. Shayer, & A. Efklides (Eds.), *The modern theories of cognitive development go to school.* London: Routledge.

Riley, M. S., & Greeno, J. G. (1988). Developmental analysis of understanding language about quantities and of solving problems. *Cognition and Instruction, 5,* 49–101.

Riley, M. S., Greeno, J. G., & Heller, J. I. (1983). Development of children's problem-solving ability in arithmetic. In H. P. Ginsburg (Ed.), *The develop-ment of mathematical thinking* (pp. 153–200). New York: Academic Press.

Romberg, T. A., & Carpenter, T. P. (1986). Research on teaching and learning math-ematics: Two disciplines of scientific inquiry. In M. C. Wittrock (Ed.), *Hand-book of research on teaching* (3rd ed., pp. 850–873). New York: Macmillan.

Romberg, T. A., & Tufte, F. W. (1987). Mathematics curriculum engineering: Some suggestions from cognitive science. In T. A. Romberg & D. M. Stewart (Eds.), *The monitoring of school mathematics: Background papers: Vol. 2. Implications from psychology: Outcomes of instruction* (pp. 71–108). Madison: Wisconsin Center for Education Research, University of Wisconsin–Madison.

Ross, S. H. (1989). Part, wholes, and place value. *Arithmetic Teacher, 36* (6), 47–51.

Saxe, G. B., Guberman, S. R., & Gearhart, M. (1987). Social processes in early number development. *Monographs of the Society for Research in Child Devel-opment, 52* (2, Serial No. 216).

Silver, E. A. (1989). On making sense of number sense. In J. T. Sowder & B. P. Schappelle (Eds.), *Establishing foundations for research on number sense and related topics: Report of a conference* (pp. 92–96). San Diego, CA: Center for Research in Mathematics and Science Education, San Diego State University.

Sowder, J. T., & Schappelle, B. P. (Eds.). (1989). *Establishing foundations for research on number sense and related topics: Report of a conference* San Diego, CA: Center for Research in Mathematics and Science Education, San Diego State University.

Steffe, L. P., Cobb, P., & von Glasersfeld, E. (1988). *Construction of arithmetical meanings and strategies.* New York: Springer-Verlag.

Stigler, R. S., Fuson, K. C., Ham, M., & Kim, M. S. (1986). An analysis of addition and subtraction word problems in American and Soviet elementary mathematics textbooks. *Cognition and Instruction, 3,* 153–171.

Strauss, M. S., & Curtis, L. E. (1984). Development of numerical concepts in infancy. In C. Sophian (Ed.), *Origins of cognitive skills* (pp. 131–155). Hillsdale, NJ: Lawrence Erlbaum.

Usiskin, Z. (1987). Resolving the continuing dilemmas in school geometry. In M. M. Lindquist (Ed.), *Learning and teaching geometry, K–12* (pp. 17–31). Reston, VA: National Council of Teachers of Mathematics.

van Hiele, P. M. (1986). *Structure and insight.* New York: Academic Press.

von Glasersfeld, E. (Ed.). (1991). *Radical constructivism in mathematics education.* Norwell, MA: Kluwer Academic Publishers.

Yackel, E., Cobb, P., Wood, T., Wheatley, G., & Merkel, G. (1990). The importance of social interaction in children's construction of mathematical knowledge. In T. J. Cooney & C. R. Hirsch (Eds.), *Teaching and learning mathematics in the 1990s* (pp. 12–21). Reston, VA: National Council of Teachers of Mathematics.

# CHAPTER 7

# Research on Early Science Education

GEORGE E. FORMAN AND CHRISTOPHER LANDRY

Research on early science education needs to be distinguished from research on early cognitive development. Research on cognitive development helps us determine common misconceptions children have about a science concept (e.g., Levin, Siegler, & Druyan, 1990). Research on science education helps us determine useful procedures to facilitate scientific thinking in young children. Such studies that deal with children under 7 or 8 years of age are difficult to find. In this chapter we will present what we have found in recent American and British journals. As a context for this educational research, we also will present the cognitive development research that has established the goals for much of early science education.

## SCIENTIFIC THINKING

Scientific thinking is a specific application of curiosity and intelligence. This form of thinking consists of the gradual understanding that certain events are anomalous and need to be explained (*What's wrong here?*); that observable data are essential to substantiate one's claims (*What happened here?*); and that explanations need to meet certain criteria of logic (*What's the proof here?*). These three orientations to the world occur to children at staggered times of onset, probably in the order mentioned. The orientations can be diagramed as a set of relations (see Figure 7.1).

The first orientation to the world represents a shift from a passive acceptance of an event to an active comparison of that event with something that was expected but did not result. For example, the child sees a heavy object float, and compares that with her expectation that this heavy object should sink. The child, through his or her advance to comparative thinking, has asked the first question. What's wrong here?

**Figure 7.1    Diagram of scientific thinking**

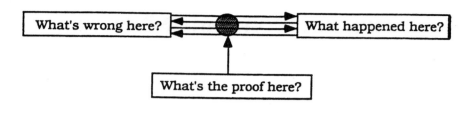

Some children may sense the anomaly but dismiss it as an isolated case. In our example, the child thinks: *This* heavy object floats. The child may not relate *what happened*, to a class of events—all heavy objects in water—but merely to the local case of one object. To proceed further the child needs to sense that one case has implications for many cases. Furthermore, if this anomalous case is accepted, the expected case (heavy objects sink) has to be reworked.

Thinking traffics between *what's wrong* and *what happened*. First the child tries an exact replication, just to see if the heavy object floats again (first arrow from left to right in Figure 7.1). On further inspection the child might realize that the object floats, but it pushes a bit into the water before it stabilizes. So the child reflects on the events and reinterprets her definition of *what's wrong* (first arrow from right to left). Instead of saying, "This heavy object floats when it should sink," the child might rephrase *what's wrong* as "This heavy object sinks a little in the water when it should sink all the way."

This revision in turn might lead to a reworking of *what happened*, for example, "The object pushes against the water." The child has now moved beyond causing and into testing (second cycle of arrow from left to right). She makes certain things happen in order to confirm a prediction. She pushes down on the object to test its strength against her finger. This shift from causing to testing is critical to scientific thinking. This cycle among causing, interpreting, and testing is the foundation for scientific thinking and occurs in preschool-aged children (see Forman & Hill, 1984).

The step toward proof comes slowly. At the intuitive level proof consists mainly in making the strange familiar. Children reason by analogy. In the higher levels of science, proofs are accomplished by relating the strange to the familiar via a set of formal procedures (e.g., math) that in turn flow one to another without gaps in logical consistency. For example, the mathematical laws of falling objects, consistently applied, can also account for the laws of orbiting satellites (i.e., Newton's apple and moon). For the child, proof begins as a case of analogy. Proof consists in realizing that the event in question is actually similar to a more familiar case. The heavy object is large; large objects are strong; therefore strong objects can hold themselves up in the water. But the proof is inconsistently applied because it applies only to heavy objects that float, not to those that sink.

An arrow in Figure 7.1 connects the proof box to the traffic between the upper two boxes. This means that proof is metacognitive. That is, proof refers to thinking about thinking, in this case, the relation between hypothesis (*what's wrong?*) and facts (*what happened?*). *What's the proof?* addresses the issue of how information constrains an answer to the only one possible and does not accept the same answer for opposite events (some sink, some float). In the description of research that follows, we will try to assess where children are in their understanding of proof.

## WHAT CHILDREN BRING TO SCIENCE

An informed approach to science teaching requires us to understand the learner. The early work in this area gave much attention to the developmental level of children. Developmental level refers to general cognitive competence, such as the ability to conserve quantity (same amount despite spatial changes) or the ability to understand class inclusion relations (some is less than all). Current research is taking us closer to specific content, such as misconceptions children have about heat or gravity or light. As a revision of its predecessor (Forman & Kaden, 1987), this chapter will concentrate on content-specific research.

### Principles

Children come to science instruction with misconceptions about how things happen. These have been called naive theories, alternative frameworks, and misconceptions. What these terms have in common is the belief that children have constructed, through high level thinking, their own theories about physical events. The developmental level of the student is not the direct issue. The misconception has a sophistication of its own (see the discussion of Figure 7.1). Thus the science teacher cannot just say to the student, "Let's forget your misconceptions and learn the correct explanations for these events." The student who is told a new explanation will concurrently hold the misconception because it is more integrated into many other assumptions he or she holds. Thus, the teacher needs to understand the procedures by which children maintain their misconceptions and help them reconstruct the misconceptions into more reliable theories.

Learning through this process of reconstructing misconceptions, called constructivism, acknowledges several principles, some obvious, some not. No one seriously assumes that the young child is a blank slate; so it is trivial to cite the tabula rasa theory as something constructivism is not. Even empiricism does not think that 4- and 5-year-olds come to science instruction without preconceptions. But beyond this obvious principle, constructivism also posits that inference is the ultimate source of knowledge, not the raw observation of noticeable events. Only the child, through inference, can organize facts into a coherent system. Furthermore, misconceptions themselves have a coherence that makes them resistant to mere replacement by new information from the teacher (Carey, 1986). This is true no matter how organized and polished a classroom lesson might be.

Constructivist education holds, as a principle of faith, that children will be conflicted when anomalies occur and the children have innate capacities to make the inferences necessary to resolve these contradictions (Wheatley, 1991). In a constructivist classroom, teachers do not directly teach these competences, but rather establish an environment that allows the children to draw on them (Duckworth, 1987). The discussion of research that follows will define and debate the tenets of constructivism within specific science domains.

## Research

The orthodoxy of constructivism is gradually being refined. Shapiro (1989) asks the practical question of why some children do not progress, even when placed in rich problem-solving environments that challenge their misconceptions. By using children's understanding of reflected light, she investigated the interaction of science learning and personality type. While this study deals with 11-year-olds, as a research methodology it is well worth reading in its entirety. In summary, she found that the social orientation of students contributed to their success or failure. Some children are socially acquiescent, that is, they defer to more dominant children. Others embrace the challenge of negotiating for equal status. While the socially acquiescent child does not profit from the confrontation of ideas, the socially embracing child does. Shapiro presents a needed refinement to the oversimplification that children universally have a fascination with contradiction.

Lawson (1988) interviewed elementary school children (aged 6, 9, and 11 years) to determine the extent to which they held naive misconceptions about biological concepts such as growth, circulation, and family resemblance. He found no evidence of coherent misconceptions, but rather scattered bits and pieces of knowledge (see also diSessa, 1988; Russell, Harlen, & Watt, 1989). If this is true, one would have to reason that didactic teaching could be justified, since the scattered facts would not be resistant to replacement. Lawson (1988) argues that, at least with these concepts, one should adopt an accretion theory of learning rather than a reconstruction theory. An accretion theory holds that knowledge builds in a quantitative manner as more and more facts are learned. A reconstruction theory holds that the system of relations among the same set of facts is reconstructed at higher levels of expertise.

Mintzes (1989) writes a rebuttal of Lawson by reviewing other early childhood research on naive theories of biology (Carey, 1985; Wandersee, Mintzes, & Arnaudin, 1987), but admits that the construction of a well-formed naive theory of biology may take longer than the construction of a well-formed naive theory about physical objects. He attributes this delay to the relative inaccessibility of observable events necessary to found naive theories of biology. One can also see in the case studies that Lawson (1988) provides that the youngest child was socially acquiescent. Thus the lack of a well-formed theory could be either real or simply not expressed (see Shapiro, 1989).

The possibility remains that children younger than 10 years form loosely held analogies, rather than coherent theories. For example, the rain cycle is understood as analogous to "raining up" and "raining down," without the children understanding the necessity for state changes in the water during evaporation and condensation. Does this imply that we should encourage children younger than 10 to forget their wrong analogies and to accept totally the more useful analogies of the teacher? Russell, Harlen, and Watt (1989) argue that even if children construct loosely knit systems of attributes, they are still constructing relations. The learning child does more than accrete new facts. Thus if we tell a child to forget a wrong fact without our understanding her loose system of relations, that wrong fact will be reinvented in some other form to support her loose system.

The issue of didactic teaching also depends on what one is trying to teach. Most teachers are trying to teach *sciencing* as well as science (see Wasserman, 1988). Sciencing includes the methods of asking good questions, so the issue of naive analogy versus naive theory has no implications for sciencing education. A constructivist approach seems appropriate for even the younger ages.

On the other hand, Elkind (1989) warns us not to rush 4- and 5-year-olds into performing controlled experiments. Children this young do not possess the cognitive wherewithal to isolate variables or to understand the interaction of two or more causes (see also Rudnitsky & Hunt, 1986). Elkind's warning pertains more to *What's the proof?* in Figure 7.1 than to the wonderful messing about that young children can handle when perplexed by some anomalous event. Sciencing for these young children is quite possible, if by sciencing one means the construction of some expectation, trying something out to confirm than expectation, and modifying the expectation based on observables. This type of sciencing can happen even in the absence of an appeal to proof or logical necessity (concrete operational thinking). In contrast to learning sciencing, we will have more to say about learning science in the following sections.

## CHILDREN'S CONSTRUCTION OF SCIENCE CONCEPTS

As a continuation of the alternative frameworks perspective, we will consider form and development of misconceptions. We will explain how these misconceptions are more than quaint, but are intuitively reasonable. When a teacher understands why a student's misconception is reasonable, the teacher has an entry point for instruction. In the service of this objective, we will use one science concept, evaporation, as a case in point so that we might more fully trace the misconceptions children bring to their classwork.

### Evaporation as a Case in Point

Most of us have seen the surprise in a child's face when the untouched water dish, wet an hour ago, is now dry. This surprise itself comes from a rather elementary theory about liquids: (1) liquids do not "spill" up, and (2) liquids do not disappear into thin air. Yet the water is gone, but the dish remains. The observation of the missing water in the presence of the empty dish violates these assumptions and leads to the first stage of Figure 7.1, *what's wrong*. From this point on, children have a variety of explanations about what happened.

Some children will cling to their theory about liquids and consider the nature of the dish. Children in the 7- to 8-year range think that the dish absorbed the water (Bar, 1989). They have some understanding of how water seeps into the ground, or into a sponge, so why not into a dish. This explanation is a first attempt to say what happened here. Since the children do not know that water can change from a liquid to a gas (called a *phase change* in science), they feel compelled to justify the what's-wrong question with a reworking of their assumptions about solid containers.

By the 9- to 10-year range children begin to talk about vapor, but it is a transitory concept and situationally applied. They believe that water can turn into vapor, but they still think that this vapor is contained in the clouds but does not constitute clouds (Bar, 1989). The children are comfortable with the idea of vapor because they think vapor is similar to air. They know that air is present but cannot be seen. But since they still think that vapor must be contained by something (the cloud), we can surmise that their understanding of phase change is incomplete. They understand that the water becomes vapor, but that is not the same as understanding that the water is transformed into vapor. To say that water becomes vapor is not much more than saying that water becomes invisible. They have not tried to account for what is it about vapor that makes it invisible (drops too tiny to see). Vapor is just water that one cannot see; therefore it still has all the other properties of water (e.g., existence and weight) and thereby requires a container if it is to be "held" in the sky.

Figure 7.1 is again helpful in discussing the children's construction and reconstruction of theory. The first what-happened referred to the absorbent dish; the second what-happened referred to the water becoming invisible and residing inside clouds. This progress is usually the result of a reworking of the what's-wrong question. They try to make the dish soak up the water; it doesn't, so the first what-happened makes no sense. The children find it unavoidable to construct the idea of water moving because they are not willing to posit the annihilation and recreation of matter. The theory about water moving comes when they relate the evaporation dish to a pan of boiling water. Vapor is invisible steam. In this way the children do not have to violate their belief about matter. They just add that some matter is invisible!

It is not until age 11 or 12 that children construct a coherent theory that accounts for both the invisibility and the movement of water (Bar, 1989). The water vapor is made of drops that are so tiny that they cannot be seen (i.e., "They are scattered everywhere in the air"), and because they are so tiny they can be moved by the air. Thus the phase change of water into particles accounts for the invisible movement. Likewise the particle theory explains how clouds can be made of vapor rather than containing vapor. For these older children, the proof that water vapor exists comes from their understanding that it *must* exist. Given the constraints that liquid water is heavier than air, and all the other constraints, water vapor is a case of logical necessity. Similar findings come from Beveridge (1985), who extended his research to include condensation.

## Other Science Concepts

Evaporation has been a popular topic for early science education, but there are a number of other interesting science concepts that have been extensively researched. For example, the research base of the National Curriculum in England (Department of Education and Science, 1989) includes children's construction of theories about growth, evaporation and condensation, light, change in nonliving materials, sound, electricity, forces, and living things and their environment. For slightly older, but still quite relevant, research, see also the studies cited in our earlier chapter (Forman & Kaden, 1987). The reader is referred to the sources cited below to extend the information presented in this chapter.

Feher (1990) and Rice and Feher (1987) have done careful work on children's understanding of paths of light. By using the inversion of an image through a pinhole, these researchers discovered some intriguing misconceptions about light rays being "squeezed" and then "bulging out" as they pass through holes.

Carey (1985) compared the naive theories children (aged 4, 6, and 10 years) have about eating, breathing, sleeping, and dying. The younger children explained these bodily processes in terms of social and psychological needs. For example, to the question, "Why do we eat?" the young child might say, "To grow big and strong." By age 10, an autonomous domain of "intuitive biology" emerges, with explanations similar to those of naive adults. For example, children may answer "Yes" to the question, "Can you gain a pound of weight by eating a half pound of Boston cream pie?" Carey's point is that these early theories are qualitatively different from the later theories, even though they both may be incorrect. This qualitative difference challenges the accretion model of learning science (Lawson, 1988) mentioned in the previous section.

## CHILDREN'S CONSTRUCTION OF MIND

Science involves not only the construction of new knowledge, but also the construction of some means to communicate the discoveries. One may know but not be able to explain. At a more philosophical level, such egocentric knowledge may not qualify as knowledge at all. Communication necessarily requires a certain level of stepping back and reflecting on one's own thoughts (metacognitive processing). Children require a reasonably developed theory of mind before they understand the necessity to explicate their knowledge for others. These issues bring the children's concept of mind into the center of research on science education.

Research on cognition has attempted to determine when children develop an understanding of mental states and activities: belief, desire, memory, inference, and so forth. For those involved in early science education, this research can perhaps shed some light on two aspects of children's science: the child's interpretation of a physical event, and the child's ability to engage in meaningful conversation with others about that event.

Pillow (1988), in a summary of research into children's beliefs about the mental world, cites several studies showing that young children often miss helpful cues about their own cognitive processes. Six-year-olds, for example, when given instructions that could not possibly be carried out, tried to carry out the instructions instead of realizing that they had failed to comprehend the impossibility. Flavell (1988) found that while 5-year-olds showed non-verbal signs of comprehension problems, such as pauses and puzzled expressions, they did not report an awareness of their own comprehension difficulty when asked. Older children had a higher degree of awareness. Young children may not realize the significance of their fleeting feelings of uncertainty. In other words, their puzzlement does not cause them to reflect on its source.

What happens when we carry these findings over to our model of science thinking? Clearly, it becomes difficult to assume that the young child will necessarily recognize a conflict (*What's wrong here?*) between her existing knowledge structure and a physical event she observes. Cognitive conflict may not occur. If the child, for example, ignores her puzzlement upon seeing a heavy object float, and if this child does not reflect on her own prior conceptions (metacognition), then the existing knowledge structure remains unchallenged.

Having briefly dealt with knowledge of mind as it affects the child's interpretation of physical events, we now turn to knowledge of mind as it relates to communication with others. Science, for children as well as adults, is not done in a vacuum but in a social realm within which ideas are discussed, are debated, and take shape. For any meaningful give-and-take to occur, there must be agreement about the facts (*What happened here?*) even if there are differences of interpretation. Konicek, King, and Teece (1990) report on the care taken by fourth graders to distinguish "floating" from "not sinking" objects. But, as Pillow (1988) summarizes, younger children's incomplete understanding of mind often prevents them from taking the perspective of others that useful dialogue requires. Young children do not, for example, understand that a person's prior knowledge or expectations may affect that person's interpretation of a physical event. Pillow offers another example. Children see an object and then are shown an uninformative patch of that same object. Next they are asked whether someone seeing just the patch could identify the object. Most 4- and 5-year-olds incorrectly said yes. They confused their own privileged information about the whole object with the partial information given to a new viewer. Such a failure to take the other's perspective would make it difficult for a young child to debate alternative views. Nevertheless, these early struggles at communication are the origins of social perspective taking and collaborative problem solving. By 8 years of age these egocentric errors are rarely made.

What emerges is a picture of the young child only gradually developing an ability to decenter, to be objective enough to fruitfully compare her experience with that of her peers. We might expect that our young learner at water play would be unperturbed by the claim of a peer that a heavy object floated, but eventually perplexed if she discovered this herself. Later, perhaps at age 6 or 7, she will more readily agree with her peers that these facts present alternative views that need to be reconciled. Then she will begin to traffic between *what happened* and *what's wrong*. At this point children are ready to learn a routine format of studying science, perhaps the model suggested by Wasserman (1988), described in the next section.

## RESEARCH ON METHODS OF TEACHING EARLY SCIENCE

What is an early science teacher to do? The research in this area suggests several forms of intervention, which, at times, includes no direct intervention. Duckworth (1987) makes an eloquent case for allowing students to discover and frame their own questions. The intervention, in this case, consists mainly in providing the children with a rich problem-solving environment and a teacher who reflects and records the evolution of the children's thinking. Wasserman (1988) offers a model described as play-debrief-replay. This model puts heavy emphasis on group discussion and repeated alternations among messing about, summarizing, and a higher level of messing about. As mentioned above, teachers need to monitor the communication competence of children before launching these more routinized formats of instruction. More specific research on science teaching techniques is discussed next.

### Elicitation and Confrontation of Ideas

Beveridge (1985); and Russell, Harlen, and Watt (1989) compared several methods of eliciting from children rich theories about the water cycle. For example, Russell and colleagues (1989) used drawings and group discussions to help children modify their theories toward greater generality and coherence. Beveridge (1985) used conflict inducement. Some children were asked to test water absorption using paper towels, a plastic saucer, a sponge, aluminum foil, and a metal plate. The results of these tests were meant to conflict with the students' assumption that evaporated water had been absorbed by the dish. Other children were given a lesson on steam. A mirror was placed in front of a boiling kettle and the condensation was noted.

It is interesting that these demonstrations did little to facilitate reconstruction of naive theories. Beveridge concludes that these demonstrations were ineffective because the alternative theories were resistant to change.

While this borders on circular reasoning, we appreciate the intent of that conclusion. The techniques were didactic. Instead of placing the children in a situation where they would invent their own tests (and therefore their own understanding of what the test tested), the teacher presented the test and demonstration as a given. The elicitation techniques (drawings and group discussions) used by Russell, Harlen, and Watt (1989) are themselves teaching techniques consistent with constructivism (see next section). The elicitation techniques are more likely to help children invent their own tests and thereby understand the implication of subsequent test results.

## Drawing to Learn

There is a movement at work in education to place more emphasis on how children represent science questions. It is clear from the history of science that solutions are determined, in part, by how one represents the problem. For example, one may try to improve his chess game by drawing a sequence of boards with all the pieces in each frame or by writing out a column of letters and numbers to represent a sequence of moves piece by space. The drawings are more likely to elicit strategies about board development; the alphanumeric list is more likely to identify a weakness in overusing the Queen or underusing pawns (see Forman, 1985).

For some years now, Roselyn Driver (1989) has asked science students to draw posters of their concepts, such as their naive theories about solids, liquids, and gases. From these early drawings children begin to ask wonderfully paradoxical questions: "What's the stuff between the particles of matter?" "What holds the particles together in solids that is not there in liquids?" But this work, so far, has been done with older children. Driver uses the drawings primarily to identify the children's misconceptions. By extending Driver's work, one could understand how drawing provides a source of new knowledge, not just a record of existing knowledge.

At the University of Massachusetts we are developing a graduate seminar titled Drawing to Learn. The thrust of the course is to understand the mechanism by which children, in the act of drawing their theories, gain a better understanding of their misconceptions and thereby reconstruct their misconceptions into a more sensible theory. This course refers to work by Driver (1989), Larkin and Simon (1987), and others, but for the early education years, the course gives careful attention to work that is coming from the preschools in Reggio Emilia, Italy. We can consider the following example of a 5-½-year-old, named Simone, who drew her understanding of the rain cycle (see Figure 7.2).

Simone has drawn what appears to be a complete representation of the rain cycle. She says:

**Figure 7.2   Simone's drawing of the rain cycle. The arrows (added to the original drawing) point to the free fall water in the open on the left and the "pipes" for the water going up on the right.**

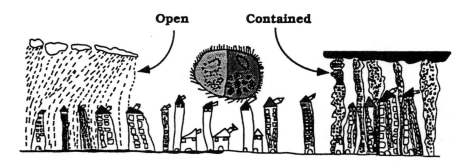

The rain falls on the houses, on the umbrellas and on the trees, then it goes on the earth, in the courtyards, then things dry up when it's sunny. Instead of continuing to go around the houses, the rain dries up, the sun heats the rain that has fallen and that's how it goes away afterwards, it goes back into the clouds and then it starts to rain again. (Cited in traveling exhibit, The Hundred Languages of Children, The Commune of Reggio Emilia, Italy)

From this description it seems that Simone has a rather complete understanding of rainfall and evaporation. But a closer look at her drawing reveals that the rain going up needs to be contained inside something like a tube (see arrow on right of Figure 7.2). These marks suggest that she is still thinking of water as liquid, and therefore this heavier-than-air substance needs to be contained in order to be transported back into the clouds.

At this point the teacher in Reggio would intervene with a comment such as this: "These marks [the tube] are very interesting, Simone. Could you tell me why you drew them?" The drawing becomes a platform for discussion among teacher and children. Drawings are frequently shared with the group, usually about four children, and the children discuss what the drawings mean. The drawings help the children develop a common referent, and this in turn helps them reconstruct their misconceptions about a science topic (see Forman, 1989). The teachers in Reggio have used drawing to teach other concepts, such as shadows, mirror reflections, gravity on the bottom of the earth, and algorithms for making tea.

We have extended drawing to learn in the United States with other themes, such as simple machines and crystalline growth (see Edwards, For-

man, & Gandini, in press). Through careful analysis of the process of drawing, we have determined that children must make a shift from drawing how
something looks to drawing how something works. This means children
have to go beyond the literal stage so common around age 6 or 7, when they
are overly concerned with picture realism (Gardner, 1980). Teachers and
children should not confuse *drawing to learn* with *learning to draw*. These
are fundamentally different enterprises.

## Collaborative Problem Solving

Educators have appreciated the power of group discussion for some
time, but only recently have begun to formalize the dynamics of collaborative problem solving. Group problem-solving research has moved beyond
the realm of teaching good citizenship and into mainstream cognitive science. Through a revival of interest in Vygotsky (1978) and the reconstruction
of Piaget's theory of knowledge (Doise & Mugny, 1984), basic and applied
research has been forthcoming on how knowledge construction is essentially
a social endeavor.

Tudge and Caruso (1988) present the implications of this research base
for early childhood education. In summary, they describe the type of setups
that generate quality collaborative problem solving, such as balance beams
and marble rollways. They then proceed to explain just what the children
do in collaborative learning that deepens their understanding. This list includes the role of cognitive conflict, the need to explicate thinking for others, and the use of inferences that go beyond what can be seen. These processes are more probable within social debate than when a child is working
alone.

We can look again at practices in Reggio Emilia, Italy, for wonderful
examples of collaborative problem solving in science. In one project, four
children, ages 5-½ to 6, volunteered to design an athletic event, the long
jump. In the course of this project they were faced with problems of many
types: rules of fairness, how to measure the long jump, how to divide the
school into ability flights, and how to read the symbols on a 10-meter tape
(see Forman & Gandini, 1991). Of particular interest was the following episode on how (and whether) to offer girls an advantage. This episode brings
into conflict two interacting variables, speed and fatigue, as well as a challenge of sexism from the girls. The episode begins as follows:

> In order to focus the discussion of rules the teacher helps by asking the
> children to make a small replica of the track itself. This serves as a common
> referent from which the children can discuss rules of fair competition. The
> children have made the sand pit from a highly textured paper and the

**Figure 7.3   Representation of the debate among four children on what it means to give the girls a handicap in a long jump contest.**

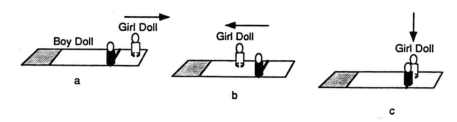

runway from a less textured paper. To facilitate the discussion the teacher provides the children with small wooden dolls that the children can move around to clarify something said.

A discussion ensues about the girl and boy runners. Augusto offers his opinion that girls cannot jump as far as boys. Silvia and Stephania listen, but do not agree. Silvia says, "I told you a thousand times, woman also do sports and can do things even stronger than the Long Jump."

Augusto pushes his point that the girls need some sort of handicap to make the competition fair. "But, do you want more run up? Yes or no?" The girls need to start further back, so they will have more space to run before they jump, Augusto explains as he positions the girl doll further back [Figure 7.3a]. The girl doll, in the red pants, is placed several inches behind the starting line.

Stephania protests, "But if they are tired, they can not make it, they cannot jump."

Lorenzo intervenes. He says, "Maybe I have misunderstood. She has to start further up, because she has very little strength and this way she doesn't get tired." He moves the girl doll, in red pants, in advance of the boy doll [Figure 7.3b]. Lorenzo no doubt believes that he is being fair.

Stephania takes a definite stand on this issue. "Hey no, come on. We have already decided the rule. The girls should start from the same line of departure as the boys." Silvia agrees completely with Stephania.

And with this assertion, Silvia moves the girl doll back to the start line with the boy doll [Figure 7.3c]. But for the boys the problem persists and will only be resolved toward the end of the project when they implement their rules for the actual event. (Forman & Gandini, 1991).

If we review this sequence, we can better understand the learning that takes place when children discuss issues among themselves. First, the medium of the collage layout and the dolls improve the chances that the children can communicate effectively. Young children have a tendency to use indefinite words like, "do this" and "not that," which makes it difficult to share meanings verbally. So the tangible materials, combined with their movement and the children's gestures, make it possible for the children to focus on the debate rather than the verbal skills of making their words unambiguous.

Then, the issues themselves were wonderfully rich. Just for the moment, let's accept Augusto's premise that girls should be given an advantage. How could this be done fairly? Augusto reasons that the girls should be moved back to increase the distance from the jumping point. This is a reasonable suggestion given his premise that more distance means more speed, which in turn means longer jumps. Of course, this assumption is true only if the girls cannot reach maximum speed in the original running space. The extra running space is superfluous beyond the point of maximum speed. So, extra running space may not mean more speed.

Stephania counters Augusto with her concern about the runner getting too tired. If you move the runner back, the greater distance will make the runner more fatigued. Perhaps since this girl doll represented herself, she related more to the tired feelings than did Augusto.

But Lorenzo counters Stephania by saying the lesser distance means less fatigue, so he moves the girl doll up. Thus we see the advantage of having several children relate to the same issue. They do so in different ways, and the system of relations becomes richer for all children. More distance increases speed, which increases the jump for Augusto, but more distance increases fatigue, which decreases the jump for Stephania. Then does it follow that less distance decreases fatigue, which increases the jump, in Lorenzo's solution? Lorenzo does not consider that the effects of speed and fatigue might cancel each other out. For children to combine two relations, they need representations more formal than wooden dolls.

The problem is simply short-circuited for the moment by Stephania, who insists that there is no reason to give girls an advantage. End of sequence, but the stage has been set for a return to this problem during the actual long jump event. The children decide that it is all right for the jumpers to begin wherever they like. The children learn to distinguish rules of fairness from strategies of choice.

## CONCLUSION

The flow of thinking, represented in Figure 7.1, can help us summarize what we have said so far about teaching. Teachers can enter this three-part dynamic flow in a variety of places. Class activities can be structured to increase the probability of unexpected events (*What's wrong here?*). Teachers can help children make better and better representations of what happened through drawings, diagrams, charts, lists, and observational records

(*What happened here?*). Teachers can encourage children to debate and thereby reflect upon the quality of their proofs (*What's the proof here?*). The intent of group discussions is to challenge the face validity of the familiar.

Special attention should be given to the developmental level of children within each content area. Proof for young children can be a summary of the events as observed, but for older children, proofs can rely on necessary truths of deduction. For the younger child, heavy objects made of wood float; heavy objects made of metal sink. The older child will want more than an endless list of floaters and sinkers. So for older children, proof goes beyond the givens.

Scientific reasoning begins with a question. The question might be presented by the teacher, but before scientific reasoning kicks in, the children have to sense the conflict between what was expected and what was observed. We know from the diaries of Susan Isaacs, Nathan Isaacs, Jean Piaget, Francis Hawkins, and David Hawkins that children are indeed curious about a multitude of events. But these do not include all of science. Children ask about the beginning of the universe, but not about the coexistence of a star and its light. They ask about animal growth, but not about predator–prey ecosystems. They ask, "Why does it rain when the sun is out?" but not, "Why are the daylight hours shortening?" Questions are themselves mini-theories, and a theory means that the child already has the cognitive wherewithal to relate two or more facts. But since some questions are more complicated mini-theories, children cannot grasp the question itself. These questions they do not ask.

Research in early scientific thinking can inform us about why certain questions are more complex than others. This, indirectly, helps us understand why young children ask some questions and do not ask other questions. The questions that children ask can then be organized into a flexible curriculum for early science education. Research shows that an emphasis on thinking skills has an impact on achievement (Tilgner, 1990). But the implementation of basic research into science curriculum continues to be a slow and sometimes bureaucratic process. As Tilgner (1990) points out, the resistance to teaching science in the younger years is as common today as it was 20 years ago. We have a clearly identified need to advocate for early science education.

## REFERENCES

Bar, V. (1989). Children's views about the water cycle. *Science Education*, 73 (4), 481–500.

Beveridge, M. (1985). The development of young children's understanding of the process of evaporation. *British Journal of Educational Psychology, 55,* 84–90.

Carey, S. (1985). *Conceptual change in childhood.* Cambridge, MA: MIT Press.

Carey S. (1986). Cognitive science and science education. *American Psychologist, 41* (10), 1123–1130.

Department of Education and Science. (1989). *Science in the national curriculum.* London: Department of Education and Science and the Welsh Office, Her Majesty's Services.

DiSessa, A. A. (1988). Knowledge in pieces. In G. Forman & P. Pufall (Eds.), *Constructivism in the computer age* (pp. 49–70). Hillsdale, NJ: Lawrence Erlbaum.

Doise, W., & Mugny, G. (1984). *The social development of the intellect.* Oxford, England: Pergamon.

Driver, R. (1989). Students' conceptions and the learning of science. [Special issue]. *International Journal of Science Education, 11,* 481–490.

Duckworth, E. (1987). *"The having of wonderful ideas" and other essays on teaching and learning.* New York: Teachers College Press.

Edwards, C., Forman, G., & Gandini, L. (Eds.). (in press). *Education for all the children: The multisymbolic approach to early education in Reggio Emilia, Italy.* Norwood, NJ: Ablex.

Elkind, D. (1989). Developmentally appropriate education for four year olds. *Theory into Practice, 28* (1), 47–52.

Feher, E. (1990). Interactive museum exhibits as tools for learning: Explorations with light. *International Journal of Science Education, 12* (1), 33–49.

Flavell, J. H. (1988). The development of children's knowledge about the mind: From cognitive connections to mental representations. In J. W. Astington, P. Harris, & D. Olson (Eds.), Developmental theories of mind (pp. 244–267). New York: Cambridge University Press.

Forman, G. (1985). The value of kinetic print in computer graphics for young children. In E. Klein (Ed.), *Children and computers* (pp. 61–75). San Francisco: Jossey-Bass.

Forman, G. (1989). Helping children ask good questions. In B. Neugebauer (Ed.), *The wonder of it: Exploring how the world works* (pp. 21–25). Redmond, WA: Exchange Press.

Forman, G., & Gandini, L. (1991). *The long jump: Using small group projects in Reggio Emilia, Italy* [160-minute VHS video]. Amherst: School of Education, University of Massachusetts.

Forman, G., & Hill, F. (1984). *Constructive play: Applying Piaget in the preschool.* Menlo Park, CA: Addison-Wesley.

Forman, G., & Kaden, M. (1987). Research on science education for young children. In C. Seefeldt (Ed.), *The early childhood curriculum: A review of current research* (1st ed., pp. 141–164). New York: Teachers College Press.

Gardner, H. (1980). *Artful scribbles: The significance of children's drawings.* New York: Basic Books.

Konicek, D., King, S., & Teece, D. (1990). Beneath the surface. *Science and Children, 27* (5), 27–28.

Larkin, J. H., & Simon, H. A. (1987). Why a diagram is (sometimes) worth ten thousand words. *Cognitive Science, 19*, 65–100.

Lawson, A. (1988). The acquisition of biological knowledge during childhood: Cognitive conflict or tabula rasa? *Journal of Research in Science Teaching, 25* (3), 185–199.

Levin, I., Siegler, R. S., & Druyan, S. (1990). Misconceptions about motion: Development and training effects. *Child Development, 61*, 1544–1557.

Mintzes, J. J. (1989). The acquisition of biological knowledge during childhood: An alternative conception. *Journal of Research in Science Teaching, 26* (9), 823–824.

Pillow, B. H. (1988). The development of children's beliefs about the mental world. *Merrill-Palmer Quarterly, 34* (1), 1–29.

Rice, K., & Feher, E. (1987). Pinholes and images: Children's conceptions of light and vision. *Science Education, 71* (4), 629–639.

Rudnitsky, A. N., & Hunt, C. R. (1986). Children's strategies for discovering cause–effect relationships. *Journal of Research in Science Teaching, 23* (5), 451–464.

Russell, T., Harlen, W., & Watt, D. (1989). Children's ideas about evaporation. *International Journal of Science Education, 11* (Special Issue), 566–576.

Shapiro, B. L. (1989). What children bring to light: Giving high status to learners' views and actions in science. *Science Education, 73* (6), 711–733.

Tilgner, P. J. (1990). Avoiding science in the elementary school. *Science Education, 74* (4), 421–431.

Tudge, J., & Caruso, D. (1988, November). Cooperative problem solving in the classroom: Enhancing young children's cognitive development. *Young Children*, pp. 46–52.

Wandersee, J. H., Mintzes, J. J., & Arnaudin, M. W. (1987). Children's biology: A content analysis of conceptual development in the life sciences. In J. D. Novak (Ed.), *Proceedings of the Second International Seminar on Misconceptions and Educational Strategies in Science and Mathematics*. Ithaca, NY: Cornell University.

Wasserman, S. (1988). Play-debrief-replay: An instructional model for science. *Childhood Education, 64* (4), 232–234.

Wheatley, G. H. (1991). Constructivist perspective on science and mathematics learning. *Science Education, 75* (1), 9–21.

Vygotsky, L. S. (1978). *Mind in society: The development of higher psychological processes* (M. Cole, V. John-Steiner, S. Scribner, & E. Souberman, Eds.). Cambridge, MA: Harvard University Press.

# CHAPTER 8

# The Social Studies in Early Childhood Education

CAROL SEEFELDT

Disparate yet similar, the fields of early childhood education and the social studies share a number of commonalities. The social studies, comprising three complex and multidisciplinary strands—knowledge, attitudes, and skills—has as its purpose "to prepare young people to be able to identify, understand, and work to solve the problems that face our diverse nation and interdependent world" (National Council for the Social Studies [NCSS], 1989, p. 15). Early childhood education, as well, is multi-and interdisciplinary and has as its overarching purpose fostering the development of children to become informed citizens capable of thinking, making decisions, and participating fully in our democracy (National Association for the Education of Young Children [NAEYC] & National Association of Early Childhood Specialists in State Departments of Education [NAECS], 1991, p. 29).

In addition to sharing the same broad, ambitious yet ambiguous purpose, the fields of social studies and early childhood education are similar in another way. Because of the multidisciplinary nature and breadth of each field, each is hindered in achieving its ambitious purpose by lack of clarity of definition, absence of specificity of goals and objectives, and uncertainty about how these goals and objectives are to be accomplished.

This chapter will (1) describe the differing definitions of the social studies and show that although early childhood education has clarity of definition, the breadth and multidisciplinary nature of the field affect clarity; (2) relate the lack of clarity of definition to the present diversity of goals and objectives in both the social studies and early childhood education; (3) examine the social studies in early childhood education by reviewing the key concepts of children's understanding of them in three social science disciplines—history, geography, and economics—briefly discussing issues surrounding the implementation of these disciplines; and (4) conclude by speculating on the future of the social studies in the early childhood curriculum.

## DIFFERING DEFINITIONS

Definitions have the function of determining direction, or specifying limits to curriculum. As such, definitions in the social studies and early childhood education can bring a preciseness and clarity to the curriculum. Because of the multidisciplinary nature of the social studies, there are many differing voices and opinions. The result is imprecise definitions of the nature and scope of the field. Early childhood education, on the other hand, does have clarity of definition. Nevertheless, the breadth of early childhood education as a field also serves to limit the potential usefulness of its clear definition.

### Defining the Social Studies

Deriving from differing perspectives of social studies, there are at least three different categories of definitions. The first group defines the social studies as discipline-based. Social science disciplines, including anthropology, economics, geography, history, sociology, psychology, and political science, are listed as constituting the social studies (Michaelis, 1988). A second grouping of definitions revolves around the overarching goal of the social studies, that of developing citizens who are prepared to participate in a democratic society. The transmission of those moral and ethical values accepted as basic to American life forms the core of this group of definitions (Holmes, 1991; Michaelis, 1988; Parker, 1991). Still others define the social studies as being primarily concerned with reflective thinking or decision making. "The mark of the good citizen is the quality of decisions which he, or she, reaches on public and private matters of social concern" (Mitsakos, 1981, p. 15; see also Litogot, 1991; Sears & Parsons, 1991).

Combining these divergent views, the National Council for the Social Studies (1989) defines the social studies as

> the study of political, economic, cultural, and environmental aspects of societies in the past, present, and future. The social studies equip [children] with the knowledge and understanding of the past necessary for coping with the present and planning for the future, enable them to understand and participate effectively in their world, and explain their relationship to other people and to social, economic, and political institutions. (p. 15)

The National Commission on Social Studies in the Schools (NCSSS, 1989)

> believes that the social studies in today's schools includes history, geography, government and civics, economics, anthropology, sociology and psy-

chology, as well as subject matter drawn from the humanities—religion, literature and the arts—and that social studies combines those fields and uses them in a direct way to develop a systematic and interrelated study of people in societies, past and present. (p. ix)

Given these broad, even global and often conflicting definitions of social studies, there is little agreement on the goals and objectives in this expansive field. Lack of specificity of goals and objectives, in turn, leads to basic confusion over what to teach young children or how to know what children have learned.

### Definitions in Early Childhood Education

The field of early childhood education, on the other hand, has clarity of definition: "that education taking place between birth and age 8" (NAEYC & NAECS, 1991, p. 21). Early childhood educators generally agree that "it serves children ranging in age from birth to about 8 years of age; sometimes parents of these children are also viewed as clients. Its purposes include education, child care, and the nurturing of development" (Spodek, 1982, p. xvii). Nevertheless, in the field of early childhood education there is no greater clarity of goals and objectives or methods by which to achieve them, than there is in the field of social studies. This, too, is directly related to the diversity of disciplines constituting the field of early childhood education. The field includes, but is not limited to, the disciplines of health (physical, dental, and mental), parent and community involvement, nutrition, social welfare, and career development.

Although the age range of early childhood, 8 years, is not exceptionally long, the developmental stages within this range vary dramatically. Infants and toddlers require a very different type of educational setting and experience than do preschoolers, whose development in turn demands a different type of educational experience than that appropriate for children in kindergarten and the primary grades. Linked to these differing developmental stages is the fact that young children's educational experiences are under different sponsorship and take place in a variety of settings.

As a result, the field of early childhood education is as complicated by differing goals and opinions on how these goals can best be achieved as is social studies. For example, the goal of child-care programs is to provide care for children whose parents are employed outside the home. Those of the nursery or preschool revolve around providing children with opportunities for socialization. Goals for kindergarten generally include preparation for the primary grades, and goals of the primary grades focus around gaining knowledge and the skills of reading, writing, and computation.

## DIVERSITY OF GOALS AND OBJECTIVES

Diversity enriches. Without diversity and the expertise provided by the disparate disciplines constituting both early childhood education and the social studies, either would be unlikely to achieve its overarching purpose of preparing children to take their place as functioning members of a democratic society.

On the other hand, diversity can hinder. The philosophies, theories, and methods of the disparate disciplines that make up the two fields are too dissimilar and divergent to permit agreement or consensus within either field. With differing terminology and ideas, there is confusion.

While the purpose of providing children with the knowledge, skills, and attitudes required to participate in a democratic society has remained constant throughout the history of the social studies, the specific goals and how to accomplish them have always differed. Intertwined with those of early childhood education, the goals of the social studies have responded to societal needs and demands, and social forces, and have reflected current societal values.

### Historical Perspectives

Both social studies and early childhood education had their beginnings in the late 1880s when the prevalent American societal need was to accommodate the wave of immigrants. In 1886 the National Education Association passed a resolution that the common, or elementary, school "be required by legislation to teach the principles of American government, both state and national," for the purposes of "inculcating love of country and encouraging respect for authority and obedience to the law" (Handler, 1985, p. 10).

Early childhood education, as well, responded to society's need to accommodate the vast number of immigrants. The kindergarten, even before it became institutionalized in the public school, and child-care programs, established by charitable organizations as the nursery school, were viewed as vehicles that would enculturate immigrant or poor children and their families into the American way of life. In order to ground poor and immigrant children in the moral, social, and mental habits basic to functioning in a democracy, "the kindergarteners [what the teachers, not the pupils, were called] professed to be more interested in preparing children for life than in teaching the preliminary skills necessary to do well in school" (Beatty, 1989, p. 65).

Early on, social studies content became an important component of early childhood curriculum. Right from the start, however, conflicting philosophies and ideas resulted in differing goals and disparate conceptions of how the broad purpose of preparing children for life in a democracy would be achieved through the social studies.

In the early 1900s, Patty Smith Hill (1923), attempting to apply "the principles of democracy to school organization" (p. iii), initiated a curriculum around the goal of habit and skill development. The goal of preparing children for participation in a democracy was expected to be achieved by training children in the skills and habits necessary to function in a democratic society. *A Conduct Curriculum for the Kindergarten and First-Grade* (Burke, 1923) provided an inventory of habits stated in measurable form, primarily in the realm of moral and social conduct. This specification of skills "became not merely an appendix to the curriculum but a gradual transformer of it" (Weber, 1969, p. 133), and the development of habits and skills became the dominant goal of the kindergarten. Rather than following the theories of Dewey in preparing children for democracy, the social studies curriculum of skills development, more congruent with the theories of Thorndike, prepared children to follow directions and know their place by knowing what was expected of them in a learning environment.

If report cards are indicators of program objectives, philosophy, and curriculum content, then the development of skills and work habits, just as in the early 1900s, seems to dominate in schools for young children today (Freeman & Hatch, 1989). In an analysis of report cards from the state of Ohio, it was found that over 80% included social skills items, and 100% had items categorized as work or habit skills.

At the same time that Hill was focusing on habit training, others during the early 1900s were conceiving broader goals and objectives for early childhood curriculum. Influenced by the philosophy and writings of John Dewey, Alice Temple in 1919 categorized early childhood subject matter into the categories of (1) natural objects and phenomena—nature study; (2) human beings and human activities—home and community life; and (3) the products of human intelligence—literature, music, and art (Weber, 1969, p. 93). The second category corresponded to today's conception of social studies. To study human beings and their activities, children took excursions into their immediate environment to study community life, worked in groups preparing meals, and constructed doll houses and furniture. As seasonal and holiday activities were a part of home activities, they were also included as a part of the curriculum.

Dewey's philosophy was reflected as well in the expanding community curriculum designed by Lucy Sprague Mitchell. Based on Dewey's philosophy that curriculum content stems directly from the child's interactions with his or her immediate environment, Mitchell (1934) developed a social studies curriculum built on the content of children's here and now lives.

Beginning with the study of their home and family, and gradually expanding to that of their neighborhood, community, the state, the nation, and the world, children would be exposed to a logical, holistic, and coordinated approach to the study of people living in societies (Brophy, 1990). By enlarging and enriching children's understanding of the immediate environment and the world and their place in it, Mitchell's goal was to develop children's intellectual capabilities in terms of relationship thinking, generalizing from experience, and the re-creation of concrete experience through symbolic, dramatic play.

Quickly adopted as the "Here and Now" curriculum, social studies in early childhood programs and the elementary school was constructed as a continual, sequential, and expanding program that began with the study of self, home, school, and community in the kindergarten and expanded to that of families in grade 1. In grade 2, children learned about neighborhoods, and in grade 3, communities. This expanding community approach continues today to dominate not only the early childhood social studies curriculum, but that of the elementary school as well (Brophy, 1990).

Inroads into this approach were made during the 1960s when curriculum reform and reconstruction were rampant. During this post-Sputnik era, the demands for education that would prepare children to compete scientifically in the world community led to a focus on teaching for concept formation. Based on Bruner's *Toward a Theory of Instruction* (1966) and *The Process of Education* (1960), the idea of planning social studies instruction around key concepts dominated.

Bruner proposed a spiral approach to the curriculum. The big ideas, or key concepts, could be used to coordinate the knowledge or content sequences with the cognitive stages of the learner so that at each successive stage children would be dealing with concepts they could understand, but in progressively greater complexity and depth. Reflecting the view that young children were not only interested in learning concepts but able to do so if these were introduced appropriately, Wann, Dorn, and Liddle (1962) wrote *Fostering Intellectual Development in Young Children*. Robison and Spodek's (1965) *New Directions in the Kindergarten*, as well, built on Bruner's philosophy that children and concepts could be brought together.

The difficulty of identifying key concepts in any given subject, lack of agreement on what these consisted of, and confusion over which were critical for young children negated full implementation of Bruner's ideas. Other problems hindered. Teachers of young children rarely had adequate background in the social sciences to be able to identify key concepts, nor did they have experience in translating these concepts into appropriate learning experiences for children. More important perhaps was the advent of the back-to-basics movement of the late 1970s. Reflecting society's growing conservatism, the emphasis on skills accumulation continues today as a major force in curriculum development.

Nevertheless, the use of key concepts continues today, and the utility of using them to organize subject matter continues. Recent position statements (discussed below) and most of the social sciences disciplines are organized around statements of key concepts or main ideas.

## Current Conceptions of the Social Studies

These historic approaches to the social studies curriculum continue today, but not without criticism. Both the expanding community approach and the skills approach are criticized on the basis that they are devoid of social studies content or intellectual stimulation (Bennett, 1986; Finn & Ravitch, 1988). Viewed as trite, boring, and intellectually sterile, Temple's approach has been labeled stereotypical as well.

Criticism of the key concept approach to the social studies is also found. Organizing curriculum around key concepts, according to cognitive theory, is contrary to the way humans organize knowledge. Presenting children with isolated segments of information would only lead to fragmented learning.

The real question is, however, whether any of these approaches to the social studies actually fulfill the stated purpose of either social studies or early childhood education.

> Are children developing skills to absorb new information in light of the information explosion? Are they learning structures for understanding and adapting to changes in technology, the marketplace, and their own family organization? Are they beginning to learn about interdependence and the relationship of technology to social conditions? (NCSS, 1989, p. 14)

Answering these questions with a resounding no, three commissions—the National Commission on Social Studies in the Schools, the National Council for the Social Studies Task Force on Early Childhood/Elementary Social Studies, and the California State Department of Education (CSDE)—have prepared statements of goals and objectives for today's social studies. Agreeing on the sterility of traditional social studies curriculum, and the fact that lack of clarity over goals and objectives exists, the commissions disagree on what the nature of the social studies curriculum should be. Descriptions of the reports on each commission follow.

1. *Social Studies for Early Childhood and Elementary School Children: Preparing for the 21st Century* by the National Council for the Social Stud-

ies (1989) has been labeled too traditional, even backward looking (Risinger, 1991). This report continues the traditional identification of three separate social studies strands: (1) knowledge and understandings, (2) skills, and (3) attitudes and values.

The knowledge strand is defined as the social science disciplines of history, geographic concepts, concepts from anthropology and sociology, and economics. The skills strand includes skills that are primary to social studies, such as those related to maps and globes, and those that enhance students' abilities to learn, make decisions, and develop as competent, self-directed citizens. Also identified by the task force are research skills, such as collecting, organizing, and interpreting data; thinking skills, such as hypothesizing, comparing, and drawing inferences; and decision-making skills, such as seeing others' points of view, accepting responsibility, and dealing with conflict.

Stating that "the early years are ideal for children to begin to understand democratic norms and values (justice, equality, etc.)" (NCSS, 1989, p. 16), the Council suggests that children can achieve a positive self-concept within the social studies, understand the similarities and differences between people, and "understand that they are unique in themselves but share many similar feelings and concerns with other children. They need to understand how as individuals, they can contribute to society" (p. 17).

2. *Charting a Course: Social Studies for the 21st Century* was prepared by the National Commission on Social Studies in the Schools (1989), a task force representing politicians, teachers, professors, scholars, and other educational leaders. The purpose was to bring clarity to the question, "What should be the goals and vision of the social studies as we set about to prepare young people for citizenship and leadership in the next century?" (NCSSS, 1989, p. v).

To do so, the National Commission on Social Studies in the Schools selected the core of knowledge from history, geography, and the American economic system as the curriculum for a "unifying and coherent framework for the social studies in the schools" (p. viii).

3. *History-Social Science Framework*, by the California State Department of Education (1987), has as its object to "set forth, in an organized way, the knowledge and understanding that our students need to function intelligently now and in the future" (p. 3). The report suggests that "knowledge of the history-social science disciplines (history, geography, economics, political science, anthropology, psychology, sociology, and the humanities) is essential in developing individual and social intelligence" (p. 3).

Centered in the chronological study of history, this framework proposes an integrated and correlated approach to the teaching of history-social science and introduces a new approach for the K-3 grades. "Through literature, stories, myths, fairy tales, children's imaginations will be fired and their appetite whetted for understanding how the world came to be as it is" (CSDE, 1987, p. 5).

## Current Conceptions of Early Childhood

Early childhood educators have also responded to the lack of content in the early childhood curriculum with a position statement. *Guidelines for Appropriate Curriculum Content and Assessment in Programs Serving Children Ages 3 Through 8* (NAEYC & NAECS, 1991) is designed to "(1) guide teachers and supervisors to: make informed decisions about appropriate curriculum content and assessment, (2) evaluate existing curriculum and assessment practices, (3) advocate for more appropriate approaches" (p. 21).

This statement defines curriculum and assessment, states the need for guidelines on curriculum content, describes the ways children learn as curriculum theory, and lists 20 guidelines for curriculum content. Guidelines for planning instruction and communicating with parents and a model of learning and teaching are included.

There is no hint, however, in these *Guidelines* of exactly what content would be taught to young children other than a reference to the utility of the *Guidelines* as applied to the area of mathematics. For other content areas, the *Guidelines* end by encouraging teachers and educators "to think about this framework in their daily work with children and to use it as a tool for analyzing and conceptualizing appropriate curriculum expectations for individuals and groups of children" (p. 37).

## SOCIAL STUDIES IN EARLY CHILDHOOD

Despite these efforts, confusion over what social studies content children should learn abounds. Social studies alone is not responsible for this confusion. If the field of early childhood education had clarity of goals for appropriate content, then educators would have direction for selecting and refining the commissions' goals for social studies learning.

Early childhood educators can, however, using the mandate found in the conclusions of the *Guidelines for Appropriate Curriculum Content* (NAEYC & NAECS, 1991) to analyze and conceptualize appropriate curriculum, begin the process of selecting social studies curriculum. Because the disciplines of history, geography, and economics were identified by the three commissions as indispensable in the social studies curriculum for young children, the remainder of this chapter will focus on these. The key concepts or core ideas of history, geography, and economics will be described, and the research on children's knowledge in these fields will be presented. The issues surrounding the inclusion of content from history, geography, and economics in early childhood curriculum will be discussed.

## History

The recommendation that history form the core of social studies instruction in the school stems from the belief that without knowledge of the past transmitted through a common national memory of the study of history, children are unable to identify with their nation and assume their civic responsibility as adults.

> We believe that good citizenship is not just a matter of the observance of outward forms, transmitted from the old to the young, but also a matter of reasoned conviction, and the end result of people thinking for themselves. Each generation faces new challenges, for which lessons from the past have much relevance. Individuals do not think well if they do not understand their own history. (NCSSS, 1989, p. xi)

Critics of the traditional expanding community social studies curriculum believe history is the natural choice of content in schools for young children because history is a story well told and all young children, they claim, love a good story (Guzzetti & McGowan, 1991). History, in the form of myths, stories, and folktales will engage children's minds, stimulating and motivating them to learn to learn (Bennett, 1986; Finn & Ravitch, 1988). Further, for very young children, whose thinking is characterized by confusion over fact and fantasy and for whom the magical is real, stories, myths, and fairytales are believed to hold deep, personal meaning (Egan, 1988).

Children under the age of 7 or 8 have no clear meaning of historical time, nor will they until well into adolescence (Piaget & Inhelder, 1969), but they do have clear and accurate concepts of the causality that holds the stories of history together, claims Egan (1988). "They clearly do understand power and weakness, oppression, resentment, and revolt, ambition and punishment" (p. 33), all of which would permit children to gain meaning from the story of history. "Telling children dramatic stories of human cultures, and particularly of the one of which they are a part and partial product" (p. 208), is an appropriate beginning for children's lifelong study of history.

True, children are interested in stories and do make sense of all types of myths, fairytales, and nursery rhymes in much the same way they make sense of the realities in their lives. Nevertheless, if history is in fact essential in developing individual and social intelligence, without which children will be buffeted by changes that are beyond their comprehension and unable to make wise choices in their own lives or to understand the swift-moving changes in state, nation, and world affairs (CSDE, 1987, p. 3), then its study must consist of more than a well-told story.

History is a complex field of complicated ideas and concepts. Although Brophy (1990) claims that history doesn't follow structuring around key concepts or generalizations, history is time-based and involves the study of change and the past. These concepts, then, can form a framework for the beginning study of history.

*Time.* "What notion of time has our Tommy got? Does yesterday exist for him save as something very distant, vague and separate as were, a little while ago, his own toes and feet?" asked Margaret McMillan in 1919 (p. 235). Research suggests that children do have an intuitive sense of time based on their direct experiences. "I don't know what time it is, but my daddy comes to pick me up after nap," states 3-year-old Kim. Limited to their perception of the succession and duration of time, and to their ability to sequence and organize daily experiences, children's intuitive ideas of time are subjective. This subjectivity leads to errors. Five-year-olds know that waiting for 10 minutes will be harder than waiting for 5, but they also conclude that it takes less time for a fast-turning wheel to spin for 5 minutes than it does for a faucet to drip for the same amount of time (Acredolo & Schmid, 1981).

Intuitive time is distinct from operational time. Operational time, which is based on logical thinking, involves understanding of relations of succession and duration and is founded on analogous operations in logic, which may be either qualitative or quantitative (Piaget, 1946, p. 551). It is not until children enter formal operations, around the beginning of adolescence, that they are able to master operational time.

Perhaps because temporal sequencing requires only qualitative comparisons, such as little versus large, children as young as 4 or 5 are able to demonstrate some understanding of the ability to sequence events. Four- to 6-year-olds are able to order actions in sequence to achieve a goal, they know that events happen in order, and they are able to sequence their day around cyclically organized daily occurrences (French, 1989; French & Nelson, 1981; Vukelich & Thornton, 1990). Four-year-olds can accurately judge temporal order at above-chance level and by 5 are able to judge the backward order of daily activities, the forward order from multiple reference points within the day, and the lengths of intervals separating daily activities. By about 7 years, children can also judge the backward order of events from multiple reference points (Friedman, 1990).

Five-year-olds begin to understand temporal units of time, such as day, date, and calendar time, formulated on the temporal or sequential order of events and can orient themselves in time, associating time with an external event: "It is day; the sun is shining." "It is night; the stars are out." Calendar time includes the development of identifying time concepts such as first, last, next, later, sooner, before, and after. By 5 years, children can tell what day it is, and they use general terms such as "winter time" before they will use the general terms "today," "before," or "in a few days" (Ames, 1946). Children are first able to respond to a time word; next, they can use the word themselves; finally, they can use the time word to answer a question correctly. Six-, 7-, and 8-year-olds can begin to use conventional methods to orient themselves in time, and clocks, watches, and calendars begin to have some meaning.

Dunfee (1970), from an extensive review of the literature, suggests that young children are receptive to planned instruction in the concepts of time. This instruction, however, is based on the cyclical, recurring, and sequential events of children's day and life. Although it would be inappropriate to ask children to memorize the names of the days or months, to tell time, or to learn operational time concepts, it may be appropriate for adults to give children labels for these things and make certain their life has routine, and to introduce measurement of time through arbitrary measures (Forman & Kaden, 1987).

*Change.*    Over time things change. If children are to gain a sense of history, they must have some understanding of the concept of change. For young children, however, whose thought is dominated by their perception, change is a difficult concept to attain. Since children have little or no ability to conserve until after 7 or 8, changes that occur with the passage of time must appear as magical and unrelated to logic as any of the other changes that children experience.

Without an understanding of change, children are even unsure of the constancy and continuity of their own lives. Under 5, children are uncertain of the stability of their own gender (Slaby & Frey, 1975). Nor do they understand the changes that occur with illness and death. Because children blame themselves for both illness and death—"she was naughty and she got sick" or "he died because he was bad"—the conclusion is reached that their concepts of change are indeed primitive (White, Elsom, & Prawat, 1978).

According to children under the age of 5, death is something that might suddenly occur, either as the result of contagion or imminent justice. "Can I catch them?" asked a 4-year-old pointing to an old man's wrinkles. "I won't grow old because I'm real good," stated a 3-year-old. Galper, Jantz, Seefeldt, and Serock (1980) found that kindergarten and elementary school children were unable to understand aging as a continuous process in time. Children asserted that people grow older at different rates, and were quite willing to say that their father would stay the same age while they would get older, or that neither they themselves nor their grandmother grew older each year. Aging, for young children, seems related specifically to events in the time interval involved rather than to the passage of time.

Under 7 or 8, time is discontinuous as well as local since it can stop with any partial motion. This is why, for young children, adults are believed to have stopped aging, or why a tree is thought to age if it still grows, but not otherwise. Only with the introduction of operational time will duration and the changes that occur with the passage of time be understood as a continuous flux.

*The past.*    To understand the past, children must not only be able to understand that the present is but a single moment in a continuous process, but also be able to store and retrieve memories. The research on children's memory development is vast and readily available (Brainerd, Reyna, Howe, & Kingma, 1990). The various theoretical positions on memory development, the importance of storage failure versus retrieval failure, the relative importance of true forgetting processes versus test-induced processes, and the importance of store-based reminiscence versus retrieval-based reminiscence have been widely researched.

For Piaget and Inhelder (1969), however, the development of memory parallels that of perception and imagery. The process of being able to recall the past, to Piaget, is based on a changing operational structure that continually governs and transforms what has been stored.

*How Will History Be Taught?*    Rather than unifying and giving direction to the social studies by specifying the study of history through myths and stories for young children, the commissions have only added confusion and controversy to an already confounded field. By taking a simplistic view of both young children's thinking abilities and the study of history, the commissions have demonstrated limited knowledge of both children and history.

Considering the fact that the study of history is complex, and little is known of how children can gain an understanding of this complexity, it is unlikely that the study of history will become the foundation for the social studies in programs for young children. The belief that young children can learn history through story and myth is flawed.

Even if the telling of stories were found to be an efficient and sufficient method of transmitting all the knowledge of the past necessary to maintain and continually improve our democracy, early childhood educators might still resist this method. Early childhood interest has its own history. This history has always had difficulty with the idea of teaching children through folktales, myths, and fantasy stories. Montessori (1929) decried presenting children, who she claimed were in the process of trying to separate fact from fantasy, with stories in which bunnies talked and cats dressed in hats and held tea parties.

Lucy Sprague Mitchell (1934), who also thought children would be more interested in developing an understanding of their immediate world, believed that stories should revolve around the "Here and Now," not some fanciful, far-off and make-believe world.

> Indeed, it is only by exploring the here and now that children grow in the capacity to discover relations—to think. We find that the transition to the far-away and long-ago seldom takes place in schools before seven. History and distant geography appear, consequently, only as occasional episodes in kindergarten and first-grades; engines, boats, markets and stores take the place of the Eskimo and primitive men. (p. 23)

Today, myths and folktales or fantasy are considered inappropriate for other reasons. Many of these portray women and minorities in racist and sexist ways and are not appropriate for use with young children. Even when folktales and myths are not racist and sexist, they "hardly represent a complete or accurate picture of life either past or present" (Derman-Sparks & the ABC Task Force, 1989, p. 119).

Brophy (1990) reminds us as well that stories and folktales may be inaccurate and serve to perpetuate untruths rather than the reality of history. Children, Brophy claims, expect teachers to tell the truth and to teach them facts. Should teachers use myths and fantasy as a means of teaching history, children may come to question the credibility of their teachers.

Then, too, it's long been accepted that instruction should begin with what children know (Brophy, 1990; Dewey, 1916/1944; Prawatt, 1989). One could question, then, whether children really do know concepts present in folktales and myths. Given the difficulty children have in understanding time and the changes that occur in their own bodies as they age, and in recalling the past, one might question whether children really do understand the abstract and complex concepts present in stories, myths, and folktales. Beginning the study of history with myths and stories may have no more historic meaning for children than beginning with any other concept in history.

Still, teaching history through myths and stories puts children in touch with heroes and heroines. This personification entices children and leads them to identify with the past (NCSSS, 1989). It may be that, in order to teach history to young children, personification actually is the key, not, however, through identification with heroes and heroines found in myths and folktales, but through personification of history. The study of history begins with children and their daily activities. By recording their personal history through observations, records of growth in photographs, history books of their year in the preschool program, portfolios, and displays in the classroom, children have a record of their own past. This type of personification leads children to develop a sense of self in time—past, present, and future.

The most we know about teaching history to young children is the fact that history is a complex field, rich in difficult, abstract concepts, including, but not limited to, those of time, change, and the past. Perhaps those recommending that the study of history form the foundation for social studies have in fact aided in bringing order and clarity to the social studies. The recommendations of the California State Department of Education and the National Commission for Social Studies in the Schools that history become the core of the social studies may serve as an impetus for researchers and scholars to begin the systematic definition of the concepts of history and exploring the role of stories and myths in fostering these concepts in children.

## Geography

Geography, a science concerned with the study and description of the earth, has traditionally been considered of central importance in the social studies. Even though there isn't total agreement about the themes and key concepts of geography, there is a set of concepts, goals, and objectives considered key to children's learning of geography. Described as "noteworthy" by Brophy (1990, p. 373), these organizing themes and concepts suggest that children should be able to

- *Locate* themselves in space in relative terms, in relation to land forms or other natural resources, and eventually in absolute terms, that is, latitude and longitude
- Develop an understanding of the physical characteristics of *place*— land forms and water bodies, climate, soils, natural vegetation, and animal life
- Understand that there is a *relationship between humans and the environment*
- Know the *patterns of movement* of people, products, and information
- Have a concept of how *regions* form and change
- Develop skills of *mapping*

Based largely on Piaget's (1948) study of children's understanding of space and perceptual development, there is general understanding of how children understand these basic concepts of geography. The stages of children's understanding of the concepts of location, place, and the development of mapping skills have been researched and will be discussed in this section.

*Location.*     Children appear to progress through distinct stages in the development of geographic concepts (Stiles-Davis, Kritchevsky, & Bellugi, 1988). From birth through 14 months, geography learning consists of infants exploring and attending to the qualities of things in their environment, including their own bodies and visual and tactile senses. As object permanence develops, children begin to comprehend the relationships that exist between objects in the environment and themselves.

From 14 months through 3 years, children are able to distinguish between objects that are near and can be grasped, and those further away, as well as the space boundaries of their immediate environment, such as the bedroom or yard. Initially, they work out their own location and then go on to discern the whereabouts of other objects in their environment. With increasing visual skills and mobility, children expand their space boundaries. During this time, the development of children's geographic concepts has been directly related to their opportunities to actively explore their physical world. The greater children's opportunities to roam and move about, the greater their ability to locate objects and self in space (Stiles-Davis, Kritchevsky, & Bellugi, 1988).

By the early preschool years there is growing awareness that objects exist outside of the immediate environment. The spatial relationships between objects is also understood. Children express these concepts as they play with blocks, sands, and water, and construct with other materials. From preschool through the primary grades, children use language as well as drawings of maps and other symbols to represent their perceptions of their environment (Catling, 1978; Hewes, 1982).

*Place.*     Piaget (1948) also described children's growing awareness of concepts of the earth as the place they live. Dominated by artificialism and animism, children attribute life and consciousness to the earth, sun, moon, and stars as well as to living things. Throughout the early years, children are even confused about what constitutes life. Three-year-olds will attribute life to things that move. Until age 7 or so, children believe that cars, planes, rivers, and clouds have life and consciousness. Around 8 or 9, children begin to distinguish between movement caused by machines or imposed externally and that stemming from the internal life of organisms.

Until about 9 or 10, children also retain the belief that every object, including natural bodies, was made for a purpose (Piaget & Inhelder, 1969).

A natural object, such as the sun, a lake, or a mountain, is made for warmth, boating, or climbing, and because it has been made for humans, is closely allied to them. Children believe either that things were made by humans or that the things created themselves for the purpose of humans.

Children's understanding of the earth as a globe is primitive and intuitive. Until they are 8 or 9 years old, children seem to hold the same beliefs about the earth that people held before the fifteenth century. To young children, the earth is flat and all objects fall to that surface (Nussbaum & Novak, 1976). Children progress to higher levels as they mature, but even after 10 or 11 are still confused about the nature of the earth and globe (Sneider & Pulos, 1983).

*Mapping.*    Because of Piaget's work, an understanding of how children develop the ability to understand and use maps and globes is present. Although it's clear that children must be able to reason formally before they can fully understand the concepts involved in mapping, there is evidence that children do have personal and intuitive knowledge of maps.

As young as 3, without hesitation or need for prompting, young children interpret aerial photographs and maps in geographical terms (Spencer, Harrison, & Darvizeh, 1980). Children can identify roads and decode other environmental features. Even though they cannot explain perspective, or how the photos and maps were constructed or produced, they can read aerial photographs as maps. When not confused with the need to explain perspective or representation, or to explain distance and scale, direction or abstract locations, children seem to have a basic understanding of maps (Atkins, 1981).

Kindergarten children have also demonstrated some understanding of maps. Children as young as 5, when introduced to the concepts of mapping, were able to understand the basic relationship between the earth and sun (Portugaly, 1967). Robison and Spodek (1965) introduced kindergarten children to concepts of distance, direction, and scale and concluded that children were able to develop the skills needed to relate a map to a geographic area, locate places using distance and direction, and abstract information from map symbols.

By the first grade, the majority of children have some knowledge of perspective and can juxtapose streets, cities, states, and countries on the same plane instead of placing them in hierarchical order on a map, and by the second grade they demonstrate even greater understanding (Mugge, 1968).

Children spontaneously draw and build maps before they read them. Between the ages of 5 and 7, children spontaneously draw and build rough maps. These sometimes include roads, rivers, and highways, with pictures of houses or cars. Although not correct in abstract mapping terms, these drawings serve to illustrate children's basic ability to use and see symbols on a map. Between the ages of 7 and 9, children can draw maps relating symbols to the actual environment, for instance, using blue to represent water, or coloring an area green to symbolize a park. After 9, children are able to picture reality on a map, but it is not until after 11 or 12 that children are able to conceptualize the total relationship of the objects they draw on a map to the actual items (Stoltman, 1979).

*Geography in Early Childhood Education Today.*    It would seem, given the clarity of goals and objectives in the field of geography, and our understanding of how children progress in understanding them, that the study of geography would be central in the early childhood curriculum. Despite this clarity, the study of geography is limited in schools for young children, and Americans continue to be labeled geographic illiterates (NCSSS, 1989). This is surprising because not only do educators have direction from both geography and knowledge of children, but they also have a guide on how to implement geography curriculum in schools for young children.

Since 1934 educators have understood how geography and children can be brought together with integrity. In her book *Young Geographers*, Mitchell (1934) illustrated how geographic concepts can be made meaningful to young children. Mitchell listed on a chart the key concepts of geography; the interests of children from birth through age 13; the geographic relations children had already discovered at each age range; and the kinds of symbols children used in their play, art, space relations, human geography, and natural phenomena. On the other side of the chart were listed the procedures and practices teachers could use to match and foster children's development of geographic concepts.

The neglect of geography in the early childhood curriculum may be related to the field of early childhood education. Many who teach young children have little or no geographic knowledge. For those not teaching in a public school, no formal qualifications, standards, or formal education is required (Seefeldt, 1988). As a result, the majority of teachers working in child-care, nursery, or preschool may not even have completed high school, much less hold a baccalaureate degree. These teachers most likely have limited understanding of geography and may not even be able to use a map.

Public school teachers, who are required to hold a baccalaureate, may also be geographically illiterate. As part of the requirements for the baccalaureate, these teachers may take a course in geography; most, however, do not. Generally, undergraduates are required to select one or two courses from those categorized as the social sciences. The course(s) selected may not have anything to do with geography (Thornton & Wenger, 1990).

Without a knowledge base of geography themselves, teachers are unable to transmit knowledge to children (Prawatt, 1991) or even utilize the chart created by Lucy Sprague Mitchell (1934). Mitchell envisioned teachers who could, based on their own study of children's environment, create their own geography curriculum for each group of young children. Teachers can do this only if they themselves have a highly developed understanding of geography.

Coupled with the lack of geography knowledge is the unfortunate fact that many early childhood teachers may also lack knowledge of children (Goodlad, 1984). With the elimination of methods courses at universities in favor of a Holmes Group model of teacher education, teachers holding baccalaureate degrees may have as little as one course in child development. This course, typically a life-span course, often does not equip future teachers with an adequate understanding of the psychology of the young child. Those teachers without a baccalaureate have no formal training in child development and limited knowledge of children's thought processes or learning.

Teachers are limited in another way. Again, despite the clarity of geographic goals and children's understandings of them, teachers have limited access to this information. Cursory examination of early childhood introductory textbooks indicates that undergraduate students are not exposed to Mitchell's ideas, nor to information on how geography can be made accessible to young children. Nor do county and state early childhood curriculum guides or preschool curriculum materials typically include information on the teaching of geography.

Further, even the National Council for the Social Studies (1989) and the National Commission on Social Studies in the Schools (1989), while selecting geography as an essential subject, offer only vague and unspecific suggestions on how geography would be taught. They, like Alice Temple, suggest teachers have children take walks to examine their own immediate environment and that they expose children to environments far away in space and time through pictures and films. Mitchell's philosophy and contributions are not reflected in these statements. While criticizing the "Here and Now" and expanding community approach to the curriculum as boring and intellectually sterile, these guides completely miss the complexity of Mitchell's (1934) concept of education.

Mitchell (1934) did not see the child's immediate environment as simplistic and sterile. Rather, she saw it as complex. She wrote that at first glance her suggestion that geography learning begin with the child and his or her explorations of the immediate environment seemed preposterous because the environment was too complex.

Modern children are born into an appalling complicated world. The complications of their surrounding culture, however, instead of making this attack impossible, make it imperative. Simplification is necessary, but it is a simplification of the immediate and the everyday rather than a resource to a vicarious or alien culture. (p. 12)

Thus, despite the general agreement on the themes, key concepts, and specific goals and objectives within the field of geography, its inclusion in the early childhood curriculum is limited. Without knowledgeable teachers who understand the complexity of both children's immediate geographic environment and their thought processes, young children will have little exposure to the study of geography.

## Economics

"Economic illiteracy is an unfortunate way of life for the great majority of American people" (Kourilsky, 1981, p. 86). Economic literacy, in common with historical and geographic literacy, is believed essential for citizens of a democracy. According to the National Council for the Social Studies (1989), children "need useful and powerful economic knowledge and the formal development of critical-thinking skills." (p. 16)

*Definition and Key Concepts.*     Since 1948, when the Joint Council on Economic Education, representing business, labor, education, agriculture, and other groups, was organized, a clear definition and set of key economic concepts have existed. Defined as the study of how goods and services are produced and distributed and the activities of people who produce, save, spend, pay taxes, and perform personal services to satisfy their wants for food and shelter, their desire for new conveniences and comforts, and their collective wants for things such as education and natural defense, economics includes the following key concepts or main ideas.

- The wants of people everywhere are unlimited but resources are limited—there is scarcity.
- Because there are limited resources but unlimited wants, decisions must be made in the use of resources.
- The function of production, to some extent, is to meet the unlimited wants of consumers.
- People are interdependent on others for distribution, consumption, and savings.
- Money and barter are used to purchase goods.

*Children's Understanding of Economics.*     Children experience these economic concepts early in life. They observe parents exchanging money for goods, and they themselves participate in paying for some of the things they purchase. They receive money for gifts, sometimes saving it in a bank; they may even participate in opening bank accounts. Advertising convinces children they need more than they can have, and early in life they make decisions between the things they really need and those they only want.

In their play, children reveal some understanding of these concepts. They use economic scripts as they play store, pretending to purchase and sell goods, and use money to obtain services. Nevertheless, economic concepts, like those from geography and history, are far from fully developed. It is not until after 9 years of age that children understand the value of money are able to compare all coins, or understand the idea of credit or profit (Strauss, 1951, 1954). Following Piagetian theory, children's stages of economic understandings have been identified as

1. Unreflective and preoperational, exemplified by a highly literal reasoning based on the physical characteristics of objects or processes
2. Transitional or emergent reasoning, exemplified by higher order reasoning and similar to Piaget's concrete operational stage
3. Reflective, based on children's ability to use abstract ideas and approximating Piaget's formal operations level (Kourilsky, 1985; Mugge, 1968; Schug & Birkey, 1985)

Based on the work of Strauss (1952, 1954), Berti and Bombi (1988) found that 3-year-olds can distinguish between money and other objects but are unable to differentiate between types of coins. Until around 4-1/2, children are generally unaware that money is needed to purchase things. Three-year-olds may take candy or toys from a store, totally unaware of the fact that money is exchanged for goods, yet they have rudimentary knowledge about economics, knowing that they buy things in stores, recognizing money, and pretending to pay for things.

Between 4 and 5, children are still unable to distinguish and name coins, but their scripts of pretending to ask for and get goods, give and receive money, and go to work suggest that children do have concepts of economic exchanges. They do not, however, understand the function of money in buying and selling (Berti & Bombi, 1988), but believe that the shopkeeper gives money to the customer and that any type of coin is suitable for any type of purchase. No concept of production is present. Children believe shopkeepers get their goods from some other shop, which gives them away without asking for money, and they do not understand that shopkeepers are customers as well (Berti & Bombi, 1988, p. 8). Even though they understand that people go to work to get money, they do not understand the relationship between work and pay. "One works AND one gets money," rather than "one gets money BECAUSE one works" (Berti & Bombi, 1988, p. 175).

By 6, when children are progressing into concrete operations, they have a clearer understanding of money; they can distinguish and name the various denominations of coins and know which of them will buy more things. They continue to believe that the shopkeeper gives customers money, but are moving toward the idea that there is a manufacturer who produces goods that the shopkeeper has to pay for.

Between 6 and 7 years, children know that although one does not have to have the exact money to pay for a purchase, one does need enough. They also are moving toward some clarity of employer–employee relations, but are still far from a clear understanding of customer and producer concepts.

Seven-year-olds are able to compare coins and understand the value of money. Work is no longer considered as going someplace to get money, but a connection between the activity and the benefits begins (Berti & Bombi, 1988, p. 178), and children now have some idea of production and selling. They can describe a few paid occupations that they can observe directly and with which they have direct experience, such as police officer or bus driver.

Between the ages of 7 and 10, pre-economic ideas are replaced by more accurate and conventional ideas of economics (Berti & Bombi, 1988). Nevertheless, it is not until the period of formal operations that children are able to understand that the price of goods is based on the costs of production, which includes the cost of labor. Nor do they understand that the materials necessary for production are other than old or broken things, and there is still confusion between the concepts of making something and mending something.

*Teaching Economics.*    At whatever age children enter school, they bring with them their "economic knapsacks" of attitudes about economics, direct experiences, and cognitive capacities (Fox, 1978). The interplay of these three things accounts for the formal economics children are able to learn and for the extent to which children become economic actors once in school (Kourilsky, 1985).

Children's "knapsacks" of understanding are fragmented and little understood, but some educators believe that when economic information and experiences are presented to children in appropriate ways, economic concepts can be made accessible (Davison & Kilgore, 1971; Koeller, 1981), Kourilsky (1985), in her project, the Kinder-Economy and the Mini-Society, introduced children to concepts of scarcity, production and consumption, specialization, money and barter, and the skills of decision making. Through the use of games, filmstrips, simulations, and direct experiences, she concluded that children as young as 5 can be taught economic concepts such as scarcity, production, consumption, and exchange.

Berti and Bombi (1988), however, found that although some third-grade children were able to acquire more developed conceptions of economics, many were still somewhat resistant to instruction. The belief that price depends on the quality of goods or that low prices in some stores reflect the ability to "sell a lot" is resistant to instruction (p. 201). They concluded that "economic thought does not exist as a general notion that develops globally from one age to the next, but that it consists, rather, in a series of distinct economic notions that develop relatively independently for each child according to their experience and their individual capacity" (p. 202).

Over 25 years ago Robison and Spodek (1965) also concluded that some economic concepts were resistant to instruction. Kourlisky (1985), even though concluding that direct instruction in economic concepts leads to an increase in understanding, also found that some concepts, such as cost–benefit analysis, were dependent on the student's age and maturation, rather than instruction.

*Some Issues.*     Despite the knowledge of economic concepts and children's understanding of them, there is much more to learn about teaching economics during the period of early childhood. First, although Berti and Bombi (1988) have researched a number of economic concepts, many concepts remain unexplored, such as scarcity, economic interdependence, and trade.

Further, how children gain an understanding of any economic concepts is still little understood: "The picture of children's economic ideas is still incomplete" (Berti & Bombi, 1988, p. 215). The studies illustrating children's understanding of economic concepts are not matched by those describing the "mechanisms through which these conceptions are transformed in the course of the child's development" (p. 214).

Then, too, the study of economics includes more than concepts. Related to the concept of scarcity and the necessity of making reasoned choices from among limited resources, the skill of decision making is believed to be an essential part of the study of economics. For those who define social studies as skill development, the processes of decision making are viewed as paramount (Brophy, 1990).

Children are believed to grow in ability to make decisions through the naturally occurring events of a quality early childhood program. In developmentally appropriate programs, children decide on which centers of interest to work in; once this decision is made, they have to decide what to do in the centers, how to do it, with whom, and when they have finished.

Group decisions are structured into the program as well. Children are asked to decide what to name the guinea pig, which story to hear, or what piece of playground equipment to purchase. Project work in groups is encouraged, for this activity is believed to foster children's ability to make decisions that affect others. Nevertheless, the question of whether these normally occurring experiences foster children's ability to make decisions remains unanswered.

## WHAT SOCIAL STUDIES?

Spanning every social science discipline and including the development of attitudes and skills, the breadth and depth of social studies are overwhelming. Even when limited to a cursory examination of the key concepts and children's understanding of them in three disciplines—history, geography, and economics—it is clear that social studies is a highly complex, complicated field. When the complexities of the field meet the confounding factors of early childhood education, the problems involved in specifying appropriate social studies content expand, and the question of how either field can effectively fulfill its overarching purpose—that of preparing children to become members of a democracy—remains unanswered.

Stimulating more rhetoric than agreement, the position statements of the National Council for the Social Studies, the National Commission on Social Studies in the Schools, and the California State Department of Education have done little to bring order, direction, or clarity to the question of what social studies content should be included in the curriculum. If social studies is to prepare children to have not only knowledge of the world in which they live but also the skills and attitudes necessary to participate in democracy, decisions must now be made by the fields of both social studies and early childhood education as to what social studies is worth knowing and teaching during the period of early childhood.

Obviously, decisions about what social studies is worth knowing relate to the goals and purposes of individual early childhood programs (Brophy & Alleman, 1991). There is no disagreement that the purposes of any educational program dictate the curriculum (Kessler, 1991), but in the field of early childhood education, discord resulting from the multidisciplinary nature of the field and the age range covered, rather than consensus, exists as to the purposes of a program.

Additionally, the identification of what is worth knowing cannot be addressed without consideration of young children's preoperational thought. Spodek (1982) rightly points out that what is worth knowing can't be dictated by children's growth and development; nevertheless, it is impossible to ignore the nature of their preoperational thinking.

Both social studies and early childhood education are ready to bring definition and clarity of goals and objectives to the question of what is worth knowing. The development of *Guidelines for Appropriate Curriculum Content and Assessment in Programs Serving Children Ages 3 Through 8* (NAEYC & NAECS, 1991) is a clear beginning. These *Guidelines* are being followed by a book on what young children should know in various curriculum content areas and when (Bredekamp, in press), demonstrating a new willingness in the field of early childhood education to address the question. The next step should be a systematic study of children's understanding of social studies concepts.

Following Lucy Sprague Mitchell's model for geography learning, a model of social studies content could be created by taking key concepts in every social science discipline and matching them with children's understandings. Educators, along with social scientists, could begin the step-by-step process of bringing together social studies content in history, economics, and other disciplines with children's understandings of these concepts. This systematic, multidisciplinary effort would require more support than that possible from independent associations and organizations. Leadership and support at the federal level seems necessary if clarity is to result.

## REFERENCES

Acredolo, C., & Schmid, J. (1981). The understanding of relative speeds, distances, and durations of movement. *Developmental Psychology, 17*, 490–493.

Ames, L. (1946). The development of the sense of time in the young child. *Journal of Genetic Psychology, 68*, 97–125.

Atkins, C. L. (1981). Introducing basic map and globe concepts to young children. *Journal of Geography, 30*, 228–233.

Beatty, B. (1989). Child gardening: The teaching of children in American schools. In D. Warren (Ed.), *American teachers: Histories of a profession at work* (pp. 65–98). New York: Macmillan.

Bennett, W. (1986). *First lessons: A report on elementary education in America.* Washington, DC: U.S. Department of Education.

Berti, A. E., & Bombi, A. S. (1988). *The child's construction of economics.* Cambridge: Cambridge University Press.

Brainerd, C. J., Reyna, V. F., Howe, M. L., & Kingma, J. (1990). The development of forgetting and reminiscence. With commentary by Robert E. Guttentag; and a reply by C. J. Brainerd. *Monographs of the Society for Research in Child Development, 55* (3–4, Serial No. 222).

Bredekamp, S. (in press). *Curriculum content in early childhood.* Washington, DC: National Association for the Education of Young Children.

Brophy, J. (1990). Teaching social studies for understanding and higher-order applications. *The Elementary School Journal, 90*, 351–419.

Brophy, J., & Alleman, J. (1991). Activities as instructional tools: A framework for analysis and evaluation. *Educational Researcher, 90*, 351–417.

Bruner, J. (1960). *The process of education*. Cambridge, MA: Harvard University Press.

Bruner, J. (1966). *Toward a theory of instruction*. Cambridge, MA: Harvard University Press.

Burke, A. (1923). *A conduct curriculum for the kindergarten and first-grade*. New York: Scribner's.

California State Department of Education (1987). *History-social science framework*. Sacramento: Author.

Catling, S. J. (1978). The child's spatial conception and geographic education. *Journal of Geography, 71*, 24–28.

Davison, D. G., & Kilgore, J. H. (1971). A model for evaluating the effectiveness of economics education in the primary grades. *Journal of Economic Education, 3*, 17–25.

Derman-Sparks & the ABC Task Force. (1989). *Anti-bias curriculum: Tools for empowering young children*. Washington, DC: National Association for the Education of Young Children.

Dewey, J. (1944). *Democracy and education*. New York: Free Press. (Original work published 1916).

Dunfee, M. (1970). *Elementary school social studies: A guide to current research*. Washington, DC: Association for Supervision and Curriculum Development.

Egan, K. (1988). *Primary understanding*. New York: Routledge, Chapman & Hall.

Finn, C. E., & Ravitch, D. (1988). No trivial pursuit. *Phi Delta Kappan, 69*, 559–564.

Forman, G., & Kaden, M. (1987). Research on science education for young children. In C. Seefeldt (Ed.), *The early childhood curriculum: A review of current research* (1st ed., pp. 141–164). New York: Teachers College Press.

Fox, D. (1978). What children bring to school: The beginnings of economic education. *Social Education, 42*, 478–481.

Freeman, E. B., & Hatch, J. A. (1989). What schools expect young children to know and do: An analysis of kindergarten report cards. *The Elementary School Journal, 89*, 595–607.

French, L. A. (1989). Young children's responses to "When" questions: Issues of directionality. *Child Development, 60*, 225–237.

French, L. A., & Nelson, K. (1981). Temporal knowledge expressed in preschoolers' descriptions of familiar activities. *Papers and Reports on Child Language Development, 20*, 61–69.

Friedman, W. J. (1990). Children's representations of the pattern of daily activities. *Child Development, 61*, 1399–1413.

Galper, A., Jantz, R. K., Seefeldt, C., & Serock, K. (1980). Children's concepts of age. *International Journal of Aging and Human Development, 12*, 129–157.

Goodlad, J. (1984). *A place called school*. New York: McGraw-Hill.

Guzzetti, B., & McGowan, T. (1991). Promoting social studies understanding through literature-based instruction. *The Social Studies, 82*, 1.

Handler, B. S. (1985). *Women in the NEA and in the field of social studies, 1857–1912.* Paper presented at the annual meeting of the American Educational Research Association, Chicago.

Hewes, D. W. (1982). Preschool geography: Developing a sense of self in time and space. *Journal of Geography, 31*, 94–97.

Hill, P. S. (1923). Introduction. In A. Burke, *A conduct curriculum for the kindergarten and first-grade* (pp. x–xix). New York: Scribner's.

Holmes, E. E. (1991). Democracy in elementary school classrooms. *Social Education, 55*(3), 176–181.

Kessler, S. A. (1991). Alternative perspectives on early childhood education. *Early Childhood Research Quarterly, 6*, 183–199.

Koeller, S. (1981). Economics education applied to early childhood. *Childhood Education, 57*, 293–296.

Kourilsky, M. (1981). Economic education: Making the most of the curriculum. *The Social Studies, 72*(2), 86–89.

Kourilsky, M. (1985). *Children's use of cost-benefit analysis: Development or nonexistent?* Paper presented at the annual meeting of the American Educational Research Association, Chicago.

Litogot, S. A. (1991). Using higher-order skills in American history. *The Social Studies, 82*(1), 22–25.

McMillan, M. (1919). *The nursery school.* London: Dent.

Michaelis, J. (1988). *Social studies for children: A guide to basic instruction* (9th ed.). Englewood Cliffs, NJ: Prentice-Hall.

Mitchell, L. S. (1934). *Young geographers.* New York: Bank Street College.

Mitsakos, C. L. (1981). The nature and purposes of social studies. In J. Allen (Ed.), *Education in the 80s: Social studies* (pp. 13–22). Washington, DC: National Education Association.

Montessori, M. (1962). *The discovery of the child.* Translated from the third Italian edition of "The method of scientific pedagogy applied to child education in the children's houses." Madras, India: Kalakshetra Publications, distributed by the Theosophical Press, Wheaton, IL.

Mugge, D. (1968). Are young children ready to study the social studies? *The Elementary School Journal, 68*, 233–240.

National Association for the Education of Young Children & National Association of Early Childhood Specialists in State Departments of Education. (1991). *Position statement: Guidelines for appropriate curriculum content and assessment in programs serving children ages 3 through 8.* Washington, DC: Author.

National Commission on Social Studies in the Schools (1989). *Charting a course: Social studies for the 21st century.* New York: Author.

National Council for the Social Studies. (1989). *Social studies for early childhood and elementary school children: Preparing for the 21st century.* Washington, DC: Author.

Nussbaum, J., & Novak, J. D. (1976). An assessment of children's concepts of the earth utilizing structured interviews. *Science Education, 60*, 535–550.

Parker, W. C. (1991). *Renewing the social studies curriculum.* Alexandria, VA: Association for Supervision and Curriculum Development.

Piaget, J. (1946). The child's conception of time. In H. E. Gruber & J. J. Voneche (Eds.), *The essential Piaget* (pp. 547–576). London: Routledge & Kegan Paul.

Piaget, J. (1948). The child's conception of space. In H. E. Gruber and J. J. Voneche (Eds.), *The essential Piaget* (pp. 576–645). London: Routledge & Kegan Paul.

Piaget, J., & Inhelder, B. (1969). *The psychology of the child* (C. Gattegno & F. M. Hodgson, Trans.). New York: Basic Books.

Portugaly, D. (1967). *A study of the development of disadvantaged kindergarten children's understanding of the earth as a globe.* Unpublished doctoral dissertation, Columbia University, New York.

Prawat, R. S. (1989). Promoting access to knowledge. *Review of Educational Research, 59*, 1–43.

Prawat, R. S. (1991). The value of ideas: The immersion approach to the development of thinking. *Educational Researcher, 20*(2), 3–11.

Risinger, C. F. (1991). Unkept promises and new opportunities. *Social Education, 55*(2), 138–141.

Robison, H., & Spodek, B. (1965). *New directions in the kindergarten.* New York: Teachers College Press.

Schug, M. C., & Birkey, C. J. (1985). *The development of children's economic reasoning.* Paper presented at the annual meeting of the American Educational Research Association, Chicago.

Sears, A., & Parsons, J. (1991). Toward critical thinking as an ethic. *Teaching and Research in Social Education, 19*(1), 45–68.

Seefeldt, C. (1988). Teacher certification and accreditation in early childhood education. *The Elementary School Journal, 89*, 241–252.

Slaby, R. G., & Frey, J. S. (1975). Development of gender constancy and selective attention to same-sex models. *Child Development, 49*, 1263–1265.

Sneider, C., & Pulos, S. (1983). Children's cosmographics: Understanding the earth's shape and gravity. *Science Education, 67*, 205–221.

Spencer, C., Harrison, M., & Darvizeh, Z. (1980). The development of iconic mapping ability in young children. *International Journal of Early Childhood, 21*(2), 57–64.

Spodek, B. (1982). Introduction. In B. Spodek (Ed.), *Handbook of research in early childhood education* (p. xvii). New York: Free Press.

Stiles-Davis, J., Kritchevsky, M., & Bellugi, U. (1988). *Spatial cognition: Brain bases and development.* Hillsdale, NJ: Lawrence Erlbaum.

Stoltman, J. P. (1979). Geographic skills in early elementary years. *Indiana Social Studies Quarterly, 32*, 27–32.

Strauss, A. (1952). The development and transformation of monetary meaning in the child. *American Sociological Review, 17*, 275–286.

Strauss, A. (1954). The development of conceptions of rules in children. *Child Development, 25*, 193–208.

Thornton, S. J., & Wenger, R. N. (1990). Geography curriculum and instruction in three fourth-grade classrooms. *The Elementary School Journal, 90,* 515–533.

Vukelich, R., & Thornton, S. J. (1990). *Childhood Education, 66,* 22–25.

Wann, K., Dorn, M., & Liddle, E. (1962). *Fostering intellectual development in young children.* New York: Teachers College Press.

Weber, E. (1969). *The kindergarten: Its encounter with educational thought in America.* New York: Teachers College Press.

White, E., Elsom, B., & Prawat, R. (1978). Children's conception of death. *Child Development, 49,* 307–310.

# CHAPTER 9

# Early Childhood Trends in Movement Development

BILL STINSON

For the past 2 decades, research in early childhood motor development and movement experiences has slowly shifted its attention from emphasis on the tasks to be performed to the individual development of each child's movement potential. Haywood (1986) emphasized that all children are not the same and one child's abilities in a particular age span cannot be used alone to determine the growth and development status of all children in that age span. Furthermore, it can be frustrating and possibly harmful to attempt to teach children skills before they are physically ready. Robertson and Halverson (1984) further clarify this child-centered approach by citing the necessity of a "working knowledge" of motor development to intelligently teach motor skills to children.

Movement to the young child means life itself. Movement helps the young child in the discovery of self and the environment; enhances the concepts of time, space, and direction; allows for more freedom to explore; helps develop skills that make the child less prone to accidents in pursuit of play; enhances communicative skills; creates emotional enjoyment; and opens the door to acceptance by others (Whitehurst, 1971). These benefits have prompted many child development specialists to cite play, and particularly movement, as major educational techniques in early childhood (Dyson, 1987; Elkind, 1988; Gilbert, 1977; Riggs, 1990; Rogers & Sawyers, 1988).

## HISTORICAL PERSPECTIVES

Much of the earlier information on motor development were data collected through observation and interpreted into scales during the 1930s and 1940s by Shirley (1931), Bayley (1936), and Gesell and Amatruda (1947).

This information focused on specific task behaviors exhibited by children at various ages. These scales were universally used by individuals in child development and the medical professions; yet, unsettled issues persisted such as (1) nature vs. nurture, (2) critical periods, (3) research methodology, and (4) stages of development (Haywood, 1986).

The 1960s brought a renewed interest in motor development research and its implications for the total development and education of the child. Keogh (1977) believed that studying children with disabilities helped increase interest in motor development research. Specifically, the area of mind–body relationships, coupled with Kephart's *The Slow Learner in the Classroom* (1960), helped bring about this resurgence in motor development research. Also, the emergence of more biomechanical analyses of movement and perceptual-motor theory added to this renewal (Clark & Whitall, 1989). In addition, a total development approach was sparked by a psychological publication, *Mechanisms of Motor Skill Development* (Connolly, 1970). This publication attempted to understand the processes of motor development by using information processing theory.

In the 1970s, movement programs were slowly becoming centered on the child and not the activity to be taught. This trend came about through the awareness of educators who were looking for more effective means to help young children develop higher levels of motor skill performance. Previous techniques were not effective for various reasons. One reason was that most books and curricula pointed out "faults" in performance of various movement skills used in children's games, dances, and individualized activities based on adult standards, not the developmental readiness of children for the demands of the skill involved (Halverson, 1990). As a result, researchers and educators alike began to develop movement curricular experiences in an attempt to design activities to meet the needs of the child rather than requiring the child to fit into the activity (Gallahue, 1982; Graham, Holt/Hale, & Parker, 1987; Hoffman, Young, & Klesius, 1985; Logsdon et al., 1984; Riley, Barrett, Martinek, & Roberton, 1980). Despite this trend toward developmentally appropriate activities, Halverson (1990) related that activity-centered programs still persist due to emphasis on competitive sports, the fitness craze, and the notion that the earlier children are "trained," the better they will develop cognitively and motorically.

The 1970s and 1980s have been looked upon as a renaissance age in motor development studies. Researchers began to study and utilize several disciplines: developmental psychology, movement analysis, research skills and techniques, and biomechanics (Halverson, 1990). Research studies became more continuous and varied in their efforts to explore more fully specific questions, much like the earlier works of McGraw (1945/1969) and Gesell (1946). Haywood (1986) verified that research results are reinforced if two or more research strategies are employed prudently in motor development issues. In addition, various developmental changes are now being looked at through a variety of perspectives. For example, it is not enough to know what the execution of the movement pattern is, but how and why changes in execution have occurred must also be understood.

## CONTEMPORARY MOTOR DEVELOPMENT INVESTIGATIONS

This renaissance has created interest in three areas of motor development. One is a renewed effort to observe and note more detailed descriptions of motor skills and to validate various developmental sequences of these skills. Roberton and Halverson (1984) classified developmental sequences as either inter-task or intra-task sequencing. Inter-task sequencing deals with recognizing a significant event or a "milestone," the first appearance of the skill. The motor skills are ordered (sequenced) according to the time first noticed, such as standing before walking, walking before running, and so forth. McGraw (1945/1969), who originated this concept in an effort to understand the developmental process, noted that obvious changes in movement patterns (milestones) did not enlighten us as to what the underlying forces were in progressing to the next milestone.

The study of intra-task sequencing was promoted as a means of enlightening these underlying processes. Intra-task sequencing tried to distinguish what the predictable movement changes are within a single motor task. Can one tell if and when a child who is now standing is ready to walk? Is the child becoming more coordinated and controlled in walking? For example, one study on early walking noted that the arms are held high to protect the child in case of balance problems (Milani-Comparetti & Gidoni, 1967). Later the arms are lowered, eventually swinging out more in opposition to the legs for a more coordinated walking pattern (Roberton, 1984). The more practical and descriptive this approach is, the more it helps the teacher in planning effective and appropriate movement experiences for each child. Several researchers have developed informative research on when and how to intervene in helping the motor progress of children (Branta, Haubenstricker, & Seefeldt, 1984; Gallahue, 1982; Ridenour, 1984; Roberton, 1984; Roberton & Halverson, 1984).

A second major area of contemporary research has been the study of how immediate environmental factors influence motor development. Research is emerging on various systematic approaches to structuring the learning environment to enhance motor development (Barnett, 1980; Barnett & Higgens, 1983; Herkowitz, 1978, 1984; Higgens, 1972; Higgens & Spaeth, 1972; Roberton, 1987). The techniques and ideas teachers use in helping a child to accomplish a motor task are of utmost concern. Is the activity doing what it is supposed to be doing in "helping" a child to learn a skill? (Halverson, 1990). For example, a large ball size might dictate that a child catch it with a primitive, catching-with-arms pattern rather than using a higher level pattern with the hands, which might enhance catching skill development (Victors, 1961). Morris (1976) discovered children had varying degrees of success in catching different colored balls against different colored backgrounds. What teachers say, the equipment used, and the design of movement experiences are all immediate environmental factors that affect movement skill development. Kovar (1991) suggested using acronyms to cue skill knowledge in improving skill performance, citing the television show, Sesame Street, as an example of how young children are challenged to remember through mediation skills of verbal rehearsal, word association, and labeling. Herkowitz (1978) designed a chart for teachers, showing environmental factors that might affect the developmental performance level a child demonstrates to the teacher. Such factors might include using a larger or smaller ball or catching with a bean bag first. Williams (1983) found that young children have more success adjusting to moving objects at a preferred speed rather than at slower or faster speeds. For example, a young batter may swing before a slow pitch ever gets to him. The teacher can time the pitch with the batter's reaction swing to ensure a better possibility of success. Making careful observations of children's developmental level skills helps teachers plan appropriate environmental conditions to ensure optimal practice and success.

The third area of research has been attempting to ascertain what the underlying structures and processes are that lead to understanding and explaining developmental changes. Studies in the 1930s and 1940s produced a neuro-maturation theory, which utilized the idea of "stages" due mainly to chronological growth and development characteristics to explain motor development and movement pattern changes or capabilities. This theory still predominates among child development specialists, teachers, and parents.

The 1970s and 1980s brought about the information processing theory, which explored developmental differences in terms of sensory input, long- and short-term memory storage, and the speed of processing information. Much of this information has been researched in the realm of cognitive development with respect to motor development (Clark, 1978; Haywood, 1986; Schmidt, 1982; Thomas, 1980, 1984; Williams, 1983). The child's potential for information processing is affected by teachers and parents. It can be enhanced by well-planned movement experiences through play, self-practice, and exploratory activities. Thus, having a command of one's movement patterns is related to one's mental development. For example, through the analysis of several studies, Haywood (1986) suggested that children benefit in performance by practicing under a variety of conditions instead of in a restricted setting. A study by Kerr and Booth (1977) in target tossing revealed that better performances were made by children practicing at different distances than by children who practiced only at the testing distance. Age differences reflect the ability or inability of children to sort out relevant from irrelevant stimuli in pursuing a task (Smith, Kemler, & Aronfield, 1975).

A newer theory—dynamical systems—was initially proposed by Kugler, Kelso, and Turvey (1982). This theory proposes that the body is made up of many systems, each with its own complexities and developmental sequences. In turn, these systems are constantly changing in terms of functioning levels and responses to various environmental conditions. Above all, these systems must somehow function in an integrated manner to produce a coordinated motor action (Thelen, Ulrich, & Jensen, 1989). For example, the eye may go through a progression of nine sensory developmental steps in completing the sequence of tracking a moving object successfully. The hands negotiate a six-step process toward the maturation level of responding to and handling a ball. It takes both systems to catch the ball, but each one may be at different "stage" of development at a given moment. To catch the ball, each independent system's functioning level is important, but somehow the actions must be integrated for the child to catch the ball successfully. Motor development is shaped by a variety of physiological, task, and environmental factors—not just specific information from the central nervous system (Whitall, 1990). This approach shows promise for positive, early intervention situations if teachers can recognize where each dynamic system is and how it is affecting and being affected by other factors in executing a motor skill.

Graham, Holt/Hale, and Parker (1987) suggest that, at the very least, teachers of movement should

1. Understand the progression and development of basic skills and related movement concepts
2. Learn to assess each child's level of motor skill proficiency
3. Become skillful in observing young children more

If teachers can achieve at least these minimal competencies, then they can provide quality movement experiences for young children.

## MOVEMENT EXPERIENCES AND THEIR CURRICULAR IMPLICATIONS

The acquisition of motor skills is a significant factor in the growth and development of young children. It is imperative to study, analyze, and carefully implement movement experiences to enhance the whole child. The significance of play in the lives of young children, and how its structure should influence teaching at critical stages of psychomotor, cognitive, and affective development, also need to be observed and recognized (see Chapter 3, this volume). Payne (1990) related that success in movement transcends to how successful children will be in other aspects of their lives. Besides the obvious psychomotor benefits of movement experiences, a child's cognitive potential in the areas of perception, memory retrieval, and language arts can be enhanced. In addition, mastering self-control in various movement tasks can improve self-concept (Flinchum, 1988).

## Developing Critical Thinking

Although the emphasis in play and movement programs has been on acquiring motor skills, many teachers think that developing intellectual or critical thinking skills is a goal of an effective movement program. Buschner (1990) states that skillful moving requires skillful thought on the child's part. The child's innate desire for play and learning by discovery provides exciting ways to learn. Elkind (1988) related that children do not separate feelings from thinking, acting, and socialization; hence, play is the most effective mode in which to learn. There has been an increased interest in utilizing movement as a vehicle for problem-solving activities. Early childhood movement programs are enhancing cognitive problem-solving skills through body awareness activities such as, "Can you make your body in the letter (or shape) of _____? or, "Let's see if you can balance on three body parts?"

Problem solving as a teaching technique for aiding preschool children in acquiring movement skills is an exciting way for them to explore and discover what their bodies can do. Young children are at the beginning level of movement skill learning (Gallahue, 1987), thereby making this approach an appropriate child-centered, active way of learning concepts and relationships. For example, a child may hop backward, forward, and sideways; or tap a balloon high, with an elbow or with the right hand; or move quickly across the room as a fluffy cloud. Boucher (1988) contended that a child's early movement experiences are the foundation for all learning. As children solve movement problems, they are not only learning to move but also moving to learn.

Buschner (1990) suggested the following steps in using movement to develop precritical thinking skills:

1. Construct a movement environment with trial and error situations
2. Select appropriate movement skills for each child
3. Encourage fantasy and independence

4. Use guided imagery
5. Match or associate concepts such as up and down, large and small

Roberton and Halverson (1984) indicate children must explore and think actively about the movement problem at hand for assimilation and accommodation to occur in precritical thinking skills; then the teacher must help the child to verbalize why the movement solution was efficient and effective. These indirect ways of teaching do not automatically ensure quality learning. Rink (1985) implied that the selection of tasks, clarity of presentation, and sequential development of tasks are the responsibility of an effective teacher. Visual and kinesthetic sensory modalities, movement awareness, inquiry, creativity, relationships, and academic reinforcement incorporated into movement experiences enhance a child's cognitive development (Curtis, 1987; Gallahue, 1982). There is a need to further investigate the areas of problems solving, guided discovery, and play as to their roles in the total education of the young child.

## Adapting Games

Recently, games for young children have been undergoing structural changes to fit the concept of the total child. The "developmental theme approach" emphasizes that games should enhance and utilize the fundamental movement abilities of children instead of being the primary objective of a lesson. Gabbard, LeBlanc, & Lowy (1987) reported that games can provide opportunities not only for motor skill enhancement but also for the cognitive and affective development of the child. Cognitive skills provided by participation in games include (1) learning and applying rules and strategies, and (2) modifying and creating new games for one's own needs and enjoyment. Values such as cooperation, honesty, respect for others, and sportsmanship are naturally aided by the use of games with young children. In addition, utilizing a games approach in teaching reinforces academic concepts introduced in the classroom.

Morris (1976) promoted the idea of changing games to accommodate the lesson objectives and the needs of children at the moment. He suggested a multitude of ways: changing the number or organization of players, equipment used, rules, or scoring contingencies. For the benefit of younger children, one large group game might be changed into several smaller ones not only to aid their short attention spans but also to create more opportunities to be active and to practice skills. Maybe a balloon should be used instead of a ball for easier tracking of a thrown object. Perhaps scoring might be in numerical terms one day and alphabetical letters another day. Morris's

(1976) suggestions allowed teachers to change traditional games without feeling sacrilege had been committed.

Two major game vehicles have resulted from the idea that games can be changed to fit lesson objectives and learners' needs: cooperative and creative games. Each approach has generated attention from educators for its versatility in promoting total child development in movement curricula. Cooperative learning strategies such as those described by Lyman and Foyle (1990) formed the basis of these two approaches. Cooperative learning strategies have four basic characteristics.

1. Students work in small heterogeneous groups.
2. The learning task is structured so that everyone must work together for the group to be successful.
3. Group and interpersonal skills are developed by the encouragement of peer approval and support.
4. Individual accountability is required of each student to demonstrate individual mastery of the task.

Orlick (1982) described the cooperative game concept as people playing with each other, not against each other, and changing the game's structure to ensure the enjoyment of the play experience itself. Cooperative games come in many variations because they must be individually tailored to fit the needs of the learners involved and the concepts they are to learn. For example, "Help Your Neighbor" is a game in which each child wears a bean bag on his head and walks around the room. If the bean bag falls off a child's head, he must freeze. He cannot move until another person bends down, picks up the bean bag, and places back on his head. This game is to make young children socially aware of others who need help. The teacher reinforces this awareness by alerting the children to others who have "lost" their bean bags and praising those who help their neighbors as the game is played (Stinson, 1991a).

Cooperative learning is a natural part of early childhood movement experiences. Utilizing the characteristics of cooperative learning in developmentally appropriate movement activities can help ensure maximum activity, less frustration, a more developmentally appropriate competitive perspective, and greater assurance for success for the individual as well as the group of children as a whole.

Creative activities also fit the needs of the learner. Riley (1977) recommended that creative activities be balanced with traditional ones and noted that they not only meet lesson objectives but challenge children cognitively in learning situations. With the "new games" concept, Fluegelman (1976) encouraged physical educators to modify traditional games as well as create "new games." Guided discovery and problem-solving situations become common in these movement lessons. For example, simple activity can be structured to fit the developmental level of a group of children by emphasizing various learning concepts and outcomes. "Busy Bee" is a creative activity for K-1 students. A body part is called out, and the children must figure out a way to touch that body part to their partner's body part. When "Busy Bee" is called, the children must move in creative ways to find a different partner (Stinson, 1991a). This encourages creative expression and moving among the children at the same time as it reinforces body part identification, introduces the concept of teamwork to these young children, and enhances better space awareness in their pursuit to find another partner.

## Coping with Stress

There is increasing concern about the stress encountered by young children in their lives. Lang (1983) noted that 42% of over 5,000 K-3 children surveyed in a Kansas study displayed health risk behaviors related to stress, such as head and neck aches, restlessness, difficulty in concentrating, chronic irritability, nail-biting, and hair pulling. Elkind (1981) expressed concern that parents and teachers alike were "hurrying" children into situations for which they were not ready. Children need to have time to be children. He also noted that play is nature's way of dealing with stress for children. Children do not understand how the body reacts to stress, let alone how to deal positively with it through talking, exercising, or other management skills (Johns & Johns, 1983). Honig (1990) suggested that children need to have the freedom to positively express their emotional and bodily feelings through play, particularly large-muscle games, not only to develop specific motor skills but also to serve as emotional outlets.

As a result, there is a growing trend to use play and movement activities, especially body awareness activities, as a way of coping with bodily tensions related to stressful events in young children's lives. Rogers (1990) cited play as a medium for expressing emotions and dealing with them through dramatic and imaginary activities. Dance activities illustrating the concepts of tension/relaxation help children not only to maintain control in their movements but also to realize when tension can be a positive, constructive factor in their movement activity (Stinson, 1988). Weimer (1987) found that progressive relaxation training reduced the frequency of classroom disruptions of low income first-grade students. Yoga exercises combined with guided imagery gradually reduced "stress" among 4-year-olds (Piper, 1988). These are representative views and approaches to using movement as a vehicle in quieting and managing stress of young children.

To date, only a few specific resource books have been published that describe quieting and relaxation activities for young children (Cherry, 1981; Lang & Stinson, 1986; Scott, 1986; Stinson, 1991b). Cherry (1981) noted that young children settled down more easily when activities centering around active play were followed by quieting experiences. Resting was not enough; the child must be relaxed and totally involved in the experience. Activities varied from finger games, to swaying to gentle music, to breathing exercises, to stretching. Scott (1986) contended that children need to learn how to relax. Rhythmics can help children bring order to their thoughts and control within their bodily actions through a range of movements and imagery. Movement activities for the young child must have the connotation of play and an exploratory spirit in order to be most effective in positive attitude formation and coping skill development, with focuses on body image, space awareness, and relationships with others/objects (Stinson, 1991b).

As society becomes more attuned to the fact that young children do experience stress, more programs will be designed specifically to either eliminate unnecessary stressors or guide children into making positive, effective responses to the situation at hand. Johns & Johns (1983) indicate that the goal is not to shelter children from stressful situations but to help them develop the ability to respond in a more positive, constructive way to this absolute in life. Developmentally appropriate play and movement experiences appear to be guiding influences in this endeavor.

## SUMMARY

Movement is the first language of children. Through it, they express themselves and their curiosity for the world around them. Historically, motor development and movement theory have evolved from a task-oriented process to a child-centered focus. Three directions in research for studying and analyzing the movement-skills development of the young child have currently emerged.

1. The pursuit of more carefully observed and enlightened descriptors of various developmental movement sequences
2. The study of how immediate environmental factors influence motor development
3. The attempt to understand and explain more thoroughly the structures and processes of developmental changes

Answers to these pursuits will help teachers in providing more quality movement experiences in early childhood programs and pave the way toward earlier positive intervention practices with young children experiencing motor skill dysfunctions.

The acquisition of motor skills is a significant factor in the growth and development of the young child. Gallahue (1989) noted that a worthy goal of any early childhood educational program should be quality movement experiences to enhance not only a child's movement abilities but also the cognitive and affective development of the child. Movement experiences for young children are being designed to aid teaching in such conceptual areas as (1) problem solving, (2) cooperative learning, and (3) coping with stress. Through the natural joys of movement and play in a young child's life, it is hoped that a more effective and positive educational setting will be established in current early childhood programs.

## REFERENCES

Barnett, B. (1980). Movement organization as reflected in the jumping patterns of young children in different environmental contexts [Abstract]. *Proceedings of the Research Section, National Convention of the American Alliance for Health, Physical Education, Recreation and Dance, 39*, 1–5.

Barnett, B., & Higgens, J. R. (1983). The effect of environmental and optic field flow changes on the organization of movements by children [Abstract]. National Convention of the American Alliance for Health, Physical Education, Recreation and Dance, *98*, 65–67.

Bayley, N. (1936). *The California infant scale of motor development.* Berkeley: University of California Press.

Boucher, A. (1988). Good beginnings. *Journal of Physical Education, Recreation and Dance, 59*(7), 42.

Branta, G., Haubenstricker, J., & Seefeldt, C. (1984). Age changes in motor skills during childhood and adolescence. In R. L. Terjung (Ed.), *Exercise and sport science reviews* (Vol. 12, pp. 467–520). Lexington, MA: Collamore Press.

Buschner, C. (1990). Can we help children move and think critically? In B. Stinson (Ed.), *Moving and learning for the young child* (pp. 51–66). Reston, VA: American Alliance for Health, Physical Education, Recreation and Dance.

Cherry, C. (1981). *Think of something quiet: A guide for achieving serenity in early childhood classrooms.* Belmont, CA: David S. Lake Publishers.

Clark, J. E., & Whitall, J. (1989). Changing patterns of locomotion from walking to skipping. In M. Woollacott & A. Shumway-Cook (Eds.), *A development of posture and gait across the lifespan* (pp. 128–154). Columbia: University of South Carolina Press.

Clark, S. (1978). Memory processes in the early acquisition of motor skills. In M. Ridenour (Ed.), *Motor development: Issues and applications* (pp. 99–112). Princeton, NJ: Princeton Book Co.

Connolly, K. (1970). *Mechanisms of motor skill development*. London: Academic Press.

Curtis, S. (1987). New views on movement development and the implications for curriculum in early childhood. In C. Seefeldt (Ed.), *The early childhood curriculum: A review of current research* (1st ed., pp. 256–270). New York: Teachers College Press.

Dyson, A. (1987). The value of time off task: Young children's spontaneous talk and deliberate text. *Harvard Educational Review, 57*, 396–420.

Elkind, D. (1981) *The hurried child: Growing up too fast too soon*. Reading, MA: Addison-Wesley.

Elkind, D. (1988). The resistance to developmentally appropriate educational practice with young children: The real issue. In C. Warger (Ed.), *A resource guide to public school early childhood programs* (pp. 53–62). Alexandria, VA: Association for Supervision and Curriculum Development.

Flinchum, B. (1988, September). Early childhood movement programs: Preparing teachers for tomorrow. *Journal of Physical Education, Recreation and Dance*, pp. 62–69.

Fluegelman, A. (1976). *The new games book*. New York: Doubleday.

Gabbard, C., LeBlanc, B., & Lowy, S. (1987). Physical education for children: Building a foundation. Englewood Cliffs, NJ: Prentice-Hall.

Gallahue, D. (1982). *Developmental movement experiences for children*. New York: John Wiley.

Gallahue, D. (1987). *Developmental physical education for today's elementary school child*. New York: Macmillan.

Gallahue, D. (1989). *Understanding motor development: Infants, children, adolescents* (2nd ed.). Carmel, IN: Benchmark Press.

Gesell, A. (1946). The ontogenesis of infant behavior. In L. Carmichael (Ed.), *Manual of child psychology* (pp. 295–331). New York: John Wiley.

Gesell, A., & Amatruda, C. (1947). *Developmental diagnosis* (2nd ed.). New York: Harper & Row.

Gilbert, A. (1977). *Teaching the three R's through movement experiences*. Minneapolis, NM: Burgess.

Graham, G., Holt/Hale, S., & Parker, M. (1987). *Children moving: A teacher's guide to developing a successful physical education program* (2nd ed.). Palo Alto, CA: Mayfield.

Halverson, L. (1990). Motor development and physical education for young children. In B. Stinson (Ed.), *Moving and learning for the young child* (pp. 85–103). Reston, VA: American Alliance for Health, Physical Education, Recreation and Dance.

Haywood, K. (1986). *Lifespan motor development*. Champaign, IL: Human Kinetics.

Herkowitz, J. (1978). Developmental task analysis: The design of movement experiences and evaluation of motor development status. In M. Ridenour (Ed.), *Motor development: Issues and applications* (pp. 139–164). Princeton, NJ: Princeton Book Co.

Herkowitz, J. (1984). Developmentally engineered equipment and playgrounds. In J. Thomas (Ed.), *Motor development during childhood and adolescence* (pp. 139–173). Minneapolis, MI: Burgess.

Higgens, J. (1972). Movement to match environmental demands. *Research Quarterly, 43*, 313–336.

Higgens, J., & Spaeth, R. (1972). Relationship between consistency of movement and environmental condition. *Quest 17*, 61–69.

Hoffman, H., Young, J., & Klesius, S. (1985). *Meaningful movement for children: A developmental theme approach to physical education.* Dubuque, IA: Kendall/ Hunt.

Honig, A. (1990). Baby moves: Relation to learning. In B. Stinson (Ed.), *Moving and learning for the young child* (pp. 31–41). Reston, VA: American Alliance for Health, Physical Education, Recreation and Dance.

Johns, B., & Johns, M. (1983). Stress burns out kids too. *Education Digest, 49(2)*, 44–46.

Keogh, J. (1977). The study of movement skill development. *Quest, 28*, 76–88.

Kephart, N. (1960). *The slow learner in the classroom.* Columbus, OH: Charles E. Merrill.

Kerr, R., & Booth, B. (1977). Skill acquisition in elementary school children and schema theory. In R. Christine & D. Landers (Eds.), *Psychology of motor behavior and sport* (pp. 243–247). Champaign, IL: Human Kinetics.

Kovar, S. (1991). Where's the beef? *Kansas Journal of Health, Physical Education, Recreation and Dance, 60*, 13.

Kugler, P., Kelso, J., & Turvey, M. (1982). On control and coordination of naturally developing systems. In J. Kelso & J. Clark (Eds.), *The development of movement and coordination* (pp. 5–78). New York: John Wiley.

Lang, D. (1983). *A comparison of selected health behaviors of Kansas students enrolled grades K-12.* Unpublished doctoral dissertation, Oklahoma State University, Stillwater.

Lang, D., & Stinson, B. (1986). *Lazy dogs and snoozing frogs: Quieting/relaxation activities for children.* LaCrosse, WI: Coulee Press.

Logsdon, B., Ammons, M., Barrett, K., Broer, M., Halverson, L., McGee, R., & Roberton, M. (1984). *Physical education for children: A focus on the teaching process* (2nd ed.). Philadelphia: Lea & Febiger.

Lyman, L., & Foyle, H. (1990). *Cooperative grouping for interactive learning: Students, teachers, administrators.* West Haven, CT: National Education Association.

McGraw, M. (1969). *The neuromuscular maturation of the human infant.* New York: Hafner. (Original work published 1945)

Milani-Comparetti, A., & Gidoni, E. (1967). Routine developmental examination in normal and retarded children. *Developmental Medicine and Child Neurology, 9*, 631–638.

Morris, G. (1976). Effects a ball and background color have upon the catching performance of elementary school children. *Research Quarterly for Exercise and Sport, 47*, 409–416.

Orlick, T. (1982). *The second cooperative sports and games book.* New York: Pantheon.

Payne, V. (1990). Observing and facilitating skill sequencing. In B. Stinson (Ed.), *Moving and learning for the young child* (pp. 107–116). Reston, VA: American Alliance for Health, Physical Education, Recreation and Dance.

Piper, F. (1988). *Stress management techniques for young children.* Unpublished master's thesis, Nova University, Florida.

Ridenour, M. (1984). Influence of object size, speed, and direction on the perception of a movement object. *Research Quarterly for Exercise and Sport, 45,* 193–301.

Riggs, M. (1990). The linkage between movement and learning. In B. Stinson (Ed.), *Moving and learning for the young child* (pp. 17–20). Reston, VA: American Alliance for Health, Physical Education, Recreation and Dance.

Riley, M. (1977). Games teaching. *Journal of Physical Education and Recreation, 48(7),* 17–35.

Riley, M., Barrett, K., Martinek, T., & Roberton, M. (1980). *Children and youth in action: Physical activities and sports.* Washington, DC: U.S. Government Printing Office.

Rink, J. (1985). *Teaching physical education for learning.* St. Louis: Times Mirror/Mosby.

Roberton, M. (1984). Changing motor patterns in childhood. In J. Thomas (Ed.), *Motor development during childhood and adolescence* (pp. 48–90). Minneapolis, MN: Burgess.

Roberton, M. (1987). Developmental level as a function of the immediate environment. In J. Clark & J. Humphrey (Eds.), *Advances in motor development research* (pp. 1–15). New York: ANS Press.

Roberton, M., & Halverson, L. (1984). *Developing children: Their changing movement: A guide for teachers.* Philadelphia: Lea & Febiger.

Rogers, C. (1990). The importance of play. In B. Stinson (Ed.), *Moving and learning for the young child* (pp. 43–50). Reston, VA: American Alliance for Health, Physical Education, Recreation and Dance.

Rogers, C., & Sawyers, J. (1988). *Play in the lives of children.* Washington, DC: National Association for the Education of Young Children.

Schmidt, R. (1982). *Motor control and learning: A behavioral emphasis.* Champaign, IL: Human Kinetics.

Scott, L. (1986). *Quiet times: Relaxation techniques for early childhood.* Minneapolis, MN: T. S. Denison.

Shirley, M. (1931). *The first two years: A study of twenty-five babies: Vol. 1. Postural and locomotor development.* Minneapolis: University of Minnesota Press.

Smith, L., Kemler, D., & Aronfield, J. (1975). Developmental trends in voluntary selective attention: Differential aspects of source distinctiveness. *Journal of Experimental Child Psychology, 20,* 353–362.

Stinson, B. (1991a). *To move to learn to grow: Movement experiences for young children* (2nd ed.). Emporia, KS: W & W Press.

Stinson, B. (1991b). *Calming and reassuring the young child: A guide for teachers and parents.* Emporia, KS: W & W Press.

Stinson, S. (1988). *Dance for young children: Finding the magic in movement.* Reston, VA: American Alliance for Health, Physical Education, Recreation and Dance.

Thelen, E., Ulrich, D., & Jensen, J. (1989). The developmental origins of locomotion. In M. Woollacott & A. Shumway-Cook (Eds.), *A development of posture and gait: across the lifespan* (pp. 25–47). Columbia: University of South Carolina Press.

Thomas, J. (1980). Acquisition of motor skills: Information processing differences between children and adults. *Research Quarterly for Exercise and Sport, 51,* 158–173.

Thomas, J. (1984). *Motor development during childhood and adolescence.* Minneapolis, MN: Burgess.

Thomas, J., & Thomas, K. (1984). Planning kiddie research: Little kids but big problems. In J. Thomas (Ed.), *Motor development during childhood and adolescence* (pp. 260–273). Minneapolis, MN: Burgess.

Victors, E. (1961). *A cinematrographical analysis of catching behavior of a selected group of seven and nine year old boys.* Unpublished doctoral dissertation, University of Wisconsin–Madison.

Weimer, K. (1987). *The effects of progressive relaxation on the frequency of classroom disruptions of low income first grade students.* Unpublished doctoral dissertation, Mercer University, Macon, GA.

Whitall, J. (1990). A dynamical systems approach to motor development: Applying new theory to practice. In B. Stinson (Ed.), *Moving and learning for the young child* (pp. 105–106). Reston, VA: American Alliance for Health, Physical Education, Recreation and Dance.

Whitehurst, K. (1971). The young child: What movement means to him. In G. Engstrom (Ed.), *The significance of the young child's motor development* (pp. 51–55). *Proceedings of a conference sponsored by the American Association for Health, Physical Education and Recreation, and the National Association for the Education of Young Children.* Washington, DC.

Williams, H. (1983). *Perceptual and motor development.* Englewood Cliffs, NJ: Prentice-Hall.

# CHAPTER 10

# Early Childhood Music Education

## CLIFFORD D. ALPER

> Art and appreciation of art constitute a general capacity or talent of man, and should be cared for early, at the latest in boyhood. . . . A universal and comprehensive plan of human education must, therefore, necessarily consider at an early period singing, drawing, painting and modeling; it will not leave them to an arbitrary, frivolous whimsicalness, but treat them as serious objects of the school. Its intention will not be to make each pupil an artist in some one or all of the arts, but to secure each human being full and all-sided development, to enable him to see man in the universality and all-sided energy of his nature, and, particularly, to enable him to understand and appreciate the products of true art.
>
> —*Friedrich Froebel (1782–1852)*
> *The Education of Man*

These prophetic, though obviously sexist, comments by the German-born founder of modern early childhood education, Friedrich Froebel, have important implications for current theories in music education for young children (see Mark, 1982). In nineteenth-century Germany, Froebel was among the first to speak out in favor of children's natural capacities, in an era when child passivity and obedience were the rule. With the advantage of hindsight, we can see Froebel's principles as having prevailed, although the specific methodologies he advocated have now been discarded. Among the current practices in music education that can be traced to Froebelian theory, one can cite the ideas of Dalcroze, Orff, and conceptual education. Kodaly methodology, while not particularly Froebelian, also plays a vital role in current music education practices, having had considerable impact on education for very young children, as well as for older students.

## APPROACHES TO MUSIC EDUCATION

Emile Jacques-Dalcroze (1865–1950), born in Vienna of Swiss parents, advocated using one's entire body as a kind of musical entity, "becoming" the music, so to speak. The term *eurhythmics* is associated with his work, in which children, through the use of their bodies, increase their understanding by having consistent and increasingly complex experiences with music and movement (Reimer, 1989). At the early childhood level, for example, students might move in new directions or in different ways when a previously unheard section or melodic idea occurs in the music. Or, if dynamics are being emphasized, students might alter their patterns of movement when the volume of sound increases or decreases. Dalcrozian techniques thus enable teachers to observe, in behavioral terms, how students respond to musical tasks. In addition, motivation is ensured, due to the intensity of psychomotor, cognitive, and affective involvement required. Dalcroze's writings reflect Froebelian thought, particularly Froebel's principle of self-activity, where the objective is to attain fulfillment and self-realization almost simultaneously. How better to achieve this than through Dalcroze's total physical and mental immersion in musical experience?

The *Schulwerk* of the German composer Carl Orff (1895–1982) also has played an important role in music education during the past several years (Reimer, 1989). Orff's system employs experiences using such instruments as metallophones, xylophones, and glockenspiels. Children play these pitched percussion instruments, producing borduns and ostinati for mainly pentatonic songs. This provides musical experiences with a great deal of interest and variety, and even lends a "professional" sound to the music made by children. At the early childhood level, Orff methodology might include instrumental borduns and ostinati with simple nursery rhyme-type songs based entirely on the pitches *so* and *mi*, such as "Rain, Rain, Go Away." This simple song becomes a truly aesthetic experience when combined with Orff instruments playing a bordun and one or two ostinati. Indeed, youngsters become real musicians when engaging in these endeavors.

The conceptual approach offers yet another valid way of working with children in music. This system, which came into use in the late 1960s and continues to have current implications, tends to avoid mere singing of songs as a total music education program (Gray, 1967). Instead, when music is taught, children are exposed not only to the music itself, but also to melody, rhythm, harmony, form, tone color, dynamics, and tempo. For example, in addition to singing a song, children may learn to notice when pitches go up, down, or are repeated, and when pitches move stepwise or by leaps. Or, if rhythm is stressed, children might be exposed to the fact that music always involves rhythm, or that music usually embodies a recurring pulse, called the beat. In order to facilitate comprehension of the beat, children might engage in physical movement or instrumental experiences to illustrate and reinforce this concept. Although singing remains an important element in the conceptual approach, as it does in most systems, songs and listening activities must be augmented by an introduction to the elements of music, thus providing comprehensive musical experiences for children.

The music education system devised by the Hungarian composer Zoltan Kodaly (1882–1967) has had a tremendous impact all over the United States (Reimer, 1989). The Kodaly system enables children, even at a very early age, to read and articulate rhythmic and melodic notation, encouraging them to internalize the elements of music and their concomitant skills. The methodology includes so-called stick notation, which leaves out the head part of quarter, eighth, sixteenth, thirty-second, and sixty-fourth notes. Whole and half notes are notated in the usual manner. The teacher shows the children how to assign rhythmic syllables to specific note values according to this notation. For melodic reading experiences, children learn to use the familiar pitch syllables, *do-re-mi-fa-so-la-ti-do*. Extensive listening activities and playing instruments other than recorders are not used very often.

The so-called Eclectic Curriculum combines elements of Dalcroze, Orff, and Kodaly, using representative elements from each. Although not looked upon favorably by purists who advocate exclusive use of just one of these methods, the Eclectic Curriculum has proven to be a viable and practical way to combine the most representative components of these various methods. Each of these methods will be discussed in more detail in the following sections.

## Dalcroze

Young children, filled with physical energy, react very favorably to Dalcrozian movement activities, especially when introduced to them at an early age. When children feel comfortable with Dalcrozian activities, and these are used consistently, gradually increasing in difficulty and complexity, children have a foundation of music skills and knowledge that enables them to be competent musicians even at the high school level. It is essential, therefore, to build an atmosphere of trust, confidence, and psychological safety, so that initial hurdles are surmounted and aesthetic considerations can begin to prevail.

One of many advantages of the Dalcrozian idea is that it becomes no longer necessary to imitate or "be" something (an animal, airplane, robot, etc.) when moving to music. Children instead can react to music in terms of its own components, rather than to extraneous constructs such as stories or pictures. In terms of aesthetic theory, reacting to the integral parts of music (melody, rhythm, tone color, and form) falls into the area of absolute expressionism or absolute formalism. In *absolute expressionism*, one acknowledges the emotive/affective elements in art, but does not conjure up stories or pictures extraneous to the artwork, especially if its originator indicated no such intentions. *Absolute formalism*, on the other hand, deals solely with an artwork's constituents, which in the case of music would involve rhythm, melody, harmony and counterpoint, form, dynamics, timbre, and tempo. If one prefers to adopt a *referential* view of music, however, one could add all kinds of stories, pictures, and other extramusical factors not really part of the artwork itself. The trend today, which Dalcroze foreshadowed in his integration-of-movement-with-music concept, is toward an absolute expressionist way of dealing with the arts in education (Reimer, 1989).

If teachers accept *absolute expressionism* as a desirable and aesthetic way of incorporating music into early childhood education, they will gear their activities to the component parts of music itself, regardless of whether it is considered to be "program music" or "absolute music." So, if rhythmic elements are to be presented, children will be asked to respond to basic pulse (beat), then perhaps to the rhythm of the words. Initially, such rhythmic factors should be repetitious enough to enable youngsters to internalize patterns they hear, and to solidify specific ideas about the music in their minds. Listed below are some possibilities for initiating Dalcroze-like activities with young children, using an absolute expressionist point of view as the aesthetic framework.

- *Melody.* Children move in certain ways or directions for
    1. Legato (smooth) melody segments and staccato (detached) melody segments
    2. Melody lines that move by steps and those that move by leaps
    3. Melody lines that ascend or descend
    4. Melody lines that contain repeated notes and changed notes
- *Rhythm.* Children move in certain ways or directions for
    1. Music with longer or shorter sounds, or silences (rests)
    2. Groups of longer or shorter sounds, or silences (rests)
    3. The recurring pulse (beat), and any changes in that pulse
    4. Music that stops suddenly or unexpectedly, and then resumes immediately
- *Harmony.* Children move in certain ways or directions
    1. Each time underlying chords should be (or are) changed
    2. When two melodies are being sounded simultaneously
    3. When accompaniment patterns (chordal, triadic, oom-pah-pah, and so forth) are changed
    4. When a major key is changed to minor, or minor to major
- *Form.* Children move in certain ways or directions when
    1. They hear like and unlike phrases in music
    2. Entire sections are repeated, or contrasting sections are introduced

3. They hear melodic sequences (patterns immediately repeated in pitches higher or lower than in their first appearance)

4. A familiar idea is altered or varied, but is still recognizable as being based on the original

- *Tempo.* Children move in certain ways, directions, or at varying speeds when

  1. Music becomes faster or slower

  2. Selected tempo seems "appropriate" or "inappropriate" to the type of music being played

- *Dynamics.* Children move in certain ways or directions when

  1. Music is very loud or very soft

  2. Music gets louder (crescendo) and softer (descrescendo)

  3. Selected dynamic levels are "appropriate" or "inappropriate"

- *Timbre* (tone color). Children move in certain ways or directions when

  1. They hear vocal sounds, then instrumental sounds

  2. They hear strong contrasts between instruments, such as between flute and double bass or cello, or clarinet and tuba

  3. They perceive "thin" tone qualities, then "thicker" ones

  4. They hear male, then female voices

  5. They hear high-pitched, then low-pitched instruments or voices

  6. They hear a small group performing, such as a string quartet or woodwind ensemble, then a larger group, such as an orchestra or chorus

  7. The same melody is played by a different group of instruments

Although teachers need not adhere solely to a particular philosophical view, their options are increased by thinking in wider aesthetic terms. The tendency for most teachers has been to embrace referentialism when dealing with the arts, mainly because it is easier, or seems easier, to tell stories or evoke pictures of specific things. When adults become comfortable with the intrinsic elements of the arts, however, it can follow naturally that these, when properly presented, can provide important and less subjective opportunities for children. The students themselves draw conclusions as to the music's emotional climate and the moods it conveys. Teachers are freed from making such banal comments to children as: "Is this music happy or sad?" "How does this music make you feel?" and "Major keys signify happiness and minor keys, sadness." Instead, children respond in various ways to music's constituent elements, and eventually draw their own conclusions about the "messages" contained therein. If children, on their own, prefer to adopt a referentialist view, so be it. But also having had experiences with absolute expressionism or formalism provides them with a larger group of viewpoints from which they may select. Does this not support

Froebel's still valid plea to let children develop naturally, with minimal interference from adults?

## Orff

Whereas Dalcroze emphasized movement, Orff dealt primarily with instrumental experiences, often combined with song. Dalcroze and Orff had certain philosophical elements in common, however, including an interest in children's gradual development and natural growth processes. In that sense, Dalcroze and Orff are related to each other more than either one is related to Kodaly, despite certain superficial resemblances in methodology between the latter two. Key words to keep in mind with regard to Orff are *bordun, ostinato*, and *rhythmic chant*. Borduns, frequently open fifths such as the partial chords C–G or D–A, are repeated consistently, providing a drone to everything else happening in the music. In addition, these borduns supply needed rhythmic consistency to music in which young children participate, facilitating their ability to maintain accuracy. After the bordun is consistent and reasonably accurate, an ostinato can be added, superimposed upon the already sounding bordun(s). Since many songs in Orff methodology are pentatonic—that is, songs using only the five tones *do, re, mi, so,* and *la* in varying order—even if children err in their articulation of an ostinato, they cannot really "make a mistake" in pitch if all inappropriate tone bells or bars on xylophones and metallophones are removed in advance. This constitutes one distinct advantage of using pentatonic material, since harmonic success is virtually ensured. At the early childhood level this is of particular importance, for not only subject matter but, perhaps more important, feelings of self-worth and confidence are being taught. Once children have achieved such perceptions of themselves, their learning is vastly improved and expedited.

For an example of an Orff approach, let us take the familiar children's tune "Rain, Rain, Go Away." Sung only on the syllables *so* and *mi*, this song, with these or other words, is known to children the world over. Researchers have found that the melodic minor third interval—in the key of C, this would be G (*so*) and E (*mi*)—is sung spontaneously by all youngsters, regardless of their race or nationality. We can remember our own childhood days, when we sang "Johnny is a baby" (*so-so-mi-la-so-mi*). Nobody knows for sure why we sang it on just those pitch levels, but we all sang them on those levels. After the children's memories of the tune and the words of "Rain, Rain, Go Away" have been refreshed, a bordun consisting of, say, *do* and *so* (C and G) played simultaneously is sounded on a bass xylophone. If the children's accuracy on this falters, they can be tapped gently on the shoulder in the correct rhythm and tempo, to help bring them up to stan-

dard. At this point, "Rain, Rain, Go Away" is sung while the bordun continues to sound. If all goes well up to this point, an ostinato is added, perhaps
on a soprano xylophone, metallophone, or glockenspiel. This ostinato might
be as simple as Ć-E-G

repeated consistently throughout the song, in combination with the bordun.
When the song has been sung two or three times, the ostinato can cease,
then the bordun, or the reverse. If the children prefer to have a feeling of
closure, in the tonal sense, an ostinato can be devised that ends on *do,* thus
giving a feeling of finality to the music, especially if the ostinato ceases after
everything else has stopped. All this results in a belief by the children that
they have made real music, something they probably did not think themselves capable of previously. Their musical accomplishment has led also to
psychological well-being, a not inconsiderable achievement, and extremely
important for this very young age level.

## The Conceptual Approach

When the Music Educators National Conference published *The Study
of Music in the Elementary School—A Conceptual Approach* (Gray, 1967),
that organization was responding to trends that had intensified during the
previous decade. There had been criticism that general music programs encompassed only singing of songs, with occasional listening lessons thrown
in. To some extent, these criticisms were well founded and have since been
addressed.

In the excellent scope and sequence chart included with that book, the
authors make the following statement:

> The conceptual learnings outlined in the scope and sequence chart re-
> quire *aural perception* which, in turn, is developed through *listening,
> kinesthetic rhythmic responses, singing,* and *playing of instruments.*
> Within a carefully planned musical environment, children will be stimu-
> lated through these activities to

| | |
|---|---|
| Imitate | Differentiate |
| Explore | Verbalize |
| Discover | Memorize |
| Recognize | Recall |
| Identify | Evaluate |

These processes are essential in the development and clarification of musical concepts. (Gray, 1967, pp. 128–129)

When one considers all 10 of these processes, one begins to understand exactly what the conceptual approach encompasses. In many cases, children have been taught merely to memorize, then spew back that exact information, at which time they were considered to "know" the material. However, looking at this list of verbs immediately reveals that memorization is but one of 10 activities in which children engage in order to conceptualize, and memorization is not even necessarily the most important among them. The valid assumption in the conceptual approach is that if youngsters have opportunities to engage in many or all of these processes, their ability to internalize increases. It follows, then, that if teachers are interested in providing more conceptually oriented activities, they must allow for more of these experiences to take place. They might ask themselves: "Am I merely a purveyor of information?" "Do I tell a lot, or do I encourage responses and comments from children?" "When I review, do I encourage the children to recall what they can before I 'fill in' any gaps?" "Must my children's responses be only verbal?" "What nonverbal options do children have in my classroom?"

If we return to the concepts of music mentioned earlier in this chapter (melody, rhythm, harmony, and so forth), and choose harmony as the example to be dealt with, how might we go about enabling children to conceive of this important aspect of music? One way would be through listening in which the children, after hearing and singing a song that has become familiar, respond to where the chords should change on an accompanying instrument (autoharp, guitar, or piano). It can be presented to children as a game in which they are asked to raise their hands each time they think the currently used chord should be changed. At first, responses are tentative and reluctant, but this soon improves as the children naturally begin to understand the concept and have greater faith in what they hear. Not everyone in the group grasps this immediately, but there usually are enough who do to constitute a nucleus from which the others can be motivated. After many of the children have grasped the idea, they are ready to play the autoharp themselves on a simple one- or two-chord song. It is necessary, however, to help children with the motor skills required in strumming the autoharp while holding down the bars; for the youngest children, the teacher should hold down the bars as the child strums. Initially, the teacher will also need to tell the children exactly what chords to play. Eventually, however, they should be weaned from this, so that they can begin to decide which of two chords is preferable at any given moment in the song being accompanied. (A one-chord song such as a round, of course, does not require chord changes.) When this freedom is ultimately achieved, and the children feel comfortable with this activity, their aural perception can be extended further by adding tone bells in chords (I, IV, and/or $V^7$ are the usual chords needed in many children's songs). One group can play the bells, then another play the autoharp, or both groups can play at the same time. Not only is this great fun for youngsters of all ages, but also they are beginning to conceive of harmonic principles, albeit on a simple level. The "fun" element should not be underestimated. As Froebel indicated in his prophetic writings in the last century, children's play activities provide the seeds from which their adulthood springs. If they perceive their learning experiences as "play" or "fun," and teachers can facilitate that perception, so much the better. Only adults differentiate between work and play. Since play *is* children's work, they make no such differentiation, and neither should their teachers.

## Kodaly

Unlike the Orff system, Kodaly emphasized music literacy, that is, children's ability to read music notation and to use this skill in various ways, which leads ultimately to comprehensive musical understanding (Reimer, 1989). Early in the program, children learn to read and articulate rhythmic figures through the use of echo clapping and stick notation. The most frequently used notes for early childhood and their rhythmic syllables are given in Figure 10.1, mostly in the Kodaly stick notation, which omits the head part of notes where feasible.

In behavioral terms, echo-clapping experiences enable teachers to observe and evaluate their students' understanding of rhythmic concepts. The teacher claps a simple rhythmic pattern at a consistent tempo (not too fast), say,

Another suitable pattern for clapping might be

where on the rest, either silence with hands to the sides and palms facing the ceiling (preferable), or actually saying the word rest is indicated. After children have engaged in many such experiences over weeks and months,

## Figure 10.1  Frequently used notes and their rhythmic syllables

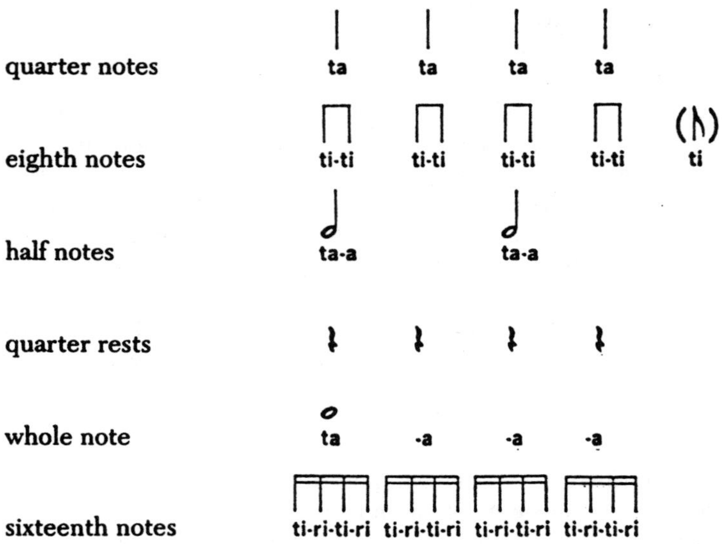

| | | | | |
|---|---|---|---|---|
| quarter notes | ta   ta   ta   ta | | | |
| eighth notes | ti-ti   ti-ti   ti-ti   ti-ti   (♪) ti | | | |
| half notes | ta-a   ta-a | | | |
| quarter rests | ᛁ   ᛁ   ᛁ   ᛁ | | | |
| whole note | ta   -a   -a   -a | | | |
| sixteenth notes | ti-ri-ti-ri  ti-ri-ti-ri  ti-ri-ti-ri  ti-ri-ti-ri | | | |

including performing these rhythm patterns on classroom percussion instruments, further development and extensions are possible. For example, four patterns, such as those illustrated in Figure 10.2, numbered for quick identification, might be on a chart or chalkboard. (It is always desirable in education to include visual presentations when feasible.) As the teacher claps each pattern, the children determine which one they hear and indicate their choice by calling out the proper number. Later, they might invent and articulate their own rhythms for other class members' responses. If approximately 5 minutes of each period are devoted to such rhythm activities, children's ability to read music can become almost second nature.

In terms of melody experiences, the Kodaly system at the outset uses primarily pentatonic songs. Initially, Kodaly uses *so-mi* songs almost exclusively, with *do, la, fa, re,* and *ti* gradually introduced later, after the children have grasped many of the concepts related to *so* and *mi.* Although seemingly restrictive, the *so-mi,* song idea can be applied to literally hundreds of nursery rhymes and children's jingles, enabling them to "set to music" any of their favorites. Let us consider, as an example, "Humpty Dumpty." The entire rhyme is chanted on *so* and *mi,* using Kodaly hand signs (these signs actually were developed by an Englishman named John Curwen, but have

**Figure 10.2    Four rhythmic patterns**

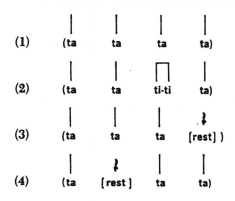

since been integrated into the Kodaly system). Using hand signs for *so* and *mi* (see Figure 10.3) provides added dimension to the simplicity of the rhyme and its "tune." After children have mastered signing while making hand signs, and this usually requires time and effort for them to learn, they can play on pitched percussion instruments, such as tone bells, the *so-mi* pattern to accompany their singing of "Humpty Dumpty." Since *so-mi* is part of the "universal chant of childhood," the entire experience can take on an inevitable natural quality for all to enjoy. If, at the early childhood level, one applied Kodaly methodology strictly, *so* and *mi* would be used almost exclusively for as long as the first year, after which time the other syllables would be introduced gradually. If, however, teachers felt that their children were capable and interested, and they usually are, songs using the entire pentatonic scale (*do, re, mi, so,* and *la;* or, in the key of C Major: C, D, E, G, and A) could be used, as well as song materials using any tones of the major and minor keys.

## The Eclectic Curriculum

The Eclectic Curriculum utilizes elements of Dalcroze, Orff, and Kodaly in ways deemed appropriate for the particular children being taught (Reimer, 1989). For example, Orff-like borduns and ostinati might be played as children sing and others move to the music being performed. These might be included with Kodaly-type activity, such as vocally articulating TA's or TI's or hearing recorded selections of important music, thus involving children in "listening" experience. Or, a conceptual approach might be in-

**Figure 10.3   Kodaly hand signs**

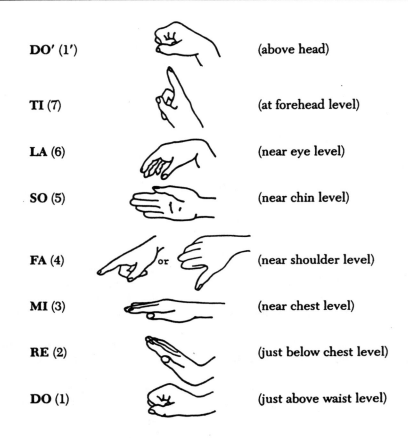

DO' (1')          (above head)

TI (7)            (at forehead level)

LA (6)            (near eye level)

SO (5)            (near chin level)

FA (4)      or    (near shoulder level)

MI (3)            (near chest level)

RE (2)            (just below chest level)

DO (1)            (just above waist level)

cluded, involving such experiences as listening, singing, instruments, improvisation, physical movement, and skills activities. Goals including rhythm, melody, harmony, form, tempo, dynamics, tone color, and mood would play important roles here.

It is possible that the so-called listening activity may be the most important music experience in schools, for most people will become consumers of music (concert and opera goers, record buyers, radio listeners) rather than professional musicians. If one accepts music listening as an important facet of the school experience, using Kodaly as the sole method would be self-defeating. Teachers usually want to include live and recorded listening experiences with which children can interact (through movement, simulta-

neous singing and/or playing of instruments, dramatization, and panto-
mime), in addition to the cognitively oriented activities such as music reading. The so-called affective area, especially in arts education, might very
well be equal in importance to the more readily evaluated cognitive domain.
For very young children, should the two be separated, or are they not two
sides of the same coin? Since one of the objectives of all education is to help
students develop insights and to embrace concepts, one can look to the arts
whose inherent nature encompasses, and often requires, internalization. If
students are expected merely to memorize information, they hardly require
education in the arts to do so, for many other fields of endeavor can teach
this as well or better. Reimer (1989) sees the intent of art as providing insight rather than being just informational. If this is indeed the case, the arts
can nurture those abilities and attitudes that enable students to develop
insights, leading to their interest in seeking out information when needed.
For maximum comprehension to take place, should insight precede information, or should the reverse occur? If one agrees with Reimer, and there
are reasons to believe his point is well taken, the former is more desirable.
If one has insight, finding needed information becomes less difficult. If one
merely has information, however, it does not necessarily follow that the uses
and import of that information are known to the learner. In other words,
developing insights can help one to gain concepts, while information alone
may be isolated and out of the learner's mainstream of thought. Ausubel
theorized that meaningful reception learning takes place only when ideas
and understandings are properly classified hierarchically ("subsumed") by
learners in relation to what they already know, thus becoming part of what
he calls their cognitive structure (Leonhard, 1965a). In the connections that
Ausubel views as essential to meaningful learning and retention, conceptualization and internalization form the core. What better vehicle to accomplish this than education in the arts?

## IMPLICATIONS OF RESEARCH FOR CURRICULUM

One of the problems with music education research and philosophy is
the fact that, until recently, the primary work was done not by music educators, but by psychologists, philosophers, and generalists. "It is the responsibility of music educators themselves to systematize and verify their principles and to develop a theoretical rationale for music education" (Leonhard,
1965b, p. 48). A major response to this suggestion was Bennett Reimer's *A
Philosophy of Music Education* (1989), in which the author offered guidelines based on aesthetic principles. Although Reimer does not deal specifically with the early childhood level, his commentary has implications for

very young children, especially in the area of music listening, in which he advocates absolute expressionism, rather than referentialism or absolute formalism, as the most desirable framework in which to operate. This, however, does not preclude the possibility of utilizing referentialism or formalism on those occasions when they are deemed to be appropriate.

Research on the musical potential of young children indicates that, even at the ages of say, 4 to 5, they can learn to match pitch, accurately replicate rhythmic and melodic patterns (through such experiences as echo clapping and repeating sung patterns), and, for the most part, correctly sing simple songs. Nye (1979) states that "writers in the field of music education conclude that early musical experiences must develop musical percepts in order that musical concepts can be acquired" (p. 2). Implied in Nye's statement is that percepts—not only in music but perhaps in all learning—must be presented and received in such a way as to encourage and lead logically to conceptualization. Experiences in music must become, therefore, not isolated or merely entertaining, but integral parts of children's total learning process. If this occurs, the probability of retention and utilization increases considerably.

Nye also advocates, in addition to its being taught in its own right, music as "an integral part of all activities in the educational program—science, social studies, language, health, safety, values, and mathematical concepts" (p. 3). If one accepts this viewpoint as valid, one's anxieties about teaching music simply due to "lack of training" or "not being musically inclined" can be reduced or eliminated. Most early childhood teachers are not "scientists," "mathematicians," "language experts," "historians," "artists," or "geographers," yet they teach all these subjects, usually free of undue anxiety. Why view music differently?

Authors who contributed to *The Young Child and Music* (Boswell, 1985) deal with such important topics of concern to early childhood music education as concepts of play, stressed children, practical applications, and state-of-the-art in early childhood music and research. Other essays in that book offer suggestions for expanding youngsters' listening preferences and ways of nurturing and assessing preschool children's aesthetic responses. In *Promising Practices: Prekindergarten Music Education* (Andress, 1989), the authors offer up-to-date information in such areas as (1) a music experience laboratory; (2) music programs for infants and toddlers; (3) the arts as part of a core curriculum; and (4) promising practices for kindergarten program planners, including community involvement, music and movement environments for preschool children, and musical understanding through creative movement.

The next sections of this chapter discuss the components of music education in detail. These include singing, movement, instrumental experiences, listening, and creative improvisational experiences.

## Singing

Young children's sense of pitch tends to be variable according to each individual. Some youngsters match pitches with ease, while others need further experiences and sometimes hard work to "find" themselves in terms of singing.

Nye and Nye (1985) offer some useful and valuable guidelines for dealing with many kinds of musical problems for ages 4 to 8 or 9. For singing, they suggest using tone-matching games, singing conversations, and the use of pitch-giving devices (autoharp, bells, piano, and the like) to help ensure proper ranges for young children.

A good rule to remember is that those pitches right on the lines and spaces of the treble staff usually are within the comfortable ranges of children. Middle C, although used occasionally, tends to be a bit low for youngsters, while F or G at the top of the treble staff tends to be a little high for them.

Using a pitch-giving device, therefore, followed by a clear "ready, *sing*" or "ready, *begin*" sung on the beginning pitch of the song, helps to ensure that everyone will begin simultaneously and at the same pitch. Consistent use of this essential procedure not only increases the teacher's accuracy, but improves student musicality as well.

When a child has difficulty matching the teacher's pitch, a useful device is for the teacher to match the child's pitch, then go on from there. This procedure is helpful not only because it shows that the teacher accepts psychologically what the child is about, but it enables the child, perhaps for the first time, to hear exactly what constitutes matching of pitches. This can be an important first step to help students internalize this intangible but essential aspect of musical understanding.

So-called monotones—people said to have but one tone in their singing repertoire—do not really exist, since almost everyone can sing on more than one pitch level. If a child tends to dwell on one or two pitches, such exercises as imitating ambulance and fire engine sirens, or "singing way up high" and "way down low" can alleviate this problem. Since these activities can be presented in game formats, they need not be embarrassing for the individuals in question, especially if *all* the children, regardless of their singing abilities, are asked, one at a time, to engage in this experience.

Another valuable game to determine pitch accuracy in children involves a "getting acquainted" activity, which enables the teacher to learn students' names while also determining their singing abilities. On the pitch levels *so-mi-la-so-mi*, the teacher sings, "My name is such-and-such, what is your name?" The children individually answer, hopefully at the same pitches, "My name is such-and-such." If a child's response is not accurate, the teacher can repeat, perhaps at the child's pitch levels, the same patterns, to determine the child's ability to match pitches. It is *not* recommended, however, that children at this point be drilled into "getting it right." The purposes here are to determine musical status and to provide experiences on which later presentations involving singing can be based. Many times, especially at the early childhood level, just experiencing and maturing in themselves bring on solutions. There is something to be said for allowing things to "sink in" over a period of time, rather than looking for immediate success.

Piaget classified children up to around age 8 as being in the pre-operational stage of development. In this stage, "the child uses symbols crudely but manipulates reality by intuitive regulation rather than by symbolic operations" (Leonhard, 1965a, p. 54). If one accepts the Piagetian theory that children at early stages of development simply are not ready to engage in certain experiences, teachers can patiently allow for time to do its job, not just with singing, or with music, but in all areas of the curriculum. It is with these kinds of insights that research and experimentation make valuable contributions to education.

In terms of song material, children should have opportunities to sing a wide assortment under various musical conditions. For example, singing with and without accompaniment, singing with recordings, and singing with accompaniments provided by other children each present distinct advantages. Nye and Nye (1985), in reminding teachers of children's interest in immediate goals and need for feelings of success, suggest songs about "everyday experiences such as mother and family, playthings, people they know, pets and animals" (p. 11). One is reminded here of Froebel's prophetic writings in the last century, for it was he who called attention to the importance of mother and family, children's play, and respect for all living things in an era when what youngsters were about was hardly of major interest to most adults (Alper, 1980).

When teaching new songs to youngsters, teachers need to keep in mind certain factors in order to determine how the song material can be conveyed most effectively (Alper, 1980). For example, short, simple songs with only a few words can be presented in their entirety. After hearing the song two or three times, the children are asked to sing the song or join in as they feel comfortable. This is called the whole-song method and works well with repetitious and brief songs, including many of those with refrains. Introducing longer and more complex songs requires a different methodology. Children hear the entire song once or twice (live and/or recorded) then echo, phrase by phrase or segment by segment, until they have sung the whole song. Repetitions, it is hoped, with variations such as instruments and dramatization, help the song to become part of their repertoire. This echo method, if presented in large enough segments to avoid tedium, can be very effective in song presentation.

Four general factors for determining appropriateness of song materials for young children include (1) length, (2) amount of repetition, (3) text, and (4) degree of musical complexity (Hoffer & Hoffer, 1982). Short songs, due to youngsters' limited attention spans, usually have greater impact on them. If there is repetition of text and/or music, such as a refrain or repeated phrases, young children can grasp musical meaning more easily, thus facilitating learning. Texts need to be on children's level and within their frame of reference, while the degree of musical complexity must be geared to their limited experience at this stage of their lives. Up-to-date though these recommendations seem, they nevertheless relate to those of an earlier era. For example, in her books, Eleanor Smith (1858–1942), an excellent children's song composer, acknowledged Froebel's philosophy by stressing children's natural abilities and inclinations, their aesthetic development, and the need for brevity in song materials to be used with very young children (Alper, 1980). Such lessons of history not only continue to teach about the future, but also help to determine its direction.

## Movement

Rhythmic activities for young children always have been acknowledged as essential to a comprehensive educational program. As most teachers and parents know, it is almost impossible and perhaps even unnatural for youngsters to remain quiet and still for long periods. Realizing this, teachers need to provide children with many kinds of physical opportunities that can be related to music. An effective and readily perceived way to do this is to use an Orff-oriented pattern, in which youngsters keep time to music they sing or hear by "patsching" (slapping one's thighs or just above one's knees with both hands, usually while seated), followed immediately by clapping. In a duple meter, such as 2/4, the patsch-clap alternation pattern occurs as the children sing, thus improving their accuracy in rhythm and tempo. In a triple meter, such as 3/4, the pattern would be changed to patsch-clap-clap (Wheeler & Raebeck, 1985). Not only are such experiences perceived positively, but they offer the additional benefit of implementing Orff's recommendation that children have opportunities to do two things simultaneously. Careful attention, however, should be given to articulation here: Clapping must be graceful and aesthetic, totally in keeping with the feeling and mood of the music being used. Patsch-clap techniques are also suitable for use when *chanting* nursery rhyme-type poems, in which the objective is to improve skills in rhythm and tempo, leaving pitch and other melody considerations for another time.

The most desirable and aesthetic movement experiences for children are those that relate to factors inherent in music, such as form, tone, color, melody, tempo, and the like. By eliminating the need to pretend to be something unrelated to music, such as an animal or thing, one can encourage a child to concentrate on music itself as the primary focus.

Singing games—songs like "Here We Go Round the Mulberry Bush" in which the words tell or imply specific kinds of movement activities in which to engage—have always played important roles in music experiences for young children. But even here, in "going around the mulberry bush," some basically musical factors enter. The song is strophic, that is, it has the same music for all its verses. Each time the child changes an activity to correspond with the words, the fact that only the words have changed, and not the music itself, needs to be brought out.

On the other hand, in a song like "Shoo, Fly," which is in a ternary form—three parts, designated as A–B–A—the formal design can determine types and directions of movement. For example, in part 1 ("Shoo, fly, don't bother me") children might move in a circle from left to right while holding hands. On the middle part of the song (section B: "I feel, I feel, I feel, etc.), being different music, they might take small steps inward, raising their arms as they reach the center (corresponding to the end of phrase 1), then back out while continuing to hold hands for phrase 2. When section A returns, accompanied by the same circular movement patterns, the fact that this is the same music as sung initially is reinforced intrinsically. The ternary (A–B–A) design of "Shoo, Fly" may begin to solidify in the child's mind.

It is desirable to use this kind of traditional song literature with young children, teaching through participation, even if students initially tend to concentrate on actions rather than on music. The objective is to develop proficiency in singing-and-moving simultaneously (Haines & Gerber, 1988). More experiences with A–B–A form, such as with the minuets and scherzi of most symphonies by Haydn, Mozart, Beethoven, and Schubert, can help youngsters to internalize further about this commonly encountered design in music. Physical activity can enhance children's understanding of a form concept in music, in this case A–B–A, where movement serves as the means, and understanding of specific formal design, the end.

Movement, of course, may be used to achieve other goals as well. Children might make up suitable physical responses to songs they sing, interpreting and dramatizing the words, or reacting to contours of melody. Some of the Dalcroze-like activities listed earlier might serve as starting points to encourage imagination and ingenuity. Movement for its own intrinsic purposes constitutes yet another valid use of this indispensable experience. In an essay entitled "The Initiation into Rhythm," Dalcroze (1921/1973) summarized its implications.

(1) Rhythm is movement; (2) rhythm is essentially physical; (3) every movement involves time and space; (4) musical consciousness is the result

of physical experience; (5) the perfecting of physical resources results in clarity of perception; (6) the perfecting of movements in time assures consciousness of musical rhythm; (7) the perfecting of movements in space assures consciousness of plastic rhythm; (8) the perfecting of movements in time and space can only be accompanied by exercises in rhythmic movement. (pp. 39–40)

Dalcroze's fourth observation about consciousness and physical experience anticipates current views of how young children learn, and his fifth poses an intriguing idea, traceable to Froebel, about the "outer" eventually penetrating and nurturing one's "inner" modes of perception. Froebelian also in Dalcroze's eight-tiered summarization is his choice of a hierarchy to define the total implications of rhythm and movement. The father of modern early childhood education thus influenced the renowned movement expert, who currently enjoys renewed popularity. Considering the fact that Orff techniques also are in extensive current use, the spirit of Froebel's philosophy still looms large and is not confined to the early childhood level.

### Instrumental Experiences

Activities involving instruments should play an important role in young children's experiences with music. In addition to hearing many instruments, live and recorded, youngsters should perform on various kinds, including orchestral as well as the familiar classroom percussion types of so-called rhythm instruments. In addition, children, with adult guidance, can make their own instruments. It is essential, however, that the products have musical and aesthetic tone qualities. A "tambourine," for example, does not emit a musical tone quality if it merely sounds like a paper plate with bottle caps attached. Easily overlooked, but also important, are other "sound producers," like parts of one's own body, as well as such commonly found items as twigs, stones, keys, coins, paper, and the like.

Swanson (1981) categorized "raw" sound sources as (1) body sounds, (2) vocal sounds, and (3) striking or rubbing sounds. In her "Sources of Instruments" section, she offers suggestions on how to make a drum, sandblocks, maracas and guiro, rhythm sticks, and tone blocks. To implement Swanson's suggestions, however, older children or adults are needed, since very young children do not yet possess the necessary skills. Perhaps the only successful instruments, in terms of sound, that very young children can make themselves are various kinds of shakers, using uncooked beans or rice within cardboard oatmeal containers or frozen juice cans, or perhaps drumlike instruments, if they truly sound good. Aesthetically speaking, one is better off buying high quality classroom instruments, if those that are self-made fail to reach a valid level of sound quality. Ideally, both types of instruments should be available; however, the manufactured variety is clearly preferable when considered for purely musical reasons.

Regular orchestral instruments, such as bowed strings, clarinets, or trumpets, often are overlooked by teachers as not being available or as being too difficult for young children. As a result of this view, many people go through their entire lives without ever experiencing the joy of physical contact with orchestral instruments. It is suggested, therefore, that teachers of early childhood request that band and orchestra teachers in their schools bring instruments to the classroom for children's exploration and lend a few instruments to the class for day-to-day use and experimentation. Opposition by band and orchestra directors to such suggestions may be encountered, mainly because these teachers tend to view very young children as having little relationship with their instrumental programs. When it is pointed out to them that today's youngsters become tomorrow's participants in band and orchestra, this view can change. Classroom teachers also might consider purchasing secondhand orchestra instruments with funds from curriculum budgets or the PTA.

Young children will have fun "buzzing" on woodwind and brass mouthpieces, with or without the instrument itself attached. (It is necessary, of course, to sterilize mouthpieces before each use.) Making oral "raspberries" seems to come naturally to children, so they delight in applying this technique to a music activity in school. Learning to hold a violin or cello bow, then applying it to the instrument's strings, is a thrill no one should miss. Having such contacts can result in

1. Positive and successful feelings about orchestral and band instruments
2. Opportunities to realize possible latent talent
3. Perception by children that instruments are "fun"
4. Enhanced knowledge of pitch, dynamics, and tempo when orchestral and band instruments are used to demonstrate these concepts

Discussions of classroom instruments and how they can be used appear in many textbooks. Sally Moomaw (1984) offers a particularly clear discussion, and the accompanying illustrations provide further clarification. She gives specific suggestions as to how teachers may go about introducing instruments to children and various ways instruments can enhance a comprehensive program. Moomaw classifies into three categories instruments suitable for children.

1. Rhythm instruments, to be struck or scraped, producing a variety of nonpitched sounds
2. Melody instruments, producing specific pitches
3. Accompanying instruments, producing several tones simultaneously, thus creating chords that can accompany melodies

Particularly helpful to classroom teachers are Moomaw's sections on ethnic or exotic self-made instruments and her selected bibliography of books on instruments suitable for use at the early childhood level. With current recommendations that multicultural factors be included in education, Moomaw's discussion of ethnic and exotic instruments seems particularly timely and apropos.

The "Developmental Sequence" and "Suggestions to the Teacher" on playing instruments by Leeper, Skipper, and Witherspoon (1979) are interesting and helpful. These authors' recommendations recall the conceptual approach: The child manipulates and experiments with instruments, listens to an instrument, uses an instrument as accompaniment, listens to music and identifies an instrument, plays an instrument, learns names of instruments, and so forth (p. 453). Land and Vaughn (1978) offer pictures of most classroom instruments, including some unusual ones from Asia, Africa, and India. These authors' diagram of a seating plan for an orchestra and list of orchestral instruments provide further valuable information for teachers of early childhood.

Andress, Heimann, Rinehart, and Talbert (1973) offer unique suggestions for using instruments with young children, such as sound-exploration carrels in which children try out various sound-producing devices. The "sound plays" on instruments include a "feel me, hear me" box, in which the musical environment is arranged in various ways. And one should not forget the possibility of using instruments and other sound producers in songs and stories presented to or by children, preferably having the children themselves decide which instruments to use, where, and in what combinations. This ensures that they will consider timbres and dynamic qualities of available instruments to determine their suitability. Andress and colleagues also suggest setting up a music corner, in which an old piano with its strings exposed might be placed. Such an instrument might be "prepared" by children, that is, its tone quality altered by attaching, for instance, paper, rubber bands, or metal pieces like paper clips or bottle caps, to its strings. This technique, it might be pointed out to children, is used by contemporary composers like George Crumb and John Cage. A recording of prepared piano music (see Cage, Wergo #60074) might be played for children to hear and react to, preferably after they have done their own experimenting.

Possibilities and directions for instrumental experiences need be confined only by the limits of one's imagination, ingenuity, and willingness to experiment, even if in "unknown" territory. All this is very much in keeping with Froebel's view that, in addition to calling on receptive and reflective qualities, early education should encourage creative and executive attributes as well. This, of course, applies equally to children and teachers.

### Listening

With the possible exception of singing, listening experiences are more likely to be retained and utilized in later life than all others one encounters in school music. Effectively teaching suitable listening techniques to children, therefore, should occupy an important place in each classroom teachers' methodology. Key to achieving this goal are

1. Inventing and finding materials and methodologies that have aesthetic and educational merit
2. Using compositions worthy of the time spent in thinking about them
3. Actively stimulating children to use their mental and physical capabilities

Formidable though it may seem, implementing this is not as difficult as one might think, for once children's interest is captured, they learn with eagerness and the rest usually falls into place.

Some examples of techniques that are likely to capture children's interest in listening to music include

1. Mirroring, in which children follow the teacher's, then each other's, hand, arm, face, and/or torso movements, which correspond to the phrases of (preferably slow and legato) music, such as the Intermezzo from Bizet's *Carmen*
2. Bouncing or rolling large balls in time to slow or moderate music
3. Moving in various ways or directions when changes (in melody, tempo, dynamics, rhythm, harmony) occur in the music being played
4. Using visuals (charts, pictures, diagrams) to increase interest and to focus children's attention on specific elements
5. Outlining melodic contour (children move their bodies or arms to the general contours of the melody being heard, drawing outlines of these structures in the air)
6. Moving to music that is stopped suddenly or unexpectedly, at which point children "freeze" into pretzel or other shapes, shortly after which the music resumes
7. Placing on a chart or chalkboard in stick notation the rhythm of a melody,

which children follow by singing the pitches on TA and TI as they are heard on a recording, or children point to each note as it is played
8. Using veil-like scarves as extensions of one's body to illustrate, through movement, the mood, shape, or form of a particular piece of music

These are just a few of many possibilities for relating music listening to the spontaneous interests and experiences of children, without the encumbrance of telling stories or conjuring up pictures not really related to music. Music is about music. If it illustrates stories or pictures at all, it does so only tangentially.

Excellent and specific suggestions for presenting listening activities can be found in Lewis's (1983) booklets and recordings, which, although specially arranged for this series,[1] include a variety of compositions suitable for use at the early childhood level. For example, children are asked to follow stick notation patterns that show the rhythm of a melody and to sing on TA and TI as these are heard on the recording of an instrumental piece.[2] Or the teacher places two melodic patterns on the board, with tone syllables indicated under each note. Children initially sing each pattern using tone syllables—at this level, so and mi, possibly also do and la—thus helping to solidify the music in their minds before they are asked to utilize this new information. Children then raise one finger when they hear pattern 1, and two fingers for pattern 2. Another effective technique in Lewis's series is for third graders to step in three meters, that is, to begin feeling changes in meter from two, to three, to four, counting aloud as these changes occur and moving accordingly. These activities have implications for behavioral objectives. Teachers can observe exactly what students perceive, as reflected in their physical responses to music.

Another interesting suggestion, among hundreds in Lewis's series of books, is for first graders to

1. Raise their hands when a certain melodic or rhythmic pattern occurs
2. Perform so-mi hand signs with these patterns when appropriate
3. Make a mark on a piece of paper or on the chalkboard each time they hear the pattern
4. Play the pattern (if it is a simple one, like so-mi) on a melody instrument, such as bells or metallophone

Lewis's lessons, by dealing with music on an intrinsic basis—that is, in terms of melody, rhythm, form, and the like—tend to illustrate absolute expressionism or formalism, rather than referentialism. Rarely in Lewis's outlines do stories or pictorial elements interfere with essentially musical considerations. If it is deemed desirable to tell the story of, say, a piece of programmatic music, or to provide children with extramusical background information, the optimum time to do this is after children have explored the music through listening, movement, instruments, and notation.

## Creative and Improvisational Experiences

Opportunities for children to invent, originate, or implement on their own probably receive inadequate time and attention in most classrooms. Whether this is due to fear of the unknown on the part of teachers, trepidation about "losing control," or queasy feelings about not being able to predict an outcome, there are several activities in which children can initiate musical experiences, with minimum risk of things going awry. Among these is the technique of clapping patterns to individual children for them to respond to with a clapped "answer." Initially, some children will be reluctant or lacking in ideas, but enough can do this activity to keep it going. Everyone is asked to keep a steady beat by patsching/clapping until their individual turn arrives. The teacher, of course, should demonstrate typical "questions" and "answers" before calling on individuals. A "question" might be a clapped pattern such as TA TA TA TA or TA TA TI-TI TA, to which the child might respond with TA TA TA (*rest*) or TA TA TA TA. "Questions" and their "answers" can be clapped, vocalized with TA's and TI's, or both. Once children become comfortable with these activities, they can make up their own antecedent patterns for their peers to respond to with consequent models. This can turn out to be fun for everyone.

Bergethon and Boardman (1979) suggest that children learn to play a rhythm pattern of long (♩) and short (♪) notes as given, then make up some new ones using long and short sounds in their own original combinations. These authors suggest also that children write simple rhythmic patterns and then compose a musical story, after they have had experience with hearing existing examples. Other possibilities include encouraging children to create their own movement or dramatization patterns when the teacher plays steady beats on a drum, altering the tempo to emphasize that concept, or changing the volume to illustrate dynamics. Findlay (1971) gives specific suggestions for games with balls, after which children could make up their own variations or invent new games of their own. Children might be asked to show how they move when they are tired, when it is dark, when it is slippery, when they are in a hurry, or when they come home from school. Although such experiences are initiated by the teacher, exactly how individuals respond differs with each child, and these differences should be encouraged and acknowledged. Landis and Carder (1990) include a picture of youngsters physically illustrating the end of a musical phrase. If recognition of phrases and where they begin or end is the goal, teachers would encourage children to show these musical phenomena *in their own ways*. The possibilities for individual expression are great, but they are successful only in an atmosphere of safety, trust, and acceptance.

What, then, should music provide for youngsters at the early childhood level? It can be the door that, when opened, discloses realizations and insights about their lives, their relationships, themselves. It can be an important source for what Maslow (1968) termed "peak experiences," moments where one becomes complete and serene with, and within, oneself. Maslow viewed having many such experiences as leading to what he termed "self-actualization," an extremely positive process of "becoming," toward which most of us consciously or subconsciously strive. Although it might sound mundane, music also adds, from the many choices available to children, a further option for something to do. Because of its manifold phases and infinite possibilities for mental and physical activity, music helps to fill those gaps that, when overlooked, frequently lead to boredom. To recall Froebel once again, music offers to children a psychological and historical link with the past, something that the great German educator-philosopher believed they sense instinctively, as revealed in their simple yet spontaneous games and pastimes. Education in the arts can be difficult to explain or justify to those administrators and members of the community who tend to think solely in terms of tangibility and utility. What educators need to make more widely known is the fact that the arts, in providing insight, inner understanding, and appreciation of one's own being, contribute significantly to the facilitation of learning.

## NOTES

1. In order to render Lewis's recorded musical examples suitable for use with children, many have been specifically arranged. When feasible, however, it is preferable to use recordings of musical compositions performed as far as possible as they were envisioned by their composers, without arrangement or simplification. One of many advantages to the now difficult-to-obtain RCA "Adventures in Music" series of recordings is its variety of fine listening selections performed in their entirety.

2. Certain types of (East) Indian music feature the *tabla* (drum) player singing the beats of the drum as they are played with the hands. Children like listening to such recordings and enjoy trying to mimic the sounds.

## REFERENCES

Alper, C. (1980). The early childhood song books of Eleanor Smith: Their affinity with the philosophy of Friedrich Froebel. *Journal of Research in Music Education, 28*(2), pp. 16–20.

Andress, B. (Ed.). (1989). *Promising practices: Prekindergarten music education.* Reston, VA: Music Educators National Conference.

Andress, B. L., Heimann, H. M., Rinehart, C. A., & Talbert, E. G. (1973). *Music in early childhood.* Washington, DC: Music Educators National Conference.

Bergethon, B., & Boardman, E. (1979). *Musical growth in the elementary school* (4th ed.). New York: Holt, Rinehart and Winston.

Boswell, J. (Ed.). (1985). *The young child and music: Contemporary principles in child development and music education.* Reston, VA: Music Educators National Conference.

Cage, J. *Sonatas and interludes for prepared piano.* Wergo 60074.

Dalcroze, E. J. (1973). Rhythm, music and education (H. F. Rubinstein, Trans.). Aylesbury, Bucks, UK: Hazell Watson and Viney. (Original work published 1921)

Findlay, E. (1971). *Rhythm and movement: Applications of Dalcroze eurhythmic.* Evanston, IL: Summy-Birchard.

Gray, C. L. (Ed.). (1967). *The study of music in the elementary school—A conceptual approach.* Washington, DC: Music Educators National Conference.

Haines, J. E., & Gerber, L. L. (1988). *Leading young children to music* (3rd ed.). Columbus, OH: Charles E. Merrill.

Hoffer, C., & Hoffer, M. (1982). *Teaching music in the elementary classroom.* New York: Harcourt Brace Jovanovich.

Land, L. R., & Vaughn, M. A. (1978). *Music in today's classroom: Creating, listening, performing* (2nd ed.). New York: Harcourt Brace Jovanovich.

Landis, B., & Carder, P. (Eds.). (1990). *The eclectic curriculum in American music education: Contributions of Dalcroze, Kodaly, and Orff.* Reston, VA: Music Educators National Conference.

Leeper, S., Skipper, D., & Witherspoon, R. (1979). *Good schools for young children* (4th ed.). New York: Macmillan.

Leonhard, C. (1965a). Learning theory and music teaching. In *Comprehensive musicianship* (pp. 134–137). Washington, DC: Music Educators National Conference.

Leonhard, C. (1965b). The philosophy of music education—present and future. In *Comprehensive musicianship* (pp. 104–107). Washington, DC: Music Educators National Conference.

Lewis, A. G. (1983). *Listen, look, and sing (Grades 1, 2, and 3).* Morristown, NJ: Silver Burdett.

Mark, M. (1982). *Source readings in music education history.* New York: Schirmer.

Maslow, M. (1968). *Toward a psychology of being* (2nd ed.). New York: Van Nostrand.

Moomaw, S. (1984). *Discovering music in early childhood.* Newton, MA: Allyn & Bacon.

Nye, R., & Nye, V. (1985). *Music in the elementary school* (5th ed.). Englewood Cliffs, NJ: Prentice-Hall.

Nye, V. (1979). *Music for young children* (2nd ed.). Dubuque, IA: William C. Brown.

Reimer, B. (1989). *A philosophy of music education* (2nd ed.). Englewood Cliffs, NJ: Prentice-Hall.

Swanson, B. (1981). *Music in the education of children* (4th ed.). Belmont, CA: Wadsworth.

Wheeler, L., & Raebeck, L. (1985). *Orff and Kodaly adapted for the elementary school* (3rd ed.). Dubuque, IA: William C. Brown.

# CHAPTER 11

# Art in Early Childhood Education

HAROLD J. MC WHINNIE

As Carol Seefeldt (1987) has observed, "art seems to belong to young children" (p. 183). The early childhood years have been described by Gardner (1982) "as a golden age of creativity, a time when every child sparkles with artistry" (p. 86). From the very beginning of early childhood education, art has held an honored position. The introduction of art activities into the Froebelian kindergarten in the late 1800s began a long tradition of seeing the arts as central in the education of the young child. It may well be that for the 1990s, the ideas and research of Gardner and Project Zero will be the catalyst to once more elevate art to the position it held in the 1960s under the influence of Lowenfeld. The theory of multiple intelligences (Gardner, 1982) and the theory of drawing as cognition (Eisner, 1989) demand a new evaluation of the place of the arts in the total school program. Such a reassessment of art education begins with a new look into art in early childhood. As background, let us consider a brief historical overview.

Since at least the 1930s, a golden age for art education in the life of the young child, art making and symbol development have held a central place in the education of young children and in some of the research devoted to the understanding of how the arts in general promote development and growth of the human organism. While art education has had a rather varied history in public school grades 3–6, the central role of art for early childhood education has remained in a somewhat static position. In the theoretical ideas of Dewey (1934) and in the work and writings of Florence Cane (1953), we have a strong historical tradition that may become relevant once more to the problems of our time (Lowenfeld, 1947).

That the age of progressive education, with its focus on the education of the whole child, was good to the arts in education needs no additional documentation at this point. Much of art education in the 1930s was the result of private school efforts, and this trend toward the privatization of art education is once more on the upswing with the efforts of Betty Edwards (1987) and the Monart Schools of Mona Brookes (1988). Those efforts can be better judged within the historical continuum that leads from Dewey to Cane to Gardner and finally to Brookes and Edwards. It is only hoped that the young child will benefit from some of this recent ferment.

The fact that whenever a crisis in public support of education arises it is the arts that are the first to be cut has caused periods of structural imbalance within the field of art education. This is one reason why it is to the private sector that some arts educators have looked as the more fertile place in which to teach and to conduct research. As Efland (1990) and others have pointed out, the arts and education in the arts have never been central to American culture or to the culture of the public school. The arts have always been justified within the context of the public school on the basis of instrumental values; that is, what education in the arts can do for other subjects rather than as having worth itself. It is within the education of the young child that the arts seem to retain their intrinsic values, and there is far less pressure to prove a worth by means of what art education may do for another subject. In this sense the arts in early childhood education may offer a model for other elementary school programs.

At least within the Lowenfeld theory, art in early childhood education focused on the symbolic and developmental growth of the child. It was no accident that his now classic work carried the title *Creative and Mental Growth* (1957/1974). Within the Lowenfeld theory, the individual's creative and symbolic artistic development was viewed as an important aspect of general cognitive or mental growth. Creative thinking was viewed as underlying general cognitive development; it was part of the multiple intelligences and not separate as a process to be limited to the arts.

Let us now focus specific attention on the efforts of three modern art educators—Betty Edwards, Mona Brookes, and Mark Kistler—to privatize early childhood art education, to become what some have called "pop art educators." The Monart Schools in southern California will be examined as a recent effort to meet some of the parental demands for an art education for young children that at least appears on the surface to be very different from those more accepted patterns of art education that were historically based in early childhood education. This new development will be examined in terms of art education history, the nature of early childhood learning in the arts, and some of the other new directions for art in education that have emerged in both the private and the public sectors in the past decade.

## POP ART EDUCATION AS A CHALLENGE TO TRADITION

Among other things, the decade of the 1980s ushered in a sustained criticism of public education in this country unmatched in recent history.

From the perspective of the 1990s, we are able to consider in context the "whole-child" philosophy, which might have otherwise been conceived of as a very separate pattern of development. It is part of the whole; distance allows the mosaic of change to become more apparent. The order that has emerged has not been accepted by everyone either within or without art education. As part of that all too often one-way debate, what might be called the privatization of public education was begun with proposals for alternative schools, for parental choice, for school-based management systems, and finally for private contracts to groups and even individuals to run public school systems. A variety of voucher and other programs have emerged, all of which seem to be designed to provide freedom of choice and to overcome what are perceived by a new generation of parents as egregious limitations in the curricula of public schools.

Within the field of art education, the 1980s produced several significant new directions for the visual arts within the general framework of public school education. The John Paul Getty Center for Education in the Arts began to argue for and to develop a new curriculum proposal, discipline-based art education (DBAE) (Eisner, 1983). The U.S. government prepared its own report relative to the status of art education in the United States and printed the influential book *Toward Civilization* (Wilson, 1988).

Somewhere between the idea of *Beyond Creating* (Eisner, 1983) and *Toward Civilization* was the general feeling that art education ought to de-emphasize art making as the central focus of the curriculum, in favor of programs that fostered the skills of looking at art. Approaches to visual art education based on the separate disciplines of art studio, art history, art criticism, and aesthetics were designed, but some art educators, such as Peter London (1989) were appalled by these new directions and the perceived threat that they held for the studio component of art making as the central focus of the school-based art program.

Programs of art in early childhood education, at least at the beginning of the 1980s, seemed to be at about the same levels of studio involvement and art making as when children's art-making activities and self-expression were a central focus during the Lowenfeld years of the 1960s. However, as the 1980s began to unfold, a group of art educators questioned programs of early childhood art education that focused on self-expression, symbol development, and the creative use of materials, in favor of art-learning programs that emphasized drawing skills, perceptual development, ability to copy or at least relate to adult models, and increased eye–hand coordination activities (Brookes, 1988).

These values all seem to be those artistic skills that would have horrified a generation of early childhood art educators brought up on the ideas and values found in the writings of Lowenfeld (1957/1974). These new ideas were best represented by Mona Brookes (1988) and fostered by the Monart Schools that she developed in the Los Angeles area of southern California. It may be no accident that the three representatives of what I have called "pop art education" are all located in southern California and have moved in their collective and separate ways toward the privatization of art education with a special focus on the preschool and the early elementary years. As a consequence of Proposition 13, which was passed in the late 1980s to control the rise of property taxes, the state of California has no special art teachers employed to teach in public elementary schools. This may be one reason for the development of private art education in that state.

In part at least, the theoretical framework for the ideas of Brookes and Kistler were provided by the writings of Betty Edwards. Her book, *Drawing on the Right Side of the Brain* (1978), in addition to having the largest audience (more than 1.5 million sold copies) is probably the most influential book on art and on art education that has been published in recent years. It has been translated into nine languages; it adorns many a coffee table in middle and upper middle class America, while Lowenfeld's now classic work can be found on dusty library shelves and is read more by the general educator than the art specialist.

Edwards's theory on right and left brain functions has fostered a new interest in the teaching of drawing at all levels in the curriculum (Mc Whinnie, 1990). Edwards believes that anyone at any age level can learn to draw without reference to a special talent in art and that the process of learning to draw is a consequence of learning to see. This process, which is nonverbal and nonjudgmental, and calls for perceptual and spatial skills, is believed to be the property of the right side of the brain, in contrast to the verbal and logical skills believed to exist on the left side. Her theory clearly related to a demand for a more highly structured program of art instruction, one that fostered not only art learning and creative development but perceptual abilities as well (Edwards, 1988). While Edwards did not directly address issues of early childhood art education, she did provide a theoretical framework and a method of instruction (often misunderstood) for perceptual growth and development through art.

It seems to me that many teachers on the elementary and early childhood levels have seen in Edwards's approach an answer or at least a countervailing force to DBAE (Pratt, 1990). That is, the Edwards approach satisfies the demand for a greater structure in the art program, while at the same time remaining firmly anchored in the studio domain. In addition, Edwards's ideas appear, at least on the surface, to be quite congruent with the early writings on the same topic by art educators such as Lowenfeld (1974) or Barkan (1962). In Edwards's view the active studio involvement in making art is essential to perceptual and spatial growth, and such experiences should be integrated into an overall study of the arts, both past and present, within the general context of learning to see.

Other factors such as the swelling of the younger age population and the explosion of child care and early childhood learning activities have stimulated once more an interest in and concern about the creative and artistic growth of the young child. At probably no time since Lowenfeld wrote in the 1960s has there been as much of an opportunity as there is now for the art educator to focus attention on the variables of early learning in the arts and to foster the growth of art education programs that could have the potential for extending influences well into the next century.

Mona Brookes (1988, 1989) used the opportunity to devise a set of art lessons that could be directed toward the education of the young child. Her program of art instruction placed a central emphasis on the child's ability to copy; her methods were based in part on her own experiences teaching art in a child-care setting in Los Angeles.

The idea of the use of professional artist materials is based on Brookes's observations that the child learns to devalue those art products that are made on cheap paper and done with crayons. Brookes has argued that the school encourages the making of throw-away art, which is not to be confused with adult or serious art in even the child's mind. In her view, a more serious attitude can be fostered very early in a child's education by the use of good materials and the avoidance of junk art projects in the early elementary school years.

The problem with Brookes's observations is that while they may be somewhat correct, they are based on her own experience with a rather limited population sample and to date very little research has been attempted to clarify some of the issues that she and others have raised in their writings. A study now in progress by Jeffers (1990, 1991) has tried to assess what memories and attitudes are fostered by early childhood art experiences among a group of elementary education majors now at a university. She has some findings that would both validate and discredit the observations made by Brookes.

Brookes developed a language of visual forms and shapes based on the use of five different shapes, and she proceeded to teach the children in her school this system as a visual language much the same as verbal language is taught. The children in a Monart school learn to discern these five basic shapes in their immediate environments, and they begin to try to deal with the presentation of visual forms within this basic language in the artworks that are produced. I use the term *Monart Schools* to refer to schools devoted only to learning in the arts and attended by children after the regular school day. These schools are located in various areas and are staffed by instructors that have been trained in the Monart method by Brookes.

In a general sense, the Getty program of discipline-based art education was also an attempt to interject more adult modes of thought into the artistic education of children. In general, the DBAE movement runs a course similar to that of the pop art educators, and these two streams of art education can be looked upon as different sides of the same coin. They seem to share the goals of reinforcing more adult norms and fostering adult behavior in the arts at an earlier age and with a greater degree of structure.

Mark Kistler (Captain Mark), with his draw squad, has moved pop art education out of the classroom, out of the Monart school, and into every home by means of television. He might be described as the "Mister Rogers of Art Education." The Kistler program has many of the same ingredients as the Monart school and the approach of Brookes. The emphasis is on the use of the adult example, on a standard set of perceptual and drawing skills, and on the ability to converge upon one right answer. The target population is the young child (both in and out of school), and the emphasis is on the final art product for which the norm is the adult example.

Some more recent art educators such as Elliot Eisner (1989) have re-conceptualized the Lowenfeld theory into one more congruent with recent interests in cognitive psychology. Eisner (1989) has come to reassert that the role of art making and specifically the art of drawing as a nonverbal language is equal in importance with verbal language in the general development of the child. This linkage to the historical theory of Lowenfeld on the part of Eisner was no accident. Eisner's own early research (1965) studied the relationships between learning in art, perceptual skill development, and variables of creative thinking.

Howard Gardner (1982), more than any other cognitive theorist writing in the literature today, has linked creativity, symbol development, and drawing with cognitive or mental development in his theory of multiple intelligences. In his view, artistic activities are cognitive through and through. When education slights the arts, it neglects the development of sides of human intelligence that are as real as or perhaps more real than the I.Q. Our symbol systems use drawing, writing, gesture, and so on, as basic vehicles of understanding the world, without which the mind hardly exists, at least in a human sense (Gardner, 1982).

The common historical thread between Lowenfeld, Eisner, and Gardner is the linkage between the multiple factors found in early childhood art education and the cognitive development of the individual as a fully functioning human being worthy of that descriptive title. All three of these major theorists have proposed guidelines as to the importance of alternative modes of symbol development as a part of communication, as a fuller definition of what we mean by language development. Yet one gets the disquieting idea that art education, within the education of the young child, has remained somewhat static and seems to lack for a historical development. Part of the purpose of this chapter will be to explore that idea in considerable depth.

## SOME THEORIES OF CHILD GROWTH AND DEVELOPMENT IN ART

A number of theories have been developed over the past 150 years (since the early writings of Froebel and Rousseau) (Efland, 1990) not only to explain the role of the arts in the development of the child but to be used as a guide in the analysis and interpretation of the art of the child. These major theories can be characterized as developmental, cognitive, psychoanalytic, and perceptual-spatial. Gardner, Eisner, and I have attempted to combine elements of these various theoretical points of view into a more comprehensive theory that we describe as a "unified field theory of artistic growth" (Mc Whinnie, 1990).

### Developmental Theories

Developmental theories have been widely accepted by early childhood art educators. Those following developmental theories have endeavored to provide a secure environment that offers art activities and art materials suited to the developmental levels of the child. They have felt that instruction on matters of technique has no place in the early childhood art program. Given the right environment and the right experiences, the creative expression of children will flourish (Ebbeck & Ebbeck, 1974).

As I have already observed, the work of Lowenfeld (1947) did much to foster the widespread acceptance of developmental theories on the part of art educators and undergirded the research base of the field of art education for many years. Lowenfeld described the following stages of growth and development of the symbols found in the art of the child:

1. Scribbling, ages 2–4, first expression
2. Preschematic, ages 4–7, first representational stage
3. Schematic, ages 7–9, achievement of form
4. Gang stage, ages 9–11, dawning realism
5. Reasoning stage, ages 11–13, pseudorealism

Lowenfeld claimed that these stages were the unfolding of a genetic process, and that each one was a part of a natural and normal pattern of growth. No external teaching could move the child from one stage to another. This stand toward the role of the teacher in artistic instruction in the early childhood years became the dominant point of view for the field well into the 1960s. The developmental theorist advocated the role of the teacher as a guide (Kellogg, 1969; Lowenfeld, 1957/1974; Read, 1943). Bruner (1966) attacked the developmental point of view and argued that the structure of a discipline could be taught to any child at any age. Ausubel and Sullivan (1970) further criticized the developmental point of view toward the role of the teacher by observing that it did not recognize or accept accounts of the impact of instruction (whether formal or informal) on the nature of the symbols developed and employed in the artistic efforts of the young child.

It is obvious, I think, that the current theories of Edwards, Brookes, and Kistler are at a considerable variance with the older developmental theories of child development in art. There has not been sufficient research to date to be able to answer either theoretical position with a degree of clarity that would guide practice in the teaching of art in the early childhood years.

## Cognitive Theory

Goodenough (1926) and others argued that children drew what they knew rather than what they saw. They further argued that drawings by children were not dependent on the general developmental level of the child but rather on concept formation. "To little children, drawing is a language, a form of cognitive expression—and its purpose is not primarily aesthetic" (Goodenough, 1926, p. 14). Goodenough believed that the child's ability to form concepts was an intellectual task, which required that children be able to recognize similarities and differences among groups, objects, or ideas. By analyzing the amounts of detail and degrees of realism that appear in children's drawings, Harris (Harris & Goodenough, 1963) demonstrated that one could obtain an index of the child's intellectual growth by the use of a nonverbal drawing task. The draw-a-man test can yield a stable assessment of nonverbal intelligence and stable assessments of intelligence.

## Perceptual-Spatial Theory

June King McFee (1961) was one of the first of the writers on art education to propose using a wide range of variables, drawing from the research in perceptual psychology in the 1960s, as a basis for research and development in art education. In a recent address to the National Art Education Association, McFee (1990) reasserted the basic theme of perceptual learning in art, which was developed as part of her own doctoral studies in the late 1950s at Stanford University. She once more reaffirmed the central importance of perception as a key to the individual's ability to make perceptual and conceptual sense out of a more complicated visual environment

(McFee, 1972). The development of the visual universe (rather than a verbal-based world) has in McFee's judgment made perceptual learning an imperative for survival in general and for healthy growth and development in the lives of young children in particular.

The development of the computer, the role of television, and the use of video games—the influence of visual languages and symbol systems on all levels of society—have given to visual arts education the chance to assume a central position in the education of the young child. McFee has argued for more than 30 years that perceptual learning as a part of art education is vital to both the survival of the individual and the continued health of society.

Salome (1965), Efland (1965), and I (Mc Whinnie, 1965) all tested specific modes of perceptual learning with groups of young children and produced a body of research data that documented the essential wisdom of the McFee theory regarding the role of art instruction in the education of the young child. The specific instructional strategies tested did increase the abilities of young children toward a greater perceptual delineation, as demonstrated by their ability to handle and to process more visual information.

Both Salome and I developed programs of research in art education that were based on our doctoral work, and more than 30 years have produced data that continue to support, as well as to expand, the original McFee theories as to the central position perceptual awareness and perceptual learning holds in the development of the artistic expression of the young child. Based on this specific body of research, we would continue to conclude that

1. Perceptual learning continues to be both possible and desirable for young children.
2. The traditional developmental approach, which featured nonintervention, can be viewed as a parallel strand within the art development of the young child.
3. The targeting of specific perceptual variables offers the chance for the researcher to identify behavioral referents for early child development in art.


Psychoanalytic Theory

Children do not draw what they know, rather they draw what they feel. Their art comes from *deep down inside* (Cole, 1966). Firmly based on the concept of the unconscious—wherein a type of mental activity takes place that people are not even aware of—this theory of child art postulates a relationship between children's psychological development and their art. Children's art products are believed to reflect their emotions and are expressions of deep, subconscious feelings instead of reflections of their conscious knowledge, general development, or concept development.

According to this theory, children draw themselves as large circles with sticks that represent arms and legs, not because they are unaware of shoulders, necks, or stomachs, but because the circle represents a force deep within a child as a symbol for the womb, the breast, or some other emotionally potent object. The progression from a circle to realistic representation is explained as a growth process. As children grow, their conscious thoughts suppress the powerful force of the subconscious, and they are able to draw and paint more realistically.

Psychoanalytic thought has greatly influenced early childhood educators. The writings of Anna Freud (1955), Lois B. Murphy (1960), and Katherine B. Read (1976) contributed to early childhood educators' acceptance of the psychoanalytic theories of art. A number of practices in early childhood stem from these theories. The use of finger paints, clay, and free-flowing tempera paint is based, at least in part, on the idea that these materials allow children to release inner feelings and emotions, and do not restrict them as small crayons, pencils, or other tools might.

## RECENT RESEARCH DEVELOPMENTS

As the data to be cited in this section of the chapter will show, research in early childhood art did not remain static or adhere to either the developmental or the cognitive theories in its main conceptual point of view. I will review some of the more recent research developments in the field of art education in general as they relate to the ideas, theories, and studies of three major art education writers: Lowenfeld, Eisner, and Gardner. I will group studies that have been done in the decade of the 1980s, as they seem to relate to bodies of research inspired by these three major art educators.

A major conflict among early childhood art educators has been over the general question of the role of self-expression (the rather untutored development of visual language and symbol systems) versus the place of perceptual development and the role of more structured learning environments in the education of the young child. The developmental point of view of Lowenfeld and Gardner tends to favor at least the appearance of a "hands-off" point of view, whereas the view of Eisner would seem to be more directive in terms of active intervention in the art learning experience. This conflict will be a major theme that I will highlight in the development of the remainder of this chapter.

## Drawing as a Part of Symbol Development

This section will focus on the nature of children's drawing behaviors as described by Marjorie and Brent Wilson of Penn State University, who have undertaken cross-cultural research on the symbolic development of the young child (Wilson & Wilson, 1985). Based on a study of the drawings of Egyptian children, they have concluded that children learn to draw by copying, but not, as in the case of the Monart Schools, by copying the drawings of an adult artist or of a master. They copy the drawings of other children. The Wilsons (1983) found that in Egypt, ample models for imitation were produced by the drawings on walls and sidewalks done spontaneously by young children. One might call this a graffiti theory of art education. (The New York City transportation system has provided an abundance of models for children in our own country.)

More recently B. Wilson (Wilson & Wilson, 1989) has developed the methodology of dialogue drawing, in which he draws along with the child on the same piece of paper. In those drawings he has observed the ability of children to copy and to imitate, in response to the stimulus provided by the experimenter. Again, the mode of learning is by imitation, and the device of copying has been shown to be a vital mode in early art education. Wilson has also studied the narrative drawings of Japanese children and has observed the high levels of professional attainment at a very early age. He has shown similar characteristics of storytelling in his comparative studies of Japanese and American children. (The Japanese method of early child art education is highly structured and quite similar to the method of the Monart Schools.) Are the higher developmental norms of the Japanese child the result of that mode of instruction or, at least in part, the consequences of learning to write with a brush?

These cross-cultural studies, as well as studies done in this country on the drawings of Native Americans, seem to cast some doubt on the classic accounts of the stages of growth and development in children's art as outlined in the studies of Lowenfeld (Wilson & Wilson, 1989). What Lowenfeld (1947), Cane (1951), and Read (1943) found in the drawings of the child that so excited them may have been a confirmation of certain aesthetic qualities found in the professional arts of the early twentieth century, and specifically observed in the works of Klee, Picasso, and Kandinsky. Were the classic Lowenfeld stages of growth yet another adult model, one adopted from the work of the modern movement of the early twentieth-century art?

Praisner (1984) has looked directly at the early childhood drawings of three adult artists—Toulouse-Lautrec, Picasso, and Klee. From his studies of those early artistic products, he drew the following conclusions:

1. The earliest drawings of all three artists (done at ages 6–8) were more adultlike than the usual child's drawings at the same developmental levels.
2. These early drawings by all three artists were very different from the adult works for which they became famous. (This is somewhat ironic, for Paul Klee's adult works were a conscious adaptation of the symbolic systems of the young child, especially the works of his own son Felix.)
3. These artists as children seem to have looked upon and imitated a different set of sources from that of the typical child.

The data from the Praisner studies seem to cast some doubt on the universality of the stages of growth and development in art as outlined in the research of the classical developmental theorists. Is there an apparent conflict between theories of learning based on imitation and those based on the developmental patterns of growth? If developmental theories of child growth and development in art do not hold up on a cross-cultural basis (as in the studies of the Wilsons), then do we not have an example, in the stages of growth and development as outlined within Western culture, of adult learning or at least adult influence on the symbolic development of the child? In other words, the symbolic forms that the child employs at various stages in development within Western culture may be a consequence of the culture itself (McFee, 1961).

One of the assumptions of Goodenough (1926), which the Wilsons have challenged, is that the developmental patterns in children's art are a consequence of cognitive development as well as age-based norms of symbolic development. For the developmental theory to hold, it would have to be independent of the cultural environment and be evident in the work of children collected everywhere. The cross-cultural studies do seem to provide a rather powerful argument against Lowenfeld's assertion that the symbolic development encountered in the art of the young child is based on genetic factors. This brings us to a consideration of the work of Howard Gardner.

## Theory of Multiple Intelligences

The work of Gardner and Winner (1983) has produced a rather large body of research on the general subject of the relationships of growth and development in the arts to the more general overall development of the human mind. This research on the symbolic development in the artwork of the young child supports in part at least Lowenfeld's classical position on development in art, but it is mixed with many implications for growth from cognitive theory. Gardner's early research on the symbolic development of the young child led him to become a very strong voice in the role of the arts in education (Gardner, 1990a). In his latest book, *To Open Minds* (Gardner, 1990b), he moves the implications of his research into the prescriptive domain of what should be the education of the young child for the next century. In this domain he is on a similar track to the recent thoughts of Elliot Eisner (1991).

While the bulk of Gardner's work does not break new intellectual ground, it is a synthesis of a 20-year research program at Project Zero. Gardner believes that there are seven different forms of intelligences (linguistic, logical-mathematical, spatial, musical, bodily kinesthetic, interpersonal, and intrapersonal). He asserts that the latter five of these basic intelligences are overlooked in the conception of intellect that is embraced by many of our testing programs and by our educational system in general. Those five neglected intelligences encompass many of the domains that can be related to and derive from a healthy art education.

Eisner (1991) has made the same point and argues that our conceptions of intelligence and the manner in which we assess educational progress are flawed and that the arts in fact provide a model for education in general and a model for the assessment of the individual that goes far beyond the confines of what is tested on objective tests of intelligence and progress in schooling. It is Gardner's view that, if taken together, these forms of multiple intelligences produce a unique cognitive profile for each individual. Gardner's plan is for education up to the age of 7 to be relatively unstructured, except for the development of personal discipline and civility, so that the students can explore materials and media on their own. The arts are the central focus of such an early educational plan. The early skill building that is cherished in China (reported by Gardner, 1990b, as a result of his visits to Chinese schools) and that is becoming an increasingly large part of American preschool education and kindergarten experiences, would not be emphasized according to the overall Gardner and Eisner plans. The conflicts implicit here between the educational ideas of Eisner and Gardner and those of the pop art educators reviewed earlier are obvious.

Gardner's basic point of view has been used by many art educators as a strong counterforce to the overemphasis on test scores (Eisner, 1991) and the dependence on verbal aesthetic development (London, 1991) that seem to be so much a part of the Getty program of a discipline-based art education. What is the specific research base that has been generated by the Gardner program of research at Project Zero, and how many of those studies highlight specific questions and concerns for the early childhood educator with a special reference to education in all the arts?

## Project Zero

Gardner and Winner (1983) argue that only rarely have children's drawings been studied on their own terms for what they can tell us about the child's knowledge of the symbol system of drawing and about the child's artistic and aesthetic goals. Research on children's drawings carried out at Project Zero has been stimulated by research in the aesthetic approach rather than the deficiency approach. (The deficiency approach characterized much of the research in early children's artistic development in which the work of the child was compared with some abstract and possibly adult-based norm, in a western European mode of perception and spatial development.) Gardner and Winner (1983) have shown that:

1. There was a loss of aesthetic qualities as the child moved out of the early stages of development into the more conventional stages of growth at about age 9 or 10. "While one might slip a painting by a five-year-old into the Museum of Modern Art, one could never get away with introducing a painting by a ten-year-old" (p. 5).
2. The preschooler actually preferred pictures that were more stereotyped, realistic, and conventional. This finding may suggest that the aesthetic effects found in the drawings of the young child might be accidental rather than intentional.
3. Surprisingly, 24% of the gifted children were left-handed (the incidence of left-handedness is about 10% in the population at large). In contrast, none of the nongifted children were left-handed. There is some indication that brain laterality may play a critical role in giftedness in the visual arts. This observation would be at least a partial confirmation of the work of Betty Edwards and her theories of the critical importance of the right brain mode in acts of drawing and in creative thinking, as reviewed earlier in this chapter.
4. Perceptual skills within a domain of talent do not generalize to other domains, even in children with exceptional abilities.

Based on the work of Goodman (1976) and Arnheim (1974), research at Project Zero focused on children's sensitivity to the following three properties of drawings, which were considered to be of critical importance to the visual arts:

1. Repleteness—the fullness of the symbol when functioning as art (The child draws what he or she knows.)

2. Expression—the metamorphic convergence of emotional expressive qualities in the drawing (The child draws what he or she feels.)
3. Composition—the structural or organizational and overall balance in the artwork. (The child draws what he or she sees.)

In her research as part of Project Zero, Winner (1989) has developed what I have been describing as a "unified field theory of early artistic development," that is, a conceptual structure that combines what had been, historically speaking, three different theories of growth and development in art. For the first time in art education history, the teacher and the art researcher do not have to choose one theory of development over another but can base their research efforts as well as their classroom practice on a combination of points of view, which gives a broader scope and dimension to any description of the artistic process as it might interface with the patterns of growth and development within the young child.

For Winner, to the extent that children fail to attend to repleteness, expression, and composition, we must conclude that works of art are functioning for them as nonaesthetic symbols such as maps or graphs. (These observations would apply not only to children's own artistic products but also to their discussion and descriptions of the art of others.) In addition, Winner's (1989) correlational analyses showed no consistent relations within or across the domains of artistic intelligence. One skill, aesthetic sensitivity, seems to develop along separate paths and to be composed of several abilities. Winner also argues in her research that reflection (talk about art) should be considered along with perception and production in any assessment of the student's learning and in progress in any of the artistic domains. She has observed as follows:

> The work conducted over the years at Project Zero suggests that development in the arts involves not one unified course of growth, but rather three separate and distinct lines of development. Perception proceeds linearly and is not marked by stage-like properties. In contrast, production follows a u-shaped curve and is more clearly divided into highly characteristic stages of growth. Reflection seems to progress linearly with age but also mirrors the development of more general knowledge and conceptions of the world. (pp. 14–15)

Other researchers in the arts and human behavior, Wolfe and Perry (1989), have extended Winner's research into a description of a more complete drawing system for the young child. This research seems to have great implications for the unified field theory of child development in art. According to Wolfe and Perry, it is possible, beginning with the first 12 to 14 months of drawing activity, to observe the advent of a series of distinct systems, each one characterized by different rules about the kinds of information to be recorded and the most powerful or satisfying ways to make those records. These distinct drawing systems of the young child can be outlined as follows:

1. *Object-based representation* (12 to 14 months). Children treat art materials such as paper and markers as they tend to treat other objects in their symbolic play episodes. They use them as objects and not as tools. (Marcel Duchamp in the 1920s did the same thing with his materials and artistic productions.)
2. *Gestural representations* (early in the second year). Children focus on the representation of motions and movements. (The action paintings of Jackson Pollack reflect this stage of development on a higher plane.)
3. *Point-plot representations* (24 months). Children attempt to give meaning to their graphic expressions. (The scribble drawing is named; Paul Klee developed this mode of expression into a higher level art form.)
4. *Visual-spatial information systems* (2 years). The use of relative size and shapes to depict a geometric reality begins to appear in children's work. (Did Cezanne and Picasso operate on this level in their explorations of the antecedents of cubism?)
5. *Rule-given visual spatial systems* (5 to 7 years). A schematic and highly conventional attempt to give a geometric reality dominates children's drawing efforts. (Do the efforts of Jaspar Johns and others relate to this stage of development but again on a higher plane?)

Wolfe and Perry (1989) observe as follows:

Described as a sequence of acquisitions, this portrayal of drawing systems seems, if longer and more detailed, to be largely similar to earlier developmental descriptions of a sequence of increasingly sufficient systems for capturing information about three dimensional work in two dimensional marks. However, the point is that each of these drawing systems is not so much a stage on the way to realism as a system with distinct motives and purposes. (p. 21)

For our purpose in the discussion of early childhood art education, the key in the Wolfe and Perry study is that these five distinct drawing systems are not part of a linear development (as, say, Lowenfeld would have held) but are part of a circular theory of development in art. All five systems coexist throughout the life of the individual. Wolfe and Perry continue their discussion of these important theoretical observations with the following remarks: "While in this culture children may eventually evolve the projective geometry and control of pictorial reality that permits them to draw chair rungs or a torso correctly, this does not mean that earlier emerging drawing systems atrophy" (p. 31).

The history of the twentieth century in art, the story of the modern movement, has shown that many adult artists employ one or more of these basic systems as part of their mature work. This is what I meant by my observations above that the selected artists did in fact use an earlier development system for their mature expressions, but on a higher level of aesthetic sophistication and concern.

## Further Directions in Research

There have been a number of important research efforts based on the Gardner model and reported in the literature in the past several years. The Gardner research, the theory of multiple intelligences, and the use of the computer with the young child have sparked what might well be described as a ferment of research activity involving the artistic development of young children that has had few, if any, antecedents, at least in recent art education history. Let us at least mention some of these studies, which are, in my judgment, a welcome change in the research focus that has characterized so much of art education efforts in the past few years under the influence of the DBAE movement.

Castle (1989) has studied how the young child learns to draw by using the computer. Her research suggests that there will be significant influences on the child's symbolic development in general as the computer becomes an ever-increasingly familiar tool in the early childhood environment both at school and in the home. Future studies of children's art will need to carefully consider what the computer might have to offer for the various drawing systems that have been identified in the Winner research just described.

Swann (1985) has explored the methodology of naturalistic studies of the art-making behavior of young children in a preschool setting. Her methodologies suggest that there are modes of data collection relative to the artistic development of children that may offer additional insights into growth that cannot be given solely by the examination of the art product. She employed journals, interviews, films, and other passive observational methods in her data-collection process.

Tarr (1990) has reassessed the scribbling stage of development and finds that it involves more than movement or automatic gestures and drawings. Within the spontaneous scribbles, there is a formal drawing system in evidence. Her research echoes the five drawing systems outlined by Wolfe and Perry (1989).

Colbert (1984) has explored alternative methodologies for the study of art in early education. Her findings also replicate much of the Gardner work but are based on quantitative as well as qualitative data sources. Replication, or the lack of it, has always been a problem in art education research efforts.

The work of Golomb has been seminal in this research explosion that has been generally concerned with the artistic development of the child. Golomb (1981) has studied the origins of young children's drawings in terms of their expression of representation and reality. Her work needs to be balanced against the Winner hypotheses of multiple drawing systems, for Golomb's work tends to look at the development of the child more as a linear system. Golomb (1981) has studied the graphic planning strategy of the child and detailed early principles of spatial organization in the drawings, predating the basic Winner (1989) research.

Matthews (1984), like Tarr, has looked at the scribbling stage in children's symbolic development and asserts that the early scribbles contain evidence of planning, design, and composition. Again, these findings help to validate those reported later by Wolfe and Winner.

Lambert (1988) has explored, like Colbert and others, the uses of alternative research methodologies. She has documented through the art serials of four young children what the lived experiences of the art room are really like for the child within a preschool setting.

## Conclusion

As noted in the beginning of this chapter, in 1983 The John Paul Getty Center for Education in the Arts began a program of art education that has sought the radical transformation of art education on the K–12 levels. A publication by Eisner (1983) argued for a balance in art content to include art studio, art history, art criticism, and aesthetics. In calling for a balance in time and effort spent on art instruction, the DBAE approach advocated a significant reduction in the amounts of time a child would spend on the making of art. In some extreme cases it would have amounted to a 70% reduction in the time that the child could spend with art materials and in the creative mode of art activity. The Getty program placed a strong emphasis on verbal learning and on the idea of talking about art as a key part or maybe even the central focus of the art curriculum.

As pointed out earlier, the Getty proposals sparked a hot debate within the art education profession. Peter London (1989) argued strongly for the necessity of the studio production of art, for a strong place for art in the early childhood education program, and for the importance of the symbolic development of the young child. London's (1991) arguments have reaffirmed the positions of Gardner (1990a), Golomb (1981), Arnheim (1974), and of course Lowenfeld regarding the primary importance of art-making activities in the lives of all children.

The role of Elliot Eisner in the DBAE debate has been interesting to trace. He was an early advocate of DBAE and produced most of the materials found in the Getty publication *Beyond Creating*. By 1989, as a consequence of other influences, such as the work of Gardner, Eisner had developed a radically altered point of view, one that argues for the necessity of drawing as part of cognitive development. In essence, Eisner (1991) has rejected the pure division of art education programs into four parts in favor of an approach that would reaffirm the central position of art making.

In fact, within Eisner's recent position, one can discern a means of reconciliation between the ideas of Gardner and those of Betty Edwards. The DBAE movement has produced at least one strongly positive result: It is no longer taboo to show examples of adult art to the young child. In fact, many rather good programs have been developed recently that encourage the young child to look at great art, to talk about art, and to make use of historical adult images in their own artwork. The insights of Winner and Wolfe noted earlier as to both the existence of multiple drawing systems and the need for reflection about art may help to make some of these new approaches to art teaching more acceptable for the early childhood educator.

For example, Hurwitz has produced a book entitled *Drawing on Drawing* (1989), which explores a wide range of methods by which children can use, understand, discuss, and interact with adult art from a variety of historical periods. Again, Wolfe's idea of alternative symbolic systems that coexist within the individual at all times makes the use of historical images a meaningful part of the general artistic development of the young child.

Finally, the Wolf Trap Institute for Early Learning through the Arts has been established to demonstrate the ways in which the arts help preschool children learn. This institute works with teachers and parents to develop methods of making the arts an integral part of their daily interaction with children. By encouraging creative multisensory involvement in the learning process, this program helps teachers and parents improve their children's ability to master and to retain a variety of skills and concepts. Specific goals of early childhood education that can be accomplished through the use of arts techniques include

Increased self-awareness and self-confidence
Group awareness and socialization skills
Development of abstract thinking and problem-solving skills

Ability to concentrate and to remember
Increased gross and fine motor skills
Awareness of individual artistic creativity
Motivation and enthusiasm for learning

Many of the efforts of programs in art education have been given a push toward excellence by the research of Gardner and the general ideas of the DBAE movement. The studies reviewed in this chapter can provide a useful guide for early childhood educators to include the arts in their programs, and, in fact, to make the arts the central focus of early childhood education in general.

## REFERENCES

Arnheim, R. (1974). *Visual thinking*. Berkeley: University of California Press.

Ausubel, D., & Sullivan, E. V. (1970). *Theory and problems of child development* (2nd ed.). New York: Grune & Stratton.

Barkan, M. (1962). *Through art to creativity*. New York: Baron and Company.

Brookes, M. (1988). *Drawing with children*. Los Angeles: Tarcher Press.

Brookes, M. (1989). *Nondrawing and young children*. Remarks at National Art Education Association Super Session, Washington, DC.

Bruner, J. (1966). *Toward a theory of instruction*. Cambridge, MA: Harvard University Press.

Cane, F. (1951). *The artist in each of us*. New York: Pantheon Press.

Castle, S. (1989). *Young children's experience with computer images*. Unpublished doctoral dissertation. University of Maryland, College Park, MD.

Colbert, C. (1984). The relationship of language and drawing. *Studies in Art Education, 25* (2), 84–91.

Cole, N. (1940). *Arts in Classroom*. New York: John Day.

Cole, N. (1966). *Art From Deep Down Inside*. New York: John Day.

Dewey, J. (1934). *Art and experience*. New York: Minton, Balch.

Ebbeck, T. N., & Ebbeck, M. A. (1974). *Now we are four*. Columbus, OH: Charles E. Merrell.

Edwards, B. (1978). *Drawing on Right Side of Brain*. Los Angeles: Tarcher Press.

Edwards, B. (1987). *Drawing on the artist within*. Los Angeles: Tarcher Press.

Efland, A. (1965). Study of drawing training and children's drawings. Stanford, CA: Stanford University Press.

Efland, A. (1990). *A history of art education*. New York: Teachers College Press.

Eisner, E. (1965). Children's creativity in art: A study of types. *American Educational Research Journal, 2,* (3)45–53.

Eisner, E. (1983). *Beyond creating*. Los Angeles: Getty Center for Education in Art.

Eisner, E. (1989). *Drawing as cognition*. Paper presented at the Conference for the National Art Education Association, Washington, DC.

Eisner, E. (1991). *Art as a model for assessment*. Paper presented at the Conference for the National Art Education Association, Atlanta, GA.

Freud, A. (1955). *The psychoanalytic treatment of children*. New York: International University Press.

Gardner, H. (1982). *Art, mind, and brain*. New York: Basic Books.

Gardner, H. (1990a). *Art education*. An invitational address at the Conference for the National Art Education Association. Kansas City, MO.

Gardner, H. (1990b). *To open minds*. New York: Basic Books.

Gardner, H., & Winner, E. (1983). First intimations of artistry. In A. Sarno (Ed.). *U = shaped behavioral growth*. New York: Academic Press.

Golomb, C. (1981). Representation and reality. *Review of Visual Arts Education, 14*, 36–48.

Goodenough, F. L. (1926). *Children's drawings as measures of intellectual maturity*. New York: Harcourt Brace Jovanovich.

Goodman, N. (1976). *Languages of art*. New York: Bobbs-Merrill.

Harris, D. B., & Goodenough, F. (1963). *Children's drawings as measures of intellectual maturity*. New York: Harcourt Brace Jovanovich.

Hurwitz, A., & Wilson, B. (1989). *Drawing on drawing*. Boston: Davis Press.

Jeffers, C. (1990). A glimpse through the keyhole. *Art education 43*(1), 15–47.

Jeffers, C. (1991). Through the keyhole: A study of attitudes to art. Unpublished doctoral dissertation. College Park, MD: University of Maryland.

Kellogg, R. (1969). *Analyzing children's art*. Palo Alto, CA: National Press.

Lambert, N. (1988). *A documentation of form: Art serials*. Unpublished doctoral dissertation. Concordia University, Toronto, Canada.

London, P. (1989). *Beyond DBAE*. Boston: University Council of Art Education.

London, P. (1991). *No more second hand art*. Boston: Shambhala Press.

Lowenfeld, V. (1947). *Your child and his art*. New York: Macmillan.

Lowenfeld, V. (1974). *Creative and Mental Growth* (4th ed.) New York, N.Y.: Macmillan. (Original work published 1957)

Matthews, J. (1984). Children drawing: Are young children scribbling? *Early Child Development, 18*, 1–39.

McFee, J. K. (1961). *Implications for change in art education*. Paper presented at the conference for the National Art Education Association, Kansas City, MO.

McFee, J. K. (1972). *Preparation for art* (2nd ed.). Belmont, CA: Wadsworth.

McFee, J. K. (1990). *Visual literacy and art education*. Invitational address at the Conference for the National Art Education Association. Kansas City, MO.

Mc Whinnie, H. J. (1965). *Effects of perceptual training on art learning*. Unpublished doctoral dissertation, Stanford University.

Mc Whinnie, H. J. (1990). *Sherman and Betty Edwards methods of drawing*. Paper presented at the Conference for the National Art Education Association, Kansas City, MO.

Murphy, L. B. (1960). *Personality in young children* (Vols. 1–2). New York: Basic Books.

Praisner, D. (1984). Artist's drawings. *Studies in Art Education, 22* (2), 34–43.

Pratt, B. (1990). *Drawing from the right side*. Paper presented at the Conference for the National Art Education Association, Kansas City, MO.

Read, H. (1943). *Education through art.* New York: Pantheon Books.

Read, K. B. (1976). *The nursery school* (6th ed.). Philadelphia: W. B. Saunders.

Salome, R. (1965). *Effects of perceptual learning on children's art.* Unpublished doctoral dissertation. Stanford University.

Seefeldt, C. (1987). The visual arts. In C. Seefeldt (Ed.), *The early childhood curriculum: A review of current research* (1st ed., pp. 183–210). New York: Teachers College Press.

Swann, A. (1985). *A naturalistic study of art making.* Unpublished doctoral study. Indiana University, Bloomington.

Tarr, D. (1990). More than movement: Scribbling reassessed. *Visual Arts Research, 16,* (31) 123–134.

Wilson, B. (1988). *Toward civilization:* Report to Congress. Washington, DC: U.S. Government Printing Office.

Wilson, B., & Wilson, M. (1985). A view of imagery sources in drawings. In Hardimon & Zernich. (Eds.), *Foundation for curriculum development in art education,* (pp. 45–47). Boston: Davis Press.

Wilson, M., & Wilson, B. (1983). *Teaching of drawing in the schools.* University Conference at Maryland Institute, Baltimore.

Wilson, M., & Wilson, B. (1989). A tale of four cultures. In Hurwitz & McCleary (Eds.), *Art and education international* (pp. 134–147). University Park: Penn State Press.

Winner, E. (1989). Children's perception of aesthetic properties in art. *British Journal of Development Psychology, 4,* 149–160.

Wolfe, D., & Perry, M. D. (1989). From endpoints to repertories. *Journal of Aesthetic Education, 22,* 17–34.

CHAPTER 12

# The Integrated Early Childhood Curriculum: New Interpretations Based on Research and Practice

REBECCA S. NEW

What goes 'round comes 'round. *The integrated curriculum, child-centered education, informal schooling, projects, and learning centers*—indeed, much of what is currently being recommended under the rubric of developmentally appropriate practice—have a familiar ring to those of us who came of age as early childhood professionals two or more decades ago. So why the renewed interest, as represented by the inclusion of this chapter in the second edition of this volume?

There are many compelling reasons to consider—or reconsider, depending on the timing of one's entry into the field—an integrated approach to the early childhood curriculum. There is a new sense of urgency to current recommendations for educational reform at the national level, amid the ever-changing sociopolitical context of American schooling. As the knowledge sinks in that the United States is losing its competitive edge in the international world of big business and becoming "less relevant to the concerns of the world" (Graubard, 1990, p. 276), there is tremendous pressure on the educational system to do something about it.

At the same time, there is a cacophony of calls for school reform from *within* the educational system as increasing numbers of disenfranchised children and their teachers drop out of the American public schools (Ekstrom, Goertz, Pollack, & Rock, 1986; Mark & Anderson, 1985). Public Law 94–142, which in 1975 mandated the mainstreaming of special needs children into classroom settings that are also increasingly culturally diverse (Ramsey, Vold, & Williams, 1989), highlights the need for attention to such "extracurricular" components as teachers working together and the incorporation of parents into the educational process (Brantlinger, 1991; Silvern, 1988).

Taken individually, these forces suggest various and often competing goals and strategies for early education. Teachers of young children (especially those in kindergarten and the primary grades) are under pressure to produce significant gains in academic goals as measured by nationally approved forms of standardized testing, in spite of numerous and eloquent pleas from early childhood professionals to dispense with most of what characterizes formal schooling (Katz, 1991; Shepard & Smith, 1988).

Cumulatively, such forces share one point of consensus: Current educational practice as typified in American early childhood classrooms—particularly those serving children age 5 to 8 years—is inadequate in meeting the present-day needs of many young children and fails miserably in preparing them to meet the demands of the twenty-first century. While the causes of, and possible solutions to, the ills facing American public education are many and complex (Crim, 1990), a growing body of empirical knowledge and theoretical consensus about how young children interact with and learn from their physical and social surroundings has clear implications for what might better take place in the classroom. As a result, an increasing number of early childhood professionals are advocating an *integrated approach to early education*—where the child rather than the subject is the unit of concern and measure—as perhaps the most appropriate and feasible means of serving the multiple needs of contemporary young children (Bredekamp, 1987; Katz & Chard, 1989; Lay-Dopyera & Dopyera, 1990; see also Chapter 1, this volume).

The chapter begins with a brief look at historical perspectives on an integrated early childhood curriculum, followed by a review of contemporary research that has led to renewed interest in, and empirical support for, a more carefully articulated version of this curriculum model. The second part of the chapter illustrates one interpretation of an integrated curriculum in the community preschools of Reggio Emilia, Italy. The goals and practices of this Italian community's early childhood program reflect cultural values and ideologies about child development and education that expand upon current conceptions of an integrated early childhood curriculum and challenge many contemporary U.S. beliefs and practices (New, 1990). The concluding discussion will focus on implications of Reggio Emilia's integrated classroom for American early education beliefs and practice and on the importance of reconsidering traditional views of children and adults as teachers and learners in our determination of developmentally appropriate practices.

## HISTORICAL VIEWS

An historical view of an integrated curriculum is essential to the goals of this chapter for several reasons: to reiterate the point that much of what is currently being recommended comes from a long tradition of advocacy for a more "progressive" form of education; to remind us of the broader socio-historical context that accompanies any efforts at educational reform; to inform us of what worked, what didn't, and why not, so that we might better anticipate and respond to the waxing and waning of curriculum change; and to highlight what is *new* in both theory and practice about contemporary interpretations of an integrated early childhood curriculum.

Within the field of early childhood, definitions of an integrated curriculum typically, though not always, include joint emphasis on the blending of content areas into thematic or problem-focused units of study *and* a child-centered rather than teacher-directed approach to learning and instruction. Yet early uses of the term were primarily to describe the incorporation of various intellectual domains into a single task or project. Long before the three R's became ends in themselves, instruction in subjects came about in the form of apprenticeships; basis skills were "embedded in practical enterprises that had important consequences" (Farnham-Diggory, 1990, p. 118). The validity of this integrated approach to learning was eventually forgotten, however, over the course of the next few thousand years as schools and their teachers came to emphasize discrete bodies of knowledge as both the ends and the means of education.

"Contemporary" discussion of integrative—as opposed to narrowly conceived—educational goals and practice first appeared in the form of seventeenth-century educational "progressives" (Bagley, 1941) and included mention of the child-centered dimension as well. This dual concern was made explicit in the many reforms proposed by Rousseau (1762/1956) and implemented by Pestalozzi (Gutek, 1968), each of whom argued in defense of a child-centered, naturalistic approach to learning. The works of early childhood educators Froebel (1887) in the nineteenth century and Montessori (1967) in the early twentieth century thus joined a history of advocacy for teaching the "whole child" with opportunities for what they described as "real-life" activities (Krogh, 1990).

American interest in the work of Froebel and later, Montessori, reflects a continuing national intrigue with progressive education (Gardner, 1990). Yet both Froebel's and Montessori's methodologies represented a compromise between a child-centered approach and one that emphasized knowledge transmission, and their suggestions for projects that integrated the various subject areas were often highly structured. This century's best and earliest advocate for an integrated early childhood curriculum was surely John Dewey, who emphasized the *integration* of knowledge and experience, the fallacy of focusing on isolated subject matter, and the importance of child-initiated, self-directed activity (1902, 1916, 1938). As a result of Dewey's work, as well as that of other "progressives"—including William Kilpatrick, known by some as the "father of progressive education"

(Hass, 1974/1983)—a strong case was made for a curriculum built jointly by pupils and teacher, characterized by real child living in which self-initiated activity reigned (Kilpatrick, 1941). By the 1930s, progressive education represented the ideal in American early childhood classrooms, although the extent to which it reflected the norm remains questionable (Spodek, 1982).

Dewey's version of an integrative curriculum was somewhat distinct from that of others in the progressive movement. He argued that content-related goals could be achieved by blending several subject areas into theme studies, and that real-life activities could lead to more focused academic study. In fact, Dewey debated the stringent *either/or* distinctions between traditional and progressive education, arguing—along with others—that the issue was not discipline versus freedom or teacher-initiated versus learner-initiated, because each aspect represents a legitimate factor in the educational process (Bagley, 1941; Dewey, 1938). However, his position was not often acknowledged by others in the progressive movement, in spite of protestations over what he saw as a distortion of his views. Thus, while Dewey's ideal version of a progressive classroom was a stimulating environment in which students developed initiative, imagination, and a love of learning, less successful implementations often appeared to give license to "anything goes" even if "nothing happens" (Gardner, 1990, p. 88).

Eventually, in spite of initial enthusiasm for Dewey's interpretation of an integrated curriculum, the difficulties of implementation (and challenges of teacher training) amid the variety of interpretations fueled criticism of the progressive classroom, with critics citing "flabbiness and anti-intellectualism" as traits of the progressive education movement (Silberman, 1970, p. 321). And so the progressive era was but a brief interlude in the growing popularity of the industrial model—in which schools were run like factories, characterized by segmentation and regimentation (Cohen & Mohl, 1979)—with which Froebel and Montessori had competed at the turn of the century (Farnham-Diggory, 1990). By the 1940s most thoughts of a child-centered, integrated curriculum had been abandoned in favor of the Thorn-dike (1922) model of formal, content-focused instruction for young children in public schools. Child-centered approaches to early education received what appeared to be a final blow in the late 1950s, when the American public educational system was humiliated by the Sputnik episode and teachers succumbed to "the covering syndrome" (Rogers, 1973, p. 267).

Yet theoretical support for and practical examples of an integrated early childhood curriculum continued to surface in the decades following the 1950s. The writings of Piaget, finally made available in the English language (1929, 1952, 1962), clearly rejected the transmission-of-knowledge model, and provided a strong rationale for Dewey's earlier advocacy of "hands-on," activity-based learning. Piagetian theory regarding the child's need to move from the known to the unknown, from the concrete to the abstract, helped teachers begin to define developmentally appropriate teaching goals and practice (Schwebel & Raph, 1973). Piaget's emphasis on the invariance of concept acquisition and his explanations of how children interact with the environment to construct their own understanding of the world proved enormously influential in helping early childhood educators—particularly those in preschool and kindergarten classrooms—implement and defend a child-centered, activity-based early childhood curriculum. Yet the educational implications of Piaget's theories were often not clear (Ginsburg & Opper, 1969), and while his work placed a new importance on the value of play (Piaget, 1962), its applicability to an integrated curriculum was left to the imagination of the reader.

At the beginning of the 1970s, the field of early childhood education was "in a fervor" as diversity more than anything else characterized American classrooms (Weber, 1970). The sharp and growing criticism of the industrial model continued (Holt, 1964; Silberman, 1970), and critics called for humanistic learning environments that were appropriate for thinking and feeling children. Preschool early childhood educators continued their participation in the War on Poverty experiments, including the many and varied Head Start programs begun in the 1960s (Greenberg, 1965/1990; Weber, 1984). During this period of experimentation Americans became aware of an educational movement begun in England that eventually captured the imagination of classroom teachers in this country as well.

Visitors to the British infant schools in the late 1960s and early 1970s were exposed to a compelling model of an integrated, child-centered curriculum that echoed many of the goals advocated decades earlier by Dewey. Open education, seen by some as a "non-model" by nature of its emphasis on individual responsiveness, was characterized by an integrated day, a developmental classroom, and informal rather than formal education (Plowden et al. 1967; Thomas & Walberg, 1975). Advocates of open education distinguished the model from laissez-faire and traditional education by noting the extent to which the "teacher and the child cooperate in shaping the goals and means of the child's learning" (Walberg & Thomas, 1975, p. 143). The open education model questioned the notion of an orderly sequence to learning, with an appreciation for the episodic (rather than vertical or linear) nature of children's learning. The role of the teacher was *not* to control students, nor were ways of teaching to be based on compulsion (Holt, 1969, p. 51). Yet writers on the topic acknowledged that it was "difficult to say exactly what an open classroom is" (Holt, 1969, p. 12); rather, they more often noted what it was *not* (Spodek, 1975).

These somewhat mystical concepts were echoed in various curriculum design writings, and teachers were reminded of the importance of a curriculum sufficiently flexible to be responsive to student interests and needs (Dale, 1972). The British challenge of an "open classroom" ultimately inspired many American teachers to abandon their dittos, reading groups, and workbooks, and to create learning environments whereby child-initiated projects might take place. Yet there were major differences between American and British interpretations of open education in general, and an integrated curriculum in particular. With an American emphasis on individualized instruction, the open education movement was characterized by extremes, ranging from A. S. Neill's (1960) advocacy of virtual "noninterference with the growth of the child" (p. 51), to architecturally manufactured clusters of "open" classrooms grouped together in a fashion that actually served to inhibit much of the activity that might otherwise have characterized an integrated curriculum. What could have been seen as a strength—the absence of definitive statements of what open education is—ultimately proved to be a major weakness.

The eventual demise of open education in the United States was attributed as much to the lack of clarity in and understanding of both theoretical and applied aspects as to the cultural differences—including teacher autonomy in the classroom—that distinguished British from American public schooling (Rogers, 1975). When all was said and done, the general U.S. impression was that an integrated curriculum was academically lazy; the role of the teacher overly complex and poorly defined; and the accomplishments of the children, as measured by standardized tests, questionable at best (Bennett, 1976). Although the results of studies comparing open classrooms with more traditional approaches eventually proved more favorable to open education (Walberg, 1984), examples of integrated curricula in public school settings were rare by the end of the 1970s.

Interest in an informal, integrated curriculum did not disappear entirely, however. The work of Piaget continued to exert tremendous influence on the organization and structure of early childhood settings, particularly the preschool classroom. Translations of his writings supported a renewed emphasis on the development of autonomy and initiative (Kamii, 1984), and the importance of play and child-centered activities for cognitive development (Kamii & DeVries, 1978). Such features as free play, including dramatic play time, block building, and activity centers; and more structured opportunities for water play, classification, seriation, and other premath experiences characterized the growing number of preschool as well as Head Start classrooms. "Units" of study such as *The Autumn* or *My Family* served to integrate language, literacy, social studies, and science concepts, with the visual arts often playing a predominant role.

In discussions of curriculum models during the 1980s, the integrated curriculum espoused by Dewey, implied by Piaget, and implemented by the British was most recognizable under the label of the *experiential model,* "which is subjective, personalistic, heuristic, and transactional . . . a learner-centered, activity-oriented approach to teaching and learning" (Gay, 1980, p. 128). This model emphasizes such educational principles as cooperative decision making between teachers and learners, and places a high priority on educational objectives that contribute to the integration of learners as individuals and members of a social group. Other objectives include learning how to learn and how to think critically and autonomously. No mention is made in this experiential model of the actual content areas.

Yet concern with subject matter has continued to be a major characteristic of programs actually using the term *integrated curriculum.* According to a recent review of curriculum models documented over the past decade, there are currently at least three major interpretations of an integrated curriculum within the public schools: those that integrate all the subject areas within a single traditional subject; those that integrate two or more related subject areas; and those characterized by the incorporation of new curriculum information into existing subject areas (Northwest Educational Service District 189, 1989).

Each of these models may be found in early childhood settings across the United States, with greater or lesser attention to the actual subject-area distinctions depending on the age of the children and the goals of the program. Social studies is a likely subject to be integrated into other areas (Meyer, 1990), with study topics such as Japan used to integrate day-to-day decisions as well as the academic subject areas (White, 1986). Another increasingly common approach to an integrated curriculum in the primary grades includes three curriculum strands: motor activities/music, math/science, and the language arts (McGarry, 1986).

Models that pay less attention to subject-matter distinctions and are actually more consistent with the experiential model than any of the above types of "integrated" curricula are typically housed in preschool settings or university laboratory schools. The Bank Street method, for example, has long emphasized the importance of integrating the curriculum through theme units in a manner reminiscent of the British infant schools (Gilkeson & Bowman, 1976). In the DeVries and Kohlberg (1987) cognitive-developmental model, the teaching of subject matter is taken seriously so as to avoid "falling into the romantic stream" (p. 381); thus skill development is incorporated into constructivist activity components. Planning in this model begins not with subject-matter analysis, however, but by thinking about how children think about the subject.

As such, an integrated curriculum has remained a viable option throughout the past decade, albeit with varying interpretations. The extent to which the child-centered version has been implemented in settings outside university laboratory schools and preschools is surely limited. Even within the preschool setting, teachers' interpretations of an experiential-based "Piagetian" program appear to vary in the extreme (Walsh, 1991). Most curriculum models currently in place in today's early childhood classrooms—certainly with children 5 years of age and older—include few, if any, of the characteristics associated with the Dewey model of an integrated curriculum. Instead, many public school early childhood curricula more closely approximate an academic Tylerian (1949) approach: discipline-centered with a sequence determined by the "logic of academic rationality," by "expanding horizons" and spiral organizational patterns, and by the inherent structure of disciplinary content (Gay, 1980).

To summarize, we are entering into the final decade of the twentieth century with many of the same questions that faced educators at the beginning; the major discussion continues to revolve around the issue of what constitutes an appropriate curriculum for young children. In response to pressures associated with the "curriculum pushdown," along with its concomitant testing and retention policies, early childhood professionals recently joined forces in publishing guidelines for developmentally appropriate practice (DAP) for young children (Bredekamp, 1987). This landmark publication, based on the premise that education must be age-appropriate as well as individually appropriate, advocates an integrated approach to curriculum planning even as it describes the various ways of teaching in the separate content areas, specifying the importance of "learning information in meaningful context" for 4- and 5-year-olds, and the "integration of curriculum" through the provision of theme projects and learning areas for the kindergarten and primary grades (pp. 53, 63). Recommendations are supported by summaries of current research, and *inappropriate* practices, such as the isolation of subject matter, are juxtaposed next to more "developmentally appropriate" teaching strategies.

Although the publication of the DAP guidelines did not put an end to the debate about content-related goals (Spodek, 1988), methods (Gersten, Carnine, Zoref, & Cronin, 1986), or even the appropriateness of the developmental framework (Kessler, 1991), the guidelines have sparked a renewed commitment to relate educational practice to our current knowledge about how young children grow and learn. More recent evidence that informal child-centered education can produce long-term advantages over isolated, skill-focused instruction (Schweinhart & Weikart, 1988) has further contributed to the growing belief that an integrated curriculum may best meet the needs of young children.

## REVIEW OF RESEARCH

There is, cumulatively, a wealth of support to be found in research of the past decade for an early childhood curriculum that is integrated, project-focused, and child-centered. Much of this work has been summarized elsewhere (Katz & Chard, 1989), in addition to work referenced in this volume. Rather than duplicate these efforts, this discussion will focus instead on several areas of research that are especially relevant to the model of an integrated curriculum to be proposed here. Studies focusing on the contribution of cognitive conflict to intellectual development and on the role of the socio-emotional context in general cognitive functioning confirm the importance of creating a learning environment that embraces the child as a social and emotional being as well as an intellectual one. Research in the area of children's artistic development provides further support for an educational setting that recognizes and promotes all of the child's efforts at symbolic representation, as opposed to only those within the oral and written traditions. In sum, work will be reviewed that explicates the term *the whole child* and that, cumulatively, suggests an integrated curriculum as the best means of educationally responding to young children.

### Theoretical Premises

The bulk of the research to be reported owes homage, at least in part, to the work of two international intellectual figures: Jean Piaget and Lev Vygotsky. As noted previously, Piaget's early writings were emphatically in favor of hands-on learning as a precursor to more abstract levels of understanding, and he highlighted the role of the environment in supporting children's development (Piaget & Inhelder, 1969). He wrote specifically about the importance of object manipulation to children's acquisition of numerical concepts (Piaget, 1952), and about the role of play in the development of imitation, and symbolic and cognitive representation (Piaget, 1962). Perhaps most important, he described children's cognitive development as proceeding in stages, moving from the general to the abstract (Piaget, 1929). On this premise alone, an integrated curriculum has more theoretical support than an approach that would artificially—at least from the child's perspective—separate out the tasks of reading, calculating, experimenting, and negotiating from the child's ongoing activity.

The incorporation of Russian semiotician and psychologist Lev Vygotsky's sociohistorical theory of cognition into current thinking about children's social and intellectual development has further refined both the types of research questions asked and the educational implications provided (Wertsch, 1985). Vygotsky's theory of the origins and evolution of human cognition, and thus the resulting research, covers a broad area of related scientific interests, reflecting his belief in psychology as part of a unified social science. In particular, the research impetus provided by the theoretical importance attributed to the role of the sociocultural environment in children's learning has resulted in a large body of data contributing to a more sophisticated understanding of the nature of children's development (Wertsch, 1991). Studies most germane to educational settings include those related to his notions of the sociocultural origins of individual cognition and the role of instruction in development (Forman & Cazden, 1985). Two of his concepts—the cognitive value of peer interaction and the "zone of proximal development"—have direct bearing on the way in which we might conceive and implement an integrated early childhood curriculum.

Together, the works of Piaget and Vygotsky have contributed substantially to our understanding of constructivist theory and to the challenge of translating that theory into educational practice. While it is not possible to delve into the meaning of constructivism in this chapter, it is worth noting that it is a theory about knowledge structures rather than teaching (Forman, in press) and that the relationship of this theory to educational practice ("constructivist education") is in the process of being constructed (DeVries & Kohlberg, 1987, p. 397). The following discussion will join in this endeavor and make reference to the linkages between constructivist theory and research findings in four areas: (1) the contextualized nature of children's learning; (2) the role of social relations in that learning; and (3) the interplay among cognition, communication, and creativity.

## The Role of Context, Conflict, and Reflection

Work of the past decade underscores the importance of learning opportunities that are contextually based, with ample opportunities for intellectual conflict, problem solving, and reflection.

The importance of active involvement in learning situations that are genuine—that is, that are related in some way to the context of children's lives—has been noted repeatedly in generalized studies on children's creative thinking and problem-solving abilities as well as research on children's emergent literacy, numerical, and scientific thinking. In each case, children who are actively engaged in the activity are at an advantage over those who must passively observe or abstractly infer the consequences of others' actions. In math education, the importance of concrete manipulation in obtaining select mathematic principles has been illustrated many times over (see Chapter 6, this volume). Research in science education underscores the importance of science in action (Forman & Kaden, 1987; Chapter 7, this volume). In fact, action-based science has been associated with overall academic achievement, as well as math and language development (Shymansky, Kyle, & Alport, 1982).

Yet the need to further understanding of what is meant by "hands-on" active learning—by now a standard early childhood maxim—has also been noted (Forman & Fosnot, 1982). Some clarification comes from more recent research on the importance of contextualized learning, a concept related to the premise that a child's education should be "a continuation of its experiential roots" (Hawkins, 1990, p. 12). In practice, this means that reading and the other language arts no less than mathematics and science require meaning and purpose in order to be effectively developed. The theory of emergent literacy has been built on a foundation of children's use of literature that is useful as well as mind expanding (Calkins, 1986; see Chapters 4 and 5, this volume). The "writing process" approach is based on children's need to have control of their writing and to be able to select topics of relevance to their lives (Graves, 1983).

Such contextualized learning appears to have benefits for children across a wide span of interests and abilities, including those who have been identified as "special" students (Stires, 1991), and is especially useful in making classrooms compatible to children of various cultural groups (Tharp, 1989).

Contextualized instruction is facilitated through the provision of real-life problem solving. The importance of conflict reduction to cognitive development has been acknowledged by both Piaget and Vygotsky. Piaget's notions of assimilation and accommodation describe the process through which the child constructs new concepts in order to restore some semblance of organization and meaning to his or her experience following disequilibrium (Piaget's term for cognitive conflict). The concept of cognitive conflict has been further articulated by Vygotsky (1978) within the framework of his "zone of proximal development," in which children first solve problems with the aid of "more capable" others, and eventually internalize those processes in which they participated. Bruner (1986), too, acknowledges the value of portraying a subject as fraught with uncertainty, thereby inviting dialogue and a commitment to problem solving.

This concept of conflict as incentive for cognitive growth has been examined in numerous studies, and results consistently point to the value of instructional activities that give rise to problematic situations for children. Researchers have noted the relationship between problem solving and children's mathematical concepts and methods (Carpenter, Fennema, Peterson, & Carey, 1988; Kamii, 1985, 1989) as well as related cognitive abilities (Casey, 1990). Other benefits of cognitive discovery models, in comparison to "open-ed" models with less emphasis on problem-focused activities, include increased verbal skills and social development (Miller & Dyer, 1975; Sigel, 1987).

When active participation also incorporates the finding of solutions to real problems rather than make-believe problems (real money rather than pretend; classroom dilemmas rather than textbook "word problems"), the benefits that children accrue increase exponentially. Numerous studies, including cross-cultural comparisons in mathematics, associate higher levels of comprehension with real-world problems (Cobb, Wood, Yackel, Wheatley, & Merkel, 1988; Stigler & Perry, 1988). Such studies combine to suggest that teachers would do well to "exploit" children's natural predispositions to "make sense out of their environments" (Condry & Koslowski, 1979).

In addition to providing genuinely problematic situations for children to explore, current research suggests that teachers provide ample opportunity for children to *reflect* upon their various strategies and hypotheses related to the problem at hand. The value of reflective activity appears to lie in its ability to encourage students to reorganize their own conceptual understandings at increasingly complex levels of abstraction (Wood, Cobb, & Yackel, 1990). The benefits of time to reflect have been demonstrated in studies across the subject-matter spectrum. Research investigations in math (Kamii, 1990) and science (Duckworth, 1987) make it clear that the "having of wonderful ideas" requires time to ponder, while studies of emerging literacy note the importance of time to think and talk about the material children have just read (Snow, Barnes, Chandler, Goodman, & Hemphill, 1991) or written (Graves, 1983).

In relating these points to an integrated curriculum, it is useful to return again to Vygotsky's work, which emphasizes the concept of internalization as it leads to higher mental functions (Wertsch, 1985). His belief that the primary goal for education is to integrate personal and schooled knowledge leads to a practical imperative that schooled knowledge be connected with intimate personal concerns (Vygotsky, 1962). The research just reviewed supports this premise and suggests that these connections be made through school experiences that entail personal involvement in meaningful problem solving, with sufficient time to think and reflect on one's work.

The importance of personally meaningful learning experiences has been further articulated by studies on motivation, creativity, evaluation, and the concept of challenge. Several areas of investigation are worth reviewing here as they extend our understanding of an integrated curriculum. The outcome of this expansive body of literature is to highlight the importance of "connecting what is taught to what is important to the individual" (Ginsberg & Asmussen, 1988) and to consider the critical role of affective components, personality dynamics, dispositions, and the role of cognitive mediators on children's learning.

The most common strategy by which American educators have attempted to motivate student achievement is through extrinsic "rewards" based on teacher evaluation, whether in the form of report cards or gold star stickers. Yet the deleterious effects of praise have been noted (see Katz & Chard, 1989, for a review of this literature), with some noting the child's right for more honest and constructive feedback (Beane, 1991). In fact, some research suggests that drawing attention to children's *errors* in an intellectually thoughtful fashion may be a more appropriate motivating strategy. High levels of achievement have been associated with the Japanese tendency to allow children to identify and argue about erroneous approaches, a strategy that is consistent with the previously discussed value of conflict. Yet "American teachers feel more comfortable praising the student who performs well than discussing the errors that can occur in the course of problem solving," even though "praise is not a particularly good way to start a deep discussion of mathematics principles and procedures" (Stigler & Perry, 1988, p. 52).

One body of research suggests that the reasons behind a child's motivation to pursue an activity may be as critical to subsequent learning as the presence or absence of motivation. Such studies have found that children characterized as learning-based (with a genuine interest in the topic at hand) demonstrated greater transfer of learning and more active attempts to apply what they had learned to novel situations, and were significantly more magnanimous toward their peers in noncompetitive situations, in contrast to children described as performance-based (motivated by potential for reward or recognition) (Dweck, 1986). In contrast, performance-based instruction and testing have been noted to serve as a constraint on learning math (Kamii & Kamii, 1990) as well as literacy skills and concepts (Harman, 1990).

Additional internal and external factors influencing children's learning have been found. In mathematics, the need for novel problems, encouragement to seek comprehension, freedom from a need for rewards, and opportunities for dialogical interaction not only influenced children's motivation, but were associated with a greater flexibility of procedures, which in turn contributed to greater achievement of conceptual knowledge (Hatano, 1988). Such factors have been combined into a personal investment theory (Maehr & Archer, 1987), which holds that the way in which tasks are defined, expectations are established, and goals are set makes a difference in children's performance. At the heart of the theory is a familiar theme: Students invest themselves in learning tasks as they see meaning in those tasks.

One determinant of whether an activity is judged to be intrinsically rewarding or not is the extent to which it presents a challenge to the child. Thus teachers should "keep that delight alive by presenting goals that involve increasingly more complex challenges matched to the student's developing skills" (Csikszentmihalyi, 1990, p. 130). Yet the concept of a challenge is not without qualifications. Related studies of emotional anxieties associated with the study of mathematics highlight the importance of the match between the child's developing competencies and the skills necessary to follow through on the activity. The concept of "hot cognition" underscores the extent to which knowledge is bound with emotion and motive, and develops in the context of an individual personality (Ginsberg & Asmussen, 1988). The relationship between challenging activities and increased time spent processing complex information is seen as optimal within the Vygotskian concept of the "zone of proximal development," whereby children are motivated to work, *with support from more capable others*, on tasks that are just beyond their reach.

To summarize thus far, context-related instruction characterized by opportunities for real-life problem solving that are sufficiently challenging, followed by time for reflective activity, is highly motivating for young children. Motivation, in turn, is associated with increased attention and "time on task," both of which contribute to greater learning. While these features might characterize a variety of educational settings, including highly individualized ones, research and theory suggest that one more feature is essential to their manifestation: the presence of others—adults as well as children—to share in at least some of those activities.

## Contributions of the Social Environment to Children's Learning

Research of the past decade has convincingly established the critical importance of successful peer relations to children's social adjustment. Social adjustment, in turn, is significantly related to school success and mental health (Asher & Coie, 1991) while its absence is associated with at-risk behavior such as truancy and other forms of delinquency (Parker & Asher, 1987). Less well understood is the role of peer relations in cognitive development, although the work of Vygotsky has dramatically influenced current research and thinking on the topic.

Vygotsky has written extensively on the interplay of social and developmental processes; he—and, to a lesser extent, Piaget—noted the value of peer interaction as a source of conflict that results in cognitive growth (Rogoff, 1990; Vygotsky, 1978). Research on peer tutoring, peer collaboration, cooperative learning, and peer play combines to support these premises.

Research on peer collaboration suggests that peers contribute in a number of ways to the achievement of previously discussed components of learning. While some advocate pairs of equal-status peers, noting greater progress in problem-solving tasks in contrast to children working in isolation or unequal-status peer groups, others support the concept of mixed-ability grouping, noting that homogeneous groupings have much less to offer in terms of student achievement than was previously believed (Slavin, 1987).

In either case, peers certainly contribute to the identification of a "problem" to be solved as they establish their varying points of view (Forman & Cazden, 1985). Similar findings have been found in studies of children with special needs. Studies have repeatedly demonstrated that disabled and nondisabled children learn from each other as they share their respective insights and expertise (Meisel, 1986).

Opportunities for informal peer interactions that take place during children's play are especially powerful contributors to children's development. The importance of play as an integrative experience has been discussed extensively (Chapter 3, this volume). Play's influence on children's basic skill development in the content areas has also been well established, including the positive contributions of playful activity with peers to children's written language (Daiute, 1989), mathematical understandings (Kamii & DeVries, 1978), and science (Forman & Kuschner, 1977). Perhaps the most important contribution of recent research on children's peer play relates to the elaboration of constructivist theory to include an interpretive perspective.

Vygotsky's view of play as its own "zone of proximal development" underscores the extent to which children use playmates to extend their understandings of "the meanings and rules of serious life" (Rogoff, 1990, p. 186). Play and other forms of interactions among peers influence children's "appropriation of their culture" as they negotiate understandings of shared social knowledge (Corsaro, 1985). Such work on children's peer relations has extended Vygotsky's notions of culturally mediated socialization, which focused primarily on individual development, to include the notion of socialization as a collective interpretive process that takes place in a public rather than private setting (Bruner, 1986; Corsaro & Eder, 1990; Wertsch, 1991).

The cumulative effect of research on peers is to strongly suggest, given that classrooms are unusually crowded social environments, that teachers take advantage of this circumstance (Forman & Cazden, 1985). Even total-group peer interactions have been found to contribute to the challenging nature of the classroom environment, as demonstrated in studies of Japanese classrooms where students engage in public debate about mathematics (Stigler & Perry, 1988) and large class size is seen as critical to the socialization of young children's classroom comportment (Tobin, Wu, & Davidson, 1989). Results of these studies not only confirm the benefits of peers to cognitive *and* social problem-solving processes, but challenge the American assumption that an individualized learning experience is inherently a higher quality, more effective learning experience than one that can take place within the context of a large group (Stigler & Perry, 1988).

Certainly peers are not the only contributors to a child's development within the classroom setting; much has been said regarding the critical nature of the teacher's role in children's learning (see Chapter 2, this volume). Teachers are essential to the provision of an environment in which children can work together on tasks of significance, share materials and ideas of interest, and respond to challenges and disagreements in an intellectually thoughtful fashion.

Studies on the qualities of relationships between teachers and children also suggest a more direct pathway of influence. Vygotsky's concept of the "zone of proximal development" to describe the cognitive challenge created by the adult-child exchange has recently been modified to include recognition of the reciprocal nature of that exchange (Rogoff, 1990). The resulting notion of "guided participation" highlights the role of the teacher in responding to individual differences of children while facilitating children's attempts at problem identification, hypothesizing, and resolution.

This concept of teacher as guide to higher levels of cognitive functioning is supported by another body of research that points to various qualities of an adult's questioning strategies as enhancing cognitive development (Forman, 1989; Sigel & Saunders, 1979). Research on the many types of conversations between adults and children concludes that those characterized by cognitive demands (which might include discussion of possibilities outside the experiences of the child), high level distancing (asking the child to go beyond the obvious to the implied or the possible), and abstract thinking (including the identification of alternative approaches) are consistently associated with greater cognitive competence in young children.

Teachers also play a newly recognized role with respect to the arts in the early childhood curriculum as a source of and contributor to children's cognition and communication.

## Cognition, Communication, and the Arts

We have learned a lot since Lowenfeld (1947) told teachers to keep their hands off children's art. The significance of children's drawings, long recognized as a measure of a child's intelligence (Goodenough, 1926), has now been linked to many other aspects of development, including social and emotional as well as cognitive functioning (Gardner, 1982; see Chapter 11). Within school settings, art educators as well as early childhood teachers have noted their ability to provide for more meaningful experiences when art is incorporated into other subject areas (Freyberger, 1985). In fact, a growing body of research has documented the positive relationship between art and the development of children's cognitive skills (Silver, 1982) as well as specific learning in other areas. As a result, professionals in virtually every subject area, including reading (Strickland & Morrow, 1990), social studies (Seefeldt, 1989), math (Meyer, 1990), science (Forman, 1989), and art (Dixon & Chalmers, 1990), recommend that art be integrated into the early childhood curriculum.

The cumulative effect of these studies is a changing orientation to art education, especially with respect to teacher involvement (Smith, 1982). Beginning with an increased appreciation for the child's developing capacity for symbolic representation, research suggests that teachers utilize puppets, storytelling, film making, sculpture, drawing, music, dance, drama, and poetry—essentially all of the expressive arts—to meaningfully integrate children's learning (Hoffman & Lamme, 1989).

A final impetus for incorporating art into the early childhood curriculum comes from a new body of research investigating the extent to which children use symbolic representation (in most cases, drawing) as a strategy for understanding and making meaning of their experiences (see Chapter 7, this volume) as well as to construct imaginary roles (Dyson, 1990). The contribution of children's symbolic representations to concept development, with multiple symbol systems, including invented notations, is finally beginning to be recognized, researched, and utilized in some American settings, including the Prospect School in Vermont, characterized by an integrated approach that includes active recognition of different modes of learning (Carini, 1982). As the view becomes more widespread that children's artwork is as much a pathway as it is a mirror to their way of thinking and conceptualizing (Winner, 1989), its role in the early childhood curriculum will likely increase.

One such early childhood program that has provided tremendous incentive to study further the role of artistic activity in children's development is the community-based infant/toddler and preschool program in Reggio Emilia. This early childhood program includes an integrated curriculum that is characterized by many of the features advocated in this research review: contextualized learning, real-life problem solving among peers, numerous challenges for creative thinking, and ample time for reflection. The next portion of this chapter will describe the goals and program characteristics of an integrated early childhood curriculum as conceptualized and enacted in a small town in northern Italy.


### EARLY CHILDHOOD EDUCATION IN REGGIO EMILIA

Readers unfamiliar with the history behind the educational programs of the city of Reggio Emilia are urged to see other recent and forthcoming publications (cf., New, 1990; Edwards, Gandini, & Forman, in press; Gandini, 1984). In brief, this town of 130,000 people has, for the past 25 years, committed 12% of the town budget to the provision of high quality full-time child care for children under the age of 6 years. While the provision of community-supported child care is no longer unusual in Italy, there are a number of features of the Reggio Emilia program that have attracted world-wide attention, not the least of which is its emphasis on symbolic languages within the context of a project-oriented curriculum. These and other features of Reggio Emilia will be described as they relate to an expanded interpretation of an integrated curriculum.

Curriculum models are typically described by attention to three distinct program components: the theoretical foundations, administrative policies, and curriculum content and methods (Evans, 1982). While practitioners of Reggio Emilia bemoan our use of the term *model* to describe their constantly evolving ideas about their work (C. Rinaldi, personal communication, August 5, 1991), their approach to an integrated curriculum may be outlined along those same three dimensions, beginning with the latter.

### Curriculum Characteristics

There are many aspects of the curriculum that are immediately visible upon entry into one of Reggio Emilia's 22 community preschools.[1] There is clearly an emphasis on children's work products—photographs and samples of group as well as individual efforts related to completed and ongoing projects cover most of the hallway walls. There is also an interest in the ways in which children *think* about their work, as indicated by the number of transcriptions of "in-progress" discussions included in the displays. These displays of children's thinking are interspersed with visually pleasing arrays of found objects and classroom materials, all arranged in a manner that draws attention to such aesthetic details as color, shape, and texture, and stimulates children to consider abstract notions such as the relationship between form and function (Gandini, 1984).

These concerns—for process and product as well as aesthetic sensibilities—are also apparent as one steps inside a classroom. The classrooms are beautiful, furnished with plants and mirrors, mobiles and more displays of children's work; large windows serve as a link between the classroom and the outdoors. Teachers—there are two in each class—are often found working with small groups of children, as the rest of the class engages in a wide variety of self-selected activities (dramatic play, blocks, painting) typical of most preschool classrooms.

Teacher-child interactions are frequently focused on the exploration of some topic of joint interest. Their conversations are characterized by elaborate and lengthy discussions regarding children's hypotheses of events; teacher questioning is used to elicit further explanations and to provoke new ways of considering an idea (Forman, 1989). Teachers take notes and record conversations as they take place between children, serving as a recorder of their plans and their understandings. As children proceed in an area of investigation, they are encouraged to express their ideas and their knowledge through drawings, which are then critically viewed by other children. Teachers not only encourage, but often participate in, debates regarding the extent to which a child's drawing lives up to the expressed intent. Revision of drawings (and ideas) is not only tolerated, but encouraged. Teachers actively support children in their attempts to make their opinions known, and allow them to modify one another's work, assuming that both children are also in agreement. Thus teachers continually advocate children's involvement in the processes of exploration and discovery as well as evaluation, acknowledging the importance of the products of children's efforts as vehicles for further exchange.

Such lengthy conversations about children's ideas or efforts often take place within, or lead to, a project—another major characteristic of this program. In almost all classes, there will be evidence of at least one long-term project, selected as a result of (1) adult observations of something of interest and importance to the children; (2) a personal interest or curiosity on the part of the teacher about a particular topic; or (3) serendipitous events that redirect the attention of the children and teacher to another focus. Teachers especially value their ability to improvise, to accept and to *enjoy* the unexpected.

Curriculum decisions regarding projects are based on a collective understanding of the kinds of interests and processes of development that characterize a particular age period and a strong belief in the importance of giving children an occasion to use their developing skills and interests— providing them some place, in a metaphorical sense, to "play with the big idea" (C. Rinaldi, personal communication, August 6, 1991). Once a project begins, the teachers remain alert to children's interests in a new way, continually looking for ways to expand upon their initial enthusiasm and curiosity about the topic.

Teachers typically begin by observing and questioning children about the topic of interest. Based on children's responses, teachers then introduce new materials, questions, and opportunities that will provoke children to further explore the project topic. While some of these teacher-provocations may have been anticipated in advance, projects often move in unanticipated directions as a result of children's interests. Thus curriculum planning and implementation are based on the reciprocal nature of both teacher-directed and child-initiated activity.

As children generate and test their hypotheses, they are encouraged to depict their understandings through one of many symbolic languages, including drawing, sculpture, dramatic play, and writing; and they work together toward the resolution of problems that arise in the course of their activities. Curriculum goals related to these projects are broadly defined; specific objectives, such as learning the names of colors or the alphabet, are rarely identified. Instead, goals are expressed in terms of experiencing the pleasures of exploration and communication with a variety of symbols, including but not limited to colors, letters, and words. Teachers use opportunities for ongoing assessment and evaluation as they present themselves. Any information obtained about the child's knowledge of discrete information is incorporated into a broader understanding of the child, including the abilities to work with other children, follow through on a task of interest, and use verbal and other communicative skills as necessary and appropriate.

In most cases, only a small group of children participate in any one project. Their experiences, however, are observed informally and shared in a variety of ways with the rest of the class. Occasionally, a small group project will lead directly to learning opportunities for the entire class. These points are perhaps best illustrated by a project, recently shared in a presentation to a group of American educators, on "the sending and receiving of messages" (L. Rubizzi, June 5, 1991). This project grew out of teacher observations of the rich pattern of exchange among a small group of 5- and 6-year-old children as they went about the process of creating and sending messages to their friends. Discussions among preschool teachers generated several questions: What are the roots of this message-sending behavior? Is this interest limited to older children, or does it begin earlier? How have the older children acquired their understandings regarding the production and interpretation of written messages? How might the classroom serve as a support for the development of this interest and expertise?

With these questions in mind, a project on messages was initiated across several classrooms of different ages. Teacher strategies for initiating the project varied according to the age of the children. Teachers of the 5- and 6-year-old children began to observe in a more systematic fashion the types of messages being sent and to note the authors as well as the recipients of the messages. They also noted those children who could write their own and others' names, copy an address correctly, and use letters and numbers in other ways, as a part of their ongoing assessment of children's abilities and concept development. These observations were followed by asking children to share their ideas of messages as they were exchanged between children and between adults.

The next step in this project was to consider the extent to which the classroom environment fostered children's interest and expertise in message sending. There were explicit goals related to the organization of the environment in this case: One was the observed need for children to be able to give and receive messages in a direct fashion, thereby facilitating quick and reciprocal feedback. This need was met by creating individual message containers for each of the children, complete with names and letter slots. The second need, based on the teachers' desire to promote children's developing capacities in this area, was to establish both the means and the motivation to communicate to a more distant audience, thereby requiring greater precision in the message sending. Thus an "official" mailbox was created for the classroom in which only letters to individuals outside the school setting were posted. This environmental feature was incorporated with trips to the post office to purchase stamps. To aid in the creation of both types of messages, letter writing areas and materials were clearly designated.

As children utilized the various materials presented to them for their messages, they began to make distinctions between those messages that could be supplemented with verbal components and those that relied more exclusively on the written form. Throughout, teachers observed the discussion and activity taking place, and assisted in clarifying the intent of the messages as children attempted to "read" one another's efforts. Teachers also stimulated message sending among those children who had not already shown an interest, by drawing attention to others' messages, asking children if they wished to send a message to someone, and continuing to provide a variety of interesting materials for message-writing purposes. This goal of increased participation was motivated as much out of concern that all children be given the opportunity to be on the receiving end of the message sending as it was to ensure that all children were exposed to these literacy experiences.

In a classroom of 3-year-old children, a parallel project was underway. The 25 children had been sharing a classroom and two teachers for several months, and had established a variety of means of communication with one another; yet few were involved in the creation of messages. The teachers initiated the project in a straightforward fashion: They asked several children if they wanted to prepare a message for someone, knowing that the term "message" was ambiguous. As the children demonstrated their understanding of the term, the teachers discovered that they utilized many different graphic forms, objects, and abilities that they had developed previously. These younger children went to great lengths to include something beautiful—a leaf, a scrap of shimmering paper, a sprinkle of glitter—in their messages, and their delivery was typically accompanied by hugs and kisses. Teachers responded to these observations by providing additional aesthetically pleasing materials to incorporate into the messages and by creating situations whereby children could not always deliver their messages in person. As children began to distinguish between those messages that could be accompanied by verbal and physical elements and those that, of necessity, had to stand alone, they began to experiment with forms of notation that were recognizable to others, including magazine cutouts of favorite toys, children, and food.

Throughout the project, parents in each of the two classrooms were kept informed of and invited to participate in children's message-writing activities. Teachers shared the premise behind the initial investigation and the processes through which the children were moving as they became more involved in the message sending. They invited parents to share forms of message sending that they utilized in the home, and urged parents to communicate with their children through messages. As messages were exchanged between home and school, teachers of the younger children began to recognize another characteristic of the young writers: They often did not identify the recipient until the message itself became articulated.

Teachers in both classes followed this observation by engaging children in conversations prior to the creation of messages, posing questions about the purpose of the message, the characteristics of the intended recipient, and the intended content of the message. Recognition of the reciprocal nature of message sending was followed by a gradual understanding that the recipient's pleasure in receiving and interpreting the message was perhaps a more critical determinant of the form and content than the sender's pleasure. Teachers presented children with reasons to choose among several forms of communication, thereby facilitating their eventual recognition of the advantages of written messages as an efficient *and lasting* means of conveying important information.

As children in both classes worked on their messages, they encountered any number of problems, ranging from the desire to spell someone's name to the need to respond in a kind fashion to an expression of love that was not reciprocated. In each case, the problems grew out of the children's own activities, and children rather than teachers assigned the level of significance to the solution. This focus on solving real problems in the Reggio Emilia classrooms is distinct from a more general focus on problem solving that characterizes some programs. Teachers in Reggio Emilia avoid giving children problems to solve, and instead try to create opportunities where children themselves discover problems of their own. Thus most problems that children encounter are within a larger context, and the children evaluate the solutions as they contribute to the task at hand.

Final outcomes of the message project were many. There was a record of children's growth in the use of formal alphabet and numeric notations, as well as an indication of children's status within the classroom as senders and receivers of messages. In the 5-year-old group, many previously disinterested children became prolific message writers, thereby increasing their preliteracy knowledge and skills. Among the younger children, there was a dramatic increase in children's recognition of the usefulness of different forms of communication, as well as a new appreciation for the need to consider the perspective of the recipient in determining the form and content of a message. The teachers of Reggio Emilia might suggest, however, that an equally important outcome of this project was the increased understanding on the part of the adults as to how children conceptualize the communicative act of message sending and how they progress in their ability to convey information in a nonverbal fashion. Through the traditional practice of documentation and exhibition of children's project work, *all* the teachers—and a good many parents—gained a better understanding of children's emergent literacy.

This project is an apt example of Reggio Emilia's approach to an integrated curriculum. Traditional subject areas were incorporated into children's project-related activities (not only writing and reading—the frequent trips to the post office to purchase stamps promoted math skills as well as an appreciation of a vital community service). The project, in turn, was integrated with the rest of the school day. While there were designated times when a teacher would work with a small group of children creating messages, the sending and receiving of messages took place across the school day amid a variety of settings and circumstances. Assessment and evaluation procedures regarding literacy and communication skills were incorporated into teachers' regular activities with children, including but not limited to the message-writing component. The project acknowledged many aspects of children's development: It contributed to the cognitive domain associated with symbol making, it fostered language and social skills, and it provided a vehicle for emotional, affective, and creative expression. And finally, the project integrated many different people, as children sent messages back and forth; teachers shared their observations as well as their insights with each other; and parents worked with both children and teachers.

### Administrative Policies and Organizational Features

There are a number of policies that support this approach to an integrated curriculum, not the least of which is the tradition of community support for young children and their families.

*Community support and parental involvement.* The infant/toddler and preschool program is a vital part of the community of Reggio Emilia, apparent not only in the consistent and high level of financial support provided for the program, but in the degree of interest and involvement in school activities, as expressed by community membership in the school organization *La Consulta,* a committee that exerts significant influence over local government policy.

The role of parents mirrors that of the community, at the school-wide as well as classroom level. Parents are not only welcome but *expected* to take part in curriculum discussions as well as activities within the classroom. Because a majority of the parents—including mothers—are employed, meetings are held in the evenings so that all who wish to do so can participate.

*Classroom organization.*    Policy features that make possible the quality of exchanges previously described between children as well as those between teachers and parents include the placement of two teachers of equal status in each classroom and the practice of keeping the same group of children together for a 3-year period. This practice creates more than a *sense* of community; adults and children soon become a rich source of support, friendship, and information for one another (T. Filippini, personal communication, June 11, 1989).

*Teacher autonomy and professional development.*    Teachers have what we would consider to be a tremendous degree of autonomy in making curriculum decisions. In spite of meager preservice training for Italian early childhood teachers, there is no principal or head figure in the schools and no teacher's manual, curriculum guide, or achievement tests to inform practice or bind teachers to a program. Teacher autonomy is not accompanied by isolated decision making, however; instead, teachers of several schools work together with a *pedagogista*—the Italian term used to describe the coordinating role of a pedagogical team leader—as they explore avenues of entry into children's learning. Classroom teachers, including the *atelierista*—art teacher[2]—as well as parents all join in the curriculum planning process. This incorporation of multiple points of view is facilitated by weekly staff meetings characterized by lengthy debates regarding opposing interpretations of children's learning and development. The goal of such discussions is rarely to determine a final or consensus position, although decisions for the initiation and sharing of projects are made. The larger aim of staff development and curriculum planning sessions is for teachers to become keener observers of children and more reflective practitioners.

*"Space is our third teacher"*    (T. Filippini, personal communication, June 11, 1989). The design and organization of the physical environment are crucial to the implementation of this early childhood program and serve to integrate the classroom with the school and the school with the larger community. Thus classrooms include space for both large and small groups, with

play and work areas clearly designated. Linkages to the community include a central area beyond each classroom similar to the town *piazza*, and windows that open to courtyards and gardens. The availability of materials for children's project work is facilitated by ample places for supplies, which are frequently arranged in ways that draw attention to their colors, textures, and other aesthetic features. Studio spaces in the form of a large *atelier* in the center of the school as well as a smaller *mini-atelier* in each classroom serve as places where children can work for extended periods of time on projects of interest without risk of having to clean up and put away materials prematurely.

*Time as an ally, not an enemy.*   The benefits of long periods of time have already been acknowledged in the policy of keeping groups of children and their teachers together for a 3-year period. A major priority in the scheduling of the day's events is that children and teachers have time to talk and listen to one another. Thus classrooms are loosely organized around large group meetings, activity times (including project work as well as child-initiated selections), outdoor play, naps, and meals.

Time is considered vital to the successful exploration of ideas; thus children's activities may be extended well beyond the typical "free-play" period, with ample opportunity to return later to the projects in progress. With group projects, time takes on an altogether different appearance; in many cases, projects extend over a period of weeks or months. In fact, the lengths to which teachers go to expand upon children's interests suggests that it is the American teacher who has the short attention span, rather than the preschool-aged child.

## Theoretical and Ideological Bases

Loris Malaguzzi, former director and founding father of Reggio Emilia's infant/toddler centers and preschools, in a presentation identified a wide array of theorists who have influenced his thinking and that of his colleagues in their work with young children: Kilpatrick, Dewey, Bronfenbrenner, Isaacs, Wallon, Frinet, Vygotsky, Bruner, Piaget, the post-Piagetians, Hawkins, Maturana, and Varela, among others. As such, the Reggio Emilia approach has a theoretical heritage reminiscent of other progressive educational programs and puts into practice much of what currently goes by the name of a constructivist approach to early education. Yet this label falls short of describing the totality of this approach to early childhood education and gives little acknowledgment of the great importance attributed by adults in Reggio Emilia to symbolic languages as forms of expression of children's multiple intelligences (Edwards, Gandini, & Forman, in press; Gardner, 1985).

As a means of understanding the educational implications of the theoretical influences cited, as well as to acknowledge the role of cultural values and individual influences in the development and implementation of the Reggio Emilia integrated curriculum, it is appropriate to consider the expressed beliefs of those adults working with young children in this Italian community. Based on numerous conversations with and presentations by Reggio Emilia school personnel (especially Carlina Rinaldi, Tiziana Filippini, and Loris Malaguzzi), I have organized the beliefs into three categories: the processes and goals of learning, children as learners, and the roles of adults in children's learning.

*Processes and goals of learning.*    Teachers repeatedly emphasize their belief in the importance of not knowing, and not understanding, as contributors to learning. In fact, a major approach to problem solving among adults as well as children is to allow for mistakes to happen, for confusion to reign. As children ask questions, debate, reexamine, and rephrase their positions, they not only gain a better understanding of their own and others' views on the nature of things, but they learn about the importance of words and other symbols of communication.

Teachers express the belief that all children do not have to go through the same steps or share the same experiences in order to derive benefit from early schooling. There is a need, on the other hand, to place children's learning opportunities within a larger context. While it is not considered inappropriate to spend a concentrated period of time on an academic-related activity such as message writing, what is important is the sense of this time as it relates to something outside the time frame, something of great significance—whether it's the establishment of a friendship, the resolution of a problem, or the simple sharing of information.

*Children as learners.*    Adults in Reggio Emilia trust in children to be interested in things worth knowing about. They see children as capable of many things, including the expression of ideas and feelings in many forms. They emphasize the importance of providing numerous opportunities and reasons for children to utilize their developing representational skills as they attempt to articulate, refine, and communicate their understandings of their experiences. They believe that children are inherently sociable and desirous, beginning in infancy, of establishing a wide variety of social relations, with the need for each of them to be of high quality. Finally, adults regard children's predisposition to enjoy the unexpected as their most important asset for the future.

*The roles of adults.*   Teachers trust themselves to be able to respond appropriately to children's ideas and interests, to facilitate those interests, and to provoke new interests. Teacher beliefs about professionalism include the idea that one is always learning; the notion of a good "team player" is not one who is agreeable, but one who is able to contribute to the professional development of others. Finally, there is an articulated belief in the ability of parents to participate in a variety of meaningful ways to children's early education. These beliefs combine to create an atmosphere of community and collaboration that characterizes adult relationships with one another as well as their efforts with the children.

This discussion of curriculum practices, organizational policies, and theoretical premises and belief systems culminates in an *integrative* image of a community preschool program where nothing occurs in isolation. This expanded view of an early childhood curriculum as conceptualized in Reggio Emilia considers the term *integrated* in the fullest sense of the word.

- Not only the "whole" child is considered in program planning and implementation but the family as well.
- Children's work and play are not indistinguishable but instead are mutually influential.
- Experiences related to the content areas are incorporated into projects that reflect the passions of children's lives.
- Children's ways of expressing themselves through their many symbolic languages are fostered and valued.
- Staff development, curriculum planning, and ongoing pupil evaluation are all reciprocally related.
- Teachers work together with parents and other teachers.
- Children's relationships to one another are seen as *integral* to their social, communicative, and cognitive development.
- Developmental as well as sociocultural concerns influence curriculum decisions.
- Children of varying abilities and interests can all find meaning in their educational experiences.

## Implications for U.S. Early Childhood Programs

Research and practice as described in the previous two sections combine to suggest that children would be better served if academic subject areas were less salient in the divisions, distinctions, and priorities of the early childhood classroom. The example presented to us of the preschool program in Reggio Emilia moves us to consider an even broader interpretation of an integrated curriculum.

Many features of the Reggio Emilia program were mentioned or alluded to in the earlier review of the literature (including the value of contextualized learning, the role of peers, the importance of real-life problem solving, and the contribution of symbolic representation to concept development). There is also a growing body of research literature related to two other dimensions—the roles of teachers and the importance of meaningful partnerships with parents—that appear to be significant contributors to Reggio Emilia's interpretation of an integrated curriculum. These two latter points appear most essential to current reform efforts in the United States and deserve brief mention before the chapter concludes.

The conception of teachers as learners provides a strong rationale for an integrated approach to early education as described. When teaching is seen as "inherently interwoven with the process of learning" (Fosnot, 1989, p. 112), the curriculum evolves from teacher/learner interactions (p. 137; Duckworth, 1987), and learning—for children as well as adults—is an integrated process. Research on teachers and teaching emphasizes the importance of enlarging the focus from what works best for children to include the relationship between how teachers teach and what teachers need. Such studies suggest that teachers as well as children need to see what they are doing as problematic and meaningful (Ashton & Webb, 1986; Paley, 1990). Teachers in Reggio Emilia thrive on the challenges they create for themselves as they struggle to learn from, and enhance the development of, the children in their classrooms.

Other important aspects of the Reggio Emilia school environment that receive empirical support in the literature are the value of teacher collaboration and parental involvement in decision making. Research makes it clear that children as well as teachers benefit when teachers share ideas, cooperate, and assist one another's professional development (Ellis, 1990; Tye & Tye, 1984). Parental involvement also affects teachers' feelings of efficacy and satisfaction (Rosenholtz, 1989) and is associated with a wide array of school-related success stories (e.g., Hauser-Cram, Pierson, Walker, & Tivnan, 1991; Hoffman, 1991). Even as researchers remind us of the difficulties of establishing and maintaining genuine home–school partnerships (Powell, 1991), the point remains that parental involvement is considered by many to be a key factor in children's schooling (Cochran & Dean, 1991), and absolutely critical to the successful integration of culturally diverse children in American classrooms (Williams & DeGaetano, 1985). In Reggio Emilia, such partnerships are not left to chance.

So what's keeping American educators from implementing a program that fully integrates children and adults, schools and community, and bodies of knowledge and the developmental domains? Certainly, the example of Reggio Emilia presented in this chapter does more than inspire us to reflect on American ways of providing early education. As the growing number of American visitors to those Italian classrooms attests, Reggio Emilia provides many concrete ideas that are well worth emulating and other features to which we can surely aspire. Who, indeed, can argue against attractive facilities, committed teachers, supportive and involved parents, and a community of young children who are thriving in an environment that respects them as thinkers and doers?

In spite of these accolades, many of the supportive elements of Reggio Emilia's approach to early childhood education are less easily embraced by American educators. The relatively organic nature of curriculum planning and implementation, the degree of discord that is not only tolerated but encouraged in staff development sessions, and the concurrent belief that *teachers learning from children* is as important an educational objective as children learning from teachers are but a number of features that furrow the brows of U.S. early childhood professionals (New, in press).

There are also dangers inherent in copying a "model"—many of them made apparent several decades ago as teachers intrigued by the concept of open education altered appearances without a thorough understanding of the philosophical, pedagogical, and personal roots from which those practices derived (Barth, 1972). Such "religious fervor" without an understanding of cultural values and ideological differences inevitably leads to failure, conflict, and disappointment (Rogers, 1975). There is also the risk of assuming that there is one curriculum that is best for all children (NAEYC, 1991). Even such practices as the writing process approach have been found wanting by some educators (Delpit, 1986, 1988) when accompanied by an apparent lack of emphasis on skill development. Others question the value of projects focused on children's lives if their worlds are too limited (Rogers, 1975) or if projects are implemented by teachers who lack the knowledge, flexibility, and autonomy to make decisions in the best interests of the child (Webster, 1990).

Yet the adults in Reggio Emilia are sensitive to these concerns, beginning with their resistance to being viewed as a model. Indeed, their view of an integrated curriculum assumes an understanding of children's needs for varying levels of structure and routine, freedom and responsibility. Even the selection of topics for projects illustrates the responsive nature of the curriculum. While children's interests are often the starting point of an investigation, teacher and parent concerns about sociocultural issues as well as developmental domains also influence the determination of projects. Teachers are confident in using their understanding of children to introduce projects and activities that will facilitate children's developing skills, including those directly related to academic domains such as literacy and mathematics. Finally, their view of professional development as a lifelong process and the supportive elements that promote teacher learning combine to mitigate against any formulaic response to the tasks of teaching. The success that characterizes their efforts is reminiscent of Frances Hawkins's (1979) conceptualization of classrooms where children learn, and in which "teachers must continuously remain aware of their own learning, and of their own ideas being formed and stretched" (p. 13).

As American classrooms increase in the proportion of culturally, ethnically, and developmentally diverse children (including those with special needs), there are few viable options that have as much to offer as this interpretation of an integrated curriculum. When the fabric of children's lives is interwoven with their classroom experiences, when the content of children's schooling is integrated in meaningful contexts, and when the concept of teaching is inextricably intertwined with the processes of learning, children can't lose.

The ideas suggested in this chapter entail a challenge, as does any curriculum reform, that involves new ways of thinking about teachers, parents, children, and the acts of teaching and learning (Klein, 1989). Indeed, this new interpretation of an integrated curriculum requires a "deliberate moral stance" about the role of education in children's lives (Graubard, 1990), one that necessitates continued and multivocal discourse on the notion of developmentally appropriate practice in early education (Swadener & Kessler, 1991).

## NOTES

[1] While many of the features described are characteristic of the infant/toddler program as well, the focus of this discussion will be on observations and discussions with teachers of preschool classes serving children between the ages of 3 and 6.

[2] Because in American classrooms being an art teacher connotes a separate relationship to classroom activities and to children, the Italian term is used.

## REFERENCES

Asher, S., & Coie, J. (Eds.). (1991). *Peer rejection in childhood*. New York: Cambridge University Press.

Ashton, P. T., & Webb, R. B. (1986). *Making a difference: Teachers' sense of efficacy and student achievement*. New York: Longman.

Bagley, W. C. (1941). The case for essentialism in education. *Today's Education. Journal of the National Education Association, 30* (7), 201–202. This article is reproduced in G. Hass (Ed.), 1983, *Curriculum planning; A new approach* (4th ed., pp. 21–23). Boston: Allyn & Bacon.

Barth, R. (1972). *Open education and the American school.* New York: Agathon Press.

Beane, J. A. (1991). Enhancing children's self-esteem: Illusion and possibility. *Early Education and Development, 2* (2), 153–160.

Bennett, S. N. (1976). *Teaching styles and pupil progress.* London: Open Books.

Brantlinger, E. (1991). Home–school partnerships that benefit children with special needs. *Elementary School Journal, 91* (3), 249–259.

Bredekamp, S. (Ed.). (1987). *Developmentally appropriate practice in early childhood programs serving children from birth through age 8* (rev. ed.). Washington, DC: National Association for the Education of Young Children.

Bruner, J. (1986). *Actual minds, possible worlds.* Cambridge, MA: Harvard University Press.

Calkins, L. M. (1986). *The art of teaching writing.* Portsmouth, NH: Heinemann.

Carini, P. (1982). *The school lives of seven children: A five year study.* Grand Forks: University of North Dakota.

Carpenter, T. P., Fennema, E., Peterson, P., & Carey, D. (1988). Teachers' pedagogical content knowledge of students' problem solving in elementary arithmetic. *Journal for Research in Mathematics Education, 19* (5), 385–401.

Casey, M. (1990). A planning and problem-solving preschool model: The methodology of being a good learner. *Early Childhood Research Quarterly, 5,* 53–67.

Cobb, P., Wood, T., Yackel, E., Wheatley, G., & Merkel, G. (1988). From research to practice: Creating a problem solving atmosphere. *Arithmetic Teacher, 36* (1), 46–47.

Cochran, M., & Dean, C. (1991). Home–school relations and the empowerment process. *Elementary School Journal, 91* (3), 261–269.

Cohen, R., & Mohl, R. (1979). *The paradox of progressive education.* Port Washington, NY: National University.

Condry, J., & Koslowski, B. (1979). Can education be made "intrinsically interesting" to children? In L. Katz (Ed.), *Current topics in early childhood education* (Vol. II, pp. 227–260). Norwood, NJ: Ablex.

Corsaro, W. A. (1985). *Friendship and peer culture in the early years.* Norwood, NJ: Ablex.

Corsaro, W. A., & Eder, D. (1990). Children's peer cultures. *Annual Review of Sociology, 16,* 197–220.

Crim, A. (1990). Moving out of our shadows. *Daedalus, 119* (2), 280–281.

Csikszentmihalyi, M. (1990). Literacy and intrinsic motivation. *Daedalus, 119* (2), 115–140.

Daiute, C. (1989). Play as thought: Thinking strategies of young writers. *Harvard Educational Review, 59* (1), 1–23.

Dale, E. (1972). *Building a learning environment.* Bloomington, IN: Phi Delta Kappa Foundation.

Delpit, L. D. (1986). Skills and other dilemmas of a progressive black educator. *Harvard Educational Review, 56* (4), 379–385.

Delpit, L. D. (1988). The silenced dialogue: Power and pedagogy in educating other people's children. *Harvard Educational Review, 58* (3), 280–298.

DeVries, R., & Kohlberg, L. (1987). *Constructivist early education: Overview and comparison with other programs.* Washington, DC: National Association for the Education of Young Children.

Dewey, J. (1902). *The child and the curriculum.* Chicago: University of Chicago Press.

Dewey, J. (1916). *Democracy and education.* New York: Macmillan.

Dewey, J. (1938). *Experience and education.* New York: Macmillan.

Dixon, G., & Chalmers, G. (1990). The expressive arts in education. *Childhood Education, 67* (1), 12–17.

Duckworth, E. (1987). *"The having of wonderful ideas" and other essays on teaching and learning.* New York: Teachers College Press.

Dweck, C. S. (1986). Motivational processes affecting learning. *American Psychologist, 41* (10), 1040–1048.

Dyson, A. H. (1990). Symbol makers, symbol weavers: How children link play, pictures, and print. *Young Children, 45* (2), 50–57.

Educational Services District 189. (1989). "Restructuring" schools: Integrating the curriculum. Mount Vernon, WA: Educational Services.

Edwards, C., Gandini, L., & Forman, G. (Eds.). (in press). *The hundred languages of children: Education for all of the child in Reggio Emilia, Italy.* Norwood, NJ: Ablex.

Ekstrom, R., Goertz, M., Pollack, J., & Rock, D. (1986). Who drops out of high school and why? Findings from a national study. *Teachers College Record, 87,* 356–373.

Ellis, N. (1990). Collaborative interaction for improvement of teaching. *Teaching and Teacher Education, 6* (3), 267–277.

Evans, E. D. (1982). Curriculum models and early childhood education. In B. Spodek (Ed.), *Handbook of research in early childhood education.* New York: Free Press.

Farnham-Diggory, S. (1990). *Schooling.* Cambridge, MA: Harvard University Press.

Forman, E. A., & Cazden, C. B. (1985). Exploring Vygotskian perspectives in education: The cognitive value of peer interaction. In J. Wertsch (Ed.), *Culture, communication, and cognition: Vygotskian perspectives* (pp. 323–347). New York: Cambridge University Press.

Forman, G. (1989). Helping children ask good questions. In B. Neugebauer (Ed.), *The wonder of it: Exploring how the world works* (pp. 21–25). Redmond, WA: Exchange Press.

Forman, G. (in press). Constructivism. In J. Roopnarine & J. Johnson (Eds.), *Approaches to early childhood education* (rev. ed.). Columbus, OH: Charles E. Merrill.

Forman, G., & Fosnot, C. (1982). The use of Piaget's constructivism in early childhood education programs. In B. Spodek (Ed.), *Handbook of research in early childhood education.* New York: Free Press.

Forman, G., & Kaden, M. (1987). Research on science education for young children. In C. Seefeldt (Ed.), *The early childhood curriculum: A review of current research* (1st ed., pp. 141–164). New York: Teachers College Press.

Forman, G., & Kuschner, D. (1977). *The child's construction of knowledge: Piaget for teaching children.* Monterey, CA: Brooks/Cole.

Fosnot, C. T. (1989). *Enquiring teachers, enquiring learners: A constructivist approach for teaching.* New York: Teachers College Press.

Freyberger, R. M. (1985). Integration: Friend or foe of art education? *Art Education, 38* (6), 6–9.

Froebel, F. (1887). *The education of man.* New York: D. Appleton.

Gandini, L. (1984, Spring). Not just anywhere: Making child care centers into "particular" places. *Beginnings,* pp. 17–20.

Gardner, H. (1982). *Art, mind, and brain: A cognitive approach to creativity.* New York: Basic Books.

Gardner, H. (1985). *Frames of mind: The theory of multiple intelligences.* New York: Basic Books.

Gardner, H. (1990). The difficulties of school: Probable causes, possible cures. *Daedalus, 119* (2), 85–114.

Gay, G. (1980). Conceptual models of the curriculum-planning process. In A. Foshay (Ed.), *Considered action for curriculum improvement* (pp. 127–148). Alexandria, VA: Association for Supervision and Curriculum Development.

Gersten, R., Carnine, D., Zoref, L., & Cronin, D. (1986). A multifaceted study of change in seven inner city schools. *Elementary School Journal, 86* (3), 319–331.

Gilkeson, E., & Bowman, G. (1976). The focus is on children: The Bank Street approach to early childhood education as enacted in Follow Through. New York: Bank Street College of Education.

Ginsburg, A. P., & Asmussen, K. A. (1988). Hot mathematics. In G. Saxe & M. Gearhart (Eds.), Children's mathematics [Special issue], *New Directions for Child Development* (41), 89–111.

Ginsburg, H., & Opper, S. (1969). *Piaget's theory of intellectual development: An introduction.* Englewood Cliffs, NJ: Prentice-Hall.

Goodenough, F. L. (1926). *Children's drawings as a measure of intellectual maturity.* New York: Harcourt Brace Jovanovich.

Graubard, S. R. (1990). Doing badly and feeling confused. *Daedalus, 119* (2), 257–279.

Graves, D. (1983). *Writing: Teachers and children at work.* Portsmouth, NH: Heinemann.

Greenberg, P. (1990). *The devil has slippery shoes: A biased biography of the Child Development Group of Mississippi.* Washington, DC: Youth Policy Institute. (Original work published 1965)

Gutek, G. L. (1968). *Pestalozzi and education.* New York: Random House.

Harman, S. (1990). Negative effects of achievement testing in literacy development. In C. K. Kamii, *Achievement testing in the early grades: The games grown-ups play.* Washington, DC: NAEYC.

Hass, G. (Ed.). (1983). *Curriculum planning: A new approach* (4th ed.). Boston: Allyn & Bacon. (Original work published 1974)

Hatano, G. (1988). Social and motivational bases for mathematical understanding. In G. Saxe & M. Gearhart (Eds.), Children's mathematics [Special issue], *New Directions for Child Development* (41), 55–70.

Hauser-Cram, P., Pierson, D. E., Walker, D. K., & Tivnan, T. (1991). *Early education in the public schools: Lessons from a comprehensive birth-to-kindergarten program.* San Francisco: Jossey-Bass.

Hawkins, D. (1990). The roots of literacy. *Daedalus, 119* (2), 1–14.

Hawkins, F. P. (1979). The eye of the beholder. In S. J. Meisels (Ed.), *Special education and development: Perspectives on young children with special needs* (pp. 11–31). Baltimore, MD: University Park Press.

Hoffman, S. (Ed.). (1991). Educational partnerships: Home-school-community (Introduction to special issue). *Elementary School Journal, 91* (3), 193–196.

Hoffman, S., & Lamme, L. (Eds.). (1989). *Learning from the inside out: The expressive arts.* Wheaton, MD: Association for Childhood Education International.

Holt, J. (1964). *How children fail.* New York: Pitman.

Holt, J. (1969). *The open classroom.* New York: New York Review.

Kamii, C. K. (1984). Autonomy: The aim of education envisioned by Piaget. *Phi Delta Kappan, 65* (6), 410–415.

Kamii, C. K. (1985). *Young children reinvent arithmetic: Implications of Piaget's theory.* New York: Teachers College Press.

Kamii, C. K. (1989). *Young children continue to reinvent arithmetic-2nd grade: Implications of Piaget's theory.* New York: Teachers College Press.

Kamii, C. K. (1990). *Achievement testing in the early grades: The games grown-ups play.* Washington, DC: NAEYC.

Kamii, C. K., & DeVries, R. (1978). *Physical knowledge in preschool education: Implications of Piaget's theory.* Englewood Cliffs, NJ: Prentice-Hall.

Kamii, C. K., & Kamii, M. (1990). Negative effects of achievement testing in mathematics. In C. K. Kamii, *Achievement testing in the early grades: The games grown-ups play* (pp. 15–38). Washington, DC: NAEYC.

Katz, L. (1991). Pedagogical issues in early childhood education. In S. L. Kagan (Ed.), *The care and education of America's young children: Obstacles and opportunities*, 90th Yearbook of the National Society for the Study of Education (Part I, pp. 50–68). Chicago: University of Chicago Press.

Katz, L., & Chard, S. (1989). *Engaging children's minds: The project approach.* Norwood, NJ: Ablex.

Kessler, S. (1991). Early childhood education as development: Critique of the metaphor. In B. B. Swadener & S. Kessler (Eds.), Reconceptualizing early childhood education [Special issue], *Early Education and Development, 2* (2), 137–152.

Kilpatrick, W. H. (1941). The case for progressivism in education. *Today's Education: Journal of the National Education Association, 30* (8), 231–232.

Klein, M. F. (1989). *Curriculum reform in the elementary school.* New York: Teachers College Press.

Krogh, S. (1990). *The integrated early childhood curriculum.* New York: McGraw-Hill.

Lay-Dopyera, M., & Dopyera, J. (1990). The child-centered curriculum. In C. Seefeldt (Ed.), *Continuing issues in early childhood education* (pp. 207–222). Columbus, OH: Charles E. Merrill.

Lowenfeld, V. (1947). *Creative and mental growth.* New York: Macmillan.

Maehr, M., & Archer, J. (1987). Motivation and school achievement. In L. Katz (Ed.), *Current topics in early childhood education: Vol. VII.* Norwood, NJ: Ablex.

Mark, J. H., & Anderson, B. D. (1985). Teacher survival rates in St. Louis, 1969–1982. *American Educational Research Journal, 22,* 413–421.

McGarry, T. P. (1986). Integrating learning for young children. *Educational Leadership, 44* (3), 64–66.

Meisel, C. J. (Ed.). (1986). *Mainstreaming handicapped children: Outcomes, controversies, and new directions.* Hillsdale, NJ: Lawrence Erlbaum.

Meyer, M. (1990). Joining forces: Integrating the arts. *School Arts, 89* (6), 46–49.

Miller, L., & Dyer, J. L. (1975). Four preschool programs: Their dimensions and effects. *Monographs of the Society for Research in Child Development, 40* (5–6, Serial No. 162).

Montessori, M. (1967). *The Montessori method.* Cambridge, MA: Bentley. (Original work published 1912)

National Association for the Education of Young Children. (1991). Guidelines for appropriate curriculum content and assessment in programs serving children ages 3 through 8. *Young Children, 46* (3), 21–38.

Neill, A. S. (1960). *Summerhill: A radical approach to child rearing.* New York: Hart Publishing.

New, R. (1990). Excellent early education: A city in Italy has it. *Young Children, 45* (6), 4–10.

New, R. (in press). Cultural variations on developmentally appropriate practice: Challenges to theory and practice. In C. Edwards, L. Gandini, & G. Forman (Eds.), *The hundred languages of children: Education for all of the child in Reggio Emilia, Italy.* Norwood: Ablex.

Northwest Educational Service District 189. (1989). "Restructuring" schools: Integrating the curriculum. Mount Vernon, WA: Author. (ERIC Document Reproduction Service No. ED #313806)

Paley, V. G. (1990). *The boy who would be a helicopter: The uses of storytelling in the classroom.* Cambridge, MA: Harvard University Press.

Parker, J., & Asher, S. (1987). Peer relations and later personal adjustment: Are low-accepted children at risk? *Psychological Bulletin, 102* (3), 357–389.

Piaget, J. (1929). *Child's conception of the world.* London: Routledge & Kegan Paul.

Piaget, J. (1952). *The origins of intelligence in children.* New York: W. W. Norton.

Piaget, J. (1962). *Play, dreams, and imitation in childhood* (C. Gattegno & M. F. Hodgson, Trans.). New York: W. W. Norton.

Piaget, J., & Inhelder, B. (1969). *The psychology of the child* (C. Gattegno & F. M. Hodgson, Trans.). New York: Basic Books.

Plowden, Lady B., et al. (1967). *Children and their primary schools: A report of the Central Advisory Council for Education.* London: Her Majesty's Stationery Office.

Powell, D. (1991). How schools support families: Critical policy tensions. *Elementary School Journal, 91* (3), 307–319.

Ramsey, P., Vold, E., & Williams, L. (1989). *Multicultural education: A source book.* New York: Garland.

Rogers, V. R. (1973). English and American primary schools. In B. Spodek (Ed.), *Early childhood education* (pp. 263–274). Englewood Cliffs, NJ: Prentice-Hall. (Reprinted from *Phi Delta Kappan,* October 1969)

Rogers, V. R. (1975). Using the British experience. In B. Spodek & H. Walberg (Eds.), *Studies in open education* (pp. 225–241). New York: Agathon Press.

Rogoff, B. (1990). *Apprenticeship in thinking: Cognitive development in social con-*

*text.* New York: Oxford University Press.

Rosenholtz, S. J. (1989). Workplace conditions that affect teacher quality and commitment: Implications for teacher induction programs. *Elementary School Journal, 89* (4), 421–439.

Rousseau, J. (1956). *Emile for today.* London: Heinemann. (Original work published 1762)

Schwebel, M., & Raph, J. (1973). *Piaget in the classroom.* New York: Basic Books.

Schweinhart, L. J., & Weikart, D. P. (1988). Education for young children living in poverty: Child-initiated learning or teacher-directed instruction? *Elementary School Journal, 89* (2), 213–227.

Seefeldt, C. (1989). *Social studies for the preschool/primary child* (3rd ed.). Columbus, OH: Charles E. Merrill.

Shepard, L., & Smith, M. (1988). Escalating academic demand in kindergarten: Counterproductive policies. *Elementary School Journal, 89* (2), 135–146.

Shymansky, J., Kyle, W., & Alport, J. (1982). How effective were the hands-on science programs of yesterday? *Science and Children, 20,* 14–15.

Sigel, I. (1987). Educating the young thinker: A distancing model of preschool education. In J. L. Roopnarine & J. E. Johnson (Eds.), *Approaches to early childhood education.* Columbus, OH: Charles E. Merrill.

Sigel, I., & Saunders, R. (1979). An inquiry into inquiry: Question asking as an instructional model. In L. Katz (Ed.), *Current topics in early childhood education: Vol. II.* Norwood, NJ: Ablex.

Silberman, C. (1970). *Crisis in the classroom: The remaking of American education.* New York: Random House.

Silver, R. (1982). Developing cognitive skills through art. In L. Katz (Ed.), *Current topics in early childhood education: Vol. IV.* Norwood, NJ: Ablex.

Silvern, S. B. (1988). Continuity/discontinuity between home and early childhood education environments. *Elementary School Journal, 89* (2), 147–157.

Slavin, R. (1987). Ability grouping and student achievement in elementary schools: A best-evidence synthesis. *Review of Educational Research, 57,* 293–336.

Smith, N. (1982). The visual arts in early childhood education: Development and the creation of meaning. In B. Spodek (Ed.), *Handbook of research in early childhood education.* New York: Free Press.

Snow, C., Barnes, W., Chandler, J., Goodman, I., & Hemphill, L. (1991). *Unfulfilled expectations: Home and school influences on literacy.* Cambridge, MA: Harvard University Press.

Spodek, B. (1975). Open education: Romance or liberation? In B. Spodek & H. Walberg (Eds.), *Studies in open education* (pp. 3–11). New York: Agathon.

Spodek, B. (1982). The kindergarten: A retrospective and contemporary view. In L. Katz (Ed.), *Current topics in early childhood education: Vol. IV.* Norwood, NJ: Ablex.

Spodek, B. (1988). Conceptualizing today's kindergarten curriculum. *Elementary School Journal, 89* (2), 203–212.

Stigler, J. W., & Perry, M. (1988). Mathematics learning in Japanese, Chinese, and American classrooms. In G. Saxe & M. Gearhart ( Eds.), Children's mathematics [Special issue], *New Directions for Child Development* (41), 27–54.

Stires, S. (Ed.). (1991). *With promise: Redefining reading and writing for "special" students*. Portsmouth, NH: Heinemann.

Strickland, D. S., & Morrow, L. M. (1990). Integrating the emergent literacy curriculum with themes. *The Reading Teacher, 43* (8), 604–605.

Swadener, B. B., & Kessler, S. (Eds.). (1991). Reconceptualizing early childhood education [Special issue]. *Early Education and Development, 2* (2).

Tharp, R. (1989). Psychocultural variables and constants: Effects on teaching and learning in schools. *American Psychologist, 44* (2), 349–359.

Thomas, S., & Walberg, H. (1975). An analytic review of the literature. In B. Spodek & H. Walberg (Eds.), *Studies in open education* (pp. 13–44). New York: Agathon Press.

Thorndike, E. L. (1922). *The psychology of arithmetic*. New York: Macmillan.

Tobin, J., Wu, D., & Davidson, D. (1989). *Preschool in three cultures: Japan, China, and the U.S.* New Haven, CT: Yale University Press.

Tye, K., & Tye, B. (1984). Teacher isolation and school reform. *Phi Delta Kappa, 65* (5), 319–322.

Tyler, R. (1949). *Basic principles of curriculum and instruction*. Chicago: University of Chicago Press.

Vygotsky, L. S. (1962). *Thought and language*. Cambridge, MA: MIT Press.

Vygotsky, L. S. (1978). *Mind in society: The development of higher psychological processes* (M. Cole, V. John-Steiner, S. Scribner, & E. Souberman, Eds.). Cambridge, MA: Harvard University Press.

Walberg, H. (1984). Improving the productivity of Americans' schools. *Educational Leadership, 41* (8), 19–30.

Walberg, H., & Thomas, S. (1975). An analysis of American and British open education. In B. Spodek & H. Walberg (Eds.), *Studies in open education* (pp. 143–154). New York: Agathon Press.

Walsh, D. J. (1991). Extending the discourse on developmental appropriateness: A developmental perspective. *Early Education and Development, 2* (2), 109–119.

Weber, E. (1970). *Early childhood education: Perspectives on change*. Worthington, OH: Charles Jones.

Weber, E. (1984). *Ideas influencing early childhood education: A theoretical analysis*. New York: Teachers College Press.

Webster, T. (1990). Projects as curriculum: Under what conditions? *Childhood Education, 67* (1), 2–3.

Wertsch, J. (Ed.). (1985). *Culture, communication, and cognition: Vygotskian perspectives*. New York: Cambridge University Press.

Wertsch, J. V. (1991). *Voices of the mind: A sociocultural approach to mediated action*. Cambridge, MA: Harvard University Press.

White, J. (1986). Decision-making with an integrated curriculum. *Childhood Education, 62* (5), 337–343.

Williams, L., & DeGaetano, Y. (1985). *Alerta: A multicultural, bilingual approach to teaching young children*. Reading, MA: Addison-Wesley.

Winner, E. (1989). Development in the visual arts. In W. Damon (Ed.), *Child development today and tomorrow* (pp. 199–221). San Francisco: Jossey-Bass.

Wood, T., Cobb, P., & Yackel, E. (1990). The contextual nature of teaching: Mathematics and reading instruction in one second-grade classroom. *Elementary School Journal, 90* (5), 497–514.

# Index

## SUBJECTS

ABC Task Force, 100, 206
Academic learning time (ALT), 133–134
Accommodation. *See* Piaget, Jean, *in subject index*
Adults, and an integrated curriculum, 312, 313
Adult-talk-to-children (ATC), 96–98
Affective development, 50–51, 228, 249, 297
American Child Study Movement, 7
Appropriate practices: and an integrated curriculum, 293; and language, 87, 99, 103–104, 111; and movement, 223, 229, 231; and multiculturalism, 103–104; and the social studies, 201. *See also* Bredekamp, S., *in author index*
Art education: and cognition, 269, 271, 275, 282; and computers, 272, 280; and creative thinking, 265; and DBAE, 266, 267, 269, 280, 281, 282, 283; and development theory, 270–273, 275; and drawing as part of symbol development, 274–275, 282; historical approach to, 264–265; importance of, 265, 282; and an integrated curriculum, 294, 301–302, 304; and multiple intelligences, 275–276, 280; and perceptual-spatial theory, 271–272; and the pop art educators, 265–270; privatization of, 265–270; and Project Zero, 264, 276, 277–280; and psychoanalytic theory, 272–273; recent research developments in, 273–283; and scribbling, 270, 280–281; and spatial organization, 281; and television, 272; and the unified field theory of artistic growth, 270, 278; and the whole child, 266
Assessment: and an integrated curriculum, 297–298, 305, 308; and language, 107–109; and play, 46–47; of problem solving skills, 168

Assimilation. *See* Concept attainment; Piaget, Jean, *in subject index*

Back-to-basics movement, 198–199
Bank Street method, 292
Beginning Teacher Evaluation Study, 133
Behaviorism, 11, 18, 20, 25–26, 31, 90, 120–121
Bilingual Education Act (1968), 87
Bilingualism, 100–102, 111
British infant schools, 290, 291–292

California State Department of Education (CSDE), 199, 200–201, 202–203, 216
Center for the Study of Reading, 119
Centre for Primary Language Education, 108
Change, as concept, 204–205
Children: communication, 182–184; and concept attainment, 8–9; and development/education theory, 2–5; and motivation, 45–46, 297–298, 299. *See also* Early childhood education; Whole child
Classrooms: arrangement of, 9–10; and an integrated curriculum, 303, 305–306, 309; and language, 99–103; management of, 21–23, 35
Cognition: and art education, 269, 271, 275, 282, 301–302; and an integrated curriculum, 292, 294, 295, 296, 297, 300, 301–302, 308; and mathematics, 154; and movement, 228; and play, 45, 51, 52, 56, 60–63; and science, 180–184. *See also* Concept attainment
Commission on Reading, 119
Commission on Standards for School Mathematics, 152, 153, 154, 157, 169
Commission on Teaching Standards for School Mathematics, 152

## AUTHORS

# About the Editor and the Contributors

**Carol Seefeldt** is a professor at the University of Maryland, where she teaches undergraduate and graduate courses in human growth and development and is a recipient of the Distinguished Scholar/Teacher Award. She has worked in the field for over 35 years, teaching child care through the third grade. In Florida, Dr. Seefeldt opened and directed a private preschool and served as Regional Training Officer for Project Head Start. She is the author of *Social Studies for the Preschool/Primary Child, Young and Old Together, and Continuing Issues in Early Childhood Education,* and coauthor of *Early Childhood Education: An Introduction.*

**Clifford D. Alper** is Professor of Music at Towson State University near Baltimore, where he teaches in the Early Childhood and Graduate programs. Dr. Alper also teaches courses in music literature. He has authored articles on early childhood education in the *Journal of Music Education* and the *Music Educators Journal.* He has presented early childhood research at conventions of the International Society for Music Education and the Music Educators National Conference.

**Nita H. Barbour** is Chair of the Department of Education at the University of Maryland, Baltimore County, where she previously directed the Early Childhood Program. Dr. Barbour has experience teaching in early childhood, the elementary grades, and secondary schools. In addition, she was Director of the Child Development Associate programs for Head Start at the University of Maryland, Baltimore County. Dr. Barbour is coauthor of *Continuity Across the Preschool/Primary Grades* and *Early Childhood Education: An Introduction.*

**Patricia F. Campbell** is an associate professor in the Department of Curriculum and Instruction at the University of Maryland at College Park. She teaches both graduate and undergraduate courses in mathematics education. Currently she is director of an NSF-funded project that is implementing a model for primary mathematics instruction to enhance student understanding and support teachers in predominantly minority schools.

**Deborah A. Carey** is an assistant professor in the Department of Curriculum and Instruction at the University of Maryland at College Park. She received her Ph.D. from the University of Wisconsin–Madison. In addition to teaching graduate and undergraduate courses in mathematics education, her current research project involves primary school teachers and students and focuses on the development of young children's mathematical thinking.

**John E. Dopyera** has taught in the teacher education programs at Syracuse University, Pennsylvania State University, and Pacific Oaks College, where he served as Dean of Faculty. He has over 35 years experience in conducting needs assessments and in designing, conducting, and evaluating training programs for education, human services, and business and industry.

**George E. Forman,** President of the Jean Piaget Society from 1983 to 1985, is Professor of Education at the University of Massachusetts, Amherst. He is the author of *The Child's Construction of Knowledge, Constructive Play, Action and Thought,* and *Constructivism in the Computer Age.* Dr. Forman has been a research psychologist at Project Zero, an institute at Harvard University's Graduate School of Education for 4 years. His current research includes work on problem solving and the use of video replay to enhance reflective thinking in young children, and the use of animated symbols in early childhood instruction.

**Doris Pronin Fromberg** is Professor of Elementary and Early Childhood Education and Director of Early Childhood Teacher Education at Hofstra University. She has been a curriculum and administration consultant to school districts and the Director of a Teacher Corps project that developed field-based inservice consultation for teachers, administrators, and the community. Her latest books are *The Full-Day Kindergarten* and *The Successful Classroom: Management Strategies for Regular and Special Education Teachers.* She is coeditor of the *Encyclopedia of Early Childhood Education.*

**Celia Genishi** has taught at the secondary, preschool, and university levels and is currently a professor at Teachers College, Columbia University. Her areas of interest are related to language acquisition and early childhood language arts, and research on language in classrooms. She has published primarily on the subjects of children's oral language and is editor of *Ways of Assessing Children and Curriculum* and coauthor of *Language Assessment in the Early Years.*

**Christopher Landry** is Program Director of the Children's Museum at Holyoke, where he develops interactive exhibits about science, art, and culture. He is currently a graduate student at the School of Education, University of Massachusetts.

**Margaret Lay-Dopyera** has 12 years of teaching experience with young children in public schools and laboratory schools. A faculty member at Syracuse University since 1967, and currently on leave, she has had major responsibility for designing and implementing model teacher training programs and she has also served as Associate Dean for Academic Programs in the School of Education. With her husband, John Dopyera, she is coauthor of the textbook *Becoming a Teacher of Young Children.*

**Harold J. Mc Whinnie** is an associate professor at the University of Maryland at College Park, where he teaches undergraduate and graduate art education. His ceramics and other artworks are frequently exhibited in the Northeast. Among his publications are books on the use of salt glazes and teaching art.

**Rebecca S. New** is Assistant Professor of Early Childhood Education at the University of New Hampshire, where she teaches graduate and undergraduate courses. She has been conducting cross-cultural research on child rearing in Italy for the past 15 years and is author of the book *Bella, Bravo, Buno: Italian Early Childhood.* As a part of her research, she has studied early childhood education in Reggio Emilia.

**Bill Stinson** is Professor of Preschool/Elementary Health and Physical Education in the Teachers College at Empora State University, Kansas. Dr. Stinson is currently a member of the National Council on Physical Education for Children of the American Alliance for Health, Physical Education, Recreation and Dance. His professional interests are in implementing and promoting programs emphasizing movement, stress management, self-concept, and cooperative learning for young children. He is the author of several books for teachers of children, including *Move to Learn to Grow: Movement Experiences for Young Children, Calming and Reassuring the Young Child,* and *I'm Somebody and So Are You: Self-Concept Activities for Children.*

**Leslie R. Williams,** a professor at Teachers College, Columbia University, is a curriculum designer and teacher educator who focuses on the refinement of teaching practice in experienced teachers. Her special interests include multicultural education, history, and philosophy in the field; currently she is researching the all-day kindergarten movement in the United States. She is coeditor of the *Encyclopedia of Early Childhood Education* and author of articles in practitioner and research journals.